The Financial Crisis and Developing Countries

In memory of Karel Jansen

The Financial Crisis and Developing Countries

A Global Multidisciplinary Perspective

Edited by

Peter A.G. van Bergeijk, Arjan de Haan and Rolph van der Hoeven

The international Institute of Social Studies at Erasmus University, The Hague, The Netherlands

Edward Elgar
Cheltenham, UK • Northampton, MA, USA

Published by
Edward Elgar Publishing Limited
The Lypiatts
15 Lansdown Road
Cheltenham
Glos GL50 2JA
UK

Edward Elgar Publishing, Inc.
William Pratt House
9 Dewey Court
Northampton
Massachusetts 01060
USA

A catalogue record for this book
is available from the British Library

Library of Congress Control Number: 2011925712

ISBN 978 1 84980 495 0 (cased)

Printed and bound by MPG Books Group, UK

Contents

Preface and Acknowledgements

This book is based on contributions to three international scientific events and a number of research projects that were organized from 2009 at the international Institute of Social Sciences or Erasmus University. Interested readers are referred to the website http//www.iss.nl/crisis that provides details on the project and a tool to follow up on this book.

The three main public events (where preliminary versions of the chapters that make up this volume were presented and discussed) took place in a relatively short period of time:

- the international conference 'A crisis of capitalism? A crisis of development!' (October 29, 2009),
- the international workshop 'The Financial Crisis and the non OECD' (June 22, 2010) and
- the CERES Summer school/Annual meeting 'Global Governance, The Crisis and Development: New Directions in Development Cooperation' (June 23–24), 2010.

We as editors and organizers would like to thank the participants and discussants at these meetings (in particular Geske Dijkstra, Robert Lensink, Selwyn Moons, Tak-Wing Ngo, Alexandra Selms, Rob van Tulder and Robert Went) for their valuable comments on the parts that made up our project. Financial support for this project by the Netherlands Ministry of Economic Affairs, CERES Research School for Resource Studies for Development, HIVOS and the ISS innovation fund is gratefully acknowledged. Ward Warmerdam provided editorial support at ISS.

We would also like to thank the editorial staff of Edward Elgar for excellent support and the short production time for this book. The impact of the crisis in the developing world is serious and urgent and we hope that this timely book can be of help in the debate on this important global issue.

Contributors

Peter A.G. van Bergeijk is Professor of International Economics and Macroeconomics at ISS and Deputy Director of CERES, Research School for Resource Studies for Development, Utrecht University.

Fantu Cheru is Research Director at the Nordic Africa Institute in Uppsala, Sweden and Emeritus Professor of African and Development Studies at American University in Washington, DC.

Harry Clemens is Programme Officer Financial Services and Enterprise Development at HIVOS, The Hague. Before he has worked as programme manager, researcher and consultant in Latin America and in The Netherlands

Andrew Martin Fischer is Senior Lecturer of Population and Social Policy at ISS.

Jayati Ghosh is Professor of Economics at Jawaharlal Nehru University, New Delhi, India and Executive Secretary, International Development Economics Associates.

Sen Gong is Research Fellow at the Research Department of the Social Development, Development Research Centre of the State Council, China.

Duncan Green is head of research at Oxfam GB and author of *From Poverty to Power: How Active Citizens and Effective States can Change the World* (Oxfam, 2008).

Arjan de Haan is Senior Lecturer in Social Policy at ISS and has worked for ten years as adviser at the UK Department for International Development, including in China between 2006 and 2009.

Rolph van der Hoeven is Professor of Employment and Development Economics at ISS and member of the Committee on Development Cooperation of the Dutch Government.

Karel Jansen taught macroeconomic policy and international finance at ISS. He was Visiting Professor at the University of Chiangmai and the Chulalongkorn University in Bangkok, Thailand.

Astha Kapoor is a Consultant in the Planning Commission of India. She obtained her Masters at the Institute of Social Studies in 2009.

Richard King is a researcher at Oxfam GB and co-author of *The Global Economic Crisis and Developing Countries* (with Duncan Green and May Miller-Dawkins, Oxfam, May 2010).

Reynaldo Marconi is Executive Secretary of Association of Financial Entities Specialized in Microfinance (ASOFIN), Bolivia. He is Founder of Latin American and Caribbean Forum of Rural Finance (FOROLACFR).

Mahmood Messkoub is Senior Lecturer in Development Studies at ISS.

Syed Mansoob Murshed is Professor of the Economics of Conflict and Peace at ISS and Professor of International Economics at the Birmingham Business School, University of Birmingham, UK.

Freek B. Schiphorst is Senior Lecturer in Labour Relations at ISS.

Karin Astrid Siegmann is Lecturer in Labour and Gender Economics at ISS.

Max Spoor is Professor of Development Studies at ISS and Visiting Professor at the Barcelona Inter-university Institute for International Studies

Irene van Staveren is Professor of Pluralist Development Economics at ISS and editor of the *Journal of Economic Issues*, the *Review of Social Economy* and *Feminist Economics*.

Rob Vos is Director of the Development Policy and Analysis of the Department of Economic and Social Affairs of the United Nations and Affiliated Professor of Finance and Development at ISS.

Ben White is Professor of Rural Sociology at ISS and Professor in Social Sciences, University of Amsterdam.

1. Introduction: Crisis? What Crisis? For Whom?

Peter A.G. van Bergeijk, Arjan de Haan and Rolph van der Hoeven

---

The global financial and economic crisis that started in September 2007 with a rather limited problem in a market for non-tradeable goods (houses) challenges the way we have been thinking for decades about globalization, development and vulnerability. The crisis confronts social scientists, not just economists, with many issues that need reflection and therefore this book develops a critical multi-disciplinary perspective and a preliminary assessment of the causes and consequences of the global system breakdown. We will concentrate on the developing and emerging economies in order to gain fresh insights into the challenges that the crisis poses to development strategies and policies, both in the South and the North. The crisis has serious social outfalls, slows down the fight against poverty, sometimes increases poverty, deteriorates income equality and reduces access to social services. The crisis also creates political conflict (amongst others about burden sharing and the external effects of national policies), generates new sets of priorities (in both the developed and the developing world), threatens food security and illuminates the need for better global governance frameworks. From an era in which *laissez-faire* capitalism seemed to have gained dominance, the role of the state as a leading actor in fostering economic growth and well-being has remained for some and emerged for others as a new paradigm. This is accompanied by the rise of emerging economies, which present alternative development models like that of China.

We have organized the chapters in this book into four parts. Part I deals with concepts of development. One aim of this part is to show how different concepts produced different analyses and policy prescription, but also how crisis per se influences thinking about developmental questions. Part II provides a set of four heterodox (political) economic interpretations that shed a fresh light on the mainstream discourse. Part III provides a global overview by means of discussions of regional and country experiences. The final part focuses attention on the next crisis, the timing of which is still uncertain of course, but its eventual occurrence is certain. The remainder of this introductory chapter puts the contributions that build these four parts into perspective.

1. PERSPECTIVES ON THE CRISIS

An important theme in this book is that completely different perspectives on the global crisis exist in different parts of the world. Andrew Martin Fischer in Chapter 6 critically analyses the economic perspectives on the causes and culprits of the current crisis as developed in the US and UK (with sources ranging from neo-liberals to New Keynesians) from a post-Keynesian perspective, supported by insights on China. In a nutshell the different perspectives can be related to causality and endogeneity: does saving drive investment (in which case saving glut or underconsumption is the culprit) or does investment drive saving (in which case overconsumption is the culprit). In view of the central position of the saving investment nexus it is astonishing that debt dynamics and the distinction between short-run and long-run effects are often ignored in the policy debate. Analysing these effects in detail, Syed Mansoob Murshed in Chapter 7 shows that Keynesian trade policies that ignore these relations will be counterproductive.

In many countries, particularly and crucially in the poorer countries, crises are regarded as being business as usual. These countries experience and manage slow-downs without perceiving these as the unique events and potential systems breakdown that OECD observers have tended to see. Fantu Cheru (Chapter 4) points out that especially for Sub-Saharan Africa (SSA), the financial crisis was merely the third in a series of crises, as it was preceded by food and fuel crises which impacted them more severely. Also Ben White (Chapter 5) documents the reactions to various economic and social crises since the 1930s. The historical context and earlier crises determine the reactions and perceptions as his case study of Yogyakarta vividly illustrates.

This business-as-usual approach to crisis is one of the important differences between observers in the industrialized countries and in the developing world. Indeed, Jayati Ghosh (Chapter 2) starts with an analysis of earlier crises emphasizing the endemic nature of crisis in the capitalist global order. She shows how the market failed to prevent the social outfall of globalization and the present crisis. It is thus extremely relevant to analyse how countries and institutions in the South have learned lessons from previous crises and how this has influenced their response to the global crisis.

Importantly, the poorest countries, despite the resilience of their inhabitants, often lack the ability to respond adequately as Duncan Green and Richard King in Chapter 3 demonstrate. This makes the current crisis even more abject as poor countries did not contribute to the crisis in the first place.

2. MONITORING THE CRISIS

Many contemporary studies on the impact of the crisis start with the caveat that we do not yet know what has actually happened in many countries – in particular for different parts of the population – simply because adequate real time data (particularly regarding poverty and employment) are not (yet) available. This is especially true for developing and emerging economies. Analysts therefore often have to resort to basic social science detective work, if they want to say something meaningful about the impact and implications of the global crisis for developing countries and emerging markets. Basically four methods can be used in addition to monitoring of key variables:

- the study of previous (financial) crises and their impact on key development indicators,
- the use of (simulation) models,
- indirect observation, and
- field studies that generate qualitative and quantitative observations.

Historical Studies

Previous cases of financial crises and recessions can be analysed in order to provide a perspective on the potential impact of the global crisis. Well-known examples are: the analysis of the poverty impacts of selected financial crises by Gottschalk (2004), the employment and incomes impacts of financial globalization and financial instability by van der Hoeven and Luebker (2007), the lagged effect of crises on economic growth, employment and debts by Reinhart and Rogoff (2009), the impact of economic downturns on human development indicators by the World Bank (2010d) and the impact of financial crises on net ODA of Japan and the Nordics (Roodman 2008). Karel Jansen (Chapter 17) analyses the Asian crisis of the 1990s for Thailand and Ben White (Chapter 5) analyses Yogyakarta in the 1930s, 1990s and 2000s.

Simulation Models

Simulation models can be used to compare scenarios with and without crisis or to analyse differences between pre- and post-crisis periods. Examples are micro-simulation model analyses of poverty and income distribution (Habib et al. 2010 and Sugawara et al. 2010) and the impulse response analysis of external demand shocks and terms of trade losses in World Bank (2010c). Rob Vos (Chapter 18) uses the United Nations Global Policy Model to analyse the risks associated with *uncoordinated* economic recovery and Syed Mansoob Murshed (Chapter 7) uses a formal mathematical model to analyse short- and long-run effects of protectionist policies.

Indirect Observation

Indirect observation has been used to get an idea of how economic activity is developing when official statistics do not exist or become available only with considerable delay or are unreliable. Such indirect observations may relate to, for example, declining consumption, school dropouts, increased illnesses, suicide rates as in Chapter 14 by Ashta Kapoor, the impact on the micro finance sector in Latin America (Marconi and Clemens, Chapter 10) or the volume of imports (an indicator that we will use in the next section).

Field Studies

Quantitative and qualitative field studies provide cases of industries and regions that may shed an early light on the concrete local impact of the crisis on local development. An example is the study by McCulloch and Grover (2010) that combines Indonesia's national household survey with a rapid qualitative study to assess the impact of the crisis on school participation and labour market participation and unemployment in Indonesia. Freek Schiphorst (Chapter 15) traces the crisis in South Africa and the reactions of trade unions.

This book provides a mix of these methods to infer if and how the crisis hits (groups in) the developing and emerging economies. The rich sample of research approaches and methods allow therefore for an informed discussion on the crisis. Crises can impact people in many ways. Sometimes impacts are very clear, but often they are indirect, seemingly absent or less pronounced than expected. Much depends on countries' social policies in place, and the motivations of governments to respond: for example between India and China we witnessed a distinct difference with respect to governments' concerns over rising unemployment, which for the latter was directly informed by the fear of 'social unrest'.

Given the scale that the financial crisis and the preceding food and fuel crises have had, we think it remarkable how – by comparison – little empirical research has documented the impact of the crisis in countries and places where unemployment statistics are absent and living standards are poorly and infrequently measured. In a sense many contributions in this book attempt to fill this gap: Karin Astrid Siegmann (Chapter 13) reviews jobless growth and economic slumps in Bangladesh, Pakistan and India, Mahmood Messkoub (Chapter 11) deals with the impact of the crisis on employment and poverty in the Middle East and Max Spoor (Chapter 12) describes how unbalanced growth aggravated social fallout in some Eastern European countries.

3. A CRISIS IN PHASES

The world economic system is experiencing the largest financial and economic crisis since the 1930s. This crisis so far has followed the classical Minsky pattern (*cf.* Karel Jansen Chapter 17) and at the global level came in three interlocking waves (Jayati Ghosh Chapter 2 and Rob Vos Chapter 18), leading to important social and governance crises.

Collapse of the Financial Sector

The first wave was the collapse of the financial sector. Problems in the US subprime mortgage market in 2007 sparked a credit crunch and an immense financial crisis that required massive public interventions. According to UNCTAD (2009a) the developed economies (had to) spend 3.7 per cent of their gross domestic product (GDP) on fiscal stimulus and in addition an astonishing 49 per cent of GDP was made available to support their financial sectors.[1] On top of this, policy responses included spectacular drops of official interest rates and unprecedented quantitative monetary easing in the US, EU and Japan. The economies outside the OECD on average provided a somewhat stronger fiscal stimulus (about 5 per cent of GDP), but since their financial institutions had not really been infected there was no need to provide public support (the exceptions are India and Saudi Arabia who provided support to the banking sector at the tune of 6 and 20 per cent of GDP, respectively). The policy responses reflected both the global nature of the reduction in effective demand and the OECD-specificity of the shock to the banking and financial sectors.

Collapse of World Trade and Investment

At the end of 2008 much attention was drawn to the 20 per cent reduction in the volume of world trade. Many observers pointed to a lack of trade finance as an important driver of the trade collapse (Auboin, 2009). The April 2009 meeting of the G20 took action and announced additional trade financing of $250 billion, including instruments to mitigate risks and liquidity support. According to the G20 Trade Finance Expert Group (2009, p. 1) by August 2009, an increase of the G20 members involved in the trade finance initiative from 12 to 16 countries had even increased the potential support available to $400 billion. By that time the global trade cycle appeared to be at a turning point, especially for emerging countries in Asia where previous peak levels were being approached and sometimes even passed. The collapse of global investment flows drew somewhat less attention but it was just as spectacular: foreign direct investment (FDI) and cross-border mergers and acquisitions in 2009 declined by 39 and 66 per cent, respectively (UNCTAD 2010a). Again, however, by mid 2009 the foreign investment cycle appeared to be turning around in Asia, in particular in China.

Collapse of Trust in Public Debts

In April 2010 the third wave became manifest and again the source of the problems was in the OECD, but this time it was not the USA but Europe where the crisis wave started. Like in the USA, in the wake of economic stimulus and in attempts to save large banks from bankruptcy, private debts had been transformed into public debts. Large and unsustainable public debts in Greece threatened to contaminate other European countries in financial distress and trigger a round of debt default. Europe created a stabilization fund of €500 billion. The IMF co-financed the EU bail-out of Greece and determined the terms of references, supplementing an additional €250 billion – by far the largest loan arrangement in the history of the IMF. Other European countries such as Spain, Portugal and Ireland were confronted with similar problems. This sovereign risk problem occurred also in the centre and was a consequence of the 2008 crisis (Candelon and Palm 2010). The debt built up in many industrialised countries was the consequence of the stimulus and bail-out response to the crisis. National pressures to reduce the debt by means of fiscal policy may now well frustrate the earlier optimistic attempts for global governance and global stimulus; in effect repeating at an international scale the mistakes of the 1930s. The optimism expressed by the G20 in their 2009 meetings to avoid beggar-thy-neighbour policies through stimulus packages is no longer reflected in the outcome documents of the November 2010 meeting in Seoul. Ghosh (Chapter 2), Cheru (Chapter 4) and

Vos (Chapter 18) argue that much of the momentum of G20 has been lost and that the G20 can hardly been seen as an institution exercising the minimal international financial brinkmanship.

The experiences during the three crisis waves illustrate both the exceptional nature of the crisis and the insufficiency of (inter)national governance and institutions. It should be noted that policy makers so far did not make the capital mistake which prolonged the crisis of the 1930s: they did not opt for protectionism as in the 1930s (which could very well be countereffective; *cf.* Chapter 7 by Syed Mansoob Murshed). In the same spirit it is noteworthy that the amounts of public financial support and guarantees (and consequently of public debt) have been massive by any standard in the developed and several developing countries.

Table 1.1 Output growth 2008–2009 and IMF projections 2010–2011

	2008	2009	2010	2011
World	2.8	–0.6	4.8	4.2
Advanced economies	0.2	–3.2	2.7	2.2
Emerging and developing economies	6.0	2.5	7.1	6.4
China	9.6	9.1	10.5	9.6
India	6.4	5.7	9.7	8.4
Brazil	5.1	–0.2	7.5	4.1
Russia	5.2	–7.9	4.0	4.3

Source: IMF (2010c), p. 2

However, due to the crisis the global geography of economic strengths and financial fragilities has dramatically shifted. First, all shock waves appear to originate from the centre and not from the periphery as was the case during earlier threats to the global economic system (the Latin American debt crisis in the 1980s, the Russian crisis in the 1990s and the East Asian crisis in the 1990s). Second, the depth of the downturn in the national business cycles prompted some to propose the decoupling hypothesis that assumed that business cycles in the emerging-market economies were not or were less linked to those of the OECD economies. In particular in China and India recovery was relatively quick and the reduction in growth rates was mild (Table 1.1), but nevertheless the social consequences were felt by many families, as Chapter 14 on India by Astha Kapoor and Chapter 16 by Arjan de Haan and Sen Gong in China illustrate. The relatively positive outlook for developing countries and emerging markets may of course be genuine, but it also reflects the fact that their banking system was not exposed to the kind of risks that materialized during the first phase of the crisis (so that their downturn could occur later). From this perspective the observation that the world crisis of the 1930s also started in the centre, but later spread to the periphery may be relevant (Rothermund 1996). Experience of the current crisis is directly informed by recent global changes, particularly the emergence of new key players in the international arena, such as India, China, Mexico and Brazil. More than ever, global flows of capital and trade will determine the wealth; each phase of the crisis demonstrates these interdependencies.

An important aspect of the current crisis is the recognition by the major economies that emerging markets can contribute importantly to its solution. The G8 appears to have dissolved itself into the already existing, but until then rather lacklustre G20. In effect the G20 gave a boost to some form of global governance which several commentators had argued for – well before the outbreak of the crisis (ILO 2004; Stiglitz 2006). However, skirmishes about currencies and a new international financial system as well as calls for fiscal tightening risk (as was manifest in the November 2010 meeting in Seoul) dampens considerably the initial enthusiasm about the role of the G20 as the mechanism for international (financial) governance.

4. TRANSMISSION MECHANISMS

It is by now well established that the major transmission mechanisms of the crisis were the reduction in FDI and other capital transfers to developing countries, a decline in trade, a reduction or levelling off in remittance and rethinking of earlier made development aid commitments.

External Finance (FDI, Remittances, Bank Lending and Aid)

In today's world many channels exist through which economies are linked. International capital flows such as FDI, remittances, bank lending, migration and development aid are influenced by the downturn in OECD economies. International capital flows may provide resources when developing and emerging economies are under strain, but these have 'in spite of soaring needs, not risen – they have fallen' (Addison et al. 2010, p. 1). Three of these flows are especially relevant for developing and emerging economies.

- After six years of uninterrupted growth, FDI flows to developing and transition economies according to UNCTAD (2010a) declined in 2009 by 35 and 39 per cent, respectively. (Chapter 8 by Irene van Staveren provides an overview and analysis of FDI trends and volatility.)

- In the decade before 2008 remittances showed strong growth and developed into one of the most important capital sources for developing and emerging economies. In 2009 a sharp break in the upward trend occurred although the reductions were limited (see Chapter 3 by Duncan Green and Richard King and Chapter 4 by Fantu Cheru).[2]
- The OECD's *Development Co-operation Report 2009* estimated that the underlying trend growth rate of the volume of official development aid (ODA) needed to increase to 11 per cent per year in order to achieve the millennium goals. The results in 2009 were, however, disappointing as the amount of aid increased by 0.7 per cent only. Importantly this is not the result of increased spending but of exchange rate movements that contributed more than 4 percentage points. Actually total ODA in current prices and at current exchange rates decreased from $122 billion in 2008 to $119 billion in 2009. (Notably, twelve OECD countries reduced ODA.)

Import Contraction and Development Level

Figure 1.1 analyses the decline in the volume of imports in a cross-country setting for a group of 45 countries over the years 2007–09.[3] It compares the peak and the trough of the import cycle over this period. The figure first of all illustrates the large variation in country experiences. The Netherlands registers one of the smallest import contractions (of about –11 per cent); the largest contractions of some –45 per cent occur in Belarus and Venezuela.

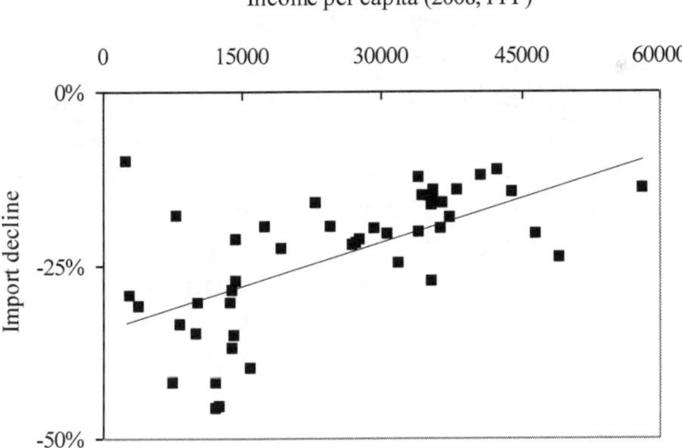

Sources: Calculations based on OECD National Accounts, IMF International Financial Statistics and World Bank indicators data sets

Figure 1.1 Import decline (peak to trough 2007–09) and per capita income

Importantly, Figure 1.1 relates this decline to the level of development (which is approximated by the income per head in US dollars). The dotted regression line indicates that lower income per head is on average associated with stronger contraction of the volume of imports. The observation that the developing and emerging economies (have to) reduce their import expenditures to a much larger extent suggests that they are hit harder by the crisis than the richer countries. Of course this is not a direct observation, but the finding that many developing and emerging economies are adversely hit by the crisis is corroborated by other recent analyses, including the fieldwork studies in this volume.

5. WHERE DOES THE CRISIS BITE?

The key World Bank (2010c) scenarios for 2005–20 still foresee a reduction in the percentage of the world population living at an income level of less than $1.25 a day, but the crisis would add between 53 and 214 million people in absolute poverty in comparison to the pre-crisis trend. Of course, these effects are different in each country and locality. According to a simulation exercise (Habib et al. 2010), in Bangladesh and the Philippines where growth slowed down, poverty is expected to be respectively 1.2 and 1.5 percentage points higher (or 1.4 and 2 million more poor people) than would have been the case without the crisis. In Mexico, where GDP contracted by nearly 7 per cent in 2009, the poverty rate may rise by nearly 4 percentage points in two years. The structure of the economy and the income distribution determine where the income declines hit most. Habib et al. (2010) show that expected income declines are largest in the middle income groups particularly in Bangladesh and the Philippines, whereas they are very significant for the lowest income group in Mexico. Their model suggests that the macroeconomic effects trickle down to the (new) poor and especially a middle income group of 'crisis vulnerable' (typically working in export-oriented industries and located in urban areas) with substantial poverty and distributional effects and potentially important effects on long-term growth (see also Khanna et al. 2010). These effects are often mirrored geographically, with areas dependent on export industries and particular sectors being affected directly, such as Guangdong in China (with a lagged impact on the rural areas from where migrants come) or Sirat in India (see Chapter 14 by Astha Kapoor).

Human development

A reduction in economic growth in the past has been associated with worse performance on human development goals such as health, education and gender. The World Bank (2010c) has analysed the experiences in 163 countries over the period 1980–2008 finding that contractions of economic activity have been associated with deteriorating social indicators.

Moreover, the impact of growth and decline on human development is not symmetrical (Figure 1.2) as the deterioration during a growth deceleration is stronger than the improvement during an upswing. Life expectancy at birth on average declines by 10 per cent as infant and child mortality increase by 50 to 75 per cent, respectively. Cuts in social expenditure may not only deteriorate performance regarding education and health directly but may in addition exert a negative influence over very long periods.

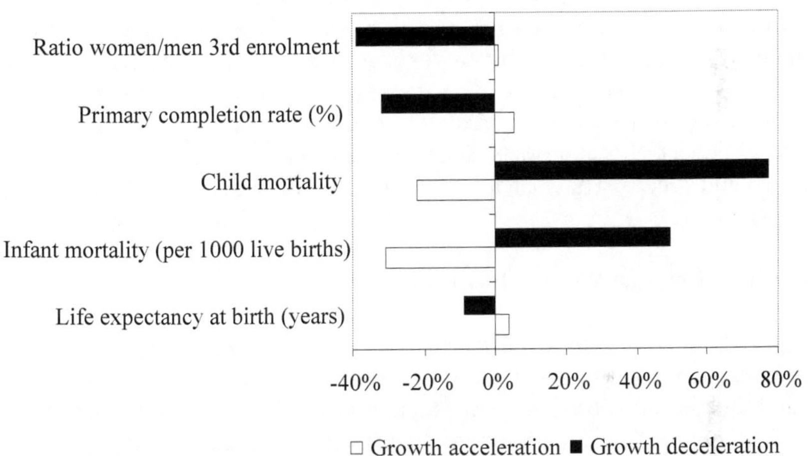

Source: Calculated from World Bank (2010c), Annex 2.1

Figure 1.2 Impact of growth accelerations and decelerations on selected human development indicators

Gender and Child Wellbeing

Duncan Green and Richard King (Chapter 3) report that many women are paying a particular price through their additional unpaid work to support their households, through migration, through additional work in the informal sector and by eating less. Karin Astrid Siegmann (Chapter 13) argues that only a few analyses have highlighted the gender impact of the crisis, not only in terms of statistics but also in terms of changing norms. In some cases the crisis reinforced existing gender norms, but the crisis has also called in question certain norms. A detailed assessment of economic and sociological phenomena is called for.

UNICEF has documented the impact of the global economic crisis on children in Ghana, Burkina Faso and Cameroon (Cockburn et al. 2010). In Ghana, child wellbeing was affected by a sharp increase in monetary poverty and hunger, while in Burkina Faso school participation dropped and child labour force participation increased (see also the next section). Friedman and Schady (2009), using household level data, show that infants die more often during crises because families tend to spend less on health and nutrition. Their estimate suggests that SSA has experienced 30,000 to 50,000 extra child deaths in 2009, and that girls are more likely to die compared to boys. World Bank research in Uganda and Madagascar shows that when household income declines, girls are first to be pulled out of schools.

In East Asia also impacts can be severe. According to Bhutta et al. (2009) the mortality rate among children younger than 5 years in severely affected countries could increase by 3 to 15 per cent, lower birth weight could increase by 5 to 10 per cent, and rates of childhood stunting could increase by 3 to 7 per cent. (Local impacts are also documented in Chapter 4 by Duncan Green and Richard King, Chapter 5 by Ben White and Chapter 14 by Astha Kapoor.)

Incomes, Employment and Inequality

It is still too early to make definite statements on the impact of the crisis on incomes, employment and inequality but nevertheless some worrying facts and trends can be observed. One should not fall into the simplistic trap of looking only at those who have been negatively affected by the crisis. This is so, because the current crisis cannot be seen as an isolated event. The crisis is related to processes of liberalization and globalization which ran out of control. Globalization itself resulted in a greater schism between those who profited and those who were excluded. It is simply wrong to argue that those who were or are excluded from globalization, and thus did not profit in the run up to crisis, can now not lose from the crisis. Indeed the situation of the socially excluded may very well deteriorate at times when governments are reducing social expenditure to reduce public debt built up to save the jobs of the bankers that created the crisis.

Table 1.1, based on information from the various chapters, traces the positions of various socioeconomic groups in various countries' groupings at several stages of the crisis. With the hindsight of the crisis we get a rather pessimistic picture to the extent that in developed countries poorer parts of the population lagged behind in profiting from the globalization bubble before the crisis. For example salaries of lower skilled workers in the USA have not increased over the last 25 years and those of German workers increased only slightly over the last 10 years. The top 1 per cent of households in the USA accounted for only 8.9 per cent of total income in 1976 compared to 23.5 per cent in 2007 (Rajan 2010).

Table 1.1 Effects on various socioeconomic groups in different countries

	Pre crisis	Crisis	Postcrisis stimulus	Postcrisis fiscal austerity	Back on track
Developed countries					
Capital owners	++	–	++	+	?
Skilled workers	++	–	+	–	?
Unskilled workers	–	–	+	–	?
Excluded	–	0	0	–	?
Emerging developing countries					
Capital owners	++	+	++	+	?
Skilled workers	++	–	+	+	?
Unskilled workers	+	–	+	–	?
Peasants	–	–	+	–	?
Poor developing countries					
Capital owners	+	0	+	+	?
Skilled workers	+	–	+	–	?
Unskilled workers	–	–	+	–	?
Peasants	–	0	+	–	?

It appears therefore that the poorer segments in the developed countries face a triple whammy: they did not profit from globalization, they were hardest hit in terms of unemployment and are now bearing the consequences of fiscal tightening following the massive stimulus and bank bail-outs.

The situation for developing countries is even more complex. The growth path of the emerging economies shows similar movements as those of developed countries but of less intensity and thus they were less affected by the crisis. However, except for some Latin American countries, the growing inequality which was building up or being reinforced is not yet being halted, and wage shares in most emerging market economies are still declining, which has a negative effect on domestic demand. The poorer developing countries, mainly in Africa, were less affected as their banking system was less developed, but suffered from slower exports proceeds, remittances and the threat of lower aid in the development of the crisis.

6. WHAT TO DO?

Bold measures have been taken to prevent a worsening of the crisis. The first reaction to the crisis was a consensus on stimulus packages and an attempt to improve global governance by resurrecting the dormant G20 structure. Here the reaction both in developed and developing countries was different than during the 1930s. However, both domestically and internationally, these initiatives have not been followed by deeper and more structural policy changes, which are definitively needed. The November 2010 meeting of the G20 did not provide the necessary breakthrough in terms of improving global governance, as discussed by Ghosh, Green and King, Cheru and Vos in their respective chapters in this volume. Renewed efforts to improve global governance are called for.

At the international level – despite some changes in the Basle guidelines – banks can still dictate markets and bonuses. The support given to banks in most western countries has quickly led to easy profits and a business-as-usual attitude by the banks. Also the absence of an integrated financial system, the continuing global imbalances and the continuing embracement of the export growth model may lead to currency wars. Fiscal policy is another area where national and international concerns intersect. After an unprecedented fiscal expansion to boost growth in all crisis-affected countries, fiscal retrenchment is now advocated by many politicians. A disorderly retrenchment, however, would make it more difficult for the world economy to grow, thus frustrating lowering debt to GDP ratios and jeopardizing job creation (Karin Astrid Siegman Chapter 13 and Mahmood Messkoub Chapter 11).

Another challenge to this crisis is policy change at the national and local level. A first requirement is to bring down the absurdly high levels of income inequality (van der Hoeven 2010). This is not only necessary for having social pacts to fend off the social effects of further crises but also to achieve a more balanced wage-led growth path with less reliance on foreign demand as Jayati Ghosh (Chapter 2) and Max Spoor (Chapter 12) argue. More attention needs to be given to employment creation. Governments have been acting during the crisis as bankers of last resort but not as employers of last resort (see Chapter 9 by Rolph van der Hoeven). Special policies to stimulate employment are necessary, since even a return to economic growth after the crisis does not lead automatically to sufficient growth in jobs. Hysteresis and ratchet effects are a reality of this crisis as they were of earlier crises (Reinhart and Reinhart, 2010).

Furthermore, increasing poverty and its very different manifestations across groups and localities make design of national policy responses a crucial topic. Policies need to be in place – preferably before a crisis hit – not only for the structurally deprived and the chronic poor, and the diversity within this group, but also for those directly affected by the crisis, or the manifold crises, particularly in SSA. While much attention has been paid recently to cash transfers, particularly those of Latin America, and how these were extended during the crisis (as in the case of Brazil's *Bolsa Familia*), the crisis has also led to renewed questions whether a strengthening of traditional social security systems and social programmes can deal with the new vulnerable, or whether systems should be expanded to take these groups into account. It has often been posited that the financial crisis provides an opportunity for the formulation of new social protection policies (Prasad and Gerecke 2010), but there is also evidence of reluctance to invest in social protection policies which are often regarded as 'unproductive' spending.

Responses to crises need to take account of the possible impact on services and human development indicators. According to Ortiz et al. (2010), the importance of social spending appears generally to be better understood during this crisis than during earlier crises. Still average growth in social spending in developing countries has slowed down to 2 per cent during 2008–09, barely exceeding population growth. As these increases were largely facilitated by an overall expansionary fiscal stance, current policies of fiscal retrenchment may well result in lower social spending.

Not all measures can be implemented centrally. The participation of those affected is needed if policy measures become grounded in political reality. Freek Schiphorst (Chapter 15) shows how difficult that is in South Africa. Fantu Cheru (Chapter 4) even calls for alternative formulations of democracy. How international solidarity can play a bigger role is truly a challenge that requires political leadership both in the North and the South.

In addition to political change at a global and national level, the development co-operation community needs to change its perspective on and its thinking about development and about development aid. Lessons related to aid effectiveness at the micro-level may not offer guidance when economies are threatened with collapse and societies may thus be in danger of disintegrating. According to Green and King (Chapter 3), the host South Korea at the November 2010 G20 meeting in Seoul was keen to establish development as a core mission of the group, and even secured an agreement for a 'Seoul Development Consensus for Shared Growth', based on nine 'pillars': infrastructure, private investment and job creation, human resource development, trade, financial inclusion, growth with resilience, food security, domestic resource mobilization and knowledge sharing. However, this call for a rethinking of development aid was overshadowed by the disagreements on reforming the international financial governance system. Giving this, it is unlikely that Western aid donors will have a strong incentive to change quickly and drastically their existing patterns of patronising (people in) developing countries. This is a missed opportunity, also because solutions for a next crisis have to be found in the development of the South, its role in global governance and a greater understanding and recognition of the South's potential and the ability to develop that, by the North.

NOTES

1 The stimulus was to be spent over a number of years. On an annual basis it is less than the fall out in aggregate demand. These numbers do not account for the countercyclical effect of automatic stabilizers.

2 Remittances continued to increase in South Asia and, on average, for low-income countries during 2009.

3 We use the method of indirect observation and analyse the relationship between the level of growth and the contraction of imports (trade, unlike more comprehensive and complex phenomena such as income, is observed reasonably accurately and published without much delay and the impact of a financial crisis should be expected to be most visible and unambiguous in the development of the volume of imports; see Van Bergeijk 2009a). We find strong indications that import contractions are larger in countries with lower per capita income and arguably this implies a stronger impact on economic activity in these countries.

PART I

The Crisis and Concepts of Development

2. Re-orienting Development in Uncertain Times

Jayati Ghosh

It did not really need a crisis to show that the economic development strategy that has been chosen in most parts of the world is flawed. Even during the previous boom, the pattern of growth in both developed and developing countries had too many limitations, paradoxes and inherent fragilities. Much was wrong with the global economic boom that preceded the crisis. It is not only that the boom proved to be unsustainable, based on speculative practices that were enabled and encouraged by financial deregulation. It was also that this boom drew recklessly on natural resources in a manner that has created a host of ecological and environmental problems especially in the developing world. Further, because it was extremely unequal in terms of the spread of benefits, most people in the developing world – even those within the most dynamic economic segment of Asia – did not really gain from that boom.

1. THE PECULIAR GLOBAL BOOM

The financial bubble in the US attracted savings from across the world, including from the poorest developing countries, so that for at least five years the South transferred net financial resources to the North (Bank for International Settlements (BIS) 2008). Developing country governments opened up their markets to trade and finance, gave up on monetary policy and pursued fiscally 'correct' deflationary policies that reduced public spending. So development projects remained incomplete and citizens were deprived of the most essential socio-economic rights. Despite popular perceptions, a net transfer of jobs from North to South did not take place. In fact, industrial employment in the South barely increased in the past decade, even in the 'factory of the world', China.[1] Instead, technological change in manufacturing and the new services meant that fewer workers could generate more output. Old jobs in the South were lost or became precarious and the majority of new jobs were fragile, insecure and low-paying, even in fast-growing China and India (Patnaik 2009). The persistent agrarian crisis in the developing world hurt peasant livelihoods and generated global food problems. Rising inequality meant that the much-hyped growth in emerging markets did not benefit most people, as profits soared but wage shares of national income declined sharply. In most countries, growth in real wages was well below increases in labour productivity in the period 1990–2006 and wage share of national income showed declines in all major regions of the world during the two decades between 1985 and 2005 (ILO 2008a).

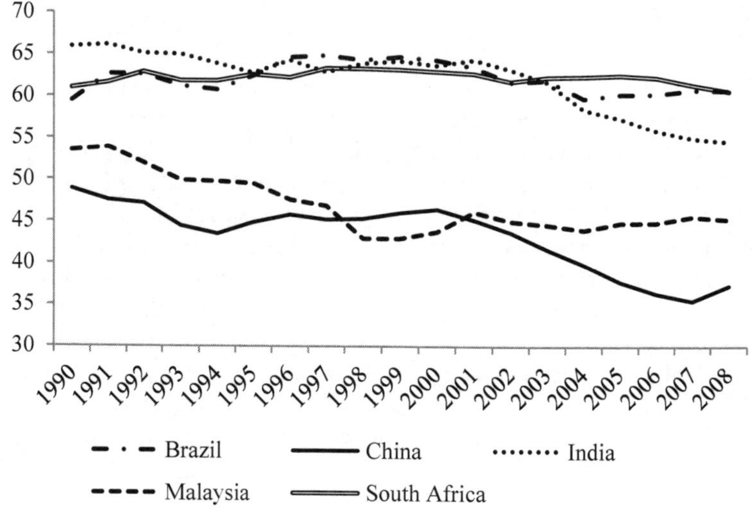

Note: Shares are calculated in current price terms for both consumption and GDP.

Source: UN Statistics Division, National Accounts, accessed 10 March 2010

Figure 2.1 Share of household consumption in GDP (per cent)

Almost all developing countries adopted an export-led growth model, which in turn was associated with suppressing wage costs and domestic consumption in order to remain internationally competitive and achieve growing shares of world markets. As evident from Figure 2.1, household consumption as share of GDP in some of the more 'successful' developing economies declined over this period, in some cases quite significantly, reflecting the strategy of suppressing the home market in order to push out more exports. This led to the peculiar situation of rising savings rates and falling investment rates in many developing countries (e.g. in South Korea and Malaysia, investment rates plummeted from 42 per cent of GDP to 21 per cent between 1998 and 2006, even as savings rates rose from already high levels to rates in excess of 40 per cent; Ghosh 2009a). This led to the holding of international reserves that were then sought to be placed in safe assets abroad. This is related to a classic dilemma of mercantilist strategy, which is evident in exaggerated form for the aggressively export-oriented economies of today: they are forced to finance the deficits of those countries that would buy their products, through capital flows that sustain the demand for their own exports, even when these countries have significantly higher per capita income than their own. The flows of capital from China and other countries of developing Asia constitute an egregious example of this.

This is why globally the previous boom was associated with the South subsidising the North: through cheaper exports of goods and services, through net capital flows from developing countries to the US in particular, through flows of cheap labour in the form of short-term migration. The collapse in export markets brought that process to a sharp stop for a time, but in any case such a strategy is unsustainable beyond a point, especially when a number of relatively large economies seek to use it at the same time. Not only was this a strategy that bred and increased global inequality, it also sowed the seeds of its own destruction by generating downward pressures on price due to increasing competition and protectionist responses in the North.

In this boom, domestic demand tended to be profit-led, based on high and growing profit shares in the economy and significant increases in the income and consumption of newly globalised middle classes, which led to bullish investment in non-tradeable sectors like financial assets and real estate and luxury goods and services. This enabled economies to keep growing even though agriculture was in crisis and employment did not expand enough.

The patterns of production and consumption that emerged meant that growth also involved rapacious and ultimately destructive exploitation of the environment. The costs – in terms of excessive congestion, environmental pollution and ecological degradation – are already being felt in most developing societies, quite apart from the implications such expansion has on the forces generating climate change. There were other negatives associated with the growth pattern. Within several developing countries, it led to an internal 'brain drain' with adverse implications for future innovation and productivity growth. The skewed structure of incentives generated by the explosive growth of finance directed the best young minds towards careers that promised quick rewards and large material gains rather than painstaking but socially necessary research and basic science. The impact of relocation of certain industries and the associated requirement for skilled and semi-skilled labour did lead to increased opportunities for educated employment, but it also led bright young people to enter into work that is typically mechanical and does not require much originality or creativity, with little opportunity to develop their intellectual capacities in such jobs. At the same time, crucial activities that are necessary for the economy were inadequately rewarded. Farming in particular became increasingly fraught with risk and subject to growing volatility and declining financial viability, and the attack on peasant livelihoods also put the crucial task on food production on a more insecure footing in many countries. Meanwhile non-farm work did not increase rapidly enough to absorb the labour force even in the fastest growing economies of the region (ILO 2008b).

Obviously such a strategy is unsustainable beyond a point, especially when a number of relatively large economies seek to use it at the same time. So not only was this a strategy that bred and increased global inequality, it also sowed the seeds of its own destruction by generating downward pressures on price because of increasing competition as well as protectionist responses in the North.

2. GLOBAL FINANCIAL CRISIS AND AFTER

While the recent boom was not stable or inclusive, either across or within countries, the slump has been rather more inclusive, forcing those who did not gain earlier to pay for the sins of irresponsible and unregulated finance.

Financial crises are not new for developing countries, but this was the first time that almost all of them were infected by a crisis that originated in financial markets in the North. The Asian crisis of 1997/98 had already brought home the fact that financial liberalisation can result in crises even in so-called 'miracle economies', whose pace and pattern of GDP growth were significantly higher than the rest of the world. The subsequent experience showed that currency and financial crises have devastating effects on the real economy. The ensuing liquidity crunch and wave of bankruptcies result in severe deflation, with attendant consequences for employment and the standard of living. The post-crisis adoption of pro-cyclical (often IMF inspired, as in Thailand and Indonesia after the Asian financial crisis) stabilisation programmes can worsen the situation by adding public policy-driven downturn to a situation of asset deflation thereby exacerbating the collapse of output and employment. Following the wave of crises during the 1990s and early 2000s, governments from developing countries became so sensitive to the possibility of future crises that they adopted very restrictive macroeconomic policies and restrain public expenditure even in crucial social sectors. When the post-crisis strategy was also associated with continued financial deregulation and lowered emphasis on credit for small borrowers, it tended to reduce financial inclusion even while it increased financial fragility, as is now evident in countries like Indonesia (Ghosh and Chandrasekhar 2009). Past experience of crisis had also led to a more cautious and calibrated approach to banking and financial sector reform in some countries. This prevented extremely adverse financial effects particularly in some countries like China and India, and also allowed the region as a whole to recover faster from this crisis.

The impact of the crisis in real economy has mostly been felt in employment, and this is where the effects of the crisis continue to be widespread and serious. Employment declined sharply in export-oriented sectors, creating negative multiplier effects across other sectors. The effects on social sectors and on human development conditions in general have been marked (Chhibber, Ghosh and Palanivel 2009; Green, King and Miller-Dawkins 2010). As economies slowed down, people faced open or disguised unemployment, loss of livelihood and deteriorating conditions of living. In the recovery, even though output has rebounded in most regions, employment expansion has remained sluggish and labour market conditions in most countries continue to remain adverse for workers. Of course, it is well known that over the standard business cycle, as well as in other past experience of financial crises, employment tends to recover more slowly and to a lesser extent than output (Reinhart and Rogoff 2009a). To that extent, the delayed recovery of employment would seem to be only normal, and not cause for excessive concern. But this current crisis has followed a boom in which, despite rapid increases in economic activity, employment – especially in the formal sector – had simply not kept pace. So labour markets across the world were increasingly characterised by more casual non-formal contracts and the growth of precarious forms of self-employment rather than 'decent work'. In other words, the boom did not generate enough productive employment, yet the crisis has already had severe effects in reducing even those inadequate levels of employment across the world.

The collapse of employment that occurred over the course of the crisis is evident from Figure 2.2, which shows the percentage change in total employment in developed and developing countries.[2] Obviously, the fall was greatest for developed countries. The recent slight recovery in employment growth rates in developing countries may be interpreted as a sign that the worst is now over for the developing world even on the employment front. However, this is not really the case. Paid employment in non-agricultural activities has continued to plummet over the course of the past year (Figure 2.3). So the apparent recovery of employment in developing countries is likely to have been largely in self-employment in various forms, which reflects the lack of social security and unemployment protection in most developing countries. Where there is no real social option to continue in open unemployment, underemployment expressed in self-employed activities is much more likely to be the norm.

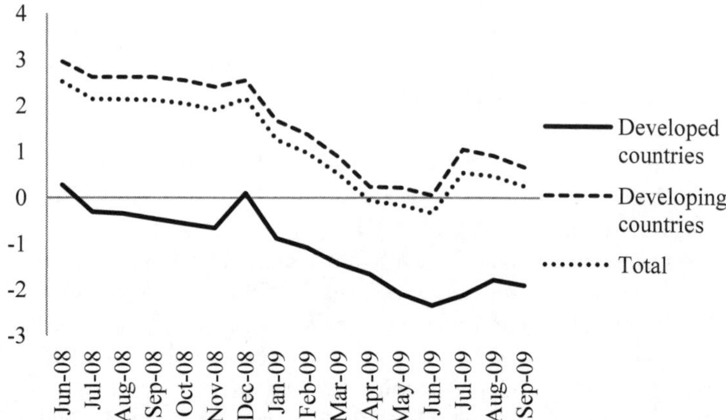

Source: ILO Global Trends in Employment, *Monthly Information Bulletin*, January 2010

Figure 2.2 Total employment (percentage change over the same period of the previous year)

Within non-agriculture, manufacturing employment has shown the sharpest recent declines, and what is more significant is that they have persisted even though manufacturing output in developing countries as a group has rebounded quite rapidly since March 2009. This suggests that even for manufacturing, and certainly in services, self-employment has been the only 'buoyant' form of job creation since the crisis broke. Self-employment in manufacturing is increasingly indicative of home-based work for complex, often global, production chains. But it does allow for more underemployment in the face of reduced demand, rather than open unemployment.

Another aspect of the same tendencies is reflected in unemployment rates. Open unemployment rates in August 2009 were around 40 per cent higher than they were a year previously in developed countries, but only around 10 per cent higher on average in developing countries taken as a group (ILO 2010a). For reasons noted above, open unemployment is only rarely a feasible option for many people in developing countries that do not have properly functioning systems of unemployment insurance or benefit, or related types of protection from job loss. As a result, many workers who lose their jobs, as well as new entrants to the labour market, have no option but to engage in some economic activity, even if it is not paid employment. This is why rates of open unemployment have been fluctuating around a largely stable trend through the crisis. However, the rapid rise in self-employment, often in very low-paying and precarious activities, is essentially a response to the lack of available opportunities for paid employment.

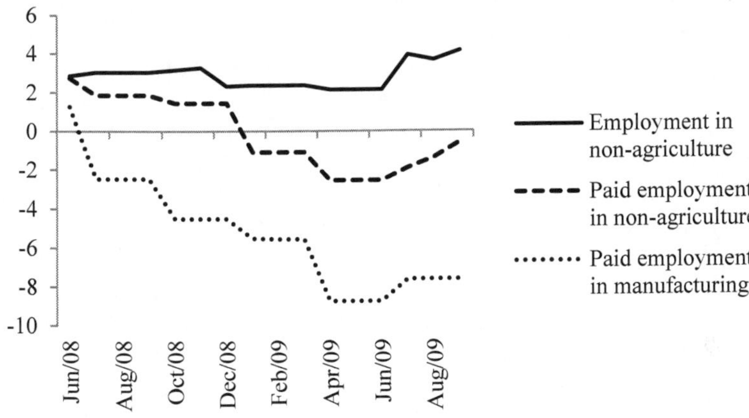

Source: ILO Global Trends in Employment, *Monthly Information Bulletin*, January 2010

Figure 2.3 Changes in employment in developing countries (per cent change over previous year)

This is of particular concern, as it is increasingly evident that the process of global economic recovery may not continue in a stable and sustained fashion. On a structural level, the three basic imbalances that caused the most recent crisis of international capitalism have still not been resolved: the imbalance between finance and the real economy; the macroeconomic imbalances between major players in the international economy; and the ecological imbalance that will necessarily become a constraint on future growth, not only because of climate change but because of other environmental problems and the demand for energy. Without resolution of these problems, sustained growth is no longer possible in the global economy. Further, the resolution of such problems is likely to be associated with severe and potentially protracted crises in many areas and countries. These structural problems in turn are associated with several business cycle problems, such that there continue to be several downside risks for future growth, particularly for the well-being of much of the world's population.

First, the problems in finance remain just below the surface. They have not been adequately addressed or dealt with, and are therefore likely to strike again quite soon. The underlying problem of stagnating or declining real estate markets and concerns with sovereign debt are compounded by continuing disincentives for 'efficient' behaviour and incentives for excessive risk-taking in financial markets. Moral hazard is greater than ever before, because bailouts were not accompanied by adequate regulation (Stiglitz 2009a; Kregel 2010). So the problems in global finance are far from over, and are likely to return with even greater ferocity in the foreseeable future. This is also true in developing countries, many of which are even being encouraged to deregulate their own financial markets.

Second, this has direct implications for certain global markets that directly affect people's lives: those for food and fuel. It is now an open secret that the huge price volatility in food and oil prices was not related to any real economic forces, but rather significantly related to the involvement of financial players in such markets (UNCTAD 2010b; Wahl 2009; Ghosh 2010a). This was particularly so because futures contracts allowed the emergence of 'index investors' who simply bet on changing prices and thus drove up prices far beyond those necessitated by any real changes in demand and supply. Commodities emerged as an attractive investment avenue for financial investors from around 2006, when the US housing market showed the initial signs of its ultimate collapse. This was aided by financial deregulation that allowed purely financial agents to enter such markets without requirements of holding physical commodities, such as the Commodity Futures Modernization Act of 2000, which effectively deregulated commodity trading in the United States, by exempting over-the-counter (OTC) commodity trading (outside of regulated exchanges) from CFTC oversight. This allowed all investors, including hedge funds, pension funds and investment banks, to trade commodity futures contracts without any position limits, disclosure requirements, or regulatory oversight. According to the Bank for International Settlements (BIS 2009), the value of outstanding amounts of OTC commodity-linked derivatives (other than gold and precious metals) increased from $5.8 trillion in June 2006 to $7.1 trillion in June 2007 to as much as $12.4 trillion in June 2008. This generated a bubble, beginning in futures markets and transmitted to spot markets.

From mid-2008 commodity prices started falling as index investors started to withdraw, accentuated by the global recession. But prices started rising again from early 2009, even before there was any real evidence of global output recovery. The price increase between January 2009 and June 2010 was 20 per cent for all food items as a group (*IMF Commodity Trade Statistics* September 2010). Once again, this increase does not reflect real economy forces: global demand and supply for most commodities remain broadly in balance. Even wheat prices, which showed the sharpest increase in this period, responded only partly to poor weather and export bans in countries like Russia, since the price change was well in excess of evident changes in current and projected supply. Such forces were able to be active because there had been no regulation of commodity futures markets and the bulk of contracts were still conducted in OTC trading rather than in regulated exchanges with sufficient margin requirements and position limits. While the Dood-Frank financial reform bill in the US aims to introduce such regulation, it is still not clear how it will be implemented and whether the rules (which are yet to be framed) will actually be effective in stemming purely speculative activity by financial index traders in commodity futures markets. The European Union is also considering some regulation in this regard, but this too has yet to be fully formulated.

Obviously this is bad news for most people in the developing world, since the international transmission of prices in most countries has been rapid for rising prices but not so marked in periods of falling prices (Ghosh 2010a). Food prices in most developing countries were in general considerably higher in early 2010 than they were two years previously (FAO 2010), and much higher than increases in nominal wage incomes (which have been mostly stagnant). The most direct way this has happened is obviously through trade. Countries in which a very large proportion of the basic food requirement is met through domestic supply (e.g. China) have experienced less volatility compared to those that import a considerable part of domestic consumption (FAO 2009). But even in these countries food price inflation has been much higher than general inflation. But the global crisis further constrained the ability of many developing countries to import more food (because of declining exports and capital flow reversals) and reduced the possibilities of enhanced public spending to ensure food distribution to the poor. For many developing countries, this has been compounded by exchange rate changes that have made imports – including of food – much more expensive in domestic currency terms.

Developing countries are caught in a pincer movement: between volatile global prices on the one hand, and reduced fiscal space on the other hand. Price volatility and changes in marketing margins mean that the benefits of price increases generally do not reach the direct producers, even as consumers (already hit by stagnant wages and falling employment) suffer from higher prices. Among more vulnerable populations, the effect of renewed food price increases on real incomes, hunger and undernutrition is likely to be devastating (Chhibber, Ghosh and Palanivel 2009).

Third, the unwinding of global macroeconomic balances that is already under way means that the United States cannot continue to be the engine of growth for the world economy. So other countries must find other sources of growth, especially in domestic demand (which should ideally be through wage-led growth) as well as by diversifying exports (UNCTAD 2010b). There is some evidence that this is occurring, but thus far this is nowhere near the extent required. Stimulating more bubbles in non-tradeable sectors like real estate and stock markets in the hope that this will once again generate more real economic growth is not a sustainable alternative to this, yet this is the direction that most policy measures have taken. In 'successful' developing countries, the relative lack of mass demand was an important element in enabling export-driven growth, both because of its association with lower wages and because it allowed more export surpluses to be squeezed out. But, in addition, it was relevant in preventing more balanced growth based on the development of domestic or regional markets. Without significant restructuring of global demand in favour of the large segments of the world's population that still has to meet basic needs, world growth will not just be more unequal, it will simply run out of steam.

Fourth, unfortunately, such re-orientation of economic growth in the world economy has been made more difficult by pro-cyclicality of adjustment measures being imposed on developing and transition economies that have been hit hardest by the crisis. Despite all the statements to the contrary, the IMF has continued to impose stringent pro-cyclical conditionality on most of the countries that seek emergency assistance, and others are being forced into deflationary measures by the combination of falling exports and capital flow reversals. For example, in Pakistan, Hungary and Ukraine, the IMF assistance has come with conditions on reducing fiscal deficits through measures such as lowering public expenditure, gradually eliminating energy subsidies, raising electricity tariffs, freezing public sector wages, placing a cap on pension payments and postponing social benefits. In monetary policy, the focus on inflation targeting has led the IMF to suggest or insist upon higher interest rates even in the context of recession in Latvia, Iceland and Pakistan and other countries (Third World Network 2009). Even in developing countries where the impact of the global crisis was less extreme, fiscal balances have been upset first by rising oil and food prices (in importing countries) and then by recession that affected tax collections. Since a lot of policy response has been directed to preventing institutions from collapse, this means that proportionately more state resources have been directed to bailouts and to monetary and fiscal incentives for business, rather than to maintaining public services or increasing employment. This has had adverse impact on social indicators in a number of countries. It has been estimated that the crisis is likely to have been associated with a deceleration or even reversal of poverty reduction especially in the developing world, with anywhere between 73 million and 100 million more people in poverty than would have been the case without the crisis (UN/DESA 2010b).

Fifth, both the nature of the previous boom and the effects of the current crisis suggest that, for various reasons, consumption demand (especially that emanating from wage incomes broadly defined) is likely to remain suppressed for some time, and this will prevent a more balanced recovery. The constraints on expanding consumption in the US and Europe are now well known: both public and private sectors have very significantly high debt to GDP ratios, and the process of rectification of these balance sheets is either already under way or likely to start very soon. In the US, where the debt-driven private consumption boom was the most marked, household savings rates have already started rising from their very low levels (Papadimitriou, Hansen and Zezza 2009) and a similar process is operating in Europe. It was expected that increased public spending would substitute for this inevitable repairing of private balance sheets, and that has actually been the case in the past year. However, the remarkably rapid political backlash against 'excessive' government spending – even though it has little validity within a Keynesian macroeconomic framework – seems to have affected both the ability and the willingness of governments in the developed economies to engage in further spending to ward off potential recession. The dangers of an early withdrawal of stimulus measures are thus very high (as noted also in ILO 2009g and UNCTAD 2010b).

3. ELEMENTS OF AN ALTERNATIVE APPROACH TO GROWTH AND DEVELOPMENT

It is now a cliché that every crisis is also an opportunity. As the global financial crisis unfolds and creates downturns in real economies everywhere, it is easy to see only the downside, as jobs are lost, many firms go bankrupt, the value of financial savings of workers is wiped out, and material insecurity becomes widespread. But in fact this global crisis offers a greater opportunity than we have had for some time now, for the world's citizens and their leaders to restructure economic relations in a more democratic and sustainable way. Clearly, if countries in which the majority of the world's population are concentrated are actually to achieve their development project in a sustainable way, new and more creative economic strategies have to be pursued. Wage-led growth, including through measures such as those outlined below, is likely to be an essential element of such strategies.

There are several necessary elements of this. First, globally, everyone now recognises the need to reform the international financial system, which has failed to meet two obvious requirements: preventing instability and crises, and transferring resources from richer to poorer economies. Not only have we experienced much greater volatility and propensity to financial meltdown across emerging markets and now even industrial countries, but even the periods of economic expansion have been based on the global poor subsidising the rich. Within national economies, this system has encouraged pro-cyclicality; it has rendered national financial systems opaque and impossible to regulate; it has encouraged bubbles and speculative fervour rather than real productive investment for future growth; it has allowed for the proliferation of parallel transactions through tax havens and loose domestic controls; it has reduced the crucial developmental role of directed credit. Given these problems, there is no alternative to systematic state regulation and control of finance. Since private players will inevitably attempt to circumvent regulation, the core of the financial system – banking – must be protected, and this is only possible through social ownership. Therefore, some degree of socialisation of banking (and not just socialisation of the risks inherent in finance) is also inevitable. In developing countries this is also important because it enables public control over the direction of credit, without which no country has industrialised.

Second, the excessively export-oriented model that has dominated the growth strategy of most developing countries and some developed countries (such as Germany) for the past few decades needs to be reconsidered. This is not a just a desirable shift – it has become a necessity given the obvious fact that the US can no longer continue to be the engine of world growth through increasing import demand in the near future. This means that countries that have relied on the US and the EU as their primary export markets and important source of final demand must seek to redirect their exports to other countries and most of all to redirect their economies towards more domestic demand. This requires a shift towards wage-led and domestic demand-led growth particularly in the countries with economies large enough to sustain this shift. This can happen not only through direct redistributive strategies but also through public expenditure to provide more basic goods and services.

In developed countries with relatively strong institutions that can affect the labour market, including collective wage bargaining, effective minimum wage legislation and the like, it is probably easier to think of wage-led growth and strategies to allow wages to keep pace (or at least grow to some extent) with labour productivity growth. But what about most developing countries, where such institutions are relatively poorly developed and where many if not most workers are in informal activities, often self-employed? How are wage increases and better working conditions to be ensured in such cases? And what does a macroeconomic policy of wage-led growth entail in such a context?

In fact, it is still both possible and desirable to get wage-led growth in such contexts. There are several important elements of such a strategy in developing countries with large informal sectors. It is possible to make the economic growth process more inclusive and employment-intensive, by directing resources to the sectors in which the poor work (such as agriculture and informal activities), areas in which they live (relatively backward regions), factors of production which they possess (unskilled labour) and outputs which they consume (such as food). This requires ensuring the greater viability of informal production, through better access to institutional credit to farmers and other small producers, greater integration into supply chains and marketing that improves their returns, and technology improvements that increase labour productivity in such activities. In addition, governments may need to provide increases in public employment that set the floor for wages (for example in schemes such as that enabled by the National Rural Employment Guarantee Act in India) and improve the bargaining power of workers. Everywhere in the developing world, and particularly in low-income countries, there is need for much better social protection, with more funding, wider coverage and consolidation, more health spending and more robust and extensive social insurance programmes including pensions and unemployment insurance.

A broader interpretation of this also requires increased focus on the public delivery of wage goods (housing, other infrastructure, health, education, even nutrition) financed by taxing surpluses. The last point is often not recognised as a crucial element of a possible wage-led strategy, but it can be extremely significant. Furthermore, such a strategy can be used effectively even in otherwise capitalist export-oriented economies, as long as surpluses from industrialisation and exports can be mobilised to provide wage goods publicly. Indeed, this has been an important and unrecognised feature of successful Asian industrialisation from Japan to the East Asian NICs to (most recently) China. The public provision of affordable and reasonably good quality housing, transport facilities, basic food, school education and basic health care all operated to improve the conditions of life of workers and (indirectly) therefore to reduce the money wages that individual employers need to pay workers. This not only reduced overall labour costs for private employers, but also provided flexibility for producers competing in external markets, since a significant part of fixed costs was effectively reduced.

Third, fiscal policy and public expenditure must be brought back to centre stage. Clearly, fiscal stimulation is now essential in both developed and developing countries, to cope with the adverse real economy effects of the current crisis and prevent economic activity and employment from falling. Fiscal expenditure is also required to undertake and promote investment to manage the effects of climate change and promote greener technologies. And public spending is crucial to advance the development project in the South and fulfil the promise of achieving minimally acceptable standards of living for everyone in the developing world. Social policy – the public responsibility for meeting the social and economic rights of citizens – is not only desirable but also contributes positively to development. It is also increasingly evident that social policies that are often seen simply as welfare or redistributive measures (employment schemes, incentivised cash transfers to particular groups, social protection like unemployment benefits) can become important macroeconomic stabilisers, by providing automatic countercyclical buffers. The National Rural Employment Guarantee Scheme in India, for example, not only provides more days of employment per amount spent than any previous employment programme in India, but has also been an important means of injecting purchasing power into a depressed rural economy and limiting the adverse effects of the economic downturn on rural effective demand. Similarly, it is likely that the new health insurance programme in China, whereby the government would cover up to 85 per cent of the costs of health care, will contribute significantly to releasing more disposable income to households and thus boost their consumption, adding to domestic demand from this quarter.

Fourth, there have to be conscious attempts to reduce economic inequalities, both between countries and within countries. We have clearly crossed the limits of what is 'acceptable' inequality in most societies, and future policies will have to reverse this trend. Globally and nationally, we have to recognise the need to reduce inequalities in income and wealth, and also most significantly in the consumption of natural resources. This is obviously important for political stability and social cohesion, but it has important economic effects as well, since basing economic growth on domestic wage-led demand tends to be more stable than reliance on external demand as the engine of growth. Emphasising workers' rights in both formal and informal economies requires employers to focus on increasing labour productivity and therefore tends to shift the fulcrum of technological change across the economy. The focus has to be on raising the aggregate productivity of labour in the economy, rather than in specific sectors or enclaves, as well as on reducing and improving the conditions of unpaid labour.

However, even with greater economic equality, the process of curbing unsustainable consumption is more complicated than might be imagined, as unsustainable patterns of production and consumption are deeply entrenched in the richer countries and are aspired to in developing countries. But many millions of citizens of the developing world still have poor or inadequate access to the most basic conditions of decent life, such as minimum physical infrastructure including electricity and transport and communication links, sanitation, health, nutrition and education. Ensuring universal provision of this will inevitably require greater per capita use of natural resources and more carbon-emitting production. So both sustainability and equity require a reduction of the excessive resource use of the rich, especially in developed countries, but also among the elites in the developing world. This means that redistributive fiscal and other economic policies must be specially oriented towards reducing inequalities of resource consumption, globally and nationally. For example, within countries essential social and developmental expenditure can be financed by taxes that penalise resource-waste.

Fifth, this requires new patterns of both demand and production. This is why the present focus on developing new means of measuring genuine progress, well-being and quality of life are so important. Quantitative GDP growth targets, that still dominate the thinking of regional policy makers, are not simply distracting from these more important goals, but can even be counterproductive. For example, a chaotic, polluting and unpleasant system of privatised urban transport involving many private vehicles and over-congested roads actually generates more GDP than a safe, efficient and affordable system of public transport that reduces vehicular congestion and provides a pleasant living and working environment. So it is not enough to talk about 'cleaner, greener technologies' to produce goods that are based on the old and now discredited pattern of consumption. Instead, we must think creatively about such consumption itself, and work out which goods and services are more necessary and desirable for our societies.

Sixth, a more comprehensive approach to agriculture and rural development is required, which recognises the role of public intervention. This remains important because agriculture still constitutes the basic source of livelihood for half the labour force in the developing world, yet there has been a prolonged period of agrarian crisis across the developing world, which has persisted through periods of commodity price booms and declines. The crisis has been largely policy-driven (although climate changes have played some still minor role) and this at some level is good news because it means it can also be reversed through appropriate policies, which bring back the role of public research and extension as well as state intervention in water management, input provision and crop price management in order to make developing country agriculture more viable and productive.

Seventh, as in agriculture, even in non-agricultural activities the required changes in patterns of demand and technologies of meeting them cannot be left to market forces, since the international demonstration effect and the power of advertising will continue to create undesirable wants and unsustainable consumption and production. But public intervention in the market cannot be knee-jerk responses to constantly changing short-term conditions. Instead, planning – not in the sense of the detailed planning that destroyed the reputation of command regimes, but strategic thinking about the social requirements and goals for the future – is absolutely essential. Fiscal and monetary policies, as well as other forms of intervention, will have to be used to redirect consumption and production towards social goals, and to reorganise economic life to be less rapacious and more sustainable. This is particularly important for the quality of urban life: the high rates of urbanisation in developing countries mean that even in many countries that are dominantly rural, within two decades half the population will live in urban areas.

Eighth, since state involvement in economic activity is now an imperative, it is necessary to develop methods and practices to make such involvement more democratic and accountable within our countries and internationally. Large amounts of public money are being used and will continue to be used for financial bailouts and to provide fiscal stimuli in the near future. How this is done will have huge implications for distribution, access to resources and living conditions of the ordinary people whose taxes will be paying for this. So it is essential that we design the global economic architecture to function more democratically. And it is even more important that states across the world, when formulating and implementing policies, are open and responsive to the needs of the majority of their citizens.

Finally, we need an international economic framework that supports all this, which means more than just that capital flows must be controlled and regulated so that they do not destabilise any of these strategies. The global institutions that form the organising framework for international trade, investment and production decisions also need to change and become not just more democratic in structure but more genuinely democratic and people-oriented in spirit, intent and functioning. Financing for development and conservation of global resources must become top priorities of the global economic institutions. In turn they cannot continue to base their approach on what is increasingly discredited as an unbalanced economic model.

4. CAN THE G20 DO IT?

This is what makes recent initiatives in the global economy – or rather, the lack of them – rather depressing. In the immediate wake of the crisis following the collapse of Lehmann Brothers in September 2008, the leaders of the major countries did indeed display a degree of co-ordination and moved to employ combined fiscal and monetary stimuli. It is generally agreed that this was crucial in saving the entire global capitalist system from collapse. But as soon as that immediate crisis was averted, earlier and newer discords between countries have emerged once again to prevent co-ordinated policy response. This is evident in the recent behaviour of the G20. The G20 is obviously at least somewhat more representative of the global economy and the world's population than the G8 that it replaced, and in the Toronto Summit of April 2009 it displayed a welcome sense of cohesion. But subsequently it has clearly lost its way, and currently seems incapable of meeting the fundamental challenges that still face the world, whether in terms of economic patterns of climate change or even security. In economic terms, there are now what are being described as apparently 'irreconcilable differences' between surplus and deficit countries, for example, or between countries that are trying to engineer lower values of their currencies through monetary policies and other measures and other countries who are trying to prevent appreciation created by the inflow of hot money. There is no doubt that these issues have emerged as significant areas of friction between some major economies. There are growing fears of currency wars and trade wars, and these fears can at best be only be partly alleviated by the platitudes coming out of summit documents. In fact the document produced by the Seoul Summit of G20 conveyed a sense of complete confusion, not just in terms of contradictions across the positions held by governments of different countries, but contradictions *within* positions, in terms of stated goals and the means to achieve them.

The obsession with imbalances obscures the lack of coherence on what should be the more significant question: what are to be the major drivers of growth for the world economy? This is important because of the absence of a global economic leader willing and able to fulfil the roles identified by Charles Kindleberger: discounting in crisis; countercyclical lending to countries affected by private investors' decisions; and providing a market for net exports of the rest of the world, especially those countries requiring it to repay debt. For obvious reasons, the US cannot currently do these, and there is no evident alternative. That is why co-ordination is so critical right now for international capitalism.

It is remarkable that the countries that ought to be the most concerned about this within the developed world seem to be the most confused, particularly from a developing country perspective. In fact, each country and each economic region is seeking to base its future expansion on net export growth, forgetting the rather obvious point that all countries cannot use net export growth as the route to expansion does not seem to have been understood, so all governments think they can export their way out of trouble. This will have inevitable implications for trade and currency wars, and the likelihood of global economic stagnation.

As it happens, the US current account deficit is already under correction: the current account deficit in 2009 was just above half its 2008 level, and the data for this year suggest that it will stay at around that level. For the rest of the world, it does not really matter whether the reduction occurs through currency movements or trade protectionism or domestic economic contraction: the point is that some other engine of growth has to be found.

Fortunately, this is actually not so difficult. Internationally, meaningful measures to enable sustained expansion of demand from low income countries can provide an equitable way out of this global dilemma. Within countries, domestic wage-led growth can prove to be a massive engine of expansion. But first our leaders have to get over their export obsession, and recognise that the first priority internationally should be to take meaningful measures to enable sustained expansion of wage-income-based demand, particularly from low income countries. This is really the only sustainable and equitable way out of the current global dilemma.

NOTES

1. It is worth noting that secondary sector employment in China was broadly stagnant in absolute numbers between 1997 and 2004, despite very rapid increases in manufacturing output in the same period (Chandrasekhar and Ghosh 2006). This reflected technological change associated with rapid per worker productivity increases. Thereafter, while secondary employment has grown, the increases are well below those in secondary sector output (*China Statistical Yearbook 2009*).
2. The most recent data provided here and in the subsequent charts should be interpreted with some caution, since they show the evidence only from reporting countries with the most recent data, and could be revised once a fuller dataset is available.

3. How have Poor Women and Men Experienced the Global Economic Crisis: What have We Learned?

Duncan Green and Richard King

> I've never made any mistake, never done anything wrong. It's probably because of my age ...it's very difficult for older people, difficult to get a new job – even youths find it hard. (41-year-old female garment worker dismissed from a factory in Serang, Indonesia)

> I feel cheated as I wonder how economic problems somewhere in America can make my cash crop suffer here in Malawi. It's a shame that I cannot boil and eat it. (Cotton farmer, Malawi)

> [My relatives in the US] are unable to send me money because the job opportunities are not there any more. Their support is a huge contribution to the family here because it helps us to support children in school and pay medical bills when one is sick. (54-year-old in Monrovia, Liberia)

In this chapter, we summarize the findings of Oxfam's research[1] on the impact of, and response to, the global economic crisis that began in 2008, and discuss the policy implications for governments, aid donors and international financial institutions. We focus on two issues in particular: resilience at household level, and the looming fiscal crunch affecting many poor countries.

1. WHAT HAS HAPPENED?

In a seismic expansion of the financial earthquake that shook the banking centres of Europe and North America, the crisis has been transmitted to the 'real economies' of poor countries along a number of fault lines, with each wave of impact having its own rhythm and amplitude. Across the world, some economic plates are already settling, while others are still being shaken. The first developing countries to experience the crisis were those with the most globally integrated financial sectors. Next came the impact on trade, as volumes and prices of commodities and manufactures collapsed across the globe. Women and men selling food on the street, doing piecework in the home, and picking through waste were affected as demand for their services dropped and more people joined their ranks. Remittances from migrant workers in rich countries fell, though not as badly as anticipated. Finally, with an even greater lag time, came the impact on government spending in poor countries and donor aid budgets – it is yet to be seen whether rich country governments will stand by their aid promises, or force poor countries and people to pay the price of their financial folly.

But how people living in poverty have personally experienced the crisis sometimes fails to conform with the 'top down' analysis in the previous paragraph. The global crisis was superimposed on a number of other processes such as the global food price spike of 2007–09, the daily struggle for survival and the impacts of climate change, with people understandably failing to distinguish between different sources of threats. According to research by the Institute of Development Studies (Hossain and Eyben 2009), in several African countries and Bangladesh, poor communities registered the food price spike as far more serious than the global meltdown (and the impact of the crisis in easing the food price pressures may even have been benign).

Moreover, impacts that may appear to be 'lost in the noise' at a local level can still be cumulatively significant at a larger scale. Although Oxfam staff reported little noticeable community impact in many African countries, subsequent research revealed a net fiscal impact that was very large indeed, with serious implications for future debt service and essential service provision, as discussed below.

Generalizations are risky with such a complex picture, but overall Oxfam has seen the crisis hit East Asia primarily through trade and labour markets, with mass layoffs in supply chains producing garments and electronics for the world's consumers, and knock-on impacts into the informal sector. In sub-Saharan Africa and the Pacific Islands, the impact has been mostly via commodity exports and reductions in trade revenues, starving governments of cash and threatening a fiscal crisis in the months and years to come. Latin America has experienced both. Eastern Europe has suffered the highest degree of financial contagion and has seen the largest falls in GDP, while Central Asia has been hard hit by its dependence on the Russian economy, which suffered both from falling oil prices and a banking crisis. South Asia has been largely insulated from the crisis, with Sri Lanka the worst affected country in the region.

2. GENDERED ASPECTS OF THE CRISIS

Few analyses have highlighted the gender impact of the crisis – a serious oversight. Oxfam's research on this issue is probably its most important and original contribution, and includes an issue of the *Gender and Development* journal[2] as well as some stand-alone papers.

In countries such as Thailand and Cambodia, women employed in the frontline of the world's consumer supply chains have lost their jobs in large numbers. Many others have suffered wage freezes, reductions of work hours or were pressured into less secure contracts, as companies have taken advantage of the crisis.

Gender norms (the ideas about women and men that shape relations between the sexes in the household, community, market and wider society) also matter. In some cases the crisis has served to reinforce existing gender norms. For example, women may be the first to lose their jobs in an office or factory, especially where they are regarded as secondary breadwinners, but the impact of this on workers and their families may be underestimated if gender norms perpetuate the notion that men are the primary providers of family income while women work to earn small amounts to cover incidental expenses.

Conversely, gender norms may be called into question by the crisis. In some cases these norms will decompose (for example, men who find themselves unemployed as a result of the crisis may temporarily take on roles within the reproductive economy that they are not accustomed to, such as cooking the family meal). There is also the possibility that in some circumstances, gender norms will be transformed on a permanent basis, with the traditional division of labour, and men's and women's overall work burden, being renegotiated within both the reproductive and productive economies. In the early days of the crisis in Hanoi, for example, women day labourers were ready to do jobs that had previously been the preserve solely of men (such as those in the construction industry) and vice versa (Nguanbanchong 2010).

To fully understand the crisis from a gender perspective, we cannot simply ask how the crisis affects women in paid employment, or indeed explore how it affects men and women differently; rather, we need to explore the impact that it has on the reproductive economy. This involves looking at the ways in which women and men in poverty struggle to survive day-to-day, at the different roles and responsibilities that each sex has in the context of care of, and support to, the family, and at the impact the crisis has on their ability to do this.

The full breadth of impacts in any gendered analysis is shown in Table 2.1.

Table 2.1 Framework for a gendered analysis of the global economic crisis

Mechanism / *Economic Sphere*	*Transmission*	*Impact*	*Response*
Finance • Gender numbers • Gender norms	Capital flight Fall in confidence Domestic bank problems Devaluation Fall in aid Fall in foreign direct investment (FDI)	Credit squeeze Fall in investment Fall in asset prices	Support for banks Use of public sector banks to direct credit Loans from international financial institutions Reduction in borrowing
Production: formal and informal • Gender numbers • Gender norms	Fall in (export) demand Fall in gross domestic product (GDP)	Fall in output Fall in employment Fall in enjoyment of rights	Fiscal stimulus Subsidies and incentives for selected industries Devaluation Increase people seeking informal paid work
Reproduction • Gender numbers • Gender norms	Fall in remittances Returning migrants Fall in government social expenditure (due to fiscal pressures)	Fall in earnings Fall in nutrition Fall in school attendance	Increase in unpaid work Social protection

Source: Adapted from Elson (2009)

Oxfam's research shows that many women are paying a particular price through their additional unpaid work to support their households. Many have migrated or taken on additional roles to prop up family income, often in the informal economy without social security or legal protection. In the home, many women have been eating less, or less nutritious food, to provide for their husbands and children.

Official responses to the crisis, as well as people's own coping mechanisms, have also often lacked gender equity. Many responses were inefficient and unjust by dint of being gender-blind. For example, in the Philippines, a day after a newspaper article reported the loss of 42,000 jobs in the female-dominated garments, semi-conductor and electronics industries, the government responded by announcing the creation of 41,000 new jobs through government infrastructure projects. Although this stimulus was badly needed, the benefits will most likely have accrued almost exclusively to men, even where women were bearing the disproportionate impact of job losses (Emmett 2009).

3. RESILIENCE

If one overriding theme emerges from Oxfam's research into the impact of the crisis, it is 'resilience' and the multiple ways countries, communities, households and individuals have been finding to weather the storm. Resilience, to date, explains the 'dogs that didn't bark' – things that we expected to happen, based on previous crises, but that have happened differently or not at all. In a surprising number of cases, migrants have not returned to their villages; people have kept their jobs, albeit with lower wages, fewer hours and worse conditions; families have managed to keep their children in school; governments haven't slashed public services and political regimes have avoided major upheavals (apart from Iceland). Although the research reveals that, to a surprising degree, many countries and households are toughing it out in the short term, it remains an open question as to how sustainable or erosive these coping mechanisms will prove to be in the long run. Individuals' lack of access to social protection and the consequent reliance on informal coping mechanisms poses a real danger of significantly depleting poor people's 'capabilities' in the longer term.

The economic crisis has confirmed that resilience to a shock such as the crisis, and the degree to which it will bolster future development, is to a large extent determined long before the crisis actually strikes. Pre-crisis factors that have strengthened resilience on this occasion include the following.

Social Networks

At a household level, resilience is largely built on the agency of poor people themselves, their friends and families, and local institutions such as religious bodies or community groups. Everywhere, people have turned to one another to share food, money and information to recover from lost jobs or reduced remittances. Families with land for subsistence farming or access to fishing have been able to survive much better than those without. Migrants with strong social networks could rely on support locally, or even (in Vietnam) on reverse-remittances from home. However, IDS research cautions against becoming too romantic over the extent of social cohesion. When researchers returned to communities in five countries a year into the crisis, they reported that a 'recurring theme [was] that neighbours and the community in general were less disposed to help each other under conditions where everyone was facing economic hardship' (Hossain et al. 2010).

Economic Structures

At the national level, as well as at the household level, dependence on one or two commodities or markets has increased the risk should they go into freefall; the degree and nature of integration with the global economy, particularly of the financial sector, has also proved a source of vulnerability. Countries such as Brazil that retain state control over a portion of the banking system have been better able to use those banks to channel credit to cash-starved small producers and small and medium enterprises. Countries with effective systems of domestic taxation in place reduced their vulnerability to sudden losses of trade taxes or foreign capital inflows. Regional trade links offered a bulwark against slumps in global markets. For example, in South-East Asia many countries benefitted from continuing strong demand from China.

Role of the State

Resilience has been enhanced when governments have entered the crisis with fiscal space, in the form of high reserves, budget surpluses and low debt burdens. Effective state bureaucracies capable of responding rapidly to the crisis with fiscal stimulus measures have also shown their worth. Well-designed and implemented labour laws are needed to deter unscrupulous employers from taking advantage of the crisis to attack workers' rights. State support for small-scale agriculture and fisheries bolstered household survival strategies in countries such as Viet Nam and Sri Lanka.

Social Policies

Countries with free health and education, and effective social protection systems, have proved more resilient, reducing the vulnerability of people living in poverty to health shocks, avoiding school dropouts in response to falling incomes, and providing shock absorbers against falls in household incomes. More generally, automaticity is beneficial in a crisis: if automatic stabilizers such as unemployment insurance, or demand-driven public works schemes like India's National Rural Employment Guarantee Scheme are already in place, they can respond immediately to a crisis rather than wait for decisions by hard-pressed governments fighting the crisis on several fronts.

The crisis has also exposed serious flaws. Even those countries that are adopting improved social protection systems seldom extend them to those working in the informal or unpaid caring economies (let alone those working as migrants), both of which have been significantly affected.

And resilience, whether national or individual, has its limits; it does not take much for 'coping' to tip over into desperation. People are best able to cope with a 'narrow V', in which shock is rapidly followed by recovery (which mercifully describes the crisis so far in many poor countries). Even then, assets once depleted take years to recoup, preventing poor people from participating in the rebound; working extra hours in second or third jobs leaves a legacy of exhaustion; loans taken on to finance consumption accumulate into crushing debt burdens; and meals forgone can affect children for their entire lifetimes.

4. HOW HAVE GOVERNMENTS RESPONDED?

Many governments have used fiscal policy to stimulate their economies. The focus of stimulus packages and counter-cyclical expenditures has included increasing public spending and infrastructure investment, as well as tax cuts and subsidies to stimulate both consumer and business demand.

This attempt at counter-cyclical policy (i.e. spending in a downturn and being prudent during an upturn) characterizes the responses of many of the poorest countries as well as some of the better off. African governments have done their best to protect public spending and those with IMF programmes initially had more success in this due to the extra resources available.

But while spending initially held up, revenue has slumped, through falling direct and indirect taxes, and lower trade taxes and royalties from commodities such as oil and minerals. Overall, the crisis has left 56 poor countries with a $65bn revenue hole, and after an initial attempt to defy fiscal gravity, in 2010 that deficit is forcing cuts in health and education. Two thirds of the countries for which social spending details were available in 2009 national budget documents (18 out of 24) were set to cut budget allocations in one or more of the priority social sectors of education, health, agriculture and social protection. Education and social protection are particularly badly affected, with average spending levels in 2010 expected to be lower even than those in 2008.

Since aid has been inadequate (see below), most LICs have resorted to domestic borrowing, which is far more expensive than concessional loans and grants. In some instances this threatens to create a new, domestic, debt crisis. In effect, many poor countries are being forced to bail themselves out of a crisis not of their own making, at huge economic and human cost.

5. BUILDING BACK BETTER?

If 'resilience' merely means the ability to return to an unacceptable status quo ante of poverty and deprivation, then it falls far short of the adaptive capacity that people living in poverty require to both recover and progress in the face of a world of shocks, general and particular. What determines whether households, communities and nations can 'build back better'?

Lessons drawn from the crisis are relevant far beyond the specifics of the global meltdown of 2008–09. Shocks are a defining feature of poor people's lives, whether they stem from economic crisis, climate change, natural disaster or more individual calamities such as accidents or illness. Many of the steps to building resilience of countries and their peoples are similar for diverse kinds of shock. What to do when a crisis hits? At a minimum, keep spending (in the medium term): governments in most countries entered the crisis in a better fiscal position than in previous crises, and initially were largely able to keep to their spending commitments, avoiding the kind of pro-cyclical cuts that have aggravated recessions in the past. In so doing, many have gone into fiscal deficit, and it remains to be seen whether they can maintain such commitments until the economy picks up again. When and if the good times return, the lesson is that countercyclicality applies in both boom and bust – governments need to accumulate the fiscal space in good times, so that they can respond in the bad. There are trade-offs here – it means governments restraining spending when economies are growing – but the crisis shifts the balance of evidence in favour of such parsimony.

Make sure the right people benefit from responses: on the ground, real-time monitoring of the impact of the crisis, and genuine dialogue with affected communities are essential to identify who has been hardest hit, and what kind of support they need. One near-universal characteristic of responses to the economic crisis to date has been gender blindness. Even where responses have addressed the symptoms thrown up by the crisis itself, seldom have they sought to go beyond and address the underlying, systemic, issues that perpetuate gender inequalities. Additionally, attempts to inject credit into cash-starved economies too often end up being pounced upon by large enterprises, who employ relatively few workers, rather than benefiting small, labour-intensive firms, or people working in the vast informal economies of the South.

6. HOW TO BUILD RESILIENCE BEFORE A CRISIS?

The key lesson here is that resilience can more easily be strengthened either side of a shock – building adaptive capacity during 'peacetime', and replenishing it when the shock is past. The crisis has marked the political coming of age of social protection as a development issue. Social protection comprises a range of 'shock absorbers', including social assistance or safety nets for the most vulnerable (e.g. cash transfers) and social insurance based on individual contributions (e.g. unemployment insurance).

What emerges from study of the crisis is that, in the 'fog of war' that prevails during a crisis, it is hard to introduce new systems from scratch, and ensure that they reach the intended beneficiaries – not that this should detract from those without established pre-crisis social infrastructure attempting to do something, but short-term responses may be preferable to trying to introduce permanent systems in a crisis. By contrast, from Burkina Faso to Brazil, governments with social protection systems already in place have been able to rapidly scale them up to cushion many people living in poverty from the worst ravages of the crisis.

Besides putting in place effective social protection systems that can be rapidly scaled up in a crisis, governments can also build resilience prior to a shock by:

- Introducing measures to ensure that loan sharks do not prey on poor people's need for finance during a crisis (e.g. interest rates caps, support to microfinance for emergency loans)
- Recognizing the role played in crisis response by community organizations and religious bodies, by investing in pre-shock disaster management training and capacity building
- Putting in place a system to prevent debt foreclosures on homes, land or other crucial assets, for example through pre-agreed repayment holidays

7. AID DONORS, IFIS AND THE G20

The crisis prompted soul-searching at the highest levels, and genuine calls for radical overhauls of a financial system that had become too big, too volatile and too impervious to public or government scrutiny. In hindsight, 2009 may prove to be a pivotal year in geopolitics: at the G20 in September, the assembled heads of state announced that 'We designated the G-20 to be the premier forum for our international economic cooperation'. This official passing of the baton from the old G8 economies to a combination of old and emerging nations was swiftly followed by the marginalization of Europe at the Copenhagen Climate Summit in December.

At the 2010 G20 in Seoul, the host South Korea was keen to establish development as a core mission of the group, and secured agreement for a 'Seoul Development Consensus for Shared Growth', based on nine 'pillars': infrastructure, private investment and job creation, human resource development, trade, financial inclusion, growth with resilience, food security, domestic resource mobilization and knowledge sharing. The pillars are developed in a multi-year action plan to be overseen by a new G20 Development Working Group. While the Seoul Consensus differs from the Washington Consensus in its greater attention to growth, and the absence of references to liberalization, it omits equity and climate change.

Discussions over financial reform continued in Seoul and were to be a major part of the French G20 presidency that took over from South Korea after the summit.

The international community can support the resilience of poor people and communities in a variety of ways.

Improve Prevention

Discussions over reform continue, in the shape of talks over improved banking supervision and regulation, ways to curb tax havens and volatile financial instruments, and the introduction of a financial transactions tax. But the danger is that as growth resumes, the appetite for reform will fade along with the memories of the crisis.

Help Respond to and Recover from Shocks that Cannot be Prevented

In the coming years, especially in low income countries, much will depend on aid donors sticking to their promises to increase aid, despite their own fiscal constraints, and poor countries having access to other forms of sustainable finance. On the supply side, a review of past banking crises in donor countries gives little cause for optimism; data from 24 donor countries between 1977 and 2007 shows banking crises are associated with a substantial fall in aid flows, in most cases by an average of 20 to 25 per cent (relative to the counterfactual). Aid flows typically bottom out approximately a decade after the banking crisis hits (Dang et al. 2009). On the demand side, the preliminary results of research for Oxfam by Development Finance International into the fiscal impacts of the crisis in the world's poorest countries are equally alarming.[3]

Despite G20 and donor country promises to help poor countries cope with the effects of the global economic crisis, only $8.2bn in grants has made its way to poor countries – plugging only 13 per cent of the revenue hole opened up by the crisis. With aid providing just one dollar for every eight lost from poor country budgets due to the crisis, countries that were already failing to meet the Millennium Development Goals on reducing poverty and guaranteeing health, education and other aspects of a decent life, are being pushed further off track through no fault of their own. If aid donors and international institutions cannot buck the historical trend of cutting aid after a crisis, the prospects for many poor countries look grim.

The conclusion is straightforward – the poorest countries need increased aid to withstand the crisis, even though aid budgets are themselves under huge political pressure from the crisis.

Knowledge Gaps

This chapter asks the question 'How have poor women and men experienced the global economic crisis?' and perhaps the most honest answer, in aggregate, would be 'we don't really know'. The crisis has revealed extraordinary gaps in the collection and dissemination of real-time data concerning shocks (other than famine) in developing countries. There is no system for collecting such data at a community level, and the only way Oxfam was able to assess the fiscal impact of the crisis in low income countries was to commission an analysis of budget statements from each individual government.

Along with a handful of organizations (including WIEGO, IDS, World Bank), Oxfam set about gathering a small amount of real-time information based on focus groups and interviews with key informants, backed up by reviews of the literature from previous crises, but the total of such research was astonishingly scant, considering that the crisis was being hailed as the greatest global crash in 60 years.

Instead, policy debates have been conducted largely on the basis of back-of-an-envelope calculations about the poverty elasticity of growth at global or (better) national levels – a very rough approximation indeed to the complex reality of the evolving crisis.

Improving on this sorry situation in future crises requires both resources and research. Real-time data is bound to be somewhat 'quick and dirty', but that can be a blessing if rigorous qualitative methods are used such as well designed focus groups. In Indonesia, where IDS employed such methods, subsequent quantitative analysis largely bore out the findings of initial qualitative work with one notable exception – qualitative work in a crisis often demonstrates a selection bias in choosing to work in communities that are likely to be affected. It therefore misses those who, for example, actually benefit from a crisis. Thus in Indonesia, some sections of the workforce saw their wages rise due to import substitution effects as international trade slumped, but this was missed by the initial qualitative work (McCulloch and Grover 2010). The lesson is that we clearly need more of both.

8. CONCLUSION

The extraordinary turbulence of 2008–09, with its 'triple F' crises of food, fuel and finance, has shifted the way we understand development. Poverty is not just about income, it is about fear and anxiety over what tomorrow may bring. These crises will not be the last, but if we heed one of the lessons that emerges, that reducing vulnerability and building resilience is the central task of development, then future crises may bring less suffering in their wake.

NOTES

1. Oxfam carried out fieldwork in 12 countries, involving some 2,500 individuals, supplemented by a review of studies by a range of universities, thinktanks and international organizations. The research paper can be found on http://www.oxfam.org.uk/resources/policy/economic_crisis/economic-crisis-developing-countries.html and all other GEC-related research on http://www.oxfam.org.uk/economiccrisis.
2. The Economic Crisis, *Gender and Development*, Volume 18, Number 2, July 2010.
3. The Impact of the Global Financial Crisis on the Budgets of Low-Income Countries: A report for Oxfam by Development Finance International, DFI and Oxfam International, July 2010, http://www.oxfam.org.uk/resources/policy/economic_crisis/economic-crisis-budget-impact-low-income-countries.html. For a broader analysis of the fiscal impact on 126 low and middle income countries, see Ortiz et al. (2010).

4. After the Gold Rush: Prospects for Africa, Economic Recovery and Long-term Growth

Fantu Cheru

> The ongoing financial chaos offers new ideological space and material justification for developing countries to chart a new course – to reimpose exchange controls and reregulate finance, and to find sources of hard currency not connected to Western donors. (Bond 2009)

> Contrary to expectations that the crisis may generate a shift away from neoliberalism, the balance is tilted against the working class. In other words, radical changes are need to the whole economic and political structure. (Beckman 2009)

The financial and economic crisis that began in the US in 2008 should not be seen from the narrow focus of the credit crunch and its relationship to the subprime mortgage crisis. The crisis goes to the very foundations of the global capitalist system and should be analyzed from that angle. The current crisis is symptomatic of some of the underlying, deeper changes that are occurring in the global economy; a shift in wealth towards the emerging markets, or what has been called the 'Rise of the Rest' (Amsden 2003).

Moreover, the crisis was provoked by a combination of massive global macroeconomic imbalances and the poor regulation of financial markets. Its severity brings to light the high degree of instability in the contemporary global financial system. The problem has been in the making for over 30 years – an indication that something is seriously amiss with a system of international finance that generates crisis with such regularity (Mexico 1994; East Asia 1998). The only exception has been that the epicentre of the current crisis lies deep inside the developed economies (Lin 2008).

Developing countries are not responsible for the crisis, but they are severely affected by it in ways that are worse than the developed countries as they also lack the means to counter the effects. There is thus growing anxiety in the south that the crisis will certainly last longer than originally expected.

1. WHAT ABOUT AFRICA?

Prior to the crisis, many countries in Africa enjoyed robust economic growth as a result of instituting sound economic policies as well as the favorable external environment, i.e., increased external support in the form of debt relief, higher aid flows and a commodity boom (IMF 2008b). More than 11 countries registered 10 per cent growth in the two years prior to the crisis. This led to an acceleration of inflation and dampened growth prospects. The financial crisis compounded the problem further, threatening some of the progress Africa has made to meet numerous MDG goals.

Predicting the impact of the financial crisis on sub-Saharan Africa is still partly guesswork. The growth forecasts of the IMF and the World Bank have repeatedly been revised downward since October 2008. The April 2009 'Global Economic Outlook' predicted a growth rate of 2 per cent compared to the actual 5.2 per cent growth rate of 2008 (IMF 2009a). A year later, the April 2010 *World Economic and Financial Survey: Regional Economic Outlook for Sub-Saharan Africa* predicts that growth in the region will rebound. Output is now projected to expand by some 4.75 per cent in 2010, up from 2 per cent in 2009 (IMF 2010b, p. 6).

Indeed, the impact of the triple crisis is not uniform across the continent. Rather it has and will affect various African national economies differently, depending on their levels of integration in the global economy and the particular type of goods and services that they produce for world markets. For example, oil and metal exporters have been hardest hit; oil prices have fallen over 60 per cent from their mid-2008 level. This has impacted negatively on fiscal and external accounts (IMF 2009c). On the other hand, oil importers benefit from falling oil prices but are affected by the decline in the prices of other commodities. Moreover, the impact of the crisis on various segments of the economy also varies, e.g. between the financial and banking sectors on the one hand, and the real economy on the other.

When examining the impact of the crisis in Africa, two contradictory realities emerge. On the one hand, Africa's marginal position in the global economy (i.e., little financialization of the economy; rigid controls on foreign exchange; limited foreign ownership of banks) appears to have shielded the continent from the disruptive effects of the crisis (apart from Kenya, South Africa and Nigeria, that are increasingly integrating into the world economy). On the other hand, as has been the case in previous global downturns, Africa is most likely to receive the most serious knock-on from the current crisis.

The continent's integration into the global economy is most visible in the areas of its exports and imports, development assistance, and foreign direct investment, which together are the conduits through which the global crisis would impact on the continent's economic and social life.

2. CHANNELS OF CRISIS TRANSMISSION

While the initial effects of the financial crisis were slow to materialize in Africa, the impact is now becoming clear. It is sweeping away firms, mines, jobs, revenues and livelihoods. In the majority of African countries, few automatic stabilizers exist, such as well-functioning social safety nets. Research (te Velde et al. 2009; IMF 2009d) has shown the main channels through which Sub-Saharan Africa is being affected. These include:

Declining Private Financial Flows

The drying up of liquidity in international financial markets has resulted in reduced levels of foreign direct investment. The large, financially integrated countries such as Egypt, Nigeria, South Africa and Kenya were the first to be affected. A visible manifestation of this has been the postponement, closure and cancelling of planned investments.[1] FDI plans in mining exploration in Tanzania, DRC, Zambia, South Africa, Cameroon and the Central African Republic were suspended; governments' attempts to raise long-term finance through sovereign bond issues have failed (South Africa), been cancelled (Ghana Telecom bond issue) or delayed (Eurobond issues for Kenya, Nigeria, Tanzania and Uganda). In addition, planned private sector projects were suspended as some investors withdrew due to uncertainty. Stock markets in South Africa, Nigeria and Kenya plunged, and tighter credit conditions were imposed in Ghana and Zambia (Cali et al. 2008).

Worsening Terms of Trade

Global recession is worsening the terms of trade for Africa due to massive drops in export receipts. Africa will experience a loss of 45–50 per cent of its exports value in 2009. The sectors most affected by the crisis are mining, tourism, textiles and manufacturing. The AfDB (2009) and IMF (2009c) have estimated losses from export revenues of $250 billion for 2009 and $277 billion for 2010, much of it based on projections of commodity price movements. As a result, from a comfortable overall current account surplus of 2.7 per cent of GDP for both 2008 and 2007, the continent will register an overall current account deficit of 4.3 per cent of GDP in 2009. Growth forecasts for Africa have been revised downward for 2009 and beyond. Global recession is worsening the terms of trade for Africa. Prices for most African commodities fell sharply, but have rebounded in recent months for commodities like oil. The China and India factor has averted the commodity crisis from being long-term. But this alone will still not provide Africa with much of a cushion. This is on top of the food, energy and climate crisis.

Declining Remittances

Remittances constitute an increasingly important source of external financing for low income countries and are integral to poverty reduction at the household level. In the past they have been relatively stable, even surpassing present levels of ODA. The World Bank now expects remittances to Africa, which had peaked at about $20 billion a year in 2008, to decline by 4.4 per cent in 2009. The impact is quite severe in countries with high dependency on remittances (measured in per cent of export earnings): Lesotho (60 per cent), Uganda (40 per cent), Senegal, Guinea-Bissau, Togo, Benin, Burkina Faso (15–25 per cent) (Ratha 2009). For example, remittances to Kenya, largely from the US, fell by 12 per cent in the first six months of 2009 compared to the same period in 2008 (Cali and ell'Erba 2009).

Decline in ODA

Even before the onset of the crisis, there has been a growing concern that the donor community has not kept its aid commitments to Africa, both in terms of volume and quality (Accra Meeting of September 2008). ODA to Africa since 2000 was approximately $40 billion a year. This is likely to decline as traditional donors redirect their attention to tend to their own domestic economic crisis. Aid is pro-cyclical in two ways: on aggregate donors tend to reduce aid flows in bad economic times; secondly, aid is pro-cyclical when countries fail to meet the targets set in agreed upon conditionalities. ODA flows are always political guesswork. It is safe to bet on the G8 not honoring commitments to double aid flow to Africa by 2010. Aid flows to Africa are already $20 billion short of the commitments made in Gleneagles in 2005.

Overall, the crisis has shrunk the fiscal space available to governments. For example, the expected shortfall in export revenue due to declining trade flows is $251 billion in 2009 and $277 billion in 2010.[2] The continent moved from a budgetary surplus accounting for 2.3 per cent of GDP in 2008 to a budgetary deficit of 5.5 per cent in 2009 (AfDB 2009, p. 12). The impact on the budget is even worse for net oil-importing countries and those with substantial food imports because of the carry-over effects of the high oil and food prices of the past two years. The combination of decreases in real wages, unemployment in labor-intensive sectors (tourism and textiles), and decelerating remittances are putting severe strain on the poor households who are already suffering from the food, energy and climate crisis (Abugre 2009). According to an ODI report, countries that rely on export markets have seen a significant decline in export receipts as well as unemployment. In Kenya, for example, the labor-intensive horticultural industry suffered a 35 per cent drop in export of flowers, with inevitable knock-on effects on its workers. Zambia had a similar experience, where nearly one in four of the workers in the mining sector lost their jobs in 2008 (te Velde et al. 2009). The AfDB estimates that, just to sustain pre-crisis levels of growth in Africa, would require an additional $50billion in 2009 and $56 billion in 2010.

3. HOW HAVE AFRICAN GOVERNMENTS RESPONDED?

The response of the African governments to the current crisis has been quite different than in previous crises. Governments have learned from the bitter experience of the adjustment decades of the 1980s and 1990s how to avoid macroeconomic mistakes, excessive borrowing and uncontrollable spending that had given rise to growth collapse in the past. Many governments have set up special monitoring units to identify the advance of the crisis and to formulate targeted responses to stimulate growth while introducing social protection programs to protect the poor and the vulnerable. The policies put in place have been rather eclectic, according to the report of the Committee of African Finance Ministers and Central Bank Governors (2009) established to monitor the crisis, and include a combination of the following:

- *Fiscal stimulus* (Mauritius, Nigeria, Liberia, Senegal and South Africa). While Mauritius proposed 10.4 billion Mauritius Rupees, or some 3 per cent of its GDP to boost domestic demand and increase job creation, Liberia proposed a 10 per cent reduction in corporate and income tax rates to stimulate private sector activity. South Africa also proposed an adjustment to personal income tax to middle and lower income earners.
- *Targeted assistance to sectors* (Nigeria, Rwanda and Uganda). In Uganda, the government provided assistance to the transport sector by writing off public loans to companies while Nigeria injected N70 billion into severely weakened textile industry.
- *Imposition of capital and exchange controls*. In Tanzania, for example, profit repatriation has been regulated to minimize contagion; new regulations in the banking sectors (e.g. in Egypt, a deposit insurance fund has been established to boost public confidence in the banking sector; and in Nigeria, the central bank has aggressively intervened in the foreign exchange market to stem the slide of the Naira).

- *Implementation of expansionary monetary policy* (e.g. cutting interest rates in Botswana and Egypt; the Central Bank of Namibia and the Reserve Bank of South Africa reduced their purchase rate to stimulate borrowing and boost private investment and consumption).
- *Freeze on government borrowing.* Unlike in the past, African governments have not gone around borrowing and they have not run down reserves. Many of them simply adjusted by cutting down budgets. They have done so in consultation with civil society and the business community so that the costs of drastic adjustment do not undermine substantially the social gains made over the past decade or so.

The pragmatic response by African governments to the crisis is a clear indication of how far development policy practices on the continent have come over the past decades. This is a very encouraging development and we need to read very carefully what is happening on the ground. African governments are no longer beholden to the one-size-fits-all 'Washington Consensus' prescriptions and are more open to experiment with 'heterodox' but pragmatic policies to stimulate growth and reduce poverty, while striving to expand policy space in determining their own development path.

4. WHAT MUST AFRICA DO NEXT?

Africa's new-found position in the global economy provides us with a compelling occasion for the continent to chart a new course – i.e. alternative conditions under which to engage economic exchanges with old and new actors that are beneficial to Africans. This will entail the adoption of key reforms at national and regional levels and greater economic policy coordination between African states.

- *Minimize exposure to risk through diversification of national economies.* The financial crisis underscored the critical role of diversification in reinforcing the resilience of economies. The focus now should be on identifying new sources of growth. Besides increasing opportunities in small-scale agriculture, attention must be made to generating employment in non-agricultural sectors: intensification of public works, such as secondary roads, irrigation, clean water supply, agro-service centres and rural electrification. This could also involve encouragement of small-scale village industries based on local materials, technology and skills.
- *Agriculture-led industrialization.* Agricultural transformation must be a critical pillar of an African renaissance. The disappointing economic performance of the continent until very recently has been caused to a

large extent by the failure of African governments to create proper conditions for an agricultural revolution to take place, which would in turn, propel the process of industrialization and social development. Kick-starting an African agricultural revolution will remain a priority for several decades and is complex and multifaceted. At a minimum, this will require the presence of a strong and effective 'enabling state' with the capacity to respond to the demands of rural producers.

- *Expand sound public investment in the infrastructure sector to support private sector activity and enhance competitiveness and diversification.* In this respect, deficit financing can be fully justified given the long-term return from infrastructure development.
- *Invest in education and basic research.* Africa cannot flourish unless the continent's intellectual capital is developed and maintained. Despite tremendous gains made since the 1960s in increasing access to education, greater challenge lies ahead. Spending on each child is half what it was twenty years ago. Fiscal crisis, poor student participation, high dropout and repetition levels, and low academic achievements are widespread, destructive trends throughout the education system. The only way to narrow the knowledge gap is by continuing to invest more in education and basic research. Specifically, strengthening African universities and retaining Africa's best and brightest professionals are important. The goal should be to climb the technological ladder and tap into the global system of information and knowledge. Transforming the educational system thus constitutes the second and most important pillar of the 'transformation' strategy (Cheru 2002).
- *Regional and integration and south–south cooperation.* Regional integration and cooperation are important aspects of the 'strategic integration' of Africa into the global economy. Such policies should support the goal of increased international competitiveness, for example, by promoting regional production chains and also nurturing the development of regional markets in order to reduce demand-side constraints on growth (UNCTAD 2009b). This could take many forms, such as the establishment of trade promotion councils, sub-regional credit and insurance system; sub-regional banks to finance production and a common framework for regional infrastructure development.
- *Appropriate management of natural resources.* How much governments get from the resource, the division of rents between extractors and governments, how they are used and how effectively public expenditures are used to diversify economics and fight poverty will require a major strategic rethinking by African governments.
- *Harness new relationship with emerging Asian powers carefully and strategically.*

In conclusion, central to Africa's economic renewal is the development of a strong, democratic, and activist state that would assert its development role within the context of a common national development vision. The lessons from China and East Asia in general demonstrate the importance of home-grown national policies that support strategic industries, develop infrastructure, invest in human capital and control financial markets.

5. MISSING FROM THE G20 REFORM AGENDA

At the very least, the global financial crisis has put the long avoided but politically sensitive topic of global governance reform back on the global policy agenda. The ability of the dominant western powers that constitute the now outdated G7/8 power structure to stifle the demands of developing countries for fundamental global reform has been significantly eroded in recent years. The rise of the G20 as the most important platform for international economic cooperation in the aftermath of the current global financial crisis is an indication of the waning of the American-dominated post-WWII Bretton Woods system of global policy coordination. The emerging powers now possess tremendous leverage in shaping the global agenda setting (Zakaria 2008).

Indeed, responses to the global financial crisis must be systematic, comprehensive, decisive and coordinated. Unfortunately, however, many of the reforms proposed by the G20 since the April 2008 London summit have focused primarily on stabilizing the financial system. The discussion among the G20 leaders has paid little attention to the urgent need to stamp out the pervasive 'financialization' of the economy – i.e., the penetration of finance into every area of economic and production structures – by putting in place stronger regulation of global finance, and an agreement on a new global financial architecture that takes into account the interests of developing countries. In the absence of radical reforms, global instability will continue and the prospects for global economic collapse, far more serious than the current crisis, is not out of the question. Below are some critical areas that future G20 summits must address head on to correct global imbalances.

Regulation of International Capital Flows

Unlike international trade, there is no global regime applying to international capital flows, including foreign direct investment. A number of proposals have been floated in the aftermath of the 1998 East Asian crisis for the creation of international institutions and mechanisms to regulate and stabilize international capital flows. While the most ambitious proposals advocate for the establishment of fully-fledged global institutions for reducing risk, such as a Board of Overseers of Major International Institutions and markets with wide-ranging powers for setting standards and for oversight and regulation of commercial banking, securities and insurance (Kaufman 1992), others advocate for less ambitious global mechanisms by reforming the mandates, membership and/or governance of existing organizations such as the IMF, the Bank for International Settlements (BIS) and the Financial Stability Board (FSB) that sets codes and standards in areas of financial regulation and supervision (Cornford 2002 and IMF 2000).

Despite the depth of the global crisis, however, the four high level G20 meetings that took place since April 2008 (London, Washington, Pittsburgh and Seoul) have focused attention more on reforming existing institutions, including new prudential requirements under Basle III and less on instituting far-reaching reforms to address the deep global imbalances, particularly the urgent need to put in place strong regulation on global finance and a new global financial architecture that gives a stronger voice to developing countries. Paragraph 41 of Seoul Leader's Declaration, e.g., reads:

> In order to deal with systemic risks in the financial sector in a comprehensive manner and on an ongoing basis, we called on the Financial Stability Board (FSB), the IMF and the Bank for International Settlements (BIS) to do further work on macro-prudential policy frameworks, including tools to mitigate the impact of excessive capital flows, and update the finance ministers and Central Bank Governors at their next meeting.[3]

What is not made explicit in the above G20 communiqué is that a growing number of emerging Asian economies are ready to go it alone and to institute appropriate national responses to protect their respective economies from predatory capitalism. This defiance by the leaders of emerging economies came out in the open at the Seoul summit when many Asian emerging countries announced a series of measures they have already taken, such as capital control, to counter the threat posed to their economies by excessive capital inflows (and pressures for appreciation) either by intervening in the currency market, or by imposing capital control such as taxes on certain types of foreign capital entering the country. This open defiance by the emerging economies of Asia is a major political development that one could not have imagined five years ago. None of these Asian governments are waiting for instructions or recommendations from the BIS, the IMF and the FSB on what to do next to protect their economies from predatory capitalism. They had already opted out for unilateral actions rather than relying on policies and guidance from the IMF, an institution very much blamed for exacerbating the 1997 Asian financial crisis. With that history in mind, Asian countries took different measures. For example, in October 2010, the Thai government introduced a 15 per cent tax on short-term inflows into its bond market, while

Indonesia introduced quasi capital control measures in June by making short-term investment less attractive to foreign funds. South Korean has moved to stabilize the won by limiting assets accessible to foreign capital, while Taiwanese officials made some bank deposits off limits to foreign investors. In fact, in the run-up to the G20 summit, ESCAP convened a meeting of its 50 plus member states to support the use of capital controls.

Modalities of Crisis Management and Crisis Prevention

Crisis management so far has relied on a combination of lending with policy adjustment designed to restore confidence and stabilize markets. However, there are problems regarding the modalities of provision of liquidity by the IMF, and conditions attached to such lending. IMF assistance always comes after the collapse of the economy, and often in the form of bailouts designed to meet the demands of creditors, to maintain capital account convertibility and to prevent default. Thus, policy proposals on crisis management and intervention would need to focus on financing (rapid response in liquidity provision), policy response and conditionality (i.e. allowing countries the right to determine appropriate macroeconomic, sectoral and social policies).

Regrettably, G20 reform of the IMF has focused singularly on governance issue while ignoring the need to define the mandates of the IMF, particularly on the scope and content of conditionalities and surveillance. The Fund continues to advocate unrestricted liberalization and deregulation of national economies, denying the right of countries to put in place appropriate measures to defend their economies, and to experiment with 'heterodox' policies to stimulate growth and reduce poverty in the process.

Creating a Stable Exchange Rate System

An important reason for international financial instability is the failure to establish a stable system of exchange rates among the major reserve currencies after the breakdown of the Bretton Woods arrangement in 1971. However, the exchange rate system has hardly figured on the G20 reform agenda (Akyüz and Cornford 1999, p. 31). In the face of persistent currency misalignments, the industrialized countries have refrained from intervening in currency markets except at times of acute imbalances that are likely to inflict huge damage on their economies. An international monetary system that enables the stability of currency exchange rates is urgently required. But this not the direction in which the G20 is heading at the moment.

The Seoul G20 Summit took place amidst the threat of a currency war between the surplus and deficit countries, particularly between the US and China, the former accusing the latter of currency manipulation.[4] In the end, the G20 concluded without any meaningful agreement on how to resolve global imbalances, other than a timid pledge to 'refrain from competitive devaluation of currencies'.[5] On the other hand, specific fault lines were brought out into the open at the meeting in Seoul, such as the growth strategies pursued by emerging economies across Asia, which have come to depend excessively on international capital flows and exports to advanced economies. The host country, closing ranks with the other Asian countries that recently embraced capital controls (Thailand, Taiwan and Indonesia), argued that developing countries need different forms of capital controls to protect their economies from the damaging effect of speculative capital inflows. Even the IMF, at one time a resolute opponent of such intervention, has been warming up to the idea of capital control.[6] This rethink by the IMF marks a dramatic shift from its position in the wake of the 1997 Asian financial crisis, when it opposed then Prime Minister Mahathir Mohamad's use of capital control to protect the Ringit and Malaysian economy.

Systematic Treatment of Debt Workout

In the event of a financial crisis, in which a country is unable to service its external debt obligations, international measures and mechanisms are required to enable the affected country to manage the crisis effectively and in which the debtors and creditors share the burden equally (Akyüz 2002). At present, there is no systemic treatment for debt workout, rescheduling and relief, and the debtor countries usually end up by carrying the bulk of the burden and the outstanding debt in many cases remains or even grows. Thus, one of the main issues in the reform agenda is how to 'involve' the private sector in crisis management and resolution so as to redress the balance of burden-sharing between official and private creditors as well as between debtors and creditor countries. A fair and transparent arbitration mechanism must strike a balance between two contradictory principles: the right of creditors to interest and repayment on one hand, and on the other, the generally recognized principle by all civilized legal systems that no one country must be forced to fulfil contracts if that leads to of human distress, endangers one's life or health, or violates human dignity (Raffer 1990).

Sovereign Insolvency

The main features of a sovereign insolvency should include: arbitration (a neutral institution assuring fair treatment); sovereignty (i.e. a country cannot go into receivership and its elected officials cannot be removed from office by court); right to be heard (pursuant to Chapter 9 of the US Civil Code, the debtor's population has a right to be heard in proceedings); equal treatment (different debtors are treated differently at the moment). The restructuring process must be enhanced through greater transparency (Raffer 2002).

Streamlining Conditionality and Enhancing Policy Space

There is an urgent need for more transparent IMF and World Bank conduct regarding the content and mechanisms of conditionality (Ahmed, Lane and Schultz-Ghattas 2001). A common perception is that IMF-supported programs remain stringent, inflexible, and in some instances punitive, leaving very little room for countries to manoeuvre. The common practice of lending with policy adjustment in the context of crisis management is not adequately governed today by a set of policies and indicators that the countries themselves have specified to achieve development outcomes and monitor them accordingly. If IMF conditionality continues to be perceived by recipient-country governments and citizens to be illegitimate, what should be the guiding principles for constructing country-specific conditionality that is not only legitimate, but that emphasizes democratic decision-making, participation and real country ownership (Collingwood 2003)?

At the end of the day, for development to be sustainable, countries must have the option to choose among appropriate fiscal, monetary, macroeconomic, trade and other sectoral and social policies without heavy-handed intervention by the IMF. Unfortunately, this important matter did not figure out in the deliberations of the G20 summit in Seoul. Instead, the focus of the summit was on IMF quota revision and increasing the voting power of emerging economies.[7] Implementation of these decisions on IMF governance will not happen overnight; the earliest this could be achieved will be in 2012. Not only have the amendments to the IMF articles to be formulated and accepted by two-thirds of the IMF membership, they also have to be ratified or accepted by national parliaments of member governments.[8]

Democratizing the Governance of the IMF and the World Bank

The debate on reforming the governance structure of the IMF and the World Bank has been going on for a long time. At the 2009 G20 leaders meeting in London convened to tackle the global financial crisis, then UK Prime Minister Gordon Brown publicly stated that the IMF and World Bank have outlived their functions and he called for a new Bretton Woods conference to establish a new global financial architecture. This was the same view expressed by the International Financial Advisory Commission (best known as the Meltzer Commission) in 2000.[9] Developing countries have repeatedly been demanding to increase their voting power in these institutions.

In response to the cataclysmic failure of the IMF in its handling of the 1998 Asian financial crisis (for which the Fund later admitted mistake and took responsibility), the Fund's Executive Board initiated a number of reviews with reference to surveillance and the content and scope of conditionality; structural and institutional reform, particularly the nature and conditions of liquidity provision in times of crisis, as well as reform on the distribution of voting power. The IMF also introduced its 'Sovereign Debt Restructuring Mechanism' (SDRM) in November 2001.[10] While the IMF proposal was warmly welcomed initially, it lost credibility quickly when the US Treasury refused to support a legally binding framework, preferring instead voluntary inclusion of so-called 'Collective Action Clauses' in bond contracts. There was also resistance from emerging market countries for fear of being locked out of future borrowing opportunities if such debt workout mechanism is up and running. Despite the resistance against the SDRM idea, the Board never took a decision to put some of the other proposals on conditionality and liquidity provision into practice, and by 2005, the relevance of the IMF itself was being questioned and many governments, including some conservative US legislators, were calling for its abolishment.

In an ironic twist, the global financial crisis of 2008 has helped salvage the IMF from extinction. The G20 leaders agreed to give more resources to the IMF to put out the financial wildfire spreading all over the world, but using its outmoded economic toolkit. This is unfortunate since the problem of today requires a different kind of medicine than what the Fund carries in its outdated toolkit. There is now an opportunity to define the mission of the IMF as a lender of last resort in times of major liquidity crisis. This must be one of the priority issues that the G20 leaders must address urgently. Central to the IMF's new role should be the need to expand 'policy space' for countries in crisis and to recognize the fact that the adjustment period will be long and that liquidity provision has to be quick and commensurate with the scope of the crisis that a country is experiencing.

The G20 Summit in Korea did take up IMF reform and the distribution of voting power. The agreement reached by the IMF Board, following the G20 finance minister's meeting on 23 October 2010, would shift the voting rights to dynamic (emerging market and developing) countries by 6 percentage points. The finance ministers also agreed to 'a comprehensive review of the quota formula by January 2013' and greater representation for emerging market developing countries (EMDCs) at the executive board through two fewer advanced European chairs and moving to an all-elected Board.[11]

The IMF has trumpeted these changes as historic. The changes will make China the third largest shareholder and will vault India, Russia and Brazil into the top ten. However, the voting rights of 'advanced countries' would be reduced by only 2 per cent and the rest of the shift in votes would come from a reduction of the share of other developing countries. The IMF's faculty classification of countries makes the numbers look bigger in favour of developing countries than it really is. For example, South Korea and Singapore are classified by the IMF's own flagship report, *World Economic Outlook,* as 'advanced countries' while also including both countries in the category of 'emerging markets and developing countries (EMDCs)' when it comes to calculating the shift in voting power.

In short, many of the reforms the G20 has tried to promote since the April 2008 London summit have been seriously questioned. The outburst of the crisis has served to reaffirm repeated calls for far-reaching structural reforms to the world's financial system, but the measures the group has adopted just amount to 'more of the same' and do not provide real solutions to the many crises the world is undergoing.

6. WHAT IS TO BE DONE? THE WAY FORWARD

What is the fate of neo-liberalism? What are the prospects for more transformative change? How do we get back to a more progressive, inclusive development policy paradigm both in the North and South? These are two important questions that we must ponder if we are ever going to embark on constructing an alternative and transformative world order that is both humane and democratic. Despite the premature exuberance from the left about the death of neoliberalism, the opportunity that the crisis provided for radical reform of the existing system may have been lost. In fact, we are entering a period of 'normalization', that is, business as usual. The 'resiliency' of neo-liberalism has been more than striking. The crisis may have given neoliberalism a 'new lease in life', as demonstrated by the way governments across the western world have responded to the crisis, and the subsequent refraining by the G20 leaders from instituting bold measures to regulate speculative capital flows and build a new global financial architecture that takes into account the needs of developing countries. At the outbreak of the crisis, there was swift action by the G20 leaders to safeguard the financial system, but not the same level of urgency given to 'safeguard' people and communities. 'Socialization of risks' and 'privatization of gains' have been at the core of the crisis response strategy of the global elites.

The challenge of the post-crisis global development agenda lies in seriously engaging in mass political mobilization across the formal–informal divide in order to create genuinely redistributive structures and institutions at the local and global levels. We need a major paradigm shift; a new analytical narrative about how global development occurs; we need to reclaim our planet (which we have successfully turned into a duty free shop); we need new ethical principles of solidarity; we need to reclaim our politics (politics which we have surrendered in exchange for embracing a new religion called 'globalization as the right to consume').

New politics

The current crisis provides new openings for activism, social pacts, public policy and debates on a number of key fronts aimed at reintegrating 'the economic' and 'the social' through democratic politics. We need fresh approaches in researching political economy and state–society relations. Who should drive the new 'emanicipatory' project aimed at popular welfare and democracy? Is it the elites? Peasants? Trade unions? The state? How do we identify potential agents of transformation in a diverse context? We need to deepen research on alternative formulations of 'people's democracy', or 'local democracy' that is being discussed and debated on the ground (Teivainen 2002). For Africa, this is quite different from the externally imposed democratic experience, which has turned out to be an ideology of domination. In the final analysis, resistance against the forces of globalization and against the vampire global elites that continue to perpetuate poverty and oppression will take many forms and the outcome will depend on the capacity of the forces of civil society to gain sufficient influence to qualify as a genuine counter-project.

New institutions

Looming in the background of these issues of analysis and action are concerns regarding global governance. It is common knowledge that global decision-making has become much less democratic, participatory and transparent as the resources, mandate and influence of the UN eroded as the power and mandate of the IMF, the World Bank and the WTO expanded. Developing countries' policy autonomy has been narrowed by loan conditions, trade rules and structural adjustment programs. Recent efforts to shift policy control to developing countries – the PRSP as one good case – have not been accompanied by democratization of multilateral institutions.

Moreover, the post-financial crisis political consensus that emerged around the G20 is unlikely to deliver real and fundamental change in global governance. This was self-evident during the political manoeuvring that took place during the climate change negotiations in Copenhagen in December 2009. Like the G8 before it, the gathering of self-appointed leaders from the 20 countries that constitute the G20 never delved into the systemic crises that bedevil the world today, with immeasurable consequences to human welfare particularly in the developing countries. As Mittelman (2010) put it succinctly, 'whereas the G-20 agenda focuses reforms for limiting executive pay and recapitalizing banks, it does not consider unsustainable debt, conditionalities that accompany loans and poverty relief measures, and social protection against jagged effects of market forces'. Global inequality, according to these leaders, is to be addressed by a well-functioning market.

Structural change requires the reconfiguration of the balance of social forces – i.e. social movements, labour movements, peasant movements, consumer movements, etc. It is all about social struggle. To borrow a line from Paulo Freire, 'the oppressors will never make changes; the oppressed themselves must make their own history'. Solutions and actions must happen at different levels: local, national, regional and global.

A strategy of recovery should center on 'transforming the production system'; transformation of 'social relations'; and transforming 'democratic governance' at the global and local levels. The market as we know it is not a god-given right; markets have always been an outcome of social struggles. Central to this is the need to employ 'social policy' as an instrument of recovery. The social question cannot be disembedded from the economy; and the economy cannot be separated from the 'social question'.

NOTES

1 Impact of the Crisis on African Economies: Sustainable Growth and Poverty Reduction', *African Perspectives and Recommendations to the G20*, A report from the Committee of African Finance Ministers and Central Bank Governors established to monitor the crisis (21 March, 2009).

2 World Economic Outlook Database, October 2008.

3 G20 Seoul Summit 2010, 'The G20 Seoul Summit Leader's Declarations, November 11–12, 2010', Seoul: South Korea, pp. 10–11.

4 Evan Ramstad, 'Currency Debate Moves on to G20', *WSJ Online*, 12 X 2010.

5 'G20 agrees on IMF quota revisions, work on reducing imbalances', TWN Info Service on Finance and Development, 9 November 2010; G20 Seoul Summit 2010, 'The G20 Seoul Summit Leader's Declaration', pp. 1–2.

6 Marwaan Macan-Markar, 'Ahead of G-20 Summit, Capital Controls Gain New Currency', Inter Press Service, Bangkok, 5 November 2010.

7 G20 Seoul Summit 2010, 'The G20 Seoul Summit Leader's Declaration', 11–12 November, 2010, Seoul: South Korea, p. 4.

8 The Bretton Woods Project report on IMF governance reform (www.brettonwoodsproject.org/art-567128); Third World Network, 'IMF Reform is less than what is claimed', TWN Info Service, 12 November, 2010.

9 IFIs Advisory Commission (2000), 'Melzer Report', Washington, DC, March.

10 'Kruger modifies sovereign debt plan', *IMF Survey*, **31** (7) (April 8, 2002).

11 G20 Seoul Summit 2010, 'The G20 Seoul Summit Leader's Declaration', 11–12 November, 2010, Seoul: South Korea, p. 4.

5. A Historical Ethnography of Recessions: Crises in Yogyakarta

Ben White

> Is the crisis receding? It has been with us for five years, it has claimed many victims, played havoc with the economy, thrown many out of work, ruined family life, in short it has done enough damage to the foundations of social life and tranquility. (*Doenia Pegadaian*, 25 January 1935)

> Clearly in Yogya many people are hungry, everywhere you hear stories of hardship. Then is nobody happy? In fact, there are also plenty of happy people. If you go out for an evening stroll in the city, it's as busy as ever. You'll see groups of people in fine clothes, three kethoprak shows are playing to full houses every night. It's not like the villages where just about everyone is suffering. In the city, those who still have work are happy, because everything is so cheap, if you have money you can really enjoy yourself. The unemployed, on the other hand, are even worse off than rural people, but you don't see them because they avoid public spaces; if you don't go to visit these people in their *kampungs*, you won't see them – people who are suffering don't want to make a noise and let everyone know. (Poerwosoedirdjo 1932)

1. HISTORICAL ETHNOGRAPHY OF ECONOMIC CRISES

In Indonesia the recent global financial crisis resulted not in recession but in a dip; after falling from 6 per cent in 2008Q3 to some 4 per cent in mid-2009, GDP growth was over 5 per cent again by late 2009 (Patunru and von Luebke 2010, p. 14). In contrast, during the previous century the economy experienced zero or negative growth for a total of 16 years, grouped in four distinct periods of economic crisis: the 1930s world recession, the Japanese occupation and independence struggle of the 1940s, the final years of Sukarno's 'guided democracy' in the 1960s and the Asian crisis of the 1990s. The last three recessions were accompanied by political crisis and regime change, so that only the 1930s can be regarded as a purely economic crisis.[1]

This chapter explores the experience of the economic crises of the 1930s, 1960s and late 1990s in the region of Yogyakarta in southern central Java. The quotations above from observers of the 1930s crisis in Yogyakarta – one from a pawnshop workers' bulletin, the other an eye-witness account – capture two important aspects of economic crisis: first, that recession threatens not only material life but also the foundations of social life and security; and second, that crisis may affect different social and occupational groups in completely opposite ways. One key aspect of historical comparison is the difference in processes generated by inflationary and deflationary crises, a dimension which separates the 1930s from subsequent shocks in the Indonesian economy. Economic crises and recessions have been regarded by some scholars, on both the right and the left, as processes of 'creative destruction'; when exploring the comparative social history of economic crises, that means exploring their role in unleashing or stimulating structural transformations in society. This underlines the importance of looking for contrasting impacts and responses both *between* and *within* regions and social groups; whether we are looking for relative wealth and poverty, asset transfers, social or political position, each crisis generates its own 'winners' as well as 'losers'. Related to this is the idea that the vulnerability or resilience of particular social groups in the face of economic shocks is rooted in much longer-term historical processes: 'impacts of crisis' are generated only in a superficial sense by the 'moment' of crisis itself. Patterns and institutions of social solidarity and 'social safety nets' may be key elements in the vulnerability or resilience of particular social groups and individuals.

The main sources used for the 1930s are published and unpublished official reports and especially five transfer memoranda (*Memories van Overgave*) of departing Dutch officials; reports of various charitable organizations operating in the region; regional or national newspapers; local bulletins of professional organizations; some eye-witness accounts by Indonesian or foreign observers; two useful earlier studies by historians, and some oral history interviews obtained during field research in the 1970s. For the 1960s the available sources are very different. I have used the Yogyakarta-based *Kedaulatan Rakyat* – a disappointing source, which during the years of crisis gave greater attention to international and national than to local news – and a series of oral-history interviews obtained in 2003 from 18 informants, as well as a special series of interviews with present and former *becak* (pedicab) drivers who were old enough to have something to say about the 1960s. For the 1990s *krismon* period, in addition a number of fieldwork-based studies by both Indonesian and foreign researchers are available from various communities in the region, providing us with detailed but often sharply contrasting accounts.

2. ON THE EVE OF THE 1930s RECESSION

In the Sultanate of Yogyakarta a 'modern' system of land-tenure, village organization and taxation had replaced the 'feudal' *apanage* system in 1918 (Stok 1939). Despite this relatively late start, the people of Yogyakarta appear to have been more heavily involved in the cash economy than many other regions. The 1930 Census, at the Depression's start, indicates the extent of the Yogyakartan population's involvement in the cash economy (Table 5.1): only 57 per cent of employed men and 22 per cent of employed women reported their (primary) occupations as peasant agriculture – as landholding peasant, tenant farmer or landless wage-labourer. One in every seven males was employed in the sugarcane sector, and two-thirds of all employed women were working in the manufacturing and trade sectors. The region's extensive sugar cane plantations yearly paid out some 4.5 million Dutch guilders to the local population in the mid-1920s, mostly wages, with smaller amounts in the form of land-lease payments to landholders. This money circulated in the local economy, providing a source of demand for local food crops and non-food products like clothing, durable goods and services.

Table 5.1 Occupational classification native population, Yogyakarta 1930

Occupation	Number (x 1000)			Per cent of total		
	Men	Women	Total	Men	Women	Total
Agriculture	277	78	355	75	28	54
(Peasant farming)	(212)	(61)	(273)	(57)	(22)	(42)
(Sugarcane)	(52)	(12)	(64)	(14)	(4)	(10)
Manufactures	32	131	163	9	46	25
(Food & beverages)	(10)	(28)	(38)	(3)	(10)	(6)
(Textiles)	(6)	(60)	(66)	(2)	(21)	(10)
Transport	6	*	7	2	*	1
Trade	9	46	55	2	16	8
Government service	18	*	18	5	*	3
Other occupations	28	28	55	8	10	8
Total	370	283	653	100	100	100

Source: 1930 Census (Volkstelling 1934)

The much-disliked poll-tax (*pajak kepala* or *hoofdgeld*) levied on all landholding peasants (*kuli*) had not yet been abolished as it had been in the regions under direct Dutch rule. Yogyakartan peasants paid this in addition to the land tax (about 10 per cent of the harvest) and were thus more heavily taxed. This was another factor requiring people to produce crops for sale, or other goods and services. Peasants needed cash both to pay taxes and to buy various basic necessities. Yogyakartan villagers were thus not insulated from the effects of the depression by peasant 'self-sufficiency'.

The 1920s had been a period of intensive administrative reorganization, and also heavy infrastructural investment in irrigation, roads, etc., and the region seemed poised for a period of solid growth. However, the mid-1920s saw signs of weakness in the economy – as elsewhere – and reduced public spending. The relative lack of large-scale industries made these problems comparatively less serious in Yogyakarta, as reported in Dingemans (1926). How then did the various social groups in the region experience the impact of the collapse of the economy in the 1930s, and how did they respond? How does a deflationary crisis make itself felt at the local level?

3. A DEFLATIONARY CRISIS: THE 1930S DEPRESSION

The most noticeable sign of the crisis in peasant agriculture was the universal, daily growing scarcity of money. Food was plentiful everywhere, but money had almost completely disappeared (Bijleveld 1939, p. 207). As sugarcane prices and markets collapsed, the area of sugarcane planted in Yogyakarta fell from 17,000 ha (1930/31) to a low of 1,100 ha (1935/36). Besides this, the contract wage rates paid for sugarcane production – from land preparation to cane delivery – declined by more than half between 1928 and 1933. Governor Bijleveld (1939, p. 206) observed, looking back on the crisis years, that the collapse of the sugarcane sector 'put heavy pressure on the peasant, through the huge reduction in employment opportunities and at the same time the reduction in wage rates'. This, together with similar developments in other agro-export sectors especially tobacco, meant an enormous drop in the volume of money circulating from the export sector into peasant agriculture, through demand for food crops and other small-scale enterprises, through demand for clothing, utensils, etc. Prices of coconuts, cassava and maize declined even more than those of rice (Sumitro 1952, p. 22); in Yogyakarta, the price of coconuts dropped by more than half (van Gesseler Verschuir 1939, p. 80).

3.1 The Differential Impacts of a Deflationary Crisis

> The influence of the crisis years on native agriculture, although clearly noticeable everywhere, still has not led to calamities anywhere in the Governorate of Jogjakarta, thanks to the incredible adaptability of the native peasant. (Bijleveld 1939, p. 206)

Pak Wishnoe Wardhana Surjodiningrat recalls seeing, as a very young boy, his father breaking down and weeping, after returning from his official tours,

> at the thought of the misery he had just witnessed among the peasantry. (O'Malley 1977, p. 344)

> The bitterness of the crisis, which is caused by the capitalist system, has to be borne by the weaker groups, that is, workers and those who share their fate. The stronger groups, those with capital, can easily avoid problems and save themselves, they can safeguard their profits, they are free to close down their businesses and fire some or all their employees. (Editorial, *Doenia Pegadaian*, 10 January 1934)

The contrasting views in the quotations suggest that the 1930s had different effects on different social groups, depending on the source of livelihood. Views on specific groups differed also depending on the author's perspective.

The agricultural population

Although there had been some threat of food shortage in early 1930, after the long *el niño* dry season of 1929, weather and harvests had been relatively good in succeeding years. By 1933 more food was stored in people's homes, due both to the expansion in food crop planting – as export-crop land reverted to food crops – and peasant retention of crops because of the very low prices they fetched on the market (van Gesseler Verschuir 1939, p. 153).

The collapse in agricultural prices resulted in a serious 'money famine' among peasants. To meet the demands of tax, debt-payments and survival, people went to the pawnshop until their possessions were exhausted. The 14 official pawnshops in the region experienced special problems due to deflation (the money value of the items held in pawn declined) and the proportion of them which were not redeemed and had to be sold at auction, often at a loss. The total number of items pawned in Yogyakarta declined from 2.1 million in 1930 (for an average loan of *f.* 3.60) to 1.2 million in 1934 (average value *f.* 2.17), and then rose slowly again to a total of 1.8 million in 1938 (Bijleveld 1939, p. 256). When credit and pawnable reserves were exhausted, the next step was pawning of land (Sumitro 1952, p. 24). Bijleveld, Governor of Yogyakarta from 1934 to 1939, ascribed the survival of Yogyakarta's peasants during these difficult years to their 'incredible adaptive capacity', a capacity which O'Malley ascribed largely to the efforts and self-sacrifice of women.

Informants whom I interviewed in the early 1970s rightly recalled that in the 1930s it was 'money that became scarce' (*larang*) or 'expensive' (*mahal*), while 'things' (*barang*) became cheap as the prices dropped. In such conditions, as one informant remarked, it was '*orang bayaran yang menjadi makmur*' (those with regular wage- or salary-incomes who prospered), while those who sold produce in order to obtain cash to pay land or poll taxes, or for other cash needs, came into severe difficulties. One in twenty employed

Javanese men in Yogyakarta was in government service. These would have seen their purchasing power grow rapidly, even after some of them experienced cuts in their salaries. The situation then was almost a mirror opposite of what would be later experienced by their children and grandchildren, in the inflationary crises of the 1960s and late 1990s.

In rural areas it is likely that the 1930s were a period of accelerated land transactions, in which the few households with access to fixed cash incomes laid the basis for their descendants' prosperity through the accumulation of land in distress sales or mortgage. One special category of agricultural workers hit by the depression was the large number of retrenched plantation coolies returning to Java from Sumatra. Of about 100,000 coolies who had returned by 1934, more than one-quarter came from Yogyakarta. They often did not find a hospitable welcome in their home villages. O'Malley cites an article in *Oetoesan Indonesia* (24 December 1934)[2] which notes that 'attitudes in the villages toward returning coolies were changing from hospitable to harsh', and himself comments:

> Since those who became coolies were never the pick of the villagers anyway (P. Wartoyo told me in February of 1975 that those who became coolies were usually young men who had angered their parents or who were considered untractable or unpromising by village authorities) … it is easy to see that they would not have been ideally fitted to returning. (O'Malley 1977, p. 380)

Raden Iskandar Poerwosoedirdjo, Labour Controller at the *Kantoor van Arbeid* (and author of the second quotation of this chapter), travelled throughout Java between 1928 and 1930 investigating the conditions of workers and the unemployed. He visited and photographed squatter settlements of returned plantation coolies who were either unwilling or unwelcome to return to their home villages and lived a hand-to-mouth existence, often resorting to petty crime. These experiences stimulated him to write an intriguing Javanese-language booklet for distribution to Javanese coolies in Sumatra, with the express intention 'to try to reverse, as much as possible, the stream of coolies returning to Java' (Poerwosoedirdjo 1932, p. 1), by persuading them that conditions of unemployment and poverty were even worse in Java than in the plantation regions outside Java.

Village schoolteachers

Teachers in Yogyakarta's newly established village schools (*volksscholen, sekolah rakyat*) were alarmed at proposals that their salaries would no longer be paid in cash but in land (like the salary-lands of the village officials). Their representatives in the regional teachers' federation PPGV (*Perikatan Perkoempoelan Goeroe Vorstenlanden*) saw this development as threatening not only the teachers' material welfare but also their status in village society:

> Remember that we have always been used to living with money ... Anyone with a sense of humanity must have some feeling for the problems facing the teachers' livelihoods and for their hurt feelings, because if they are paid in land not only will their income decline, not only will they have real problems in farming it, but also it will erode their status, they will no longer be respected by their pupils' parents, let alone by other social groups. (*Sinar Goeroe Vorstenlanden*, 4 July 1933)

The PPGV calculated that if they were paid, as proposed, with 2 *baoe* (approx. 1.5 ha) of *sawah* their monthly purchasing power would decline by 80 per cent; a teacher would need 10 *baoe* (7 ha) of good-quality land to match his present purchasing power, if he farmed the land himself; if he employed a share tenant he would only get half that much. A local teacher reacted strongly to the Director of Education's explanation to the *Volksraad* that the extra cuts in village teachers' salaries were justified by the lower prices of food in rural areas, especially root-crops like *oebi*, *keladi* and *talas* (sweet potato and taro): 'Even if *talas*, *keladi* and *oebi* cost nothing at all, we still do not plan to fill our wives' and children's bellies with these every day' (A. Djas, in *Sinar Goeroe Vorstenlanden*, 1 December 1933).

Pawnshop workers

Earlier I noted that the slump caused financial problems for Yogyakarta's government pawnshops. Some employees were made redundant, and those who remained received salary cuts. Articles and members' letters in *Doenia Pegadaian*, the bulletin of the Yogyakarta-based pawnshop workers' federation PPPB (Perserikatan Pegawai Pegadaian Boemipoetro) were quite vocally opposed to these cuts and to all measures that tried to make savings at the expense of working people (*Doenia Pegadaian*, 25 January 1934). Many such protests were expressed in the form of poems, such as this extract from 'The worker's poem' published in the pawnshop workers' bulletin:

> In the time when Indonesia prospered
> the industrialists made too much profit,
> in the time when Indonesia is bankrupt
> they must always be obliged to help.
> The high official with his big salary
> won't be bothered by a 5 percent cut –
> his salary will still be big,
> enough to afford all that he needs.
> But it's different for a lowly employee
> whose salary is only a few [guilders]
> another 5 percent cut will feel like a heavy burden
> and only increase his woes
> (Djengkol, Sair kaoem boeroeh (The workers' poem),
> *Doenia Pegadaian*, 10 August 1935)

Non-indigenous elites: Chinese and Europeans

Although Europeans and Chinese numbered only 0.5 and 0.8 per cent respectively of the total population of the region, they were quite significant in the city of Yogyakarta where one in twenty of the total population were European and one in fifteen were Chinese (Kwartanada 2002; Volkstelling 1930, II 1934). The great majority of Chinese made their living in trade (64 per cent) and manufactures (24 per cent); they were prominent in manufactures (especially wood and bamboo products) and the textile trade, as well as money lending, loaning large sums of money to the aristocracy as well as smaller sums to peasants and traders. They also dominated shop keeping and market/roadside stall business, and food and tobacco trade. All of these were very vulnerable occupations in a deflationary crisis. The Depression forced many Chinese into bankruptcy and those involved in trade faced increasing competition from both indigenous and Japanese traders (Kwartanada 2002, p. 260). But there were also Chinese businessmen who prospered in these years, establishing new businesses, expanding old ones, or purchasing them from European owners. Lie Kioen Gie's Lodji Redjo coffee and biscuit factory, established in 1928, employed 500 workers by 1939. Still more spectacular is the dynamic Liem Ing Hwie, who returned to Yogyakarta in 1932 after some years of study and work in Delft, Czechoslovakia and Shanghai, established a new trading house in the height of the Depression, purchased an ice factory in 1937 from its Dutch owners, developed a number of tile factories and became the landlord of 41 houses which he rented out. These houses may have been purchased 'when the homes of many Chinese businessmen were confiscated and auctioned off at relatively low prices when they were unable to pay their mortgages or went bankrupt' (Kwartanada 2002, pp. 265–66).

Europeans in Yogyakarta were involved in a wider variety of occupations than the Chinese, in plantation enterprises and the civil service (these two categories accounted for a good 40 per cent) and smaller numbers in private enterprise, trade, transport and industry. They were thus more dependent on salaried employment in the private or public sector, and significant numbers appear to have lost their jobs in the early Depression years. By mid-1931, 381 Europeans in Yogyakarta had registered themselves as unemployed, a relatively large number for this quite small town,[3] if we compare Batavia and Bandung where only 223 and 225 registered (Vreede 1931, p. 515).

4. GOVERNMENT AND NGO INTERVENTIONS

In 1932 Resident van Gesseler Verschuir's Committee of Enquiry reported that the food situation was favourable, that people were adapting to the situation through reduced expenditures (*versobering*), that taxes were being promptly paid and that for the time being no special measures were required (van Gesseler Verschuir 1939, pp. 150–51). Soon, however, the situation worsened due to further contractions in the plantation sector and collapsing prices of peasant crops. In January 1932 a decision was made to lighten the tax burden of those dependent on home-garden crops, reducing the land-tax on home gardens and the head-tax for the so-called *koelie karang kopek* (those who only owned a home-garden plot). The following month a more general measure was taken to reduce the head-tax by about one-third in selected districts, and reduce the land rent by 30 per cent in the coconut-dependent districts of Kebonongan and Adikarta, and by 15 per cent in other regions. These tax reductions had some impact on relieving rural distress, but still did not balance the much greater drop in peasant and worker incomes through collapsed prices and reduced wage-rates, meaning that it was still relatively harder to meet these demands than in pre-depression times.

On the other side of the coin, it did not escape the government's notice that wage- and salary-earners stood to benefit considerably in a period of falling prices, and from 1933 onwards government-salaried workers, like their counterparts in the large-scale plantation and other private or corporate sector, faced substantial wage cuts. Pawnshop workers and schoolteachers, for example, both experienced a series of nominal wage cuts amounting to some 30 per cent, plus reductions in fringe benefits.

Public and private sector retrenchment were accompanied by various measures, which today in World Bank parlance constitute the 'social safety net'. At least 15 non-profit organizations in Yogya concerned themselves with provision of relief for the poor and unemployed. These organizations provided either cash allowances, food and/or free or subsidized shelter to the poor, selecting their 'target groups' on religious, ethnic or sometimes 'neutral' grounds. In addition to these NGO efforts, the Yogyakarta branch of the government's Central Unemployment Administration provided cash support and vocational training courses for the unemployed – both (Indo-) European, Chinese and native Indonesians. By the end of 1938 the Yogyakarta branch was paying out *f.* 3,250 every month to Europeans, *f.* 300 to native Indonesians and *f.* 150 to Chinese (Bijleveld 1939, p. 16).

5. CHRONIC INFLATION AND THE CRISIS OF THE 1960s

During the revolution and early independence period, according to Selosoemardjan's pioneering study of *Social Changes in Yogyakarta*,

> importers, merchants, and large sections of the peasantry have gained considerably by the inflation. Wage labourers and particularly the large group of government officials have been seriously hit because of the lag between price rises and rises in wages and salaries. (Selosoemardjan 1962, p. 250)

During the last years of Sukarno's presidency annual inflation rates reached more than 100 per cent in Java for seven years in a row, reaching a peak of almost 900 per cent in 1966,[4] the year following the spectacular decision to re-calibrate the Rupiah by 1000 to 1 on 13 December 1965. How did people in Yogyakarta city and the rural areas experience this rapid inflation?

The 1960s crisis (with economic shrinkage estimated for the years 1963 and 1966–67) emerged in the context of an extremely weak economic base, after three decades of disruption, stagnation or recession. Infrastructures of all kinds, as well as the regional export economy, were at a very low point, with efforts to revive the sugar and tobacco sector having made little progress (Selosoemardjan 1962, Ch. IX). Comparison of the 1930 and 1960 regional census data on employment (Tables 5.1 and 5.2) provides a strong suggestion of quite drastic de-industrialization and re-agrarianization, particularly affecting women. The generally low levels of living and low purchasing power in Yogyakarta and nearby regions meant difficult times for many of the textile (weaving and *batik*), crafts and food industries that had provided employment for so many women in the 1930s. On the other hand, there is a general impression that wealth/poverty contrasts in the 1960s were at a lower level than either the 1930s or the 1990s; household reserves (cash, gold or other assets) were low, leaving both the relatively better and the relatively worse off vulnerable to economic shocks. For food producers, severe problems were caused by the *el niño* drought and pests (particularly rats) in 1963–64.

The impoverished southern region of Gunung Kidul received special media attention at the peak of the crisis in 1964–65. On 19 February 1964 the Bupati (District Head) reportedly wept as he submitted his annual report to the Minister of Home Affairs. Irregular rainfall and rat infestation had caused total crop failure in many southern districts; some farmers had planted their fields as much as four times in one season (with upland paddy, cassava or maize) and each time the rats had eaten all the seeds or young plants. Indications of distress sales were evident, and house prices dropped by more than 50 per cent (*Kedaulatan Rakjat*, 20 February 1964). Hunger oedema was widely reported and three villages had requested to be moved *en masse* to transmigration areas in Sumatra (*Kedaulatan Rakjat*, 18 January 1964).[5] At the same time it was reported that many people were now seen begging in Yogyakarta city 'who did not look like ordinary beggars', sometimes arriving in truckloads and carrying their children with them (*Kedaulatan Rakjat*, 24 January and 4 February 1964).

Besides casual or organized begging, non-violent moves for redistribution of food from the rich to the poor achieved more concerted form in Gunung Kidul's *Gerakan Rakyat Kelaparan* (hungry people's movement, also known as *Gerajak*), established by the local branches of the *BTI* (Peasant's Front) in January 1964 and including some local schoolteachers and village officials among its leaders. Besides demonstrating in front of the Bupati's office for distribution of free food to the hunger-stricken districts, groups of poor people would visit the houses of wealthy farmers and local elites, asking for food (Pratikno 2000). Government agencies were also involved in relief activities, with the accompanying incidences of corruption that were to become commonplace in subsequent decades. In January 1964 four cases of fraud in the distribution of government-purchased *gaplek* were exposed in Gunung Kidul (*Kedaulatan Rakjat*, 25 January 1964).

Food supplies in the city were also an issue of general concern. *Kedaulatan Rakjat* reported on 8 January 1964 – in the middle of the lean *paceklik* season and shortly before the end of the fasting month – that 'rice supplies for Jogjakarta were sufficient', since the Yogyakarta Paddy Procurement Foundation had managed to acquire 1900 tons of rice per month, which were to be distributed to civil servants, pensioners, students, the Taman Siswa school, permanent daily workers, the dormitories of hospital and social services personnel, state enterprises and other daily workers. Recalling that the normal monthly allocation of rice for civil servants was 10 kg per person, this amount represents rice supplies for about 190,000 people or one in every 12 of the total population of the region.

In the confused declining months of the Sukarno régime, Presidential Instruction 27 of 13 December 1965 announced that a New Rupiah would replace the old one at the rate of Rp. 1 new = Rp. 1,000 old. All old notes and coins would remain in circulation at their old value until their withdrawal; the old Rp. 5,000 and 10,000 notes would no longer be legal tender after 30 days, but could be changed at banks up to 25 February 1966 (but when changed, they were subject to a tax of 10 per cent). The same instruction ordered all 'traders not to raise their prices above those prevailing on 13 December (Survey 1966, pp. 4–5). In Yogyakarta the regional military commander ordered that traders and entrepreneurs must not use this opportunity to engage in actions that could cause harm, or chaos in the progress of the economy' (*Kedaulatan Rakjat*, 13 December 1965). Nevertheless, many traders seem to have ignored these warnings:

> Almost all the shops in South Yogyakarta were closed yesterday. The one or two that stayed open, or just opened their doors, were swamped with

> customers... Many people bought goods just to turn their money into goods, without considering whether they needed the goods they bought, and in a single morning the price of rice tripled in the city… Early in the morning the price of rice was around Rp. 1,000, but because of the rush to buy, and in some cases to buy in large quantities, the price rose to about Rp. 3,000. But finally stocks ran out completely. (*Kedaulatan Rakjat*, 13 December 1965)

These excerpts suggest a period of severe economic difficulty, reflecting at local level the larger national economic crisis of the 1960s. It is therefore quite puzzling to read the results of our interviews with urban and rural informants, which present a different picture. Most people do not seem to recall the experience of the 1960s hyperinflation as a particular calamity, and certainly not to have felt its impact more harshly than their experience of the late 1990s *krismon.* Local memories of the December 1965 currency reform are very vague and it does not seem to have been a momentous event in people's lives. Particularly in urban Yogyakarta and Kota Gede, nearly all informants have told us that the 1960s were a time of relative prosperity when 'it was easy to earn money' whether as a petty trader, a small-scale entrepreneur in the *batik* or other craft industries, or as a labourer. 'At that time, there was work for everyone', 'any kind of work brought money', and (in contrast to the 1990s) 'there were no layoffs, in fact everyone was looking for workers'; food and other basic necessities were available in the market (except, some say, for a period of a few months immediately after the September–October 1965 military coup when markets were relatively deserted and people 'afraid to go out'), and one could stand in line for distribution of subsidized rice (*beras kupon*) and oil. Many of our informants, both rural and urban, recall various kinds of distribution programmes of rice, other foods or daily necessities, either free or at reduced prices, rationed by a *kupon* system. Certainly these years were not materially disastrous for everyone; when 75 *jemaah haji* set off on the pilgrimage to Mecca in February 1965, the press commented 'in the history of the pilgrimage from Jogja, this is a very large number' (*Kedaulatan Rakjat*, 19 February 1965).

Greater hardship seems to have been felt in the rural areas where food was produced, in what seems a direct contrast to the situation of the 1990s *krismon*; informants in both Sriharjo (Bantul) and Kali Loro (Kulon Progo), two villages which at that time depended on rain-fed agriculture, recall extended periods when they ate mainly *thiwul*, *gaplek* (both dried cassava products) or maize. Real agricultural wages, however, were not lower than in the 1970s; informants mention cash wages which were kept equivalent in value to 2 kg of rice for a full days' work in Sriharjo, 1 kg for a half-day in Kali Loro and accompanied by good meals. Both rural and urban informants have mentioned the importance of *sambatan* (reciprocal labour exchange, in agriculture, house building etc.) as a source of good food, since the food provided was always *nasi lengkap* (rice with side-dishes) even when the normal daily menu was maize, *oyek* or other cassava products: 'In the most difficult periods, *sambatan* was something which many people relied on'.

One important aspect of resilience against inflation for wage and salaried workers (both unskilled and white-collar) is the payment of a part of the wage or salary in kind. This can apply both to casual farm workers and to those in large-scale plantations and factories, to teachers and civil servants. Many formal-sector employees in the 1960s received in-kind allowances of rice, cooking-oil, sugar etc., and these were also a point of negotiation between trade unions and employers. In January 1964, for example, when the Yogyakarta branch of the trade union SOBSI demanded bonuses for the Lebaran festival, their demands included (besides the normal extra one months' cash wage) 'cheap cloth, with payments to be spread over 6 months' and extra distributions of rice, sugar, cooking oil and lighting oil (*Kedaulatan Rakjat*, 2 January 1964). This may have helped to cushion the impact of inflation on wage and salary earners.

Former teachers, nurses, military personnel and others whom we interviewed all agreed that their cash wage was very small; however, all pointed to the importance of the in-kind allowances of rice and other basic commodities[6] which apparently arrived with no or little disruption throughout the 1960s. Most informants mentioned as exceptions the months immediately after September 1965, when the 10kg/person rice allowance was replaced with 6 kg of rice and 4 kg of maize or *bulgur* wheat. An urban married couple who received two low salaries – he as a primary school teacher, she as a nurse – informed us that they had never bought rice, in fact they had often sold some during this period.

Both in rural and urban areas, informants recall that indebtedness was less common than at present, although moneylenders (*rentenir*) in urban areas offered loans at 20 per cent interest. Those short of cash did, however, take gold, batik cloth or crockery to the local government pawnshop and sometimes paid village shopkeepers with such items; however, most informants told us that this was much less common than in the Japanese and revolution periods, when many people had to exchange crockery, cloth or jewellery for consumables just to eat, since at that time 'there was no work'.

Another important dimension of contrast with more recent times, both in rural and urban areas, is the contrast between the 'normal' *needs* of households in the 1960s and the 1990s. A few examples may be useful. By the 1960s, education had developed quite rapidly in the region and most children went at least to primary school, but the costs of this were minimal: there was no need to buy school uniforms (these were not introduced until some time in the 1970s); both urban and rural children were allowed to go barefoot (*cekeran*) to school, and there were no school fees – a rural teacher recalled that some children would bring him cassava, coconuts or other produce, but never cash – and even notebooks and pencils were not required in many schools which still used the *sabak*. Clothing was also simple (no brand-name clothes!) and often purchased only once in the year (at Lebaran). Basic medical care (and medicines) were, according to some informants, available free at the local *mantri* (health official); cheap traditional medicines were often used, and the more expensive medicines such as antibiotics were perhaps not available at all.

In summary then, although the economy as a whole was in a very weak state in the 1960s, these years are not recalled as years of special hardship, with the exception of certain groups and certain years, like the farmers of rain-fed regions during 1963 and 1964. The assumption that rapid inflation brings special problems for wage- and salary-earners is not entirely confirmed, given the tendency for rural cash wages to follow rice prices (although we do not have sufficient evidence to confirm whether this norm was always followed in practice) and the allowances of rice and other consumables given to salaried employees. Our view of the 1960s, like that of our informants, depends rather on whether we are comparing that period to the decades before or the decades that followed.

6. *KRISMON*: THE CRISIS OF THE LATE 1990s

On the eve of Indonesia's 1997–98 economic and political crisis, the economic situation in the Yogyakarta region was quite different from that of the 1960s. Yogyakarta's population of about 3 million was already 58 per cent urban, and the non-farm sector had grown to more than 80 per cent of GRDP.[7] Infrastructures of all kinds were relatively well-developed, Yogyakarta had become the country's second largest tourist destination with almost a million visitors per year, and a key centre of higher education with no less than 69 universities or other institutions of tertiary education and a very large student population: more than 20 per cent of the population aged 10 years and above were either students or still attending school. While the role of agriculture in GRDP had relatively declined, agriculture was still the largest single employer in the region (40 per cent of total employment in 1997) followed by trade (19 per cent), services (17 per cent), manufacturing (12 per cent) and construction (6 per cent).

The basic contours of the regional impact of *krismon* and its aftermath can be seen in statistics on sectoral changes in GRDP growth rates and employment in Yogyakarta from 1997 to the early 2000s. The overall shrinkage of the regional economy by 11 per cent in 1998 (somewhat less than the national shrinkage of 14 per cent) masks an uneven impact across sectors: the construction sector was by far the hardest hit with a contraction of about one-third, while both agriculture and manufacturing contracted by only about 6 per cent. All sectors except agriculture had returned to modest growth by 1999. Economic contraction, however, was not accompanied by widespread open unemployment, which actually declined between 1997 and 1998 (from 4.0 to 3.6 percent overall and from 8.8 to 5.7 percent in urban areas). The 2000 Census, when compared to 1990 (Table 5.2) shows a large drop in manufacturing employment (by half) and corresponding growth in services, which seems (rather than trade) to have been the main 'refuge' sector for those who had lost jobs and livelihoods.

At the sub-sectoral or branch level we can begin to see some of the more dramatic impacts of *krismon*. For example, while the financial sector as a whole shrank by only 7 per cent overall in 1998, banking itself shrank by 36 per cent. The modest overall decline in manufacturing exports (5 per cent) masks the near-collapse of some export branches (plywood for example declining by more than 50 per cent) and the 'devaluation bonanza' experienced by others (with exports in textiles, garments and leather gloves growing by around 30 per cent). The transport sector as a whole shrank by 9 per cent (but air transport by 37 per cent), while rail transport actually grew by 2 per cent as many former air passengers shifted to rail. While the construction sector overall shrank by one-third, construction employment contracted by only about 10 per cent (reflecting the fact that the contraction occurred mainly in large infrastructure and commercial construction projects while the majority of construction employment is in the more labour-intensive branches of house-building and repair).

The tourism industry suffered a number of shocks and setbacks more related to the political and security situation than to *krismon* itself. While both domestic and foreign tourist visits dropped drastically in 1998 this was both most dramatic and longer-lasting in the case of foreign tourists; the succession of episodes of violence in Jakarta, in some outer islands, bombs and the resulting 'negative travel warnings' by many countries drove foreign tourist arrivals down to only one-third or less of pre-*krismon* levels for more than a decade, while domestic tourism recovered to pre-crisis levels by 2001 (Prabawa 2010, p. 82). Yogyakarta's large hotels remained open though with reduced occupancy rates, while some smaller hotels shifted to other functions such as student lodgings (Kompas [Yogya edition] 14/7/04).

Disemployment resulting from *krismon,* while traumatic to those affected by it, was thus relatively limited to a few specific sub-sectors or branches such as banking, air transport, some tourism-related activities and specific industries such as plywood and canned mushrooms. Yogyakarta is also a major exporter of labour to the industrial, informal sector and service sectors of the Jabotabek region and other urban regions. However, the predicted return flow of out-migrants (for example from struggling or bankrupt manufacturing industries in West Java) – the 1990s equivalent of the returning plantation coolies of the 1930s – does not seem to have occurred to any large extent, and remittances continue to flow into the region.

As we have seen, the rapid price increases of the *krismon* period of 1997–98 were a relatively minor inflationary episode compared to those of the 1960s. Annual inflation rates in the region came close to 100 per cent in only one year[8] (1998, compare the seven-year period in the 1960s) and monthly inflation exceeded 10 per cent only in one month (February 1998) compared to almost every month during 1964–66. This is comparable not so much to the chronic hyperinflation of the 1960s, but to the more modest and now largely forgotten inflationary shocks experienced during the 'mini-crisis' in 1973–74 when food prices increased by 50 and 30 per cent respectively.

Table 5.2 Economically active population Yogyakarta, 1960–2000

Occupation	Numbers (x 1000)			Percentage		
	M	F	Total	M	F	Total
			1960			
Agriculture	398	218	616	76	64	71
Manufactures[1]	48	53	101	9	14	12
Transport	10	*	10	2	*	1
Trade	18	39	57	3	11	7
Services	42	29	72	8	9	8
Construction	10	*	10	2	*	1
Total	526	340	866	100	100	100
			1971			
Agriculture	358	216	574	63	48	56
Manufactures	63	101	163	11	22	16
Transport	15	*	16	3	*	2
Trade	35	96	131	6	21	13
Services	73	29	101	13	6	10
Construction	18	*	18	3	*	2
Other	9	7	18	1	2	2
Total	571	450	1021	100	100	100
			1990			
Agriculture	367	308	675	46	45	45
Manufactures	82	106	188	10	16	13
Transport	31	1	32	4	*	2
Trade	76	155	231	9	23	16
Services	139	91	230	17	13	15
Construction	83	1	84	10	*	6
Other	26	17	43	3	2	3
Total	804	680	1484	100	100	100

Table 5.2 continued

Occupation	Numbers (x 1000)			Percentage		
	M	F	Total	M	F	Total
			2000			
Agriculture	349	360	709	41	47	44
Manufactures	48	48	96	6	6	6
Transport	22	1	23	3	*	1
Trade	84	132	216	10	17	13
Services	277	155	432	32	21	27
Construction	–	–	–	–	–	–
Other	78	60	138	9	8	9
Total	859	756	1614	100	100	100

Notes: [1] Includes mining and electricity.
[2] The 2000 Census publications probably subsume construction in 'services'.

Source: Sensus Penduduk (1960, 1971, 1990, 2000)

Some groups of course are particularly hard hit by inflation. Even if real wage levels more or less keep up with inflation in the long term, wage- and salary-earners experience a temporary drop in real incomes as wage/salary increases always lag behind inflation trends. Those living on fixed incomes include not only pensioners but also the tens of thousands of out-of-town students. Among urban Yogyakarta's large student population, many out-of-town students coming from modest backgrounds and living on fixed money allowances were seen lining up for cheap mid-day meals provided by various charitable organizations on campus in the early crisis years. Most rural households were not insulated from inflation as high rates of landlessness and near-landlessness mean that the great majority of rural household are net food buyers (Kutanegara and Nooteboom 2002).

In the light of past experience, Yogyakarta's *krismon* may actually appear locally as a rather modest crisis if seen in long-term perspective and in only material terms. The *krismon* was certainly upsetting for shareholders and bankers, disastrous for those who work in certain sectors – e.g. construction, certain branches of manufacturing, and tourism-related activities – and caused hardship for those living on fixed incomes. There remain questions, however, about why this short period of serious, but relatively moderate inflation seems to have been felt to have caused such serious reversals and hardship for so many people in urban and rural areas, compared to the 1960s.

If we consider as defining feature of 'crisis' that it represents a 'turning-point … a state of affairs in which a decisive change for better or worse is imminent'[9] we may wonder if we are not exaggerating to speak of 'crisis', as applied to either urban or rural Yogyakarta, in this case. Three episodes of

Indonesian recession (the 1930s, 1960s and 1990s) all saw declines of a similar order of magnitude in per capita incomes – some 12–17 per cent – while the truly staggering decline in output in the 1940s made this the deepest, as well as the longest-lasting, of all economic crises in the twentieth century, with national income probably declining by about one-half and regaining its pre-crisis level only some 23 years later. The long period of four decades from 1930 to the end of the 1960s could be characterized as a context of recurring or near-permanent crisis in Yogyakarta, as in much or all of Indonesia. In contrast the three decades of continuous, recession-free growth from 1968 to 1997 mean that the younger generation (in fact, more than half the population) had, in contrast to their parents' generation, no 'experience of economic crisis' prior to the *krismon* of 1997. When they compare their experience of past and present economic (as well as social and political) conditions, it is not surprising that that they do this in a different way than their parents or grandparents; their experience of, and response to, contemporary crisis is qualitatively different from that of the older generation. This is why nearly all our older informants interviewed in 2003, both rural and urban, have told us that the *really* difficult times – in comparison to the 1960s and the 1990s – were the '*zaman Belanda, zaman Jepang, dan kembalinya Belanda*' ('the [end of the] Dutch time, the Japanese time, and the time when the Dutch came back again').

NOTES

1. Interestingly, the recessions of the 1930s, 1940s, 1960s and 1990s were preceded by *el niño*-type droughts.
2. I have not been able to locate this source.
3. Assuming that they were all or mostly male, this number amounts to about one in every five or six adult male European residents of Yogyakarta.
4. These inflation rates are based on food prices in urban Java, as in Papanek and Dowsett (1975) and BPS, *Indikator Ekonomi.* I have not yet been able to find comparable details for Yogyakarta.
5. In February 1964 it was announced that two of these villages (4,000 people) would be resettled in South Sumatra the following month.
6. Most seem to have received also sugar, cooking and lighting oil; some also mentioned soap, margarine, powdered milk and even chocolate.
7. All information in this paragraph is from BPS (1999).
8. In 1998, overall consumer price inflation in the Yogyakarta region reached 78 per cent, and food price inflation 115 per cent.
9. *Shorter Oxford English Dictionary*, Vol. I (1977), p. 457.

PART II

Heterodox (Political) Economic Interpretations

6. Chinese Savings Gluts or Northern Financialisation? The Ideological Expediency of Crisis Narratives

Andrew Martin Fischer

Debates on the current financial crisis have been intense and ongoing, particularly among economists intent on squirming out from under the burden of responsibility with the convenient refrain that no one saw it coming (besides those whose work was being ignored by the mainstream). However, within this debate and despite its loosely substantiated evocations of Keynes, a broadly neoclassical consensus has reasserted itself, showing little or no variance from the mainstream views that brought us into crisis in the first place. As if a refrain from past crises, the narrative is focused on blaming the peripheries for crisis in the centre. The target is China, the most obvious surplus country within global economic imbalances (besides Germany, which somehow escapes similar castigation).

China's 'savings-glut', it is argued, was a fundamental contributor to crisis in Northern financial systems. The charge is that China's interventionist economic strategies and its understandable but mistaken obsession with amassing foreign exchange has been an important, if not dominant, underlying cause of the credit bubble in the US. The logic is that a foreign exchange savings glut emanated from Asia as an outcome of specific policy choices, including currency undervaluation, taken in the aftermath of the East Asian crisis of 1997–98. This savings glut was then recycled in the US given that most foreign exchange reserves are held in US Treasury securities or, increasingly, in non-government investments, which then fuelled the notorious securitised subprime mortgages among other speculative asset bubbles in the US economy. Hence, the Asian savings glut crucially fuelled the US credit bubble. The Keynesian allusions are presumably based on the idea that such savings will ultimately be self-defeating whence bubble comes to bust and that surplus countries should be penalised. China in particular must now make painful adjustments to correct its previous policy blunders, primarily by allowing its currency to appreciate and by liberalising its financial sector in order to end the repressed consumption of its citizens.

This narrative might be called a 'G20 consensus' given its endorsement by leading central bankers and finance ministers in various international economic fora since the beginning of the crisis.[1] It has been spearheaded by leading economic commentators such as Paul Krugman or Martin Wolf, central bankers such as Ben Bernanke and Mervyn King, economists working for Goldman Sachs and other large private financial institutions, or else economists at the Peterson Institute for International Economics in Washington, such as Fred Bergsten, Nicolas Lardy, Morris Goldstein and Arvind Subramanian (indeed, some of these groups overlap). Many of these economists have called for aggressive action against China on its exchange rate, which they deem to be hugely undervalued and characterise as 'mercantilist'. It is with this logic that 130 members of the US Congress called on the Obama administration in March 2010 to label China a 'currency manipulator', which would have then allowed for other punitive measures to be taken against China. It is with the same logic that similar advocacy was made in the US in September and October 2010. Strikingly, this consensus has even captured the cognition of many on the political Left, reinforcing the potential for this narrative to appear as a self-evident and infallible truism of the current state of international economic affairs despite its very contestable theoretical foundation.

This chapter offers a critical examination of the theoretical foundations of this crisis narrative in two parts. The first reviews how the crisis was quickly framed by leading public economists such as Martin Wolf or Paul Krugman as a problem of excess savings, particularly those deriving from Chinese surpluses, thereby deflecting attention away from the fact that the crisis is more accurately rooted in the recent phase of rampant financialisation intimately connected to the maintenance of US hegemony. The second section then discusses how this logic is profoundly un-Keynesian and an alternative explanation of the sequencing between the US financial bubble and Chinese surpluses is provided. The conclusion explores some of the implications of this ideological reconstitution.

1. OF US CREDIT BUBBLES AND CHINESE SAVINGS

In order to clarify the logical steps of the savings-glut narrative in more detail, it is useful to focus on the columns of Martin Wolf from the *Financial Times*, given that he represents a powerful voice in its popularised propagation. Notably, at the end of 2008, Wolf (2008b) iconically alluded (without attribution) to the famous quote by Paul Samuelson that 'we are all Keynesians now', referring to the apparent shattering of the consensus which, it should be recalled, he had supported until it became obvious that the party was ending in 2007. In this column, he also directed his attention to the issue of rebalancing global demand. Beyond his case for a fiscal response to the crisis, his focus on global imbalances appeared to be his other claim to Keynesianism given Keynes' own efforts at the end of his life to create a balanced post-war international trading and financial system that would penalise surplus as well as deficit countries.[2] From his own side, Wolf appeals to the idea of constructing 'a new system of global financial regulation and an approach to monetary policy that curbs credit booms and asset bubbles'. Alluding also to Minsky, he argues that 'recognition of the systemic frailty of a complex financial system would be a good start'. He did not provide more guidance at this point, besides pre-empting criticism by suggesting that we must meet this task 'in a spirit of humility and pragmatism, shorn of ideological blinkers'.

In his later columns, Wolf elaborated on the more important question of how such bubbles came to be and thus how they can be undone by turning his attention to China as a primary source of savings glut, thereby maintaining the supply-side thrust of his condemnation of China's 'mercantilist' currency policies as laid out in Wolf (2008a). For instance, in Wolf (2009a), he set out a standard argument about the transmission of a global savings glut to financial debacle in the US. Citing a publically-unavailable paper from Goldman Sachs, he reasoned that a global savings glut had driven two salient features of the global economy leading up to the crisis: a huge increase in global current account imbalances (especially the emergence of huge surpluses in emerging economies) as well as a global decline in nominal and real yields on all forms of debt. Conferring with the unidentified Goldman Sachs authors, he dismissed the argument that loose monetary policy had been driving these rising imbalances and falling yields because it 'fails to explain persistently low long-term real rates'. He listed the two remaining salient features identified by the Goldman Sachs paper (an increase in global returns on physical capital and an increase in the equity risk premium) and then added one of his own; 'the strong downward pressure on the dollar prices of many manufactured goods'. These, he argued, are additionally explained by a massive increase in the effective global labour supply and the extreme risk aversion of the emerging world's new creditors. In turn, this led to the accumulation of net overseas assets, entirely accounted for by public sector acquisitions and principally channelled into reserves.

Wolf (2009a) added that Asian emerging economies (China, above all) have dominated such flows. He attributed this fact, along with his fifth salient feature (downward pressure on dollar prices of manufactured goods), to policy decisions, particularly China's exchange-rate regime. Thus, he wrapped the plot together by centring in on China's decision to keep the exchange rate undervalued. Concurring with the unidentified Goldman Sachs authors, he argued that 'the low bond yields caused by newly emerging savings gluts drove the crazy lending whose results we now see. With better regulation, the mess would have been smaller … But someone had to borrow this money.' He concluded that 'China's decision to accumulate roughly $2,000bn in foreign currency reserves was … a blunder' and it now has to accept the consequences in the quest for global rebalancing, particularly if it does not want to face default from its debtors (i.e. the US) no longer able to consume Chinese surpluses through further borrowing. In order to do this, China must, above all, correct its exchange regime.

Wolf (2009b) reaffirmed this argument later in September. He remarked that it is no wonder the huge exposure of over 2 trillion dollars-worth of foreign currency reserves makes the Chinese government nervous. However, 'nobody asked the Chinese to do this', he asserted.

> Having made what I believe was a huge mistake, the Chinese government cannot expect anybody to save them from its consequences. A substantial appreciation of the Chinese currency is inevitable and desirable in the years ahead. The longer the Chinese authorities fight it, the bigger their losses (and the pain of adjustment) are going to be.

This time he conferred with a paper by Goldstein and Lardy (2009), published by the 'nonpartisan' Washington-based Peterson Institute, that currency appreciation would also help rebalance the Chinese economy in the long term, among other policies such as further financial reform. He argued that an appreciation of the real exchange rate, 'ideally via a rise in the nominal exchange rate', is the primary means to end China's 'massive subsidy to its exports' through its 'foreign currency interventions, combined with the sterilisation of their natural monetary effects'. This in turn would also serve to increase consumption as a share of GDP. On 17 November, during Obama's visit to China, Wolf (2009c) again stepped up this tone of urgency, insisting that the 'US is entitled to protect itself against such mercantilism … We have spent long enough discussing China's exchange rate policies. It is time for action.' He has since been rutted into this tune.

It is not unsurprising, given Wolf's posturing since the beginning of the crisis, that this is more or less the same position taken by the Obama administration, and even the Bush Junior administration. Indeed, one of the first acts of Tim Geithner as US Treasury Secretary was to declare China a currency manipulator in January 2009, although he quickly stepped down from this very aggressive stance. Notably, the Bush administration had been toying with this threat for several years but had not yet taken a stand.

Similarly, on 19 October 2009, Ben Bernanke argued that Asia must guard against a return to global imbalances in the economic rebound (see Guha 2009), even while Asia was being simultaneously thrashed by what has been called 'the mother of all carry trades' by Nouriel Roubini, stemming largely from liquidity conditions in the US (see RGE 2009). Bernanke claimed that the US-centred crisis had been fuelled by giant capital inflows that overwhelmed both market discipline and regulatory safeguards against the mispricing of risk. In other words, similar to Greenspan before him, his interpretation of causality runs from surpluses to capital inflows and then to liquidity and regulatory failure. His contention is that the East Asian push into export-driven growth and trade surpluses following their experience with the 1997 crisis subsequently produced imbalances between national savings, consumption and investment. Hence, while leading the rebound, China should work towards preventing a return to surpluses and asset bubbles. One way to mitigate this risk would be 'through some greater exchange rate flexibility' offset by fiscal consolidation.

Some otherwise critical 'liberal' aka 'left' economists have reinforced this savings-glut narrative of crisis. For instance, Paul Krugman, the flag bearer for the 'New Keynesians' in the US, also places emphasis on China's exchange regime. In April 2009 he recounted that China chose, in the early 2000s, to keep the value of the yuan fixed to the dollar, resulting in the necessity to buy dollars as trade surpluses mounted (Krugman 2009a). He argued that such habits must change; 'Two years ago, we lived in a world in which China could save much more than it invested and dispose of the excess savings. That world is gone ... The bottom line is that China hasn't yet faced up to the wrenching changes that will be needed to deal with this global crisis.' He explained this further in a related blog (Krugman 2009b) by clearly identifying the current crisis as a liquidity trap, in which we are faced with an incipient excess supply of savings even at a zero interest rate. 'In this situation,' he explains, 'America has *too large a supply of desired savings* [his emphasis]. If the Chinese spend more and save less, that's a good thing from our point of view. To put it another way, we're facing a global paradox of thrift, and everyone wishes everyone else would save less.' The New Keynesian credentials of this argument seem to be based on an idea of the paradox of thrift, albeit excess savings in his version do not adjust to aggregate demand but instead keep sloshing around the system.

While he was more parsimonious with his blame in these springtime blogs, Krugman (2009c) nonetheless came out much stronger against China in his autumn op-eds, in line with the positions mentioned above. He claimed that 'China's bad behavior is posing a growing threat to the rest of the world economy. The only question now is what the world – and, in particular, the United States – will do about it.' It is interesting that in his discussion, he omitted any recognition of the revaluation of the yuan from 2005 onwards (see Section 2 below) but concluded that many 'economists, myself included, believe that China's asset-buying spree helped inflate the housing bubble, setting the stage for the global financial crisis. But China's insistence on keeping the yuan/dollar rate fixed, even when the dollar declines, may be doing even more harm now.' Krugman encouraged a more bullish approach from US officials to negotiations with China on currency manipulation. Helping to set the tone later asserted by Wolf, he insisted that 'with the world economy still in a precarious state, beggar-thy-neighbor policies by major players can't be tolerated. Something must be done about China's currency.' By March 2010, Krugman (2010a) was adamant that it is 'time to take a stand' by calling China a currency manipulator.

A similar narrative has found a hold even further to the left. A strong example is Robert Wade (2009). This is somewhat paradoxical given that he usually opposes Martin Wolf on most issues, but here he seems to find an affinity in the savings supply-side interpretation of the crisis by placing emphasis on how 'global imbalances have had an important causal role… at the domestic level, in the form of credit recycling to the agents spending more than their income' (Wade 2009, pp. 542–3). He implies that, as the US fiscal deficit fell as a share of GDP after 2003, private sector and current account deficits had to balloon due to the global imbalances. This was facilitated through 'credit recycling to the private sector,' which 'took the form of capital inflows going mainly into mortgage finance (for example, the central bank of China bought the securities issued by the government-backed mortgage lender Freddie Mac), creating a real estate boom'. He offers this perspective as a way to explain why 'the "mistakes" in monetary policy and financial regulation were made' (he implies they were the consequence of global imbalances) and why the crisis resulted in a run into the dollar rather than away from it. Hence he concludes that the issue is too important to ignore; 'the current policy responses nationally and internationally are focused too narrowly on the financial system and not enough on the imbalances and what lies behind them'. Through this logic, Wade actually finds himself quite close to the position of Wolf, arguing that much more is needed than simply correcting mistakes in monetary policy and financial regulation, although he does not explicitly spell out what this should entail for China (e.g. see Wade 2009, pp. 550–51). While he repeatedly quotes Keynes and evokes Keynesian remedies, it is interesting that his streamlined albeit somewhat ambiguous interpretation of the crisis, condensed into a mere page of text, seems to rest on a causality running from global imbalances to credit crisis, rather than, for instance, imbalances being a reflection of the US credit conditions that lead to crisis. If so, his argument is essentially in line with that of Wolf, Bernanke and Krugman.

It is precisely this *de facto* consensus across much of the Left and Right that provides the potential for a powerful ideological reconstitution. Perhaps the guise of the reconstitution would not exactly match the neoliberalism that the Left so despises, but it would effectively legitimise a strategy of shifting the burden of adjustment onto the most obvious peripheral surplus country that, in the end, is not even a serious industrial contender but instead is deeply integrated into regional and international production networks increasingly dominated by Northern corporations. In other words, despite the attention to global imbalances, these narratives ignore the underlying structures of production, distribution and ownership – or of power – that drive these imbalances. Indeed, from this latter perspective, the current crisis could well represent an important milestone in the seismic reorganisation and consolidation of these international production networks. If so, it is quite possible that repressed US wages and Chinese trade surpluses are both symptoms of larger global forces at work, encompassing financialisation in the centre and network reorganisations in East Asia since the 1997–98 crisis.

2. KEYNES IN BEIJING

In order to understand the last point, it is important to question whether these emerging narratives have understood the causality the right way around. Is it the case that emerging market surpluses have been generating a savings glut that is then transmitted and amplified through the financial sector to the US? According to this logic, the US financial sector might not be efficient in the sense of avoiding bubbles, but it definitely does its job with a vengeance, even if somewhat hectically. However, it could not do this job if the global imbalances had not provided a source of liquidity to slosh.

Despite the ritualised claims on the intellectual soul of Keynes that have become a litany accompanying these narratives, the underlying logic is profoundly un-Keynesian. To borrow the words of Geoff Tily, from a Keynesian perspective the logic amounts to the tail wagging the dog.[3] In other words, it is based on the principle that supply creates its own demand (i.e. Say's Law). To frame this in the current discussion, Asian savings drive US aggregate demand. Or, in the words of Wolf (2009a), 'someone had to borrow this money'. Or, as argued by Wade, if 'the external deficit remains constant (or rises) and the fiscal deficit falls, there must be an offsetting increase in private indebtedness' (Wade 2009, p. 542). This logic helps to clarify why both Wade and Wolf argue that the crisis cannot be fully explained by 'folly, greed and mis-regulation' (Wolf 2008b) or by '"mistakes" in monetary policy and financial regulation' (Wade 2009).

Keynes would have rejected this logic. Indeed, it was precisely this logic that was at the heart of his rejection of what he called 'the classics'. Instead, he argued that aggregate savings adjust to aggregate demand, not the other way around. To translate this into the current context, US aggregate demand drives US external imbalances, which in turn drive the imbalances of those economies oriented towards servicing US demand and/or absorbing excess US liquidity, primarily through investment and/or speculative demand in those economies, to which aggregate savings adjust. Changes in US aggregate demand are influenced by deficit spending, which in turn is influenced by warmongering and ideological obsessions with cutting taxes and subsidising the wealthy, and by private demand augmented by phases of financial deregulation, innovation and resultant credit bubbles. In other words, another phase of rampant financialisation in the centre drives global imbalances. Placing this in the context of China, China's investment rates are not high because the Chinese save a lot. Rather, China's aggregate monetary savings (which includes credit from the banking system as well as finance from abroad, as discussed below) are high because of high rates of investment, which are in part responding to aggregate demand from the US and Europe, among other factors. China's growing surpluses and building foreign exchange reserves are outcomes of these processes rather than causes.

There is a strong case to be made that this Keynesian interpretation fits the historical stylised facts quite well, at least much better than the supply-side (neoclassical) interpretation. To start with, it is important to recognise that the Chinese authorities have been keenly aware of the dilemma of the low consumption to GDP share for much longer than is typically acknowledged by western commentators. Raising this share has been an explicit government goal since at least 2003. Already in 1998 one of the first reactions of the government to the East Asia crisis was to boost domestic demand. It has since been a subject of much domestic debate. The failure to achieve this goal of lowering the investment share can, by lack of any obvious or desirable alternative, hardly be called a 'choice'. It is certainly not the case that, as suggested by Krugman (2009a), 'China acquired its $2 trillion stash – turning the People's Republic into the T-bills Republic – the same way Britain acquired its empire: in a fit of absence of mind.' However, Krugman is probably right that there was not necessarily a deep strategy behind this vast accumulation of low-yielding assets. Indeed, in recognising its inability to balance its external position, the central government quickly and very consciously opted for the contingency option of at least managing the imbalances through sterilisation. The choice to ride the wave of regional and global economic restructuring is understandable. Balanced or not, growth was a priority given the enormous challenges facing China, still a poor country, including fairly high levels of urban unemployment, persistent rural poverty, and, in this context, the planned urbanisation of the about one-third of the country's population over the course of the next generation. (For further discussion, see de Haan and Gong, Chapter 16 in this volume.)

Moreover, the common assertion that China's high savings rate derives from high household savings, which in turn drive investment versus consumption, is another caricature worthy of some attention. Notably, many of the arguments in this respect involve a blurring between a conception of savings as household savings (i.e. choices between consumption and saving out of total household income) and the residual concept of 'national savings' in national accounting (i.e. the difference between aggregate output and aggregate consumption). The latter conception assumes that aggregate savings equal aggregate investment (plus the external balance) whether by a neoclassical logic whereby savings drive investment, or else by a Keynesian logic whereby savings adjust to aggregate demand, which is driven by consumption and investment decisions. Notably, there is nothing implicit or explicit in national accounting that predisposes it to the neoclassical logic.

The distinction is important because there is, in fact, much contention around the caricature of Chinese household thrift. For instance, He and Cao (2007, pp. 3–6) point out that the high levels of national savings in China are not explained by the household sector but by the government and corporate sectors. In reality, they note that aggregate household savings accounted for a shrinking fraction of total national savings, falling from 52 per cent of national savings in 1992 to 42 per cent in 2001.[4] They further explain that the high national savings rate is in part attributable to fast growth of savings in the non-financial corporate and government sectors. Moreover, their detailed analysis reveals an implicit Keynesian slant in that, despite the high and increasing levels of savings in both the government and non-financial corporate sectors, such savings were insufficient to meet investment demand. The government was covering its shortfall by issuing large amounts of government bonds.[5] Similarly, non-financial corporate savings (i.e. retained earnings) covered only about half of that sector's investment needs up to 2001 (the most recent data covered by the authors). Bank lending was the major source of financing to cover the gap, although other sources included portfolio finance and an increasing share of financing from abroad, the latter reaching 39 per cent of bank loans already by 2001, up from 22 per cent in 1992 (ibid., pp. 10–11). Thus, the appearance of rising national savings rates in large part reflects monetary expansion, credit creation, increasing levels of foreign financing and increasing levels of reinvested corporate earnings, all in response to investment demand.

This would also help to explain the falling share of household disposable income in national income despite very high rates of growth in such household incomes that are the envy of most developing countries. It is in this sense that the high residual category of national savings should not be conflated with a notion of repressed consumption or savings-led investment but, rather, as an attribute of the speed by which China has been catching-up.[6] While He and Cao recommend a variety of government-directed redistributive policies and further reform in the domestic financial sector to deal with the resultant imbalances, currency appreciation and international financial liberalisation are absent from their recommendations.

The issue of currency revaluation reveals another fallacy of the savings–supply-side analysis of the Chinese growth experience. Namely, it is not at all clear whether revaluation would have any impact on China's external surpluses, nor is it clear whether the Chinese yuan is even undervalued in the first place.[7] Notably, the government allowed the yuan to appreciate against the US dollar by over 20 per cent from July 2005 to July 2008. At the same time, China's trade surplus in goods exploded from around 3 per cent of its GDP in 2004 to a peak of over 9 per cent in 2007.[8] More specifically, the value of the trade surplus with the US more than doubled between 2004 and 2007, increasing from about 4 per cent to 5 per cent of nominal Chinese GDP converted into US dollars at market exchange rates, i.e. even after accounting for the effect of revaluation on this nominal calculation. This simple observation suggests that the external imbalances have borne little relation to the exact relative valuation of the Chinese currency but, rather, to underlying structural changes in the organisation of international trade and production.

Revaluation advocates have retorted that the yuan was so undervalued that much more revaluation is needed. More sophisticated versions of this argument contend that other intervening factors, such as interest rate differentials, have prevented revaluation from inducing the necessary adjustments (for instance, see Pettis 2010). However, alternative explanations include China's integration into networks controlled by transnational corporations (TNCs), with the result that revaluation is unlikely to have much effect on the competitiveness of Chinese exports because so much of the inputs for these exports are imported (and priced as intra-firm transfers), cancelling out the potential effect of any currency movement.[9] Indeed, much of the trade account could actually represent capital flows given the predominance of transfer pricing practices used for intra-firm transfers within the TNC networks that dominate China's trade.[10] The disjuncture between currency appreciation and rising trade surpluses is also partly explained by rising productivity in China, which compensates for currency appreciation by lowering unit-labour costs. Hence, the real significance of the trade data must be evaluated with much caution.

Even if we reject the notion that excess savings have been driving these surpluses, an argument could still be made, as does Pettis (2009), that the excess output has been caused by artificially-high levels of investment encouraged and subsidised by government industrial policies intent on 'turbo-charging economic growth'. Hence, from this logic, it could be argued that excess output has been driving external imbalances. However, this obviously begs the question of what allows for the consumption of such output surpluses. In other words, what are the international factors that enable the government to follow such investment strategies in the first place? After all, at the end of the 1990s and in the wake of the East Asia crisis, the Chinese economy was facing serious problems with overproduction in many sectors, as well as generalised price deflation in the economy, particularly for agricultural and manufactured goods. From the vantage point of the time, it was not obvious whether the government would be able to continue an investment-driven strategy. As reasoned by Hu Angang (2000): 'We will see what is going to happen after the WTO rules take effect but for the time being it is difficult to know what will happen in those sectors.'

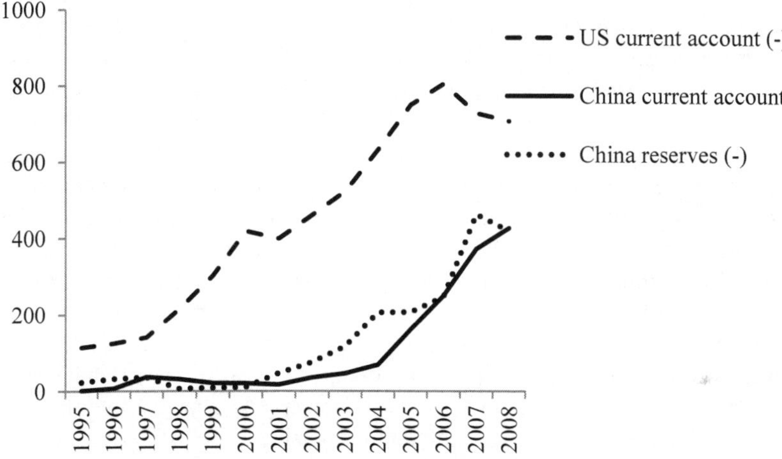

Source: China: CSY (2009: Table 2-34) and IMF IFS data base. US: IMF IFS databases (Accessed on 27 October 2009)

Figure 6.1 US current account deficit (reversed) and China current account surplus (1995–2008, billions of US dollars)

Many economic commentators in the US have suggested that the US consumption of this surplus was more or less induced by the imbalance, given the responsiveness and absorptive capacity of its mature free market economy. Hence, the reasoning that overproduction caused trade and foreign exchange surpluses, which in turn caused the credit bubble. The alternative hypothesis is that financially-lubricated corporate restructuring and expansion in the US and other Northern economies drove Asian surpluses. In order to analyse this question, it is useful to examine the sequencing of China's current account surpluses and US current account deficits, presented in Figure 6.1. The US deficits and China's reserves are presented with reversed signs in order to more effectively evaluate the evolution of this bilateral comparison. The values are in current US dollars as this best represents the respective monetary weights of the imbalances in the international economy, particularly in comparison to each other.

Through this simple comparison, it is quite clear that the argument that China's surpluses have been fuelling the credit bubble in the US equates to placing the cart in front of the donkey. China's current account surplus shrank from a brief East Asia crisis high of $40 billion in 1997 to $17.4 billion in 2001 (1.3 per cent of its GDP), while the US current account deficit simultaneously fell from –$141 billion to –$398 billion. The bursting of the dotcom bubble in 2000 and the ensuing recession in the US caused a slight correction to this trend in 2001, but thereafter the US current account deficit continued its precipitous decline, whereas the Chinese current account only started to increase at a comparable pace after 2004 (in terms of year-on-year increase in nominal value, not in terms of pace of change). Up to 2004, China's surplus had increased only gradually to $69 billion by 2004, whereas the US current account deficit had fallen to –$631 billion. In comparison to 1997, China's surplus had not even doubled by 2004, whereas the US deficit had increased 4.5 times. The nominal increment in surplus for China was only $28.7 billion between these years, whereas the US deficit had increased by $490.4 billion. In this light, the argument that the reduction in the US fiscal deficit as a proportion of GDP in 2003 caused an expansion in the private sector deficit due to the necessity to absorb global imbalances (primarily those from China) appears particularly specious, at least in the case of China. It is only from 2005 onwards that the current account surplus of China started to explode at a pace comparable to the US freefall into deficit that had been well in course since the East Asian crisis.

Notably, an equally dramatic descent into deficit with the rest of Asia (mostly East and Southeast Asia) – parallel to the rising surpluses with the US and Europe – underlay China's emerging global trade surplus in the early 2000s. China's trade balance with Asia shifted from a surplus in the 1990s, to a slight deficit in 2001, to a sudden increase in the trade deficit to about $74 billion by 2004, almost equal to the surplus with the US of $81 billion in the same year. This was the result of its phenomenally increasing import and export volumes with Asia. For instance, China's imports from Asia increased from $147 billion in 2001 to $620 billion by 2007 (over half of total imports). This exceeded the combination of its export trade volumes with the US and Europe.[11] The descent into deficit with Asia stalled from 2005 onwards because China's exports to Asia started to catch up with its imports from Asia, which again is counterintuitive given the revaluation of the yuan from 2005 onwards. The stalling of the deficit with Asia explains the sharp rise in the overall trade balance from that year onwards given that the surpluses with the US and Europe continued to rise. From this perspective, it is also clear that the recent trade surpluses have been generated through phenomenal (and phenomenally increasing) volumes of turnover, particularly in the processing trade between East Asia, the US and Europe.

Returning to the overall picture presented in Table 6.1, the trend of rising imbalances appeared sooner in China in terms of reserves, which started to increase in 2001, although still slower than the increasing US current account deficits. Notably, this was because of a huge surge of capital inflows into China in 2001–05. These would have been related, in large part, to the centrifugal capital outflows from the US during the recession in 2001 combined with increased net inflows of FDI parallel to China joining the WTO in the same year. Then, much of the inflows were related to speculation on yuan revaluation up to 2005 together with further FDI. Thus these capital flows were a reflection of financialisation in the US rather than a cause of it. It can hardly be said that reserves accumulated by China through its sterilisation of capital inflows contributed to the US credit bubble as much of these inflows derived from US credit expansion in the first place (and from credit expansion in supporting financial centres). The fact that the surge on the capital account preceded the surge on the current account by about three to four years suggests that the latter was due to international restructurings of production and distribution that were being led by the former.

While more detailed analysis of causality is required,[12] there is a strong case to be made that the Chinese current account surpluses were responding to imbalances in the US. Indeed, the US credit bubble had already been well in progress by 2005, when the Chinese current account surplus started to explode. The US current account deficit then hit its – nominal – trough in 2006, at the peak of the credit bubble in the US. As mentioned above, the Chinese trade surplus in goods hit its peak as a proportion of GDP in 2007, at the outset of the US credit crisis, after which it has since fallen. While the Chinese current account surplus has continued to increase in nominal value, in 2008 it still remained about $280 billion less than the US current account deficit in the same year. Moreover, the Chinese surplus only started to increase faster than the US deficit fell from 2006, although by this point the credit bubble in the US had already reached its zenith and was starting to wane, mutating into volatile international activities such as carry trades and other speculative pursuits by hedge funds and related financial institutional innovations (UNCTAD 2007, pp. 15–22). With the onset of crisis, Chinese surpluses have arguably played a counter-cyclical role in the US economy.

The key question in this analysis of sequencing regards the causes of the sudden emergence of China as mercantilist *tour de force* since 2001. Notably, up to the late 1990s, China's current and capital accounts were much more typical of a 'late late' peripheral industrialiser, in the sense that growth spurts usually ended in current account deficits, subsequently requiring austerity to correct. China's escape from this classic predicament of peripheral late industrialisers appears intimately related to the systemic rerouting of East Asian centred international production networks (IPNs) through China that followed the East Asian crisis in 1997–98. As discussed above, this can be inferred through a regionally disaggregated examination of its trade balances, which reveals that the pattern by which China has built very large trade surpluses with the US and Europe parallel to large trade deficits with East and Southeast Asia only emerging since the East Asian crisis.[13]

A growing body of literature on transnational corporations (TNCs) in Asia confirms this observation, providing strong evidence of China's subordinate third- or even fourth-tier position within these IPNs.[14] For instance, Athukorala and Yamashita (2009, pp. 54–5) argue that the growing trade deficit between China and the US has been related to the reorganisation of these IPNs – through the lead of US firms – consolidating the use of China as the main point of final assembly of high-end parts and components sourced from other higher-tier bases in East and Southeast Asia. Yao (2009) similarly argues – in a strong critique of Rodrik (2006b) – that it is deceptive to conclude that China has been technologically upgrading its exports to the extent suggested by trade data. Rather, China's move into higher technology exports has been 'closely associated with its processing trade regime and foreign outsourcing to China' (Yao 2009, p. 63). These arguments confer with the previous observation from He and Cao (2007) that finance from abroad has been quickly rising in prominence in the late 1990s and 2000s as a source of funding for non-financial corporations, increasingly complementing government funding and bank loans.

Arguments for yuan revaluation as part of the solution for global imbalances avoid this emerging role of China as mass processor in the final assembly of goods destined for US and European consumption through networks heavily and increasingly dominated by Northern TNC production and distribution networks. They also avoid the parallel processes of financialisation in the US and Europe that fuelled not only consumption in these final trade destinations but also Northern consolidation of control over these production networks in the 2000s. This essential missing link leads to a completely different analysis regarding the significance of China's imbalances and, more importantly, the ownership and control of the wealth that they represent. For instance, Zheng and Yi (2007, p. 19) note that China's 'foreign exchange reserves do not imply wealth that is disposable at any time, but rather a sizeable indirect debt', in the sense that a large proportion of China's foreign exchange holdings represent the investments and non-repatriated profits of foreigners. Similarly, Kregel (2008, p. 28) points out more generally that a deterioration of the recorded US trade balance might actually reflect the increased profitability observed in the past ten years of US companies operating in the global market. Athukorala and Yamashita (2009, p. 40) also conclude that observations drawn from out-of-date reporting systems designed at a time when countries were trading only in final goods are misleading. It is vital to see the current debates in this light.

3. CONCLUSION

This chapter focused on the ideological expediency of recent crisis narratives with regard to the role of China in the global financial crisis of 2007–09, which explain China's excess savings as a key driver of financial crisis in the US. An alternative interpretation of global imbalances was proposed from a Keynesian perspective, emphasising that aggregate monetary savings adjust to aggregate demand, not vice versa. Hence, financialisation in the US can be seen to drive global imbalances. China's external surpluses and reserves are outcomes of these processes rather than causes, particularly through the mediation of the systemic rerouting of East Asian-centred international production networks through China that followed the East Asian crisis in 1997–98. Arguments for revaluation of the Chinese yuan mostly avoid the implications of this emerging role of China as subordinate mass processor in the final assembly of goods destined for US and European consumption through networks heavily and increasingly dominated by Northern TNC production and distribution networks. The presumption that China has been in a position of strength during the recent crisis is one that treats China as if it were one of the central powers behind the expansion and regulation of the global monetary and trading system. A false evaluation of such strength could have dramatic implications for China, particularly if the proposed strategies of currency and financial liberalisation would result in accentuating vulnerability to volatile capital flows in the near-future reverberations of the recent crisis. This concern is all the more important given the huge surges of international liquidity – largely generated by Northern financial systems – that led to the build of crisis and that have also followed from the outcome of the crisis response, and which could quickly erode China's own foreign exchange reserves in the medium term.

The danger with the dominant narrative – which cuts across both political Left and Right – is that it facilitates an ideological reframing that legitimises strategies from the centre that are ultimately bent on discipline and subordination. Whether devised or emanating from impulsive protective responses to crisis, these strategies are oriented towards shifting the burden of adjustment away from Northern financial sectors and towards the most obvious Southern scapegoats within the international economic order. The advocated strategies are unlikely to solve the issues that they purport to address, but in the havoc potentially created they could enact a reconsolidation of US economic hegemony, albeit with dubious implications for publics in both China and the US. For, if we see US–China trade in terms of bilateral arms-length transactions of finished goods as per conventional conceptions of trade in economic theory, it is true that China cannot continue to rely on over-indebted US consumers to continue to consume its surpluses. But if we see the organisation of this trade not in terms of countries but in terms of corporations and their networks controlling wealth, then yes, the imbalances can and probably will continue because they are not expressions of market outcomes but of structures of power. The global imbalances narratives must therefore be seen as the emerging ideological discourses of such power, whether or not their proponents are aware of this implication.

NOTES

1. I am indebted to Geoff Tily for suggesting this term 'G20 consensus'.
2. Wolf is not explicit about this claim to a Keynesian legacy.
3. Geoff Tily made this point during the question period that followed a talk by Prabhat Pranaik at LSE in July 2009. See Tily (2010, p. 12).
4. This share has presumably fallen further since 2001 given rising shares of government consumption in total consumption and gross capital formation in total GDP up to 2008 (see CSY 2009: Table 2-17 and 2-18).
5. Also see the discussion of bond issuance in Sun (2009).
6. See some historical international comparisons in He and Cao (2007, p.9).
7. For a review and discussion of the currency debate, see Fischer (2010a).
8. The balances are calculated from balance of payments data from various China Statistical Yearbooks. See Fischer (2010b) for further details.
9. This point was made in 2005 by Lau and Stiglitz (2005).
10. This point is mentioned by Li et al. (2007).
11. Data are compiled and calculated from CSY (2009: Table 17-8) and equivalent tables in earlier statistical yearbooks. See Fischer (2010b).
12. See some preliminary work in Fischer (2010b).
13. See Fischer (2010b) for analysis of these data, as well as Athukorala and Yamashita (2009). Also see Fischer (2009).
14. For example, see the excellent contributions by Athukorala (2007), Li et al (2007), Athukorala and Yamashita (2009) and Yao (2009).

7. Short- and Long-run Macroeconomic Effects of Keynesian Trade Policies in the Presence of Debt Servicing

Syed Mansoob Murshed

It would be a truism to state that the current global economic contraction is deemed to be the most significant global economic crisis since the great depression of the 1930s. The present predicament originated in a financial crisis that had repercussions for the real economy, and was rapidly transmitted from the United States to the rest of the world. The national income compressions that followed were, however, asymmetric, with many dynamic Asian economies only experiencing a decline in their (positive) growth rates, while other countries (developed and developing nations) witnessed a diminution of their national income. All of this occurred against the backdrop of what has come to be known as 'global imbalances' (see Chapters 6 by Andrew Fischer and 18 by Rob Vos). This refers to the differences between deficit nations like the United States (which also simultaneously runs a huge government budget deficit), the UK and many other European nations, and the surplus countries exemplified by China (which has become the world's largest exporter of goods and the second largest economy in absolute terms), Japan, Germany and many other Asian economies. Furthermore, the vast trade surpluses of countries like China are not, in the main, absorbed domestically, but instead held in the form of safe short-term dollar-denominated assets such as US treasury bills. It has been argued that this behaviour is predicated on a precautionary principle leading China into hoarding a war chest of financial reserves (in dollars) to be deployed in the event of a speculative attack on its currency. Haunted by the spirit of financial crises past in the East Asian region, China is also reluctant to fully liberalize capital account transactions in its balance of payments.

The recent global recession has also seen a dramatic contraction in world trade, unparalleled since the inter-war period associated with the great depression. Although trade is predicted to recover, this sort of negative shock in an otherwise globalizing economy for the last half a century, can engender a phenomenon known as trade uncertainty; see van Bergeijk (2009c, 2010) and references therein. Uncertainty about the smooth functioning of the channels of future international trade can have an independent, and additional, adverse effect on the real economy. Added to that is the loss of confidence that characterizes deep depressions, as opposed to more temporary recessions. Akerlof and Shiller (2009) refer to this as the confidence multiplier, something that is unusually buoyant in the boom years prior to the recession, and equally stubbornly gloomy in refusing to revive during the course of a depression. When the confidence is low, the expansionary impact of the usual fiscal and monetary stimuli is much more muted, as in the case of Japan since the early 1990s. Akerlof and Shiller (2009) also point out that when economic confidence is at its nadir, individualized stories about corruption and other nefarious activities contributing the downturn abound in the popular mind. Apart from the usual suspects (bankers and financiers), blame has also been laid at the feet of nations such as China for 'exporting too much', and a revival of confidence might necessitate the politically attractive option of some bilateral trade policy restricting goods from China into the USA (or Europe for that matter); see Grossman and Helpman (1994) on how lobby groups induce specific forms of protectionism via political campaign contributions. There are frequent accusations levied against China for gaining 'unfair' competitive advantage by artificially engineering a real exchange rate devaluation. The Chinese are also charged with being a nation of excessive savers, compared to the negative saving propensities of American households, where arguably a different brand of consumer capitalism abounds (Akerlof and Shiller, 2009 and Chapter 6 by Andrew Fischer). Trade policy targeted specifically towards China could also serve to reduce trade uncertainty as described and analyzed in van Bergeijk (2009c, 2010). The multilateral framework governing international trade could then be complemented and supplemented by bilateral negotiations; this too can become a part of economic diplomacy (van Bergeijk, 2009d, 2010).

Recently there has been a revival of 'Keynesian' demand management policies that aim to increase output and employment via boosting aggregate demand. Keynes (1936) himself came around to the view that protectionism could also provide a macroeconomic boost during a deep recession. Exports are a component of aggregate demand and imports represent a leakage from domestic demand, hence policies that switch expenditure from foreign to domestic sources would raise domestic aggregate demand. One instrument that achieves this goal could be bilateral trade policies that restrict imports from a major source. It is not inconceivable that a powerful nation such as the United States (arguably the post-war engine of global economic growth) might convince a major foreign supplier to its market like China to restrict its sales within the USA out of fear of greater future disruption, were the American economy to falter even further. A potential future threat of greater trade disruption may induce China to reduce its current sales in the USA in order to preserve orderly economic relations in the foreseeable future, thereby granting a Keynesian boost to the US economy.

Trade policy could also become a substitute for the traditional instruments of stabilization (fiscal/monetary) policy, given the constraints placed on the other policy instruments because of growing central bank independence, and the burgeoning debt following the 2008 financial crisis in 'deficit' nations like the USA or the UK, for example. It could also be a means of redistributing income towards factors of production in certain industries. It has been argued that trade policy has small direct output effects when compared with fiscal/monetary policy. But such an assertion neglects the real exchange consequences of trade policy in its various forms. Real exchange rate changes result from the balance of payments effects of trade policy. These have consequences not only for international competitiveness, but also for debt servicing flows. Changes in debt servicing flows have, in turn, income and output repercussions. In order to explore these debt servicing implications for the macroeconomy, it is necessary to distinguish between the short and long run, as pioneered by Rodriguez (1979) who analyzed fiscal and monetary policy in the presence of debt servicing within a single small open economy setting.

The purpose of this chapter is to analyze the effect of Keynesian-minded trade policy in the form of a voluntary export restraint (VER) on the macroeconomies of both the home (imposing) country and the foreign (targeted) country. The analytical treatment of a VER differs from that applicable to a traditional tariff or quota, as it is the exporter and not the importer who obtains the revenues from the trade restriction. Trade policy in the form of a VER is inherently bilateral in nature and it is the favoured form of trade policy engaged in by countries or blocs such as the United States (or even the European Union) when the target of the trade policy is a particular country, China say. This is the example in mind in this chapter. A VER is also relatively more WTO compatible.

The literature on the macroeconomic analyses of VERs is relatively scant. Examples of the latter include Murshed (1992) who compares VERs with tariffs in the North–South context, and Murshed and Sen (1999) who analyze the capital account effects of VERs. The innovation in this chapter is the analysis of trade policy in the form of VERs when debt servicing enters the current account of the balance of payments. Current account deficits lead to the accumulation of the stock of debt which has to be repaid in the future in the form of debt servicing flows. This leads to a difference between the short-

and long-run effects of trade policy in the form of VERs. In the short run the effects of VER type trade policy impact on the current account. These current account changes eventually cause alterations in debt stocks, requiring debt servicing. In the long-run equilibrium, by definition, no changes in stocks are possible, and appropriate adjustments to bring this about must take place in the economy. Thus, in the long run, the debt servicing implications of the VER will have fully worked their way through the economies in question. This can lead to the reversal of the short-run effects of the VER in the long run. The rest of the chapter is organised as follows: Section 1 contains a sketch of the two-country macroeconomic model; Sections 2 and 3 contain the short and long-run effects respectively of trade policy. Section 4 briefly concludes.

1. THE MODEL

I will employ a two-country variant of the Rodriguez (1979) model. I ignore the monetary side of the economy as I wish to focus on the (debt servicing inclusive) current account effects of the VER. Although my model does not explicitly incorporate imperfect competition in product markets, the presence of excess capacity in goods markets brings about the same flavour in our results as imperfect (monopolistic) competition.

The equilibrium relation for the home (VER imposing) country's goods market is given by:

$$Y = E\{Y + rD; e(1+v)\} + X\left(Y^{*} - \frac{rD}{e} + vX^{*}; e\right) - eX^{*}\{Y + rD; e(1+v)\}(1+v) \qquad (1)$$

where Y stands for national income; E for expenditure; X for exports; X^{*} for imports; e for the exchange rate – a rise in e is a depreciation (appreciation) of the home (foreign) currency; the stock of debt, D, is in one unit of home currency (say dollars) and can be either positive or negative; rD represents debt servicing, r is the relevant interest rate; v is the *ad-valorem* tariff equivalent of the VER quota, following Brecher and Bhagwati (1987). Expenditure depends on debt servicing augmented disposable income, $E_1 > 0$. $E_2 > 0$; this is the Laursen–Metzler (1950) effect, see Murshed (1997, pp. 25–7) for a detailed derivation. My argument for its inclusion is that it played an important role in Mundell's (1961) seminal work on the macroeconomic effects of tariffs. $E_2 = X^{*}(1 - \varepsilon)$, $\varepsilon < 1$ is the elasticity of real expenditure with respect to real income. The intuition behind it is that an exchange rate depreciation lowers real income (defined in terms of home and imported goods prices), but real expenditure declines less than proportionately, hence nominal expenditure increases. $X_1 > 0$, $X_2 > 0$, $X_1^{*} > 0$, $X_2^{*} < 0$. Note that I have normalised domestic and foreign prices at $P = P^* = 1$. The *initial* VER rate, $v = 0$, but $dv \neq 0$. An asterisk (*) denotes foreign country variables. Goods market equilibrium in the foreign economy is given by:

$$Y^* = E^*\left(Y^* - \frac{rD}{e} + vX^*; \frac{1}{e}\right) + \{X^*Y + rD; e(1+v)\}$$
$$-\frac{X}{e}\left(Y^* - \frac{rD}{e} + vX^*; e\right) \tag{2}$$

In equation (2) the exchange rate is employed in the opposite direction of the home country. The signs of the various partial derivatives in (2) are symmetrical to those in (1). It should be borne in mind that the VER rent accrues to the exporting country, unlike a tariff or quota when rents are retained by the importer. Thus, the foreign economy potentially benefits from a positive income effect, just as the home economy should gain from a price or substitution effect shifting expenditure towards its own goods.

The current account of the balance of payments is defined for the home economy, exactly the converse applies to the foreign economy. I include debt servicing flows (rD) in addition to the difference between exports and imports (trade account) in the current account, following Rodriguez (1979). D stands for the stock of debt denominated in home currency units, rD denotes debt servicing flows where r is the interest rate on debt. The current account, therefore, has two components, trade balance and debt servicing flows so that $D = X(.) - eX^*(.)(1 + v) + rD$. This relation states that current account surpluses will contribute to the home country's becoming a creditor (or a reduction in its indebted status) as D is accumulated, similarly current account deficits will contribute to its becoming a debtor (or a diminution of its creditor ranking). In the short run the inherited debt stocks are non-zero, $D \neq 0$. Current account imbalances arising from the impact of the VER will, however, lead to changes in the stock of debt which have to be eliminated in the long-run equilibrium. I postulate that the home (foreign) country deficits (surpluses) causes the exchange rate to depreciate (appreciate), i.e. e rises:

$$e = eX^*(.)(1 + v) - X(.) - rD \tag{3}$$

In order to proceed we totally differentiate (1) – (3), and arrange them in matrix form:

$$\begin{bmatrix} a_{11} & a_{12} & a_{13}^* \\ a_{21} & a_{22} & a_{23} \\ a_{31} & a_{32} & a_{33} \end{bmatrix} \begin{bmatrix} dY \\ dY^* \\ de \end{bmatrix} = \begin{bmatrix} b_{11} \\ b_{21} \\ b_{31} \end{bmatrix} \begin{bmatrix} dR \\ dH \\ dE \end{bmatrix} \tag{4}$$

$$a_{11} = E_1 - 1 - eX_1^*$$

$$a_{12} = X_1$$

$$a_{13} = X_2 - eX_2^* + \frac{X_1 rD}{e^2} - \varepsilon X^*$$

$$a_{12} = X_1^*$$

$$a_{22} = E_1^* - 1 - \frac{X_1}{e}$$

$$a_{23} = X_2^* - \frac{X_2}{e} - \frac{X_1 rD}{e^3} + \frac{E_1^* rD + \varepsilon X}{e^2}$$

$$a_{31} = eX_1^*$$

$$a_{32} = -X_1$$

$$a_{33} = X^* + eX_2^* - X_2 - \frac{rDX_1}{e^2}$$

$$b_{11} = e\varepsilon X^* - X_1 X^* + e^2 X_2^*$$

$$b_{12} = \frac{X_1 X^*}{e} - E_1^* X^* - eX_2^*$$

$$b_{13} = X_1 X^* - e^2 X_2^* - eX^*$$

Next I investigate the stability of the model. The trace is negative if $a_{33} < 0$; the Marshall–Lerner conditions hold, i.e. if an exchange rate depreciation (rise in e) improves the domestic trade balance and vice versa. The determinant of the Jacobian J can be derived as:

$$J_{short\ run} = (E_1 - 1)\frac{rDX_1}{e^2} + (E_1 - 1)(E_1^* - 1)\left(X^* + eX_2^* - X_2 + \frac{X_1 X \epsilon}{e^2}\right) - (1 - E_1^*)eX_1^* X^* \varepsilon \quad (5)$$

A requirement of stability is that (5) is negative. This is so only if $a_{33} < 0$; if the Marshall–Lerner conditions hold. If $D > 0$, this is also sufficient; if $D < 0$, then $X > rD$, the indebted (home) country's export revenues must exceed debt servicing.

2. SHORT-RUN MULTIPLIERS

I now analyze the short-run or *impact* multipliers of the system. As far as these multipliers are concerned I next postulate, as in Rodriguez (1979), that

$dD = 0$, but $D \neq 0$. This means that on impact the historically given debt stocks cannot change, but the inherited stock of debt may be positive or negative. If $D > 0$ the home country is the creditor nation, but if $D < 0$ it is the foreign economy which is the creditor country. Turning to the multipliers I find that:

$$\frac{\mathrm{d}Y}{\mathrm{d}v} = \frac{(1-\varepsilon)\left[X^{*2}X_1 - eX_2X^*(1-E_1^*) - \frac{rDX_1X^*}{e}\right] + \frac{\epsilon X^* X}{e}(\varepsilon - X_1)}{J_{short\ run}} \tag{6}$$

Restrictive trade policy v only increases national income Y if the short-run multiplier is positive ($\mathrm{d}Y/\mathrm{d}v > 0$) which is only true if (i) $X_2 > X_1$ and (ii) $X_1 > \varepsilon$ in absolute value. So the VER on impact will lead to an improvement in the foreign country's current account as long as it receives more revenues for exporting a smaller quantity (a positive VER rent). This seems plausible, and is in conformity with the stylized facts when the VER is effected by an economy like China, whose export quality appears to be increasing. What it really implies is that the subjects of trade restrictions are high quality goods, which are inelastically demanded. The improvement in the foreign economy's current account will lead to its currency appreciating, under flexible exchange rates (see equation (8) below). This means that the home country's currency (in the stylized case: the US dollar) depreciates. This should eventually raise aggregate demand in the home country via improvements in net exports. For this to successfully occur, and raise output, X_2, the price elasticity of its exports in the foreign country, must be high. Also the home economy benefits from a positive Laursen–Metzler effect as its currency depreciates. This is greater the smaller is ε, the elasticity of absorption (expenditure) with respect to real income.

$$\frac{\mathrm{d}Y^*}{\mathrm{d}V} = (E_1 - 1)\Psi + X^*X_1^*(\varepsilon - 1)(E_1^*rD + \varepsilon X - eE_1^*X^*) \tag{7}$$

Where Ψ is $\left[-E_1^*X^*eX_2^* + E_1^*X_2^*rD - \frac{X_1X^*}{e^2}(rD + \varepsilon X) + X_2^*\varepsilon X + \frac{X}{e}(E_1^*rD + \varepsilon X) + X^{*2}\left(\frac{X}{e} - E_1^*\right) - X_2X^*(1 - E_1^*)\right]$. Now $\mathrm{d}Y^*/\mathrm{d}v$ is ambiguous in sign so that the impact of the VER on foreign income is unclear *a priori*. Even though the foreign economy benefits from the VER rent, currency appreciation potentially crowds out these gains via the deterioration in the trade balance. Also if it is a creditor economy, so that $rD < 0$, it will suffer from a negative wealth effect. This is because D is denominated in dollars, and its value in local currency declines as the dollar depreciates (each dollar fetches less in yuan units).

$$\frac{\mathrm{d}e}{\mathrm{d}v} = \frac{(E_1 - 1)[eX^*(1+\Omega)(1-E_1^*)][e^2X_1^*X^*(1-\varepsilon)]}{J_{short\ run}} > 0 \tag{8}$$

This means that the home (foreign) country's exchange rate depreciates (appreciates) as long as $\Omega = eX^*2/X^*$, the price elasticity of demand of the restricted import is inelastically demanded (less than 1 in absolute value). This is also a condition for a positive VER rent for China after the trade restriction is imposed by the US.

3. LONG-RUN MULTIPLIERS

The analysis in Section 2 was concerned with impact (short-run) multipliers. In the long-run steady-state equilibrium there must be no change in stocks, which in turn means that the current account *in totality* must balance. The debt servicing implications of the VER fully work through the two economies in the long run. A trade account surplus must be matched by a negative debt servicing inflow and vice versa. This means that in the steady state (long-run), $\mathrm{d}D = 0$ but $\mathrm{d}(rD) \neq 0$. Thus, although changes in debt stocks are zero, debt servicing inflows could be non-zero (see Rodriguez, 1979). The mechanism of change in the current account is debt servicing, $\mathrm{d}(rD)$ replaces $\mathrm{d}e$. Equation (3) is replaced by:

$$X(.) - eX^*(.)(1+v) + rD = 0 \tag{9}$$

The various a_{ij} in (4) alter as follows (the b_{ij} are unaltered):

$$a_{13} = E_1 - \frac{X_1}{e} - eX_1^*$$
$$a_{23} = -\frac{E_1^*}{e} + X_1^* + \frac{X}{e^2}$$
$$a_{33} = eX_1^* + \frac{X_1}{e} - 1$$

The model is stable and the determinant of the Jacobian now becomes:

$$J_{long\ run} = (E_1 - 1)(1 - E_1^*) - 2X_1^*X_1 < 0 \tag{5`}$$

Turning to the long-run effects of the VER:

$$\frac{\mathrm{d}Y}{\mathrm{d}v} = \frac{(1-E_1^*)[e\varepsilon X^*(1-eX_1^*) + e\Omega X^*(1-E_1) - eX^*(E_1 - eX_1^*)]}{J_{long\ run}} \tag{10}$$

$$\frac{\mathrm{d}Y*}{\mathrm{d}v} = \frac{(1 - E_1^*)[eX_2^*(E_1 - 1) - eX^*X_1^*(1 - \varepsilon)]}{J_{long\ run}} \tag{11}$$

dY/dv in the long run is negative only if $|\varepsilon(1 - eX_1^*| > |\Omega\,(1 - E_1)|$ in absolute value; dY^*/dv > 0 if $|eX_1^*| > |\Omega|$; and $|1 - \varepsilon| > |1 - E_1|$, both in absolute value.

$$\frac{\mathrm{d}(rD)}{\mathrm{d}v} = \frac{\mathrm{d}e}{\mathrm{d}v} > 0 \tag{12}$$

This is positive and can be verified by examining equation (8) above. It means that the home (foreign) economy experiences positive (negative) debt servicing flows in the long-run equilibrium.

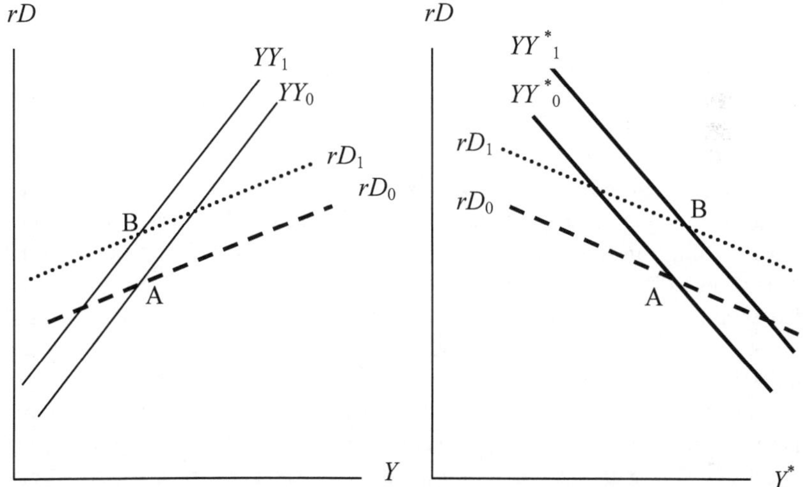

Figure 7.1 VER in the long run for imposing home economy (left-hand panel) and foreign target economy (right-hand panel)

The intuition behind the above results can be best understood by tracing the movements from the impact multipliers in the short-run to the steady-state equilibrium. The effect of the VER for the home country in the short run causes its exchange rate to depreciate, improving its trade balance. This will improve its credit standing, as either its debt is reduced or its creditor position is enhanced. For the foreign economy exchange rate appreciation worsens the trade balance in the short run. This leads to an accumulation of debt or its previous creditor status is diminished. In the long run this increased debtor (reduced creditor) status eventually requires debt servicing which needs to be financed via improved export performance. This increase in net exports is precisely what causes the foreign country's output to rise in the long-run equilibrium. We have noted that in the long-run equilibrium the current account in total must balance, there can be no changes in debt stocks. For the home economy the long-run effect of the VER leads to a reduction in its trade balance, exactly matched in value by positive debt servicing inflows. The converse results apply to the foreign country.

These results are depicted in Figure 7.1 for the home and foreign economy respectively, and are obtained from the a_{ij} coefficients above. The YY (Y^*Y^*) schedule depicts goods market equilibrium. A rise in output increases net imports which has to be matched by positive debt servicing making the schedule positive (negative) for the home (foreign) country. A similar line of reasoning is applicable to the external balance schedules, rD. The initial point before the VER is indicated at A, and the post VER long-run outcome is shown at point B.

4. CONCLUSIONS

In summary, therefore, the short (impact) and long-run effects of trade policy in the form of VERs could be diametrically opposite, given the presence of debt servicing. Indeed it can be argued that there is a trade-off between the short-run and long-run effects. In the short run the VER causes exchange rate depreciation in the home economy. This improves its current account and raises output in the home country. In the foreign economy exchange rate appreciation crowds out the benefits of the VER rent. The foreign country's current account surplus worsens as its currency gets stronger, lowering output there. In the long run, however, the signs of the impact multipliers are reversed. The increase in debt (or the reduction in its creditor status) accumulated by the foreign country following the impact effect of the VER has to be paid off through increased net exports in the future, which is beneficial to output. The converse occurs in the home economy, where the short-run benefits of the improved trade balance are lost in the long run, and its equilibrium output declines. Both the short- and long-run multipliers for the VER, as far as the home or VER initiating country is concerned, are similar to the results in Rodriguez (1979) for monetary policy in a single country. The moral of the story is that Keynesian-minded trade policies aiming to boost domestic output may not work in the long term when debt has to be repaid, and that the debtor status of countries like the United States or the creditor status of China cannot be deemed to last indefinitely.

8. FDI Volatility and Development

Irene van Staveren*

It is generally assumed that the volatility of international capital flows predominantly occurs through portfolio investments, and much less through Foreign Direct Investments (FDI). The high volatility in portfolio investments, especially in equity, is particularly stark during financial crises due to its high liquidity as compared to FDI. But this does not necessarily imply that outside crises, and over the long run, FDI is a stable capital flow. With the enormous growth in financial globalization as well as financialization of the global economy, in which companies worldwide are increasingly driven by strategies to maximize short-term shareholder value across the globe, it is possible that FDI may have become more volatile over time. If this were the case, this would add to the already high uncertainty of the sharp volatility of portfolio investments. Moreover, policies to stabilize FDI are less straightforward than those for stabilizing portfolio flows, because FDI flows depend more strongly on the non-financial performance criteria of an economy, including political stability, social climate and labour market conditions. These policies are more complex to design and to enforce, as they will partly go against existing international agreements such as those of the WTO, as Chang (2004) has shown.[1] Hence, if FDI flows were to become more volatile over time, this is likely to have a negative impact on macroeconomic stability and, through policy responses of labour market flexibilization, also negative effects on the quality of employment.

The purpose of this chapter is to describe the development in FDI volatility in developing countries over the long run, that is, the period 1970–2008. In addition, the chapter will try to indicate whether, and to what extent, FDI volatility may have an impact on real economy variables. The focus will be on GDP growth, tax revenue and labour market variables. The next section provides an overview of FDI volatility with descriptive data analysis. The following two sections present and discuss some bi-variate regression results with FDI volatility as the independent variable. The chapter ends with a conclusion.

1. FDI VOLATILITY IN THE LITERATURE

The empirical literature on FDI volatility is quite limited, as compared to the body of research on FDI volumes. A common result in the literature on FDI volumes (stocks and flows) is a positive effect on GDP growth for developed and developing countries, and so FDI moves pro-cyclically (World Bank, 1999). Although there are exceptions, as Rajan (2008) demonstrates for developing countries over the long run, and is argued in a study with long-run panel data and time series by Sarkar (2007). Sarkar shows that only in a very small group of relatively rich open economies is the relationship between FDI and growth positive, whereas for the majority of developing countries, no relationship could be established. There are only a few studies that look at other relationships than those between FDI volumes and GDP growth: Davies and Voy (2009) find a negative impact of FDI inflow on child labour and Busse and Nunnenkamp (2009) uncover for middle income developing countries a negative relationship between FDI inflow and gender disparity in education. Other studies point at low quality of FDI, for example in terms of environmental impact, skill and technology transfer, and employment (see, for example, on Latin America: Gallagher and Chudnovsky, 2009).

When turning to the scarce empirical literature on FDI volatility, we find that the empirical results of regression analyses of FDI volatility on GDP growth tend to show a negative impact (Choong and Liew, 2009; Lensink and Morrissey, 2001). The literature is rather silent on the mechanisms that would help to explain this negative impact. Because volatility tends to increase uncertainty, the explanations generally refer to Keynesian mechanisms. There are three likely mechanisms. First, the business sector may hold up domestic investment due to uncertainty about foreign technology or matching capital coming in. Second, workers are likely to experience more job insecurity due to 'a growing demand for more flexible hiring-and-firing practices as a buffer against large and unexpected swings in the overall level of economic activity' (United Nations 2008b, p. 34) which links to FDI because in developing countries FDI inflows often go to labour-intensive industries. Moreover, as the ILO has shown, the bargaining power of labour vis-à-vis foreign capital has declined with globalization (ILO, 2008a). Third, the government may not have sufficient automatic stabilizers in place through taxes, subsidies and the substitution of private sector investment by public investment through borrowing on domestic capital markets. The first and third mechanism both imply crowding out of domestic investment with higher volatility of FDI inflows, a hypothesis that was discussed, but not adequately tested, by Agosin (2008).

Another type of explanation is institutional, arguing that there is a relationship between FDI inflow and institutional strength of countries. This explanation can be divided up into the strength of national institutions and the participation in international institutions. One explanation is that countries with weak economic, social and political institutions attract relatively less portfolio investment and more direct investment, so that FDI tends to flow relatively more to less stable economies (Hausman and Fernández-Arias, 2000). Another explanation, referring to international institutions, is that countries which participate in global economic institutions of trade and investment, in particular WTO, tend to experience less FDI volatility (Büthe and Milner, 2008). Hence, stronger domestic institutions or participation in international institutions would likely decrease FDI volatility because of the stability that these institutions provide for investment. At the micro level, FDI instability may actually mirror a quick outflow of equity capital through short-term financial transactions between subsidiaries of a multinational firm, as Loungani and Razin (2001) have suggested.[2] This means that financialization at a global scale through multinational corporations' financial management could make FDI flows more similar to portfolio movements: quicker FDI flows and hence higher levels of volatility.

The FDI data used in this chapter is from UNCTAD's online world investment database. It uses FDI inflows as a ratio over GDP. The database's latest available data at the time of writing was for 2008, but a study by UNCTAD itself of the preliminary data over 2009 indicates that global FDI flows have gone down by 40% (UNCTAD, 2010c). This is likely to increase the volatility measure over the last period, if 2009 data were included.

Two methods are commonly used to measure FDI volatility. The first method is a statistical measure, the standard deviation of FDI inflows over a certain period of time. Since the measure of FDI is taken as a ratio over GDP, there will not be a bias in the measure stemming from the huge differences in actual amounts of FDI inflows between countries due to differences in the size of their economies. But since FDI (and GDP) increases over time, the statistical measure can be further refined by normalizing it, through dividing the standard deviation by the mean per period. For the disaggregation of FDI into greenfield investment and mergers and acquisitions, the volatility measure is weighted by the mean, since the disaggregated FDI data are expressed in million US dollars. The second measure is a theoretical measure, since it measures deviations from the trend of FDI inflows per country. It is calculated as the standard deviation of the residual through auto-regressions and generates an indicator of investors' reactions to the market trend. In this chapter I will use the statistical measure for two reasons. First, as others have pointed out as well, the difference with the auto-regression measure tends to be very small. Second, it is a purely macroeconomic descriptive measure, rather than reflecting a theoretical financial market perspective assuming a trend line of foreign investors' actual annual increases in investment. A final note on measurement is that it should be kept in mind that FDI is not entirely independent from GDP. FDI may increase investment and hence production (and often also exports), stimulating GDP. But FDI may also lead to increased imports, both of the capital goods invested and of raw materials or intermediate products, which has a downward affect on GDP.

2. DESCRIPTIVE DATA ANALYSIS

The data set includes 121 developing countries, from which Oceania and a few other small island economies were excluded as they appeared to be outliers and experience more volatility over the whole study period due to their deliberately sought status as investment paradises. The descriptive data analysis covers the period 1970–2008, which has been divided up in five-year periods (except for the last period due to unavailable data for the year 2009).

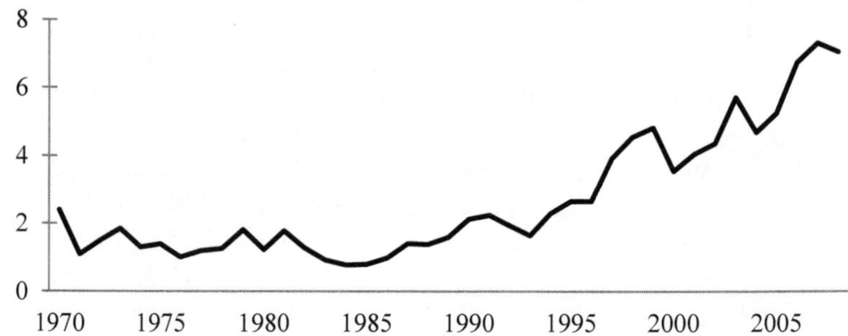

Figure 8.1 FDI inflow to GDP ratio, developing countries (N = 121), percentage, 1970–2008

Before turning to the volatility of FDI, I will first show the trend in FDI inflows to developing countries in Figure 8.1. The figure clearly shows an increase of FDI inflow, as a percentage of GDP, over the period. The line also suggests an increase in volatility with decreases during periods of (local) crises. Surprisingly, the current global financial crisis seems already reflected in the data for the year 2008, with a modest decline from 7.32 to 7.06%. One would have expected, since the crisis originated in the developed world and is concentrated in the US and European economies, that the impact on FDI in developing countries would not be noticeable, at least not immediately. The figures, however, suggest that there was a quick reaction in US and EU firms' international investment decisions, most likely because of an urgent need for liquidity by the parent companies, which may have led to either a reduction of new FDI or the use of existing subsidiaries to refund parent companies (see also footnote 2).

Figure 8.2 shows a regional breakdown of the FDI inflow to the developing world. The diagram reflects the higher inflow of FDI/GDP in Latin America over almost the whole period, followed by Africa and then Asia. The reason why Africa scores higher than Asia, except for the early 1990s, is probably, as was indicated in the literature review, because African economies tend to be weaker than Asian economies, and hence, they attract relatively less portfolio investments and more FDI.

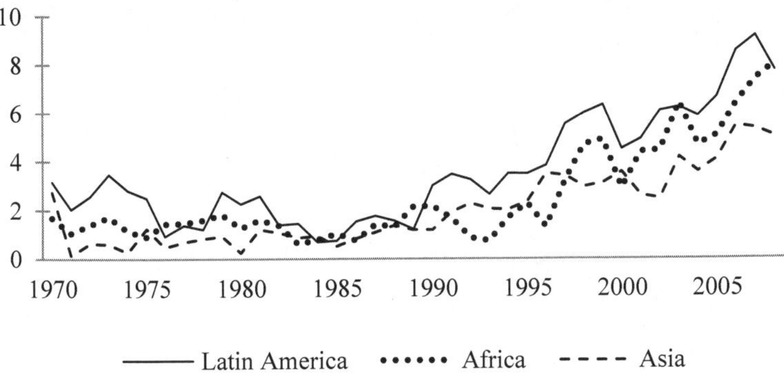

Figure 8.2 FDI inflow to GDP ratio, three regions, percentage, 1970–2008

We now turn to the volatility of FDI inflows. Figure 8.3a shows the development of volatility of FDI inflows in the developing world measured as the standard deviation of FDI as a percentage of GDP over five-year periods, between 1970 and 2008. Figure 8.3b shows the standardized measure of volatility, namely the standard deviation divided by the mean per period, which corrects for the increase in FDI/GDP over time, a trend which was shown in Figure 8.1. Figure 8.3a shows that, although volatility decreased until the early 1980s, it has increased since then with a stabilization in the first decade of the new millennium at higher levels than before, with standard deviations of FDI over GDP of around 2.65 since 1995. The last bar includes, as we have seen from the figures above, the decline of FDI inflows over 2008, which, as mentioned earlier, will further decline significantly in 2009, according to an UNCTAD (2010c) report, probably leading to a further increase of the volatility measure for the last period. The standardized measure shown in Figure 8.3b, however, shows that with increasing volumes of FDI and shares of FDI in GDP, standardized volatility tends to go down, although it still features periods of increased volatility, in the early 1990s and in the most recent period, since 2005. The standardized measure suggests that there is no reason to worry about FDI volatility over time, because increased inflows do not seem to lead to higher volatility.

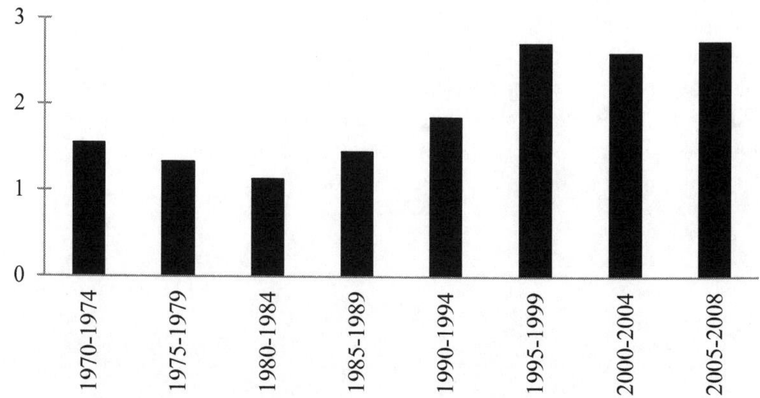

Figure 8.3a Volatility of FDI inflow (standard deviation of FDI to GDP ratio) in developing countries (N = 121), 1970–2008

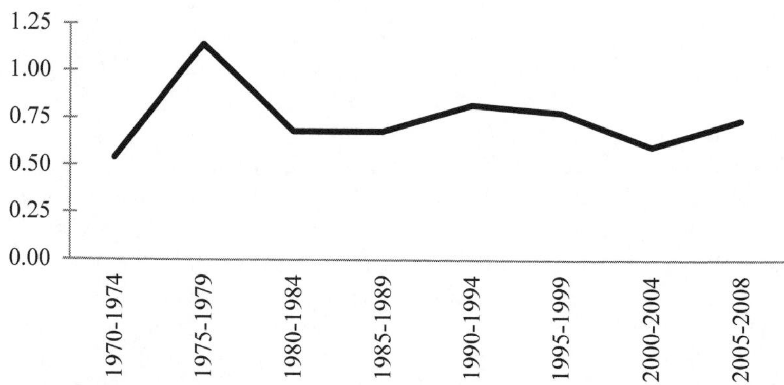

Figure 8.3b Standardized volatility of FDI inflow to GDP ratio, developing countries (N = 121), 1970–2008

But this does not mean that the increased volatility as experienced by countries, the one expressed in Figure 8.3a, has no disturbing impact on their economies. On the contrary, it may well be that the experience of higher uncertainty about the expected level of inflow of foreign investment may have effects on domestic investment, import and exports, production, labour markets and government revenues, and, through these variables, on economic growth. But we first need to get a better understanding of the volatility itself.

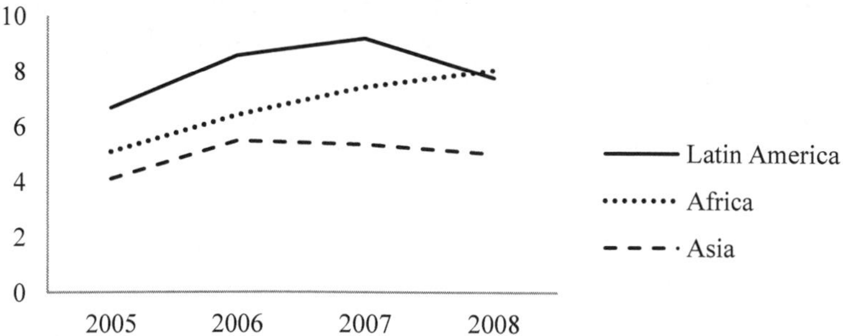

Figure 8.4 FDI inflow to GDP ratio per region, percentage, 2005–2008

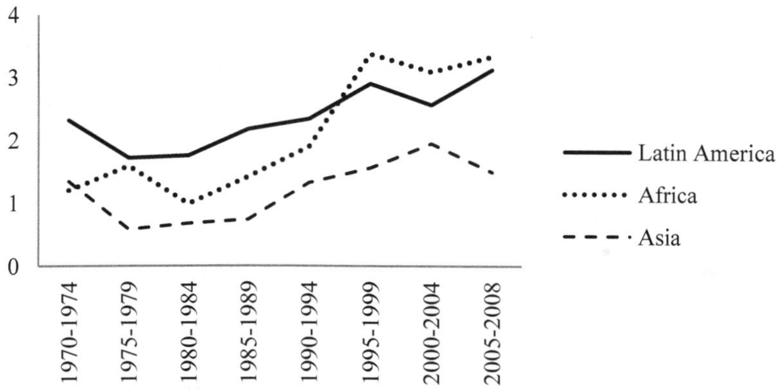

Figure 8.5 Volatility of FDI inflows (standard deviation) per region, 1970–2008

In order to get an idea of the volatility in the last four years leading up to the current global financial crisis which started in the second half of 2007, the next figure gives a breakdown of the FDI inflows (FDI/GDP) for the last period for each region. Figure 8.4 shows no disturbance from the trend for Africa but a steadily increasing trend, suggesting that FDI to Africa is not (yet) affected by the crisis. In Latin America the decline starts in 2008, whereas in Asia the decline already begins in 2007. More detailed analysis per region, in terms of type of FDI inflow, countries of origin, and economic sector may help to explain the regional differences. Figure 8.5 below shows the volatility of FDI inflows per region for the whole period, which is a breakdown of Figure 8.3a.

Figure 8.5 clearly shows that volatility in FDI inflows went up in all three regions since the 1980s, with the steepest increase in Africa. The last period shows an increase for Latin America and Africa, but a decline in volatility for Asia. To what extent the current financial crisis and/or lessons learned in Asia from the 1997 financial crisis may be responsible for this divergence can only be understood with a detailed regional analysis of trends and policies.

As a summary, Table 8.1 provides an overview of the volatility indicators for all developing countries together as well as per region. FDI inflows can be distinguished between greenfield investments and mergers and acquisitions (M&A). Note that the data includes negative numbers for greenfield investments, representing disinvestments, but not for mergers and acquisitions. Figure 8.6 shows the breakdown of FDI in M&A and greenfield investments per year between 1987 and 2005, the period for which disaggregated data was available. The figure shows that on average greenfield makes up a larger share of FDI over the whole period. The average shares are 65% for greenfield and 35% for M&A investment .

Table 8.1 Volatility of FDI inflows (std. Dev. FDI/GDP), 1970–2008

	1970–1974	1975–1979	1980–1984	1985–1989	1990–1994	1995–1999	2000–2004	2005–2008
Lat. America	2.31	1.72	1.76	2.17	2.33	2.90	2.56	3.12
Africa	1.20	1.59	0.99	1.42	1.90	3.37	3.09	3.33
Asia	1.35	0.58	0.68	0.74	1.32	1.56	1.95	1.49
All LDC	1.55	1.33	1.13	1.45	1.85	2.71	2.60	2.73
(standardized)	(0.54)	(1.14)	(0.68)	(0.68)	(0.82)	(0.78)	(0.60)	(0.74)

Figure 8.7 shows the development of the two types of FDI relative to GDP. Greenfield investment clearly makes up a larger part of GDP – on average 2.56% as compared to 0.61% for M&A. There also seems to be a difference in reaction to financial crises. For the Asian financial crisis of 1997, the figure shows only a small decline of M&A but a steep, though shorter, fall in greenfield investment. Also, the dotcom crisis of 2000 seems to have affected greenfield investment more than M&A.

In the more recent years, however, Figure 8.7 shows more volatility in M&A compared to greenfield investment. This seems to suggest that in times of financial crises, greenfield investments are more vulnerable than M&A,

perhaps because it is easier to disinvest in 100% owned self-initiated production facilities as compared to disinvestments in joint ventures and other participations in local firms. But this is a hypothesis which needs more detailed research beyond what is possible with the data that is being used in this study.

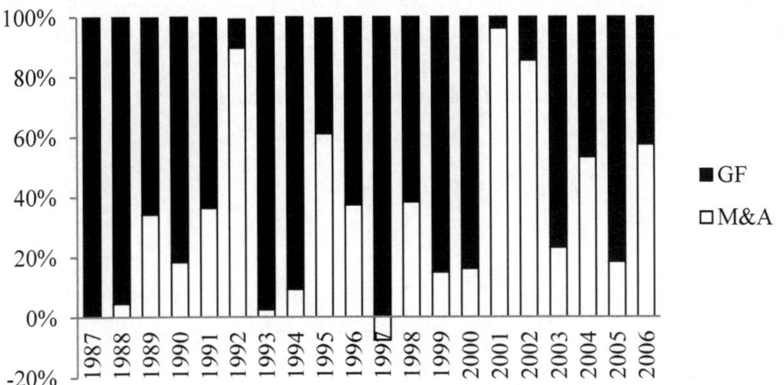

Note: three outliers were excluded: Bahamas, Cuba and South Africa

Figure 8.6 Shares of M&A and greenfield investment in FDI (N = 117), 1987–2005, in per cent

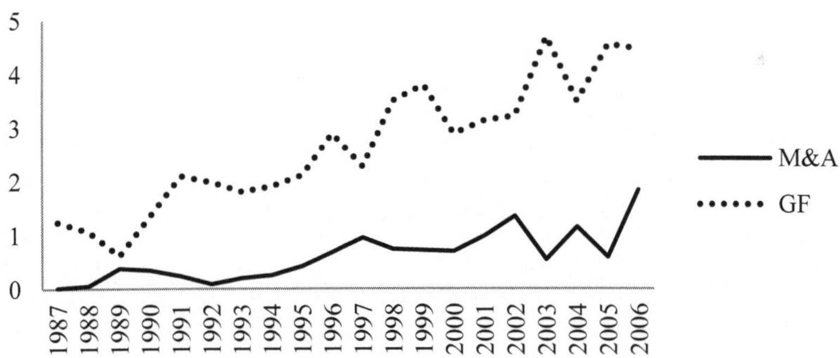

Note: three outliers were excluded: Bahamas, Cuba and South Africa

Figure 8.7 Share of M&A and greenfield investment in GDP (N = 117), percentage, 1987–2006

The database used in this study does allow the analysis of volatility in the two types of FDI, although for less periods than for the aggregate FDI data. Figure 8.8 shows the development of volatility in the two types of FDI for all developing countries, for the period 1987–2006. The figure shows that when we break down FDI, the volatility level of M&A is higher than that of greenfield investment but both have declined over time. This means that with increasing levels of both types of FDI, absolutely as well as relative to GDP as was shown in Figure 8.7, volatility has not increased simultaneously. The decrease, however, does not continue: in the last period it stabilizes for greenfield investment whereas it increases for M&A.

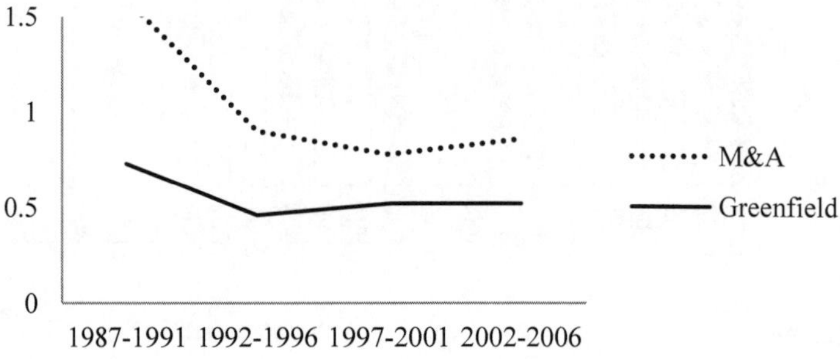

Figure 8.8 Volatility in greenfield and M&A (std./mean) (N = 120), 1987–2006

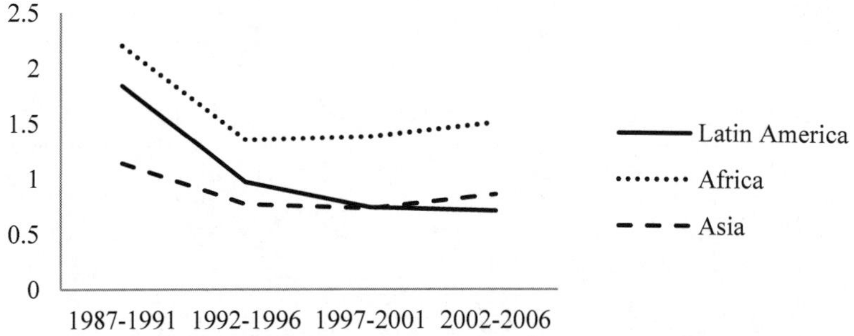

Figure 8.9 Volatility in M&A per region (std./mean)

Figure 8.9, zooming in on mergers and acquisitions, shows that the volatility in M&A is U-shaped for Africa and Asia, whereas it flattens out for Latin America. The figure suggests that volatility declined in the 1990s but rose again after the 1997 Asian financial crisis in Africa and Asia. The increase in Asia may be a side-effect of the capital controls taken by various Asian countries after the crisis, in order to stabilize portfolio investment flows: this may have led to some substitutions of investment from portfolio to mergers and acquisitions. Such substitutions may have also included some of the volatility that is inherent in portfolio investment, for example through accounting transactions between a corporation and the companies in which shares have been acquired (note that the data includes all M&A transactions with at least 10% of shares, hence, the data includes up to 100% acquisitions). Finally, Figure 8.10 shows a similar pattern of volatility for each region for greenfield investment, but now with Latin America decreasing also in the last period. There is an increase in volatility in greenfield investments in all three regions after the Asian financial crisis.

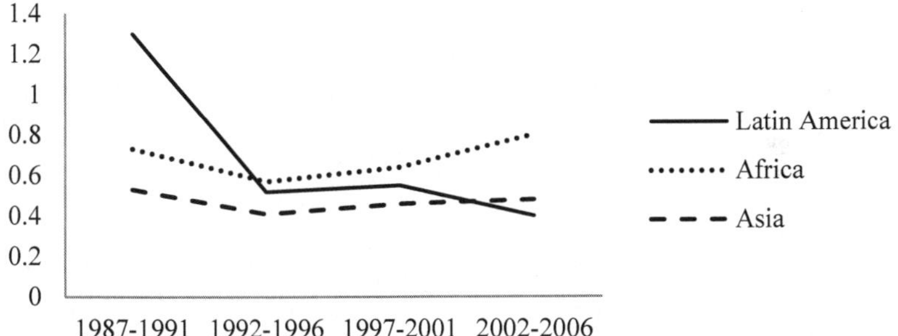

Figure 8.10 Volatility in Greenfield investment per region (std./mean)

The volatility diagrams suggest that over the long run greenfield investment is the more stable form of FDI, whereas in periods of crisis, M&A shows more stability. This would point at a dilemma for developing countries who want to stabilize their foreign capital inflows: there may be a trade-off between long-run stability and short-run stability.

3. BI-VARIATE REGRESSION ANALYSIS

With increasing FDI volatility, paralleling higher inflows of FDI, both absolutely as well as relative to GDP, it may well be that the real economy is directly or indirectly affected by the higher levels of volatility. As was briefly discussed in the introduction, possible effects are likely to run through GDP growth, tax revenues and labour market flexbilization. These possible impacts, however, will also be influenced by other trends (such as globalization with its accompanying weakening of trade unions *vis-à-vis* mobile capital) and by various policy variables as a reaction to FDI volatility (such as investment subsidies, tax competition and labour market deregulation). Therefore, the regression analysis will only include bi-variate regressions, in order to give an indication of possible impacts of FDI on the real economy, recognizing that other factors play a role as well, and that there are likely indirect effects that may either weaken the correlations, as dampening effects, or that could increase the found correlation coefficients due to positive feedback effects. The results presented in this section should therefore be taken with caution, and are only indicative of possible impacts of FDI volatility on the real economy in developing countries.

Table 8.2 provides an overview of some bi-variate regression results with FDI volatility as the independent variable and, to compare, FDI inflow as well as volatility in the two types of FDI. This allows us to compare correlations between volatility and possible impact variables with correlations of flows with the same variables. Such a comparison will give an indication whether the possible impacts would be similar or different for flows and volatility of FDI. For the dependent variables, the regression analysis includes GDP growth, tax revenue and the vulnerable employment rate for men and women. The data combines cross-section data and time-series data, leading to three periods of observations per country: 1990–1994; 1995–1999; 2000–2004. These periods were chosen as they are the most volatile periods for FDI inflows, moreover, there was insufficient data available for earlier periods and for the last period.

Table 8.2 shows quite similar results for the two aggregate independent variables in terms of signs and statistical significance. This is probably due to the fact that over the period both variables went up; FDI inflows as well as FDI volatility. Indeed, the Pearson correlation between the two variables is quite high, 0.68 ($p < 0.01$, $N = 90$). What is striking about the dependent variable GDP growth is that the sign is unexpected: whereas the macroeconomic literature finds a negative correlation between FDI volatility and GDP growth, these results show a positive and statistically significant correlation. This would suggest that not only is the increase in FDI inflows beneficial for GDP growth but even its volatility may have a positive impact on growth. It is difficult to find a theoretical explanation for this result, which should probably be attributed to the particular time period involved and the lack of control variables.[3] One explanation may be related to a policy response to higher uncertainty about foreign investments, namely an overreaction in policies to attract a steady inflow of FDI. Relevant policy variables would be tax breaks, investment subsidies and labour market deregulation, as well as complementary government investment in business parks and export processing zones. Some of these policy measures are likely to create positive externalities for domestic investment and capacity utilization in existing production facilities, which have in turn a positive impact on GDP.

The regressions with tax revenue as the dependent variable show no correlation at all and no statistically significant results. The labour market variable for flexibilization, the employment vulnerability rate for males and females, tends to confirm the hypothesis that FDI volatility goes hand in hand with labour market flexibilization. This is in line with studies finding more vulnerable employment with globalization, in both developed and developing countries (as for example reported in ILO, 2008a). Obviously, these bi-variate regressions cannot distinguish between labour market flexibilization as a trend (for example through a substitution of fixed contracts into flexible contracts) and flexibilization as a consequence of deregulation policies (for example relaxing minimum wages and labour standards).

Table 8.2 Bi-variate regression results for FDI volatility

Dependent variables →	GDP growth (constant LCU)	Tax revenue as % of GDP change	Female vulnerable employment rate change	Male vulnerable employment rate change
FDI/GDP	9.985***	0.304	2.841**	8.490***
	R^2=0.26	R^2=0.00	R^2=0.09	R^2=0.26
	N=338	N=120	N=56	N=56
Stdev (FDI/GDP)	2.837***	0.044	1.816***	3.983***
	R^2=0.02	R^2=0.00	R^2=0.12	R^2=0.19
	N=333	N=120	N=56	N=56
Stdev/mean GF	0.016	−4.488***	1.253	0.543
	R^2=0.00	R^2=0.12	^{2}R=0.04	R^2=0.00
	N=295	N=111	N=55	N=55
Stdev/mean M&A	0.853***	0.272	−0.095	−0.487
	R^2=0.02	R^2=0.01	R^2=0.00	R^2=0.04
	N=292	N=111	N=56	N=56

Notes: GF = Greenfield. Unstandardized coefficients. $^{*}p < 0.1$; $^{**}p < 0.05$; $^{***}p < 0.01$. In the dataset, country-period observations were removed when for the volatility variables stdev/mean ≥ 20 since these were outliers

The regressions for the two types of FDI suggest that each type of FDI may have partially different impacts. But since, as we have seen above, the share of M&A and greenfield investment varies greatly over the years, without a clear trend, the expected impacts of FDI are therefore also likely to vary from year to year. This variability in types of FDI over the years makes it very difficult to evaluate FDI volatility in a cross-section study and for time-series. More detailed analysis for a region or a small number of countries would be necessary in order to better understand the various possible impacts of FDI inflows on developing countries. The bi-variate regression results presented in Table 8.2 indicate that greenfield investment volatility has no impact at all on GDP growth, a result which is statistically significant, whereas volatility in mergers and acquisitions shows a positive and statistically significant effect on GDP growth. This difference may be a consequence of the fact that volatility in greenfield investment includes disinvestments, leading to sometimes negative net greenfield investments for countries in particular periods. M&A volatility refers only to ups and downs in positive net investment inflows.

For the correlation with tax revenue, a policy variable, the results are the reverse. Greenfield investment volatility shows a negative statistically significant impact on changes in tax revenue, whereas volatility in mergers and acquisitions shows no statistically significant effect. These differentiated results suggest that mergers and acquisitions may be more beneficial for developing countries in times of increasing volatile investment flows than greenfield investments; M&A seems to have a positive impact on GDP growth and no disadvantageous effect on tax revenue. Why this would be the case requires microeconomic analysis into the different characteristics of the two types of investment. It may be the case that greenfield investments are largely low value added, labour-intensive production facilities in export processing zones, attracted partly by tax breaks offered for such investments, while mergers and acquisitions may involve positive externalities through technology transfer, skill upgrading and reliance on existing forward and backward linkages in the industries in which foreign investors participate. This, in turn, is more likely to contribute to GDP growth in additional ways than only through the exports of low value added manufactured goods, while tax breaks are not a major policy instrument to attract foreign capital for mergers and acquisitions.

Finally, it is surprising to see that the regression results for the labour market flexibilization variable shows no statistically significant effects from the breakdown of FDI volatility into greenfield investment and mergers and acquisitions. It is unclear why this is the case, whereas the aggregate FDI volatility variables, both for the flows and the volatility, show positive statistically significant effects on labour market flexibility. The results suggest that labour market flexibilization and/or deregulation is related to the increase in FDI inflows and volatility as such, and not to a specific type of FDI, which, as was shown in Figure 8.6, vary extensively as a share of FDI from year to year.

4. CONCLUSIONS

This study has analyzed long-run developments of FDI inflows into developing countries, their volatility and possible impacts on the real economy. FDI inflows, relative to GDP, have increased sevenfold since 1970. The standardized volatility of these inflows have come down in the 1980s, but show an increase since 2005. The unstandardized volatility shows a much shorter period of decline of volatility, with an increase beginning in the 1990s and volatility at higher levels since then, as compared to the 1970s. The pattern is quite similar for Asia, Latin America and Africa. A breakdown of FDI in greenfield investment and mergers and acquisitions is relevant because their shares in FDI vary considerably per country and per year. Over the period 1987–2005 greenfield investment was about twice as high as a percentage of GDP compared to M&A. The volatility decline in FDI concerns both types of investment and for all three regions, although since 2005 volatility in M&A is rising again while that for greenfield investment remains stable, so far. This means that from the perspective of reducing uncertainty of foreign capital inflows, greenfield investment may be more beneficial for developing countries than M&A, for two reasons. First, the volatility level of greenfield investment is lower than that for M&A for the whole period. Second, the volatility in greenfield investment stabilizes in the last period, whereas for M&A it rises. But the descriptive data analysis of the annual inflows (rather than volatility indicators for four periods) also suggested that although greenfield investment is more stable than M&A in the long run, it seems to be more volatile in periods of crisis.

The bi-variate regression results should be taken with caution, as they ignore other variables that may explain changes in growth, tax revenue and employment vulnerability. Keeping this in mind, the results suggest that FDI volatility is not detrimental to economic growth, but it does seem to increase the rate of vulnerable employment, both for men and for women. Moreover, greenfield investment seems to have a negative impact on tax revenue, whereas this is not the case for M&A. In addition, volatility in greenfield investment has no significant impact on growth whereas M&A volatility seems to have a positive impact on growth. Hence, contrary to the descriptive data analysis, the bi-variate regression analysis seems to suggest that M&A may be the more beneficial type of FDI for developing countries, since it has no negative impact on tax revenue and a positive impact on GDP growth.

The preliminary findings presented in this chapter do not lead to straightforward policy advice on FDI for developing countries. In general, the increase in FDI inflow and volatility does not seem to harm growth, but it may affect poverty and inequality negatively due to an increase of employment vulnerability. When breaking down FDI in greenfield investment and M&A, developing countries seem to face a trade-off. On the one hand, greenfield investment shows a consistently lower level of volatility than M&A (about 50% less), while on the other hand volatility in greenfield investment seems higher during financial crises and appears to be correlated to lower tax revenues in the long run, and does not show the positive correlation with growth as M&A shows. So, stabilizing FDI inflows comes at a cost: going for more greenfield and less M&A in the FDI mix would help to stabilize direct capital inflows, but in order to increase the share of greenfield investment tax holidays and/or tax credits seem to contribute to lower tax revenues. This tax reduction may in turn, through lower social expenditures, have an additional negative effect on poverty and inequality, adding to the already negative effect of FDI inflow and volatility on employment vulnerability. In conclusion, from a policy perspective it all depends whether a country seeks to stabilize FDI inflows in the long run or during crises and to what extent it is prepared to give up tax revenue and equality, and perhaps some growth, for more stability. Further research is needed in order to provide more insight into this dilemma, as well as into possibilities to reduce the impact of FDI on vulnerable employment.

NOTES

* This chapter was written when I was fellow at the NIAS (Netherlands Institute for Advanced Study in the Humanities and Social Sciences). I greatly acknowledge the space that NIAS gave me for reflection and inspiration.

1 Chang (2004) mentions, among others, limiting ownership, limiting technology transfer, preferential local procurement and barriers to 'brownfield' investments.

2 'For instance, the foreign subsidiary can borrow against its collateral domestically and then lend the money back to the parent company. Likewise, because a significant portion of FDI is intercompany debt, the parent company can quickly recall it' (Loungani and Razin, 2001, p. 5).

3 When, in an alternative regression, both FDI inflow and FDI volatility as well as their interaction term are included, the sign for the volatility variable becomes negative. But in that exercise, only the parameter for the interaction term is statistically significant.

9. Financial Globalization, Current Crisis and Labour in Developing Countries

Rolph van der Hoeven*

The current wave of globalization starting around 1999–2000 (with the fall of the Berlin Wall, with changes in the concepts of development and with the ensuing capital market liberalization following earlier undertaken trade liberalization) has had profound effects on the labour market and on the employment situation of workers all over the world. These effects are in many cases accentuated by the current financial and economic crisis. The purpose of this chapter is to highlight especially the effects of financial globalization on labour.

Stiglitz (2009a) argues that the dominant view during the current process of globalization was that unfettered markets were judged sufficient to ensure economic efficiency. The best role for government was a limited one, and somehow the benefits of the growth that this would engender would trickle down to everybody in society. Added to that was the view of a dominant strand of economists arguing that the problem in the market economy was rigid wages, and that if it were not for wage rigidities, the economy would work in the way that classical economics predicted. According to Stiglitz, the implication of the Keynesian rigid-wage theory was very invidious but very pervasive: get rid of the rigid wages, and let labour markets be more 'flexible'. That has been the basis of a whole set of doctrines undermining job protections and labour rights. But as he rightly observes, wages are not rigid: in the Great Depression wages fell by about one-third; the problem that Keynes recognized was that wages can be too flexible. Stiglitz observes that lack of aggregate demand was the problem with the Great Depression, just as lack of aggregate demand is the problem today. Accordingly, imposing more wage flexibility can result in exacerbating the underlying problem of lack of aggregate demand. He puts the nature of the problem that we face today as follows: the people in the global economy have the same skills as before the crisis, and the machines and real resources are the same as before the crisis.

The problem is that there is an organizational failure, a coordination failure, and a macroeconomic failure.

A major question is of course whether ongoing analyses on employment, inequality and globalization remain relevant in the current context of the large financial and economic crisis. This chapter argues that such analyses remain highly relevant for at least two reasons. Firstly, several elements of the ongoing process of globalization, especially the unfettered markets, (including the labour market)[1] and the growing inequality (resulting for many households to indebt themselves in order to keep up spending on basic needs)[2] have given cause to the current crisis; therefore, the analysis of the structure and nature of current globalization and its impact on employment and inequality as well as policy recommendations to alter current globalization processes are even more relevant in times of the current crisis.

Secondly, there is growing evidence that the employment, human and social effects of the financial and economic crisis will last for a while, especially if no corrective action is taken. Reinhardt and Rogoff (2009) for example foresee that the deceleration or decline in GDP growth will lead to rising unemployment with a much longer duration than the deceleration or decline in GDP itself.[3] There is also evidence that indicators for human development exhibit a similar ratchet effect. Arbache and Page (2007), for example, show that African child mortality increases during growth decelerations, but hardly falls during growth accelerations. Further, primary school completion rates and life expectancy are and remain substantially lower in countries with growth decelerations. There are thus strong reasons to include policies for employment, income inequality and human development as priority issues in designing short-term and longer-term policies to deal with the crisis.

1. FINANCIAL GLOBALIZATION AND LABOUR

The current wave of globalization is characterized by widespread adoption of policies for financial openness.[4] Over the past two decades, many countries have liberalized their capital accounts (Lee and Jayadev 2005) and almost all policy measures related to foreign direct investment favoured a more open regime. These measures have been adopted autonomously by some countries, and also as conditions of adjustment loans. The major expected result was that it would allow developing countries to better utilize resources and to increase capital formation by stimulating foreign direct investment (FDI) and other international capital flows such as private portfolio investment. A more open national financial system was seen as a necessary complement to the lifting of impediments to international capital flows.

In spite of this substantial increase in capital flows, the expected benefits have not materialized for many countries. During the surge in foreign capital flows since the mid-1990s, actual investment into new infrastructure and productive capacity stagnated. This can in part be attributed to the fact that much FDI was spent on mergers and acquisitions, rather than on investment into new factories or equipment that would have added productive capacity.[5] Gross fixed capital formation (the most commonly used measure for physical investment) averaged 21.6 per cent of GDP in the 1990s and 21.0 per cent in the years from 2000 to 2006. Hence, it fell well short of the level reached in the 1970s and 1980s. In fact, van der Hoeven and Lübker (2007) observe an overall declining trend in capital formation since the early 1970s and not surprisingly that world GDP growth, too, was slower in the 1990s and the 2000s than in previous decades. Meanwhile, international capital movements and their sometimes sharp reversals have led to greater economic volatility, a trend that has been well documented (Diwan 2001; Prasad 2004; Cerra and Saxena 2005). That volatility has led to more frequent financial and economic crises, predominantly in developing countries (see Easterly, Islam and Stiglitz 2001; Singh 2003). While the current financial crisis had its origins in the industrialized world, the initial hope that developing countries had effectively 'de-coupled' proved to be an illusion when the upheaval in capital markets and the economic downturn spread around the globe within months. Such crises have negative effects on growth, investment and incomes, not only in the short term, but also in the long run (Diwan 2001; Cerra and Saxena 2005).

How does financial openness affect labour? There are several potential channels of influence. First is the potential effect of openness on growth. In addition to the potential direct positive effect of capital flows on growth (as countries gain additional resources that can be invested), there can also be an indirect negative effect on growth when financial liberalization forces countries to hold larger foreign reserves, which reduces consumption and/or investment and hence growth potential. If financial flows have, on balance, a positive impact on growth, this would be generally beneficial for labour, while slow growth is usually disadvantageous for labour. However, even in the case of growth, the distributional impact of financial openness on different categories of labour needs to be taken into account, and as a whole labour might benefit less than necessary from long-term institutional and human capital development and from growth of domestic consumption.

1.1 Financial Globalization, Growth and Employment

It has proven difficult to establish a robust causal relationship between financial globalization and growth.[6] A study by IMF researchers (Prasad et al. 2004) has confirmed the main findings of earlier studies, such as those undertaken in UNCTAD (2001), that find that growth depends more on the quality of domestic institutions and careful macro-economic management than on financial liberalization. Edison et al. (2004) argue in the same direction and demonstrate that the findings of previous research (that found a positive association between capital account openness and growth) crucially depended on the country coverage, the choice of time periods and the indicator for capital account openness. They also find evidence for a suggestion that was first made by Rodrik (1998), namely that conventional indicators for capital account openness closely proxy the reputation of a country's government. If governance is controlled for, capital account openness has no significant effect on economic performance (Edison et al. 2004: 243ff.).

Indirect growth effects through increased reserve holdings

The repeated financial crises of recent years have led many developing countries to build up foreign reserves. For some countries these reserves were created by surplus on the current account, while others built up reserves through capital inflows which were not spent on foreign goods. Rodrik (2006a) estimates the cost of increased reserve holdings to be 1 per cent of GDP on average for developing countries. While imposing costs on developing countries, increased reserve holdings are an indirect subsidy to the countries in whose currencies the reserves are held (see Stiglitz 2000).

The trend has accelerated in recent years to a somewhat alarming level. Overall, reserves held by low and middle income countries were equal to 27.1 per cent of their GNI in 2007, compared to 6.8 per cent in the first half of the 1990s – a fourfold increase. The increase took place in low and middle income developing countries alike, and across regions. Even a poor region like sub-Saharan Africa now holds foreign reserves equal to 17.9 per cent of its GNI, more than three times the ratio in the early 1990s. The trend is particularly strong in South Asia, East Asia and the Pacific. Even when China (the developing country with the largest foreign reserves) is excluded, there remains a substantial increase from an already high 15.0 per cent of GNI (1990–94) to 27.6 per cent in 2007 for the rest of the region (World Bank 2009e).

Financial globalization, volatility, crises and employment

Financial liberalization in developing countries is associated with increased GDP volatility and higher consumption volatility (Kose, Prasad and Terrones 2003; Prasad et al. 2004). Kaminsky, Reinhart and Végh (2004) pointed out that the absence of sound financial regulation, both at the national and international levels, makes developing countries much more vulnerable to negative impacts of capital flows. When institutions with the ability to manage greater volatility are absent or not fully effective, the generally procyclical nature of international capital flows ('when it rains it pours' syndrome) adds to the effects of fiscal policies and, to a certain extent, also macroeconomic policies, that tend to be procyclical in most developing countries. Such behaviour deepens and prolongs a crisis. Financial crises typically have a large impact on the real economy. In the five countries most affected by the East Asian crisis of 1997/98, GDP per capita fell between 2.6 per cent (Philippines) and 14.8 per cent (Indonesia). In Latin America, the Mexican crisis of 1994/95 led to a decline in incomes of 7.9 per cent, and the Argentinean crisis of 2001/02 reduced the country's per capita incomes by 16.5 per cent. Hutchison and Noy (2006) document that so-called 'sudden stop' crises (a reversal in capital flows and a simultaneous currency crisis) have a particularly harmful effect on output – over and above that of 'normal' currency crises. On average, they cause a cumulative output loss of 13 to 15 per cent of GDP over a three-year period.

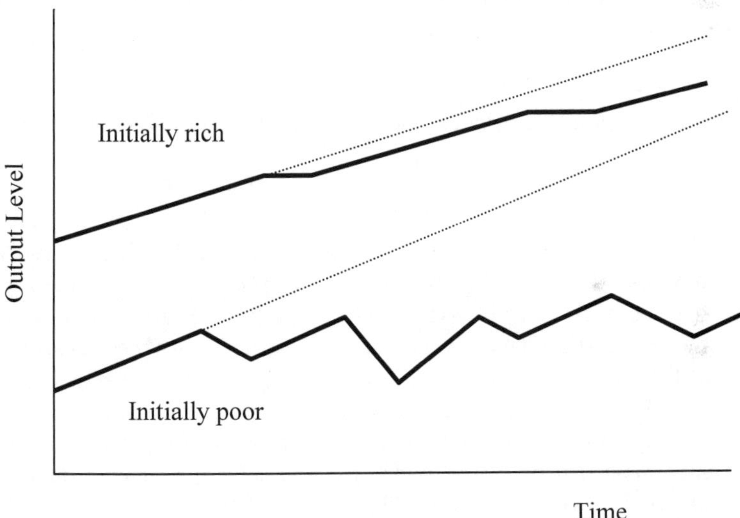

Figure 9.1 Typical growth paths after a financial crisis in rich and poor countries

The view that crises pose only a temporary set-back is challenged by Cerra and Saxena (2005), who deconstruct what they call the 'myth of recovery' by using panel data for broad datasets of countries. They document that recessions are typically not followed by high-growth recovery phases, either immediately following the trough, over several years of the subsequent expansion, or even over the complete subsequent expansion that follows a recession (Figure 9.1). When output drops, it tends to remain well below its previous trend. Cerra and Saxena also find that frequent crises and instabilities interfere with convergence between rich and poor countries:

> Countries that experience many negative shocks to output tend to get left behind and their long-term growth suffers. Thus, while standard growth theory may work well in explaining expansion, a fruitful direction for future research would be to explain the proclivity to wars, crises, and other negative shocks. (Cerra and Saxena 2005: 24)[7]

Financial crises generally provoke both economic decline and social costs. These are most prominently felt in terms of rising open unemployment, falling employment-to-population ratios, falling real wages, or a combination of the above (see e.g. Lee 1998). Moreover, the social costs are usually felt longer than the economic impact; even when GDP per capita has recovered to pre-crisis level, the other indicators usually lag behind (see World Commission on the Social Dimension of Globalization 2004: 40f.). This pattern can be observed in a majority of countries that were most affected by the financial crises of the past decade. We compare the situation before to that after a financial crisis for some of the most salient examples.

1.2 Impact of Financial Crises on Employment in Latin America and Turkey

Latin American countries experienced several periods of financial turbulence in recent years. The most prominent examples are the Mexican 'Tequila crisis' during 1994/95 and the currency crisis in several South American countries in the aftermath of the East Asian and Russian crises. Following extensive liberalization policies in Mexico, financial inflows expanded rapidly in the early 1990s, but reversed in 1994. The peso devaluation of December 1994 (see Ibarra 1999) brought the recently privatized, already fragile banking system into considerable difficulty as the peso value of foreign-denominated debt soared. Similarly, the balance sheet positions of companies which had accumulated debt in US dollars deteriorated rapidly (see Carstens and Schwartz 1998; Mishkin 1999), which in turn led to a sharp fall in investment (Aguiar 2005). Taken together, this can explain how a currency crisis rapidly turned into a crisis of the real economy and provoked a recession with an 8 per cent drop in per capita income in 1995. Unemployment, relatively stable at around 3 per cent before the crisis, started to increase during 1994 and reached 5.8 per cent in 1995, almost twice the pre-crisis rate. However, these figures mask the actual loss of jobs, since the share of informal employment rose from 30 per cent in 1993 to 35 per cent in

1995 (ILO 2005). By 1997 Mexico had achieved its pre-crisis income level, with the unemployment rate lagging the economic recovery by one year. However the share of informal employment remained above the pre-crisis level.

Brazil experienced large foreign capital inflows from 1994 onwards, when the Real Plan had introduced a new stable currency (see Cinquetti 2000). When investor sentiment swung suddenly after the Russian debt default of August 1998, Brazil responded by tightening its monetary policy in an effort to defend the exchange rate. Even though interest rates reached 40 per cent in late 1998, the capital outflows from Brazil were massive and the Central Bank allowed the Real to devalue. The currency crisis, in combination with the recessionary impact of high real interest rates, led to a relatively modest decline of per capita incomes that was accompanied by an increase in unemployment from 7.7 per cent in 1997 to 9.6 per cent in 1999 (see Figure 9.2). Despite the subsequent economic recovery, unemployment rates have hardly recovered and remained close to 9 per cent in 2004.

Like other emerging economies, Chile received large international capital inflows in the beginning of the 1990s. But unlike most other countries, Chile imposed controls on capital inflows in the form of an unremunerated reserve requirement (URR). Although it is uncertain whether this affected the overall amount of inflows, it reduced speculative capital inflows: the share of short-term debt in total external debt fell from an already low level of 19.4 per cent in 1990 to 4.8 per cent in 1997 – at a time when other countries increasingly relied on short-term financing (de Gregorio, Edwards and Valdés 2000: 70f.). At the onset of the Asian crisis, Chile was thus considerably less exposed to international volatility. The peso was also at the lower (appreciated) end of the exchange rate band at the time, leaving room for a relatively large devaluation within the band. However, the Central Bank feared that a depreciation could endanger the inflation target. Therefore, it defended the peso against growing pressure with a mix of monetary tightening and interventions on the foreign exchange market, before finally allowing the peso to float in September 1999 (Morandé and Tapia 2002: 5). Solimano and Larraín (2002: 17f.) argue that the Central Bank effectively prioritized '[l]ower inflation over higher growth and employment'. The high interest rates had a recessionary impact, and unemployment increased from 5.3 per cent in 1997 to 8.9 per cent in 1999. While GDP per capita regained its 1998 level in 2000, unemployment only fell slowly and reached 6.0 per cent only in 2006. Solimano and Larraín (2002: 38f) discuss several hypotheses that could explain the sluggish employment performance, among them firm-restructuring, continued job losses in small and medium enterprises (SMEs) and the noticeably slower rate of GDP growth after the crisis. They warn that unemployment could become a structural problem in Chile unless capital formation accelerates.

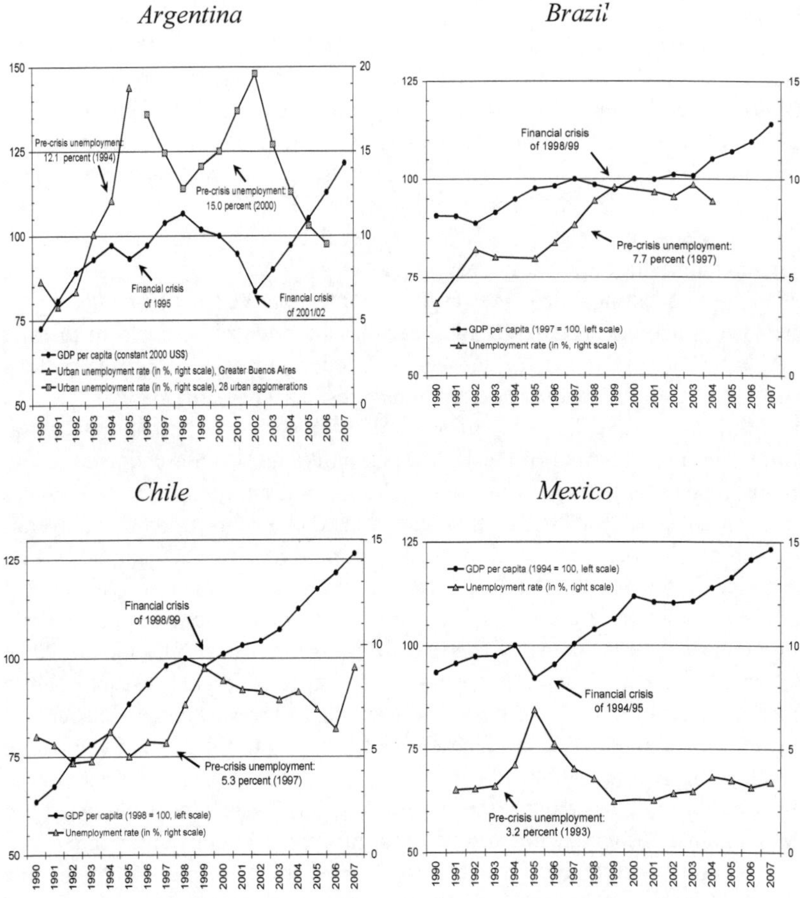

Note: Unemployment data for Brazil exclude the rural population of Rondônia, Acre, Amazonas, Roraima, Pará and Amapá. Unemployment data for Argentina refer to Greater Buenos Aires (SIAL series) or to 28 urban agglomerations (LABORSTA series)

Source: World Bank, World Development Indicators, online database as of May 2009, series 'GDP per capita (constant 2000 USD)'; International Labour Office, Key Indicators of the Labour Market, 5th edition (2009)

Figure 9.2 Medium-term effects of financial crises on unemployment in Latin American countries

The case of Argentina stands out, for the country went through two financial crises, in 1995 (when investors withdrew capital following the Tequila crisis in Mexico) and again in 2001/02, leading to the collapse of a fixed exchange rate system (see Daseking et al. 2004). The first crisis caused only a relatively mild downturn, and, with considerable foreign support, pre-crisis income levels were again reached in 1996 (see Damill, Frenkel and Maurizio 2002: 9ff.). As in other countries, the unemployment rate (that covers only urban areas in the case of Argentina) was still far above the pre-crisis level at this point, but it was approaching its 1994 level by 1998.[8] A recession that year sent unemployment up again. Argentina therefore went into the 2001/02 crisis with an already high level of (urban) unemployment (15.0 per cent in 2000), that rose to almost 20 per cent by 2002. More recent data indicate that a partial recovery had occurred by 2006, when unemployment fell below 10 per cent for the first time. Economic turbulence and the cumulative effects of two financial crises have thus caused a substantial unemployment problem in a country where unemployment rates had fluctuated around 5 per cent for most of the 1980s (ILO 2005).

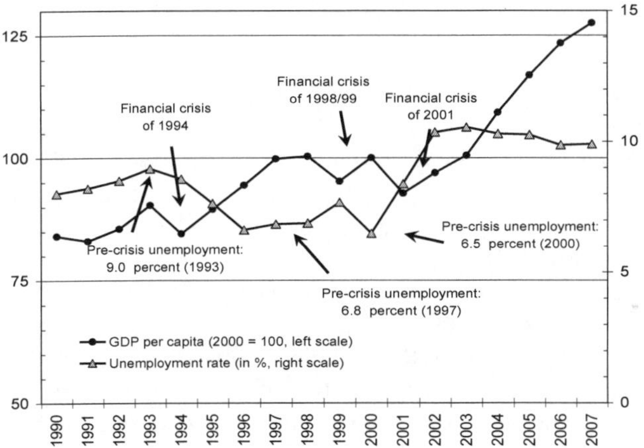

Source: World Bank, World Development Indicators, online database as of May 2009, series 'GDP per capita (constant 2000 USD)'; International Labour Office, Key Indicators of the Labour Market, 5th edition (2009)

Figure 9.3 Medium-term effects of financial crises on unemployment in Turkey

In Turkey, the frequency of crises was even higher than in Argentina. The country had liberalized its economy throughout the 1980s, but embarked on full capital account liberalization only in August 1989. Since then, capital flows have been highly volatile and have contributed to the repeated crises that affected the country in 1994, 1998/99 and 2001. As Demir (2004) argues, the country went into a vicious cycle of crises, where the loss in output reduced public revenues and increased public borrowing through short-term treasury bills that were bought by domestic banks, which re-financed themselves through short-term loans from abroad – building up currency risks and setting the stage for the next crisis. Resulting high real interest rates reduced investment and prospects for long-term growth (see also Akyüz and Boratav 2003). Whereas recovery from the first crisis in 1994 was relatively smooth – both in terms of GDP and employment – the second and especially the third crisis proved to be more severe. Their combined effect meant that per capita incomes were still at their 1997/98 level in 2003 (see Figure 9.3). Unemployment peaked briefly during 1999 and was back at its previous level of around 6.5 per cent in 2000 – before the next crisis set in. The third crisis led to a dramatic rise in unemployment to 10.4 per cent in 2002 and has remained close to 10 per cent since. While employment had recovered largely in line with GDP during the first crises, unemployment has not fallen significantly after the last, most severe crisis – despite a strong rebound in GDP.

1.3 The Employment Impact of the East Asian Crisis

That financial crises typically translate into crises of the real economy is also clearly evident from the experience of East Asia. Here, both output and capacity utilization fell sharply during the 1997/98 crisis. In a survey of firms in Korea, Thailand, Indonesia and Malaysia, entrepreneurs list the drop in domestic demand, rising costs for imported inputs and the high interest rates as the most important reasons (see Dwor-Frécaut, Colaco and Hallward-Driemeier 2000, Ch. 1). The declining capacity utilization had adverse impacts on the average profitability and liquidity of firms, and many companies abandoned or scaled down planned investments. Interest rate and currency shocks also forced many companies into bankruptcy as they found themselves unable to service their debt, much of which was denominated in foreign currency (Kawai, Lieberman and Mako 2000: 77ff.). Data from the five countries worst affected by the East Asian crisis show that many of the surviving firms reduced their workforce in 1998, while only a small fraction hired more staff (see Dwor-Frécaut, Colaco and Hallward-Driemeier 2000: 4f.). Unemployment increased throughout the region, and incomes fell – in some cases dramatically, pushing many people below the poverty line. According to ILO estimates, the number of working poor in South East Asia (using the threshold of 1 US$ per day) rose from its pre-crisis level of 33.7

million in 1996 to 50.6 million at the height of the financial crisis in 1998 – an increase of almost 17 million (see Kapsos 2004: 14f.).

A more detailed look at the country level shows that in 1996, the year before the East Asian financial crisis, some countries had virtually achieved full employment with unemployment rates of 1.1 per cent in Thailand, 2.0 per cent in Korea and 2.5 per cent in Malaysia (Figure 9.4).[9] By 1998, the combination of production cut-backs and lay-offs through bankruptcies had brought unemployment to 3.4 per cent in Thailand, or 1.1 million (up from 0.3 million). In addition, about 0.2 million workers left the labour force despite strong growth of the working age population.[10] Many workers had to find a new source of income in the informal economy which grew significantly during the crisis. This development is mirrored by a rise in the number of self-employed by 0.8 million. Hidden unemployment in the form of underemployment also increased almost two-fold (from 2.3 million to 4.4 million). A further effect of the crisis was a decline in real wages by 4 per cent within a year (see Mahmood and Aryah 2001: 266ff.).[11]

The Korean labour market suffered severely from the wave of redundancies that accompanied the bankruptcies of thirteen large conglomerates during 1997, and the reduction in the work force of surviving companies. Delays in payments by the large corporations dragged many SMEs into the crisis; 8,200 of them failed in 1997 and a further 10,500 in 1998 (see Kawai, Lieberman and Mako 2000: 77ff). Open unemployment rose to 7.0 per cent or 1.5 million (up from 0.6 million), a level not seen in decades. Among the hardest-hit groups were manual production workers and those in clerical grades. By the first quarter of 1999, total employment had fallen to 19 million, down by 2.1 million from the fourth quarter of 1997 (see Kang et al. 2001: 98f.). The disparity between the growth in unemployment and the far larger decline in employment can be attributed to the fact that around 350,000 workers (in particular women) left the labour force altogether, resulting in a decline of the labour force participation rate by almost two percentage points (ILO 2009c). The increase in unemployment was less dramatic in Malaysia, where the rate rose by less than a percentage point. Nonetheless, around 250,000 formal sector jobs were lost in 1998 (see Jomo 2001: 34 and Table 26). Many of the retrenched workers were foreign migrant workers, which cushioned the effect on the domestic labour market (see Mansor et al. 2001: 144f.) but dispersed some of the negative impact to other countries. ILO data also show that agricultural employment expanded by 135,000 in 1998. The absorption of labour by the primary sector helped to contain the rise in open unemployment, but contributed to falling labour productivity in agriculture (ILO 2009c and World Bank 2009c).

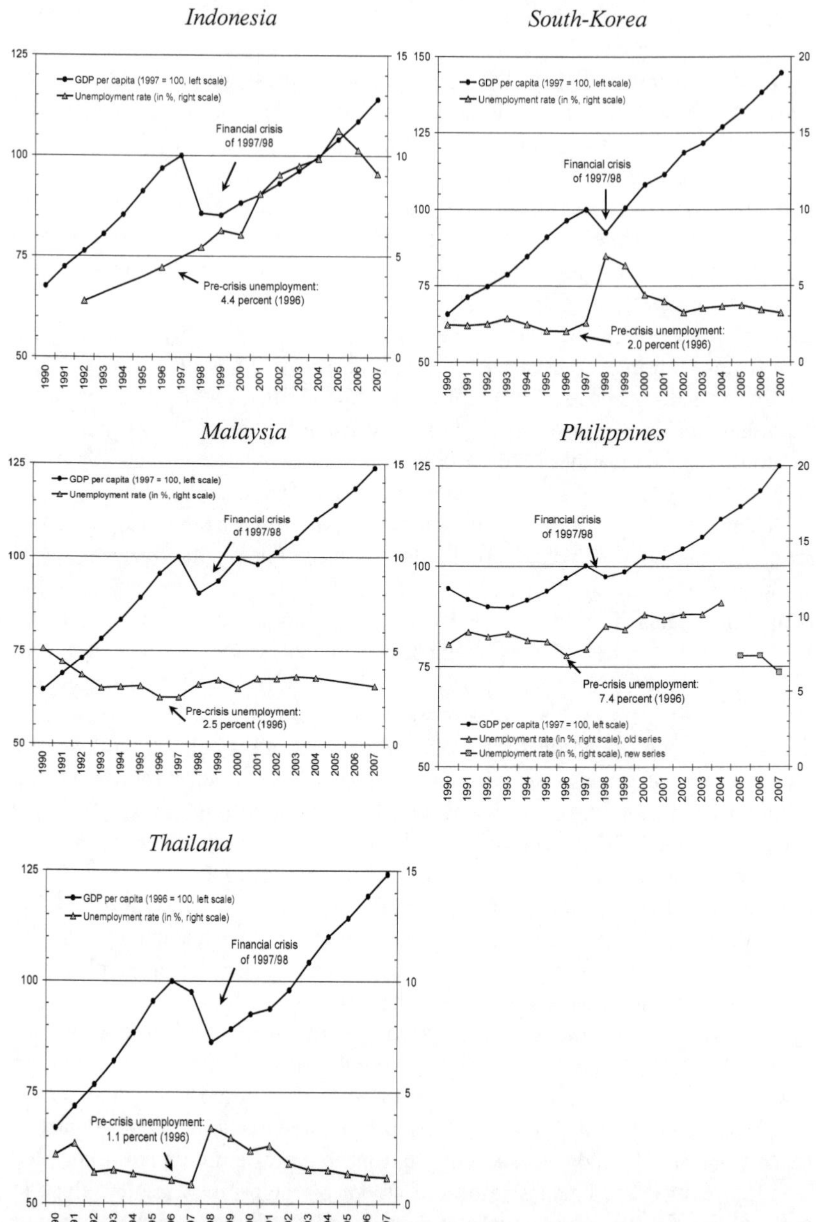

Figure 9.4 Medium-term effects of the East Asian financial crises on unemployment

Indonesia (4.4 per cent unemployment in 1996) and the Philippines (7.4 per cent) went into the financial crisis with considerably higher unemployment (Figure 9.4). From that higher base, about 2.5 million workers lost their jobs in Indonesia in 1997/1998, among them 1 million in manufacturing alone (see Islam et al. 2001: 50ff.). The fall in industry and services employment was offset by an expansion of agriculture employment, so that open unemployment grew only modestly during 1998 despite strong labour force growth. However, unemployment continued to rise in subsequent years and reached 11.2 per cent in 2005. Real earnings also fell by about 40 per cent during the crisis and were still about 10 per cent below their pre-crisis level in 2000 (Dhanani and Islam 2004: 29f.). In the Philippines, where the crisis had a comparatively mild economic impact, unemployment rose to 9.4 per cent in 1998 (+2 percentage points) and has continued on an upward path during the early 2000s.[12]

The East Asian experience shows that progress in returning to pre-crisis unemployment is generally far slower than the pace of economic recovery. Although all five countries returned to positive growth in 1999 or 2000, unemployment rates continued to increase in Indonesia, Korea, Malaysia and the Philippines and peaked only four or five years after the return to positive growth. This explains why the recovery of the labour market lagged far behind the economic recovery. Although all five countries have regained their pre-crisis GDP level – Korea as early as 1999, Indonesia only in 2005 – only Thailand had returned to pre-crisis levels of unemployment in 2007, a decade after the East Asian Crisis.[13] Thus, while countries have largely managed to recover from the economic impact of the crisis, the devastating labour market effect seems to be much more long-lived.

2. THE EFFECT OF THE CURRENT CRISIS ON LABOUR AND POSSIBLE POLICY RESPONSES

The above analysis on the effects on labour in previous crises provides a useful indicator for an analysis of the current crisis, where information on employment and labour issues is only surfacing.

A first important point to observe in this context is that the current crisis affects developing countries more than previous crises did. The recent *World Bank's Global Economic Prospects for 2010* (World Bank 2010b) argues that the severity of this recession is far larger than that of earlier recessions. These observations are at variance with earlier assessments on the effects of the current recession on developing countries. The IMF 2008 *World Economic Outlook* (IMF 2008a), for example, argued that greater delinking was taking place between industrialized and developing economies and that developing countries would be less affected by a crisis which had started in the developed world. However, the decline in trade volumes and values, the substantial shrinking of foreign direct investment as well as a reversal in fast-growing trend of increasing remittances, which some have labelled as de-globalization, have all had substantial consequences for developing countries in various ways, and especially on the poorer segment of the population (see United Nations 2010b and World Bank 2010b).

One could argue that such de-globalization might be beneficial for developing countries as it reversed the trend of increasing globalization. Indeed, the current crisis has led to somewhat greater influence in economic decision making of the larger developing countries, for example in the reborn G20 which is replacing the G7, but this is far from a necessary change in global governance to avoid future crises as Stiglitz (2009b) has argued.

Furthermore the decline in trade, FDI and remittances was not the consequence of any agreed change in international policy attitudes towards globalization, but the outcome of a serious downturn in GDP in industrialized countries, with rising tendencies of protectionism and a deterioration of attitudes to foreign workers.

The position of labour in the current crisis is actually extremely worrying: the trends over the last two decades (reported above) indicate that the economic bubble, as a consequence of financial globalization, in the second half of the first decade of the 21st century did not favour most participants in the labour market. Only a small minority has really been profiting from this. But now that the bubble has burst, we notice an asymmetric trend: most workers did not profit from the bubble (as the low employment elasticities, the growing inequality and the persistent informalization attest to), but after the bubble many workers suffered from the consequences of the bursting of the bubble (ILO 2010a). And while business as usual, including the highly skewed remuneration packages, seems to be on the cards for financial institutions, this is not the case for many in the labour market. Ravallion (2009) for example, reports a substantial increase of households in poverty as a consequence of the crisis. And earlier I noticed already the lag in employment recovery after a financial crisis, which according to the latest estimate is manifesting itself again during this crises (ILO 2010a).

To state briefly: current globalization has made labour more precarious, a trend which has been magnified by the current crisis. This picture is consistent with the policy reaction in many countries to the crisis, to the effect that the governments have (rightly) acted as a banker of last resort to avoid the collapse of the financial system, but that governments, despite stimulus plans for monetary easing and some labour market policies, have not really acted as an employer of last resort.

It seems thus important to frame policies favouring labour in the current context on two essential elements. Firstly, by introducing or by strengthening those national and international policies, which try to undo the trends of precariousness and increasing inequality as a consequence of (financial) globalization. Examples of such policies can be found in van der Hoeven and Luebker (2007), UN/DESA (2007) and World Commission on the Social Dimension of Globalisation (2004). Secondly, in addition to the policies above, by applying special policies to deal with the outfall of the current crisis, such as employment schemes (Wray 2009), special labour market policies (Cazes et al. 2009) and cash transfers (Standing 2007) etc. The costs of these policies are often a fraction of the support the financial institutions and large industries have received recently. They can in the first instance be financed as part of the current stimulus packages and, once the economy has picked up, from increased tax revenues or from reimbursements to the governments by bailed-out financial institutions.

It is important to base policy interventions simultaneously on policies dealing with the structural problems, which financial globalization has caused, and on policies assisting those who fall into poverty or experience poor working conditions as a consequence of the crisis. The current crisis is clearly the outcome of a longer trend of financial globalization which, if not arrested in its current form, may lead well to a new crisis.

NOTES

* I would like to thank Malte Lubecker for valuable inputs for Sections 1.2–1.3.

1. Part of growing inequality can be explained by the policies undertaken during the process of liberalization and adjustment, including policies to make the labour market more efficient (van der Hoeven and Taylor 2000).
2. 'over the past 30 years particularly, there has been an increase in inequality. In effect, we have been transferring money from the poor to the rich, from people who would spend the money to people who do not need to spend the money, and the result of that is weaker aggregate demand' (Stiglitz 2009, pp. 7–8).
3. Van der Hoeven and Luebker (2007) investigate the behaviour of labour shares in national incomes during recent periods of financial crises and observed a ratchet effect: labour shares decline during crises but in many cases do not return, once the economy has picked up, to their pre-crisis level.
4. Financial openness is used here as an umbrella term that includes both financial integration and financial liberalization. Financial liberalization in turn incorporates the liberalization of the capital and financial account. Congruent with the literature, we henceforth use 'capital account liberalization' as shorthand for the liberalization of the capital and financial

account; for the standard presentation of the Balance of Payments see IMF (2005).

5 UNCTAD data show that the FDI boom was in part driven by mergers and acquisitions (M&A). In 2007, the value of worldwide M&As was US$1,637 billion – some 21 per cent higher than during its previous peak in 2000. This compares to global FDI inflows of US$1,833 billion in the same year. See UNCTAD, *World Investment Report 2008*.

6 The conflicting results could in part be caused by differences in country coverage, but also by differences between the indicators employed in the literature. There is a crucial difference between *de jure* or *de facto* measures of financial openness. *De jure* openness includes abolishment or changes in rules and regulations concerning foreign capital, as is often required as part of the conditionality for financial support by the international financial institutions. By contrast, *de facto* openness relates to increases in a financial openness indicator, irrespective of whether rules have changed or not. In the latter case, the causal relationship between financial openness and growth is more difficult to establish. Did openness lead to higher growth, or did higher growth induce financial flows and integration? Rodrik (2003) and Singh (2003) argue that the latter is the case especially for India and China where growth induced greater financial integration.

7 This is related to Rodrik (2003) that policies for stimulating growth are different from policies to sustain growth and that frequent crises require frequent policy regime switches

8 Unfortunately, due to the expansion of geographical coverage from Greater Buenos Aires (until 1995) to 28 urban agglomerations (from 1996 onwards) the unemployment data are not directly comparable.

9 For the Philippines, unemployment data from 2005 onwards are not comparable to earlier figures due to a series break. Source World Bank, *World Development Indicators*, online database as of May 2009, series 'GDP per capita (constant 2000 USD)'; International Labour Office, *Key Indicators of the Labour Market*, 5th edition (2009c).

10 See ILO (2009c), *Key Indicators of the Labour Market*, 5th edition.

11 Women in urban areas suffered a disproportionate wage loss (−10.5 per cent), and workers in manufacturing (−13 per cent) and constriction (−24 per cent) were also badly affected (Mahmood and Aryah 2001: 267).

12 Due to a series break in the data from the Philippines, unemployment rates from 2005 onwards are not directly comparable to the earlier series.

13 No conclusive assessment is possible for the Philippines, where a change in survey methodology led to a series break in 2005.

PART III

Regional and Country Experiences

10. Impact of the Global Crises (Financial, Economic and Food): The Case of Microfinance in Latin America

Reynaldo Marconi and Harry Clemens

The global financial, economic and food crisis has provoked an important debate in the microfinance sector in Latin America. This debate focuses on two central questions. First, is the crisis a threat to services for poor and vulnerable clients or an opportunity to improve the sector's performance and social impact? Second, how should the microfinance sector react to the crisis and the changes that the region is going through: learn to live with it and wait until the crisis is over or treat the crisis as an opportunity? The drama of Latin America is the reproduction and persistence of rural poverty. The share of people living in poverty in Latin America fell from 46 per cent in 1994 to 34 per cent in 2007 and the share of people in extreme poverty declined from 21 per cent to 13 per cent. Although this reduction in poverty and extreme poverty was an outstanding achievement, the level of rural poverty in Latin America remains high (52 per cent and 28 per cent respectively), with a widening gap between rural and urban zones (Trivelli et al. 2009).

At the global level, microfinance has been promoted as an anti-poverty tool. The World Microfinance Summit, held in 1996, set the target of reaching 100 million clients worldwide. Almost fifteen years later, it appears that this target has been exceeded. But is it enough? Studies emphasise the success of microfinance in certain countries of the region (Bolivia, Peru, Nicaragua, etc.), but after two decades of development and experience with microfinance, poverty persists or has increased in those same countries. It is clear that microfinance will not eradicate poverty on its own. If microfinance has been successful in supporting the fight against poverty, why does poverty persist and why have microfinance services not reached those who are most in need, the rural poor? Several microfinance institutions started to ask themselves if they succeeded in reaching out to the poor, and how they can more effectively translate their social mission into effective policies, practice and social results.

This chapter has five sections. Section 1 provides a background on the effects of the recent global crisis in Latin America. Section 2 introduces the development of the microfinance sector in the region after 2000, paying particular attention to the increased attention to social performance of the sector. In order to analyse the effects of the crisis on microfinance institutions we will distinguish between different types of institutions. Section 3 describes three types of microfinance providers, while Section 4 analyses the effects of the crisis on each type. Section 5 draws conclusions regarding two questions: (i) is the crisis a threat to services for poor and vulnerable clients or an opportunity to improve the sector's performance and social impact? and (ii) how should the microfinance sector react to the crisis and the changes that the region is going through: learn to live with it and wait until the crisis is over or treat the crisis as an opportunity?

1. THE EFFECTS OF THE CRISIS IN LATIN AMERICA

The Latin American region is highly integrated in the global economy, and thus dependent on economic cycles and crises in the main centres such as the United States, Europe and, increasingly, East Asia. After the crisis in the 1980s (known as the 'lost decade') and the 1990s, the region experienced increasing growth figures. High commodity prices and improved control of income of mineral exports by governments benefited both balance of payments and fiscal balances in resource-rich countries. In 2007 some 7% of export income of the region came from China that had become the second largest export market for Peru and the second largest trade partner of Brazil.

High food prices in 2007–2008 had a dual effect: it improved terms of trade for food-exporting countries, but negatively affected purchasing power and food security, especially of poor households. Volatility of market prices affected many poor households, both producers and consumers, changed policies and trade regimes in countries such as Argentina, and changed the position and thinking of small-scale farmers in globalised markets (Murphy 2010).

Even though international trade relations had become more diversified, the US market was still very important to the region, especially for Mexico, Central America and the Caribbean. Therefore the crisis in the United States had a rapid impact in the region. At the outset of the financial crisis governments of mineral-rich countries still had reserves so that they could manage anti-cyclic policies, as opposed to during former crises such as in the 1980s. Nevertheless, the population was affected in several ways.

Table 10.1 Latin America and the Caribbean GDP growth

	1995-2005	2007	2008	2009
Regional average	2.9	5.4	4.1	−2.3
Brazil	2.4	5.7	5.1	−0.2
Mexico	3.6	3.2	1.8	−6.5
Argentina	2.3	8.7	7.0	−1.2
Peru	3.4	8.9	9.8	0.9
Ecuador	3.2	2.0	7.2	0.4
Bolivia	3.8	4.6	6.1	3.4
Central American average	3.6	3.6	2.0	−5.9

Sources: worldbank.org databank; ECLAC Economic Survey of LAC (2009–2010)

According to a study of 11 countries in the region,[1] the international financial crisis has affected the countries of the region directly, though in diverse ways. The crisis affected countries and households with least resources, through at least three mechanisms: (a) lower incomes, as a result of fewer employment opportunities (the result of a fall in demand and investment, especially in infrastructure); (b) lower incomes due to a fall in remittances by migrants; and (c) reductions in public expenditure, especially in social expenditure (which affects the poorest by reducing their income or consumption). The study maintains that, in all the countries studied, it is necessary to introduce policies to support small-scale and subsistence agriculture. The objectives of such policies must be to improve the capacity of these activities to act as a safety net during the crisis and to create the conditions to revitalise the sector. The policies to be developed should provide an opportunity to promote and revive rural areas. This presents a special challenge for rural microfinance.

According to FAO (2009) data, the food crisis increased the number of people who go hungry in Latin America from 45 million in 2008 to 53 million in 2009. Latin America produces and exports significant quantities of food, but only in certain countries and by certain types of producer. In Latin America and the Caribbean, agriculture contributes 5% of regional gross domestic product (GDP). Paradoxically, the food crisis also affected rural households. Small-scale farmers are increasingly vulnerable because of rapidly changing market prices. This highlights the need for the Latin American countries to have enhanced food security and sovereignty policies to ensure more stable prices and reduce the vulnerability of low-income sectors of the population and reduce malnutrition and food insecurity. This would provide an opportunity for rural microfinance to develop strategies for specific financial services to reduce such vulnerability and create the foundations for economic development. However this is limited by the regulatory framework, inhibiting rural savings.

Meanwhile, the political context of the region has seen the emergence of left wing and 'populist' governments of various descriptions, some of which have been receptive to the peasant sector and have included the objectives of food security, food sovereignty and the right to food in their government agendas and prioritised support for small-scale agricultural and peasant production in their anti-poverty strategies and interventions. However, it is not enough to adopt policies if the mechanisms to achieve satisfactory results do not exist. One such mechanism is access to credit for small-scale farmers and peasant food production, an area in which microfinance has achieved few results but one in which new governments feel the need to respond.

2. PROMOTION OF SOCIAL PERFORMANCE IN MICROFINANCE

For five years (2000–2004) the Ford Foundation supported the Imp-Act (Improving the Impact of Microfinance on Poverty) programme. This laid the foundations for the measuring and management of social performance in microfinance (Copestake et al. 2005). Meanwhile, in 2001, within the framework of the Solidarity Finance, a broad alliance of providers, including FOROLACFR, began to develop the first version of the Social Performance Indicators (SPI) tool, under the leadership of CERISE in France. In October 2005, the FOROLACFR organised a seminar entitled 'Measuring Social Performance in Microfinance', in Santa Cruz, Bolivia. This seminar's recommendations made a definitive distinction between measuring and managing social performance and led microfinance rating agencies to include social performance indicators in their methodologies. The development of simplified 'social auditing' (SPI) instruments was decisive in promoting systematisation. The creation of the Social Performance Task Force (SPTF) in Paris, France in June 2006 and its successive annual meetings promoted a 'global mobilisation' that gradually progressed towards the 'conceptualisation of social performance in microfinance'; the systematisation of social auditing tools (SPI) for managing social performance (ImpAct Consortium); the adoption of social performance measuring/managing schemes by microfinance rating agencies; the use of Standardised Social Performance Indicators in Microfinance, with the support of Microfinance Information Exchange (MIX); and the creation of non-repayable funds to encourage microfinance providers to gain access to Social Performance Rating services.

In the last ten years (2000–2010), there has been significant progress in various directions in the promotion of measuring, monitoring and managing social performance in microfinance. The meeting of the SPTF in June 2009 identified the provider networks as ideal actors to promote coordination of processes and initiatives because of their knowledge and proximity to microfinance providers (2). In response to this, in 2010 FOROLACFR has proposed the organisation and operation of a Social Performance Certification System for Microfinance and Popular Finance.[2]

3. A SNAPSHOT OF THE LATIN AMERICAN MICROFINANCE SECTOR

In some countries (Bolivia, Peru, Ecuador, Guatemala) the availability of microfinance grew rapidly, as a component of anti-poverty strategies directed mainly at urban and periurban centres. The World Bank estimated that access to financial services in this region reached 36% on average. However, this average hides the low coverage of financial services in rural areas, which was only 5% according to FOROLACFR and its associated networks. For example, in Bolivia the coverage of financial services in urban areas is 44% of the economically active population, compared to 22% in rural areas (Marconi 2010). A global study conducted by the Bill & Melinda Gates Foundation found that only 5% of the continent's poor population have access to financial services. This situation calls to broaden and expand financial services in rural areas, without limiting ourselves to providing loans and micro-loans. Financial services for poor rural communities must be comprehensive and appropriate for the needs and cultural practices of peasant and rural economies.

The low availability of financial services in rural areas is reflected in the limited attention paid to the peasant sector and small-scale agricultural production, which is the basis for our population's food supply. Doubts have been raised about whether microfinance is an appropriate financial instrument for the productive sector, particularly with regard to small-scale and family agricultural production. Often the interest rates of microcredit are higher than economic returns of food production. Interest rates may be affordable for petty trade and services with quick rotation of capital; they are often less affordable for agricultural producers.

In some countries, the issue of interest rates has combined with doubts about the social objectives of some of the microfinance providers. Increasingly, governments are looking for a re-introduction of agricultural development banks though they failed in former decades (Gonzales-Vega and Graham 1995). Therefore, in countries like Brazil and Guatemala agricultural development banks operate in a modified way. However, another response is the emergence of producer financial organisations and rural credit unions founded by producer organisations. The institutional maturity reached by groups of producers, particularly those involved in fair trade activities, have raised expectations that such institutions will become the new paradigm for popular finance in some countries of the region.

Table 10.2 Typology of micro finance providers

	MFIs CV (Commercial Vision)	MFIs SM (Social Mandate)	Community Finance Institutions and Producer Finance Institutions
Legal form	Private company	Civil associations and foundations	Private companies; Associations & foundations; Cooperatives
Purpose	For profit	Non-profit	Various
Focus Regulation	Microfinance as a business Regulated	Outreach to poor and vulnerable Non-regulated (with exceptions)	Autonomous development clients Regulated and non-regulated
Market	Usury	Peri-urban and rural	Rural
Main clients	Trade & services microenterprise	Trade & services microenterprise Women	Peasants and agricult. producers
Products and services	Microcredit, savings, SAF	Microcredit and village banking	Investment finance; SAF

Note: SAF: Payments and supporting financial services.

At present, there are three types of institution involved in the region's microfinance and popular finance sector, each with different approaches, as described in Table 10.2. First, there are microfinance institutions with a commercial vision (MFIs CV). Their approach is the commercialisation of microfinance. The actors here are commercial microfinance providers, whose aim is to obtain attractive financial returns for their shareholders, though they may incorporate principles of corporate social responsibility. They use business criteria and some of them depend on non-performing holdings or investors in the North. Second, there are microfinance institutions with a social mandate (MFIs SM), which primarily aim to increase and expand coverage for poor and vulnerable clients. The actors here are microfinance providers with a social vision, who have a 'social mandate'. Their civil society backers and investors require them to focus on providing services for people living in relative poverty. Third, there are community finance institutions and producer finance institutions (CFIs/PFIs) which aim to promote the autonomous socioeconomic development of their clients, who are now the owners of these financial organisations, which take the form of local producer and community financial institutions. This third group is an emerging sector. Successful models for CFIs are the FASCO and CDRO networks of Guatemalan financial institutions. PFIs are widespread in Mexico, for example microbanks, and are beginning to appear in Bolivia, for example FINCAFE and AFID.

4. THE EFFECTS OF THE CRISIS ON THE DIFFERENT TYPES OF MICROFINANCE INSTITUTION

The effects of the crisis on the microfinance sector have differed according to the type of institution, as illustrated in Table 10.3 (the arrows indicate the direct effects of the crisis and of institutional strategies on performance). Four features stand out in Table 10.3

Portfolio

The reduction for MFIs' commercial vision corresponds to microloans. Their overall portfolio is increasing as a result of upgrading (providing larger loans); for example, in Bolivia Banco PROCREDIT and in Nicaragua with Banco PROCREDIT and BANEX (that has not survived the crisis). In the case of the CFIs/PFIs, the upwards trend is the result of a strategy in response to the opportunities generated for the productive sector by the crisis, notwithstanding their cautious policies.

Clients

The reduction for MFIs' commercial vision is due to its change of strategy. The stagnation in the case of the MFIs' social mandate is due to changes in the flow of external resources and to the cautious policies of cooperative institutions and social and commercial investors. In the case of the CFIs/PFIs, the upwards trend is the result of a strategy in response to the opportunities generated for the productive sector by the crisis.

Equity

The reduction in equity of the MFIs' social mandate and CFIs/PFIs is explained by their negative financial results. In the case of the MFIs CV, there is pressure from regulators to maintain reasonable equity levels, all the more so in times of crisis.

Efficiency

The improvement in the position of the MFIs' commercial vision is due to the increase in the overall portfolio resulting from upgrading policies (larger loans). The deterioration in the position of the CFIs/PFIs is due to the adoption of financial expansion and penetration policies as a strategy for taking advantage of the current situation.

Table 10.3 Impact of crisis on MFI strategy

Detail	MFIs CV	MFIs SM	CFI/PFI
Marketing strategy	Upgrading	Expansion	Expansion and penetration
Portfolio	↘	→	↗
Clients	↘	→	↗
Deposits	↗	?	?
Innovation	↗	↗	↗
Financial return	↘	↘	↘
Equity	→	↘	↘
Efficiency (operating costs/portfolio)	↗	→	↘

5. WHAT CAN WE EXPECT FOR MICROFINANCE PROVIDERS AND THEIR CLIENTS?

Table 10.4 shows the situations faced by the various types of financial institution. Returning to the first question in the introduction, about whether the crisis is a threat to services for poor and vulnerable clients or whether it represents an opportunity to improve their performance and social impact, the response presented in this chapter is that neither applies to the MFIs' commercial vision. It is a threat to MFIs' social mandate because of the temptation to follow the example of the MFIs' commercial vision in order to protect themselves against the risks presented by the crisis and the restriction of external funds. Only in the case of the CFIs/PFIs does the crisis not threaten to reduce or weaken services for poor and vulnerable clients. On the contrary, it provides an opportunity to focus and extend the provision of microfinance services for poor and vulnerable clients and to adopt revitalised focuses.

Table 10.4 Threats and opportunities for MFIs

	MFIs CV	MFIs SM	CFI/PFI
Threat to reduce or decline outreach to poor and vulnerable clients	Indifference	Real threat: due to cautious policies and financial prudence coverage and growth is limited	Coverage is invariable and constant (no threat)
Opportunity to focus and deepen coverage	Upgrading strategies (larger loans)	These are subject to own and funding restrictions (less loan funding or more cautious apex funds)	Opportunity to focus on policies prone to food security and sovereignty

However, it is important to emphasise that the coverage of services is insufficient and services must promote change and have an impact on clients. Reality shows us that good coverage is a necessary but insufficient condition for access to financial services to provide opportunities to escape from poverty.

Finally, in order to be certain and have evidence that progress is being made in the right direction, it is essential to promote the management, monitoring and measurement of social performance in microfinance, as discussed in Section 2. As a consequence of the crisis, this is an opportunity for microfinance providers to achieve better results in terms of social performance.

With regard to the second question: how should the microfinance sector respond to the crisis and the changes that the region is going through? Learn to live with it and wait until the crisis is over or treat the crisis as an opportunity? Our proposals are: (1) strengthen the corporate social responsibility of MFIs' commercial vision, developing appropriate financial products for poor clients, including savings, microinsurance and loan products for agricultural producers (short and long term, interest rates that are financially sustainable for the institutions and for the client) and small and medium enterprises that buy products from small-scale producers (value chain finance), and respect for client protection principles; (2) support for MFIs' social mandate, including appropriate regulations so that the MFIs' social mandate can provide savings services, develop differentiated savings products, individual and group loan products, microinsurance, and rely on deposits as a stable source of funding; and (3) strengthen the financial organisations owned by the poor and vulnerable themselves, for example, agricultural producers.

Transparent markets should benefit clients as well as service providers with a social mission. If the microfinance sector recovers its original mission and MFIs are enabled to do so by regulators and favourable public policies, the sector can increase outreach and perform even better than before the crisis. Many urban poor have benefited from access to microcredit and improved livelihoods. During the crisis access has been reduced. In some cases over-indebtedness has led to impoverishment instead of improved living conditions. But if the crisis is taken as an opportunity it will be possible to turn this around, increase outreach in rural areas, improve and diversify services, ensure interest rates that are accessible to agricultural producers but also cover the costs of the financial service providers. Strategies will differ by type of institution. There is an important role to play by the three types described in this chapter, and for creating incentives for MFIs with demonstrated better social performance.

NOTES

1. Countries involved are: Mexico, Guatemala, Honduras, El Salvador, Nicaragua, Colombia, Brazil, Bolivia, Dominican Republic, Paraguay and Peru. The study was organised by RIMISP (Trivelli et al. 2009, p. 6, fn.).
2. The SPTF is a forum for the exchange and coordination of practical, research, cooperative, investor and rating agency initiatives. Its objective is to seek coherence and synergy of efforts in understanding, designing and implementing tools and methodologies for measuring and monitoring social performance in microfinance.

11. Crisis, Employment and Poverty in the Middle East and North Africa

Mahmood Messkoub

This chapter provides an overview of the impact of the financial and economic crisis on MENA (Middle East and North Africa) countries with a focus on employment and poverty in the region. For almost 20 years and up to the eve of the crisis MENA countries have been experiencing reasonable rates of growth that, however, have not been able to create sufficient number of jobs to the growing ranks of the labour force and the working age population. Neither has growth been able to reduce poverty in the region. Closer examination (using the 'growth–poverty nexus' analytical framework) of the relationship between growth, on the one hand, and employment creation and poverty reduction, on the other, shows that reliance on growth, necessary as it is, is far from sufficient to solve the problem of unemployment and poverty in the region. For the most part this can be explained by low growth elasticity of employment and inadequate social policy measures. I argue that the recent economic crisis will further aggravate the problems of unemployment and poverty in those countries in the region that have had strong labour and trade links with the international economy. The region will also be affected by the decline in capital flows to countries that rely heavily on foreign credit, aid and investment.

1. A HETEROGENEOUS REGION

In the first decade of the 21st century, and on the eve of the global financial crisis in 2008, most of the MENA countries had been experiencing an annual average GDP growth of about 5–6 per cent. This was well above the 3–4 per cent rates in the last decade of the 20th century (World Bank, 2009b). The sources of economic growth vary across countries, reflecting the heterogeneity of the region in terms of resource base and economic structure that in turn have important implications in the way each country will be affected by changes in the global financial and economic events.

The MENA region is comprised of a range of countries with diverse social and economic histories and resource bases. Following Richards and Waterbury (1990) a taxonomy of MENA countries is suggested that is based on the resources available in each country.

- Small countries that are mainly rich in oil: Libya, Kuwait, Oman, UAE, Bahrain and Qatar. These have very small markets and little resources to diversify their economies, notwithstanding the fact that Dubai in UAE has been successful in developing a vibrant *entrepot* and financial sectors and, more recently, a tourist industry. Immigrant labour from labour surplus and poorer countries of the region, as well as the Indian subcontinent and South East Asia, have been crucial to the development of these sectors in Dubai as well as the economy of this group of countries.
- The oil industrialising countries of Iran, Algeria, Saudi Arabia and Iraq that have substantial oil and gas reserves and other natural resources as well as sizable populations allowing the development of a large internal market and diversification of their economies. Iran and Algeria have been more successful industrialisers than other countries in this group though they still rely heavily on oil for their export earnings.
- The 'small' natural-resource-poor countries of Israel, Jordan, Syria and Tunisia that have been relatively successful in diversifying their economies through education and skill development and developing sizable tourism, services, financial and manufacturing sectors. The Lebanon could also fit in this group. The occupied Palestinian territory (OPT) has the potential to join this group once the Israeli invasion ends and a viable Palestinian state is established.
- The newly industrialising countries (NICs) of Turkey, Egypt and Morocco have either no oil (Turkey and Morocco) or a limited amount (Egypt) and have sizable populations and a reasonably strong agricultural sector with potential for future growth.
- The poorest countries rely mainly on agriculture and some oil export, as in the case of Sudan, or on agriculture and worker remittances who work in the oil rich countries of the region, as in the case of Yemen.

It has to be reiterated that the above taxonomy should not be treated as a map with clear demarcated boundaries, but as a general guide on the potential and constraints facing the MENA countries and how they can respond to the crisis. It should also be noted that because of strong linkages among MENA countries, through labour migration, trade and capital mobility, the impact of the crisis on individual countries may well be amplified.

2. THE GLOBAL FINANCIAL AND ECONOMIC CRISIS

In various degrees the MENA countries have been integrated in the international financial and economic structure for many decades. The pace of integration has increased in recent years and in response to the current phase of globalisation. This has exposed them to fall-outs from the recent financial and economic crisis. But the way in which the recent crisis is going to affect individual countries in the MENA region depends on their main economic and financial linkages with the world economy, as the 2009 collapse of the property market in Dubai has demonstrated.

In general the main channels of transmission of international financial and economic crisis are through trade in goods and services, finance (FDI and portfolio investment, foreign aid, and transfers such as remittances) and labour migration. One or more of these linkages, based on the taxonomy discussed earlier, dominate the relationship between MENA and the international economy. For example, Egypt as a labour-abundant country has strong links with the European labour markets and the labour-deficit countries in the MENA region through migration of Egyptian workers and remittances that are sent back, whilst at the same time it has a thriving tourism industry which is targeted at regional and international markets.

Trade Openness

The MENA is a fairly open region to international trade. On the basis of export and import to GDP ratios as measures of trade openness there is a high and varied degree of integration of MENA countries in the global economy. For the MENA (excluding Iraq) countries as a whole, export and import ratios in 2007 were 57 and 39 per cent, respectively. These figures are comparable with the openness of developing countries in the East Asian and Pacific region where export and import to GDP ratios are, respectively, 49 and 36 per cent, and in Sub-Saharan Africa where both ratios are 39 per cent. But MENA countries are much more open than the Latin American, the Caribbean (where these ratios are around 25 per cent) and South Asian countries (where these ratios are around 18 per cent). There are, however, variations in the degree of openness across the MENA region. In 2007 export to GDP ratios varied from a low of 26 per cent for the Lebanon to 99 per cent for UAE. Similarly import to GDP ratios varied from a low of 23 per cent for Kuwait to 91 per cent for Jordan (World Bank, 2009b). Similarly, the commodity composition of trade varies across MENA that in the case of the resource-rich countries is dominated by oil, whilst labour-intensive manufacturing, services and tourism dominate the trade of the resource-poor–labour-abundant countries (World Bank, 2009b). All in all the region is highly integrated with the world economy and has important international linkages; with all its potential and opportunities as well as vulnerabilities to international economic and business cycles, this is particularly true for the small open countries of the region.

Migration Flows

Migration flows in the MENA countries closely follow the pattern of available resources in each country. The resource-rich–labour-deficit countries of, for example, Emirates of the Persian Gulf are a magnet for immigrants from the resource-poor or labour-abundant countries in the region (such as Egypt) or from outside the regions (such as India and Pakistan). Egypt has the largest stock of out-migrants in the MENA region, that in 2005 was estimated to be 2.4 million (3.2 per cent of population), followed closely by Occupied Palestinian Territory (OPT) with 955 thousand emigrants, Jordan with 641 thousand and Lebanon with 622 thousand. However, a much larger proportion of the population of smaller countries emigrate; in 2005 that was 25 per cent for OPT, 11.2 per cent for Lebanon and 11.2 per cent for Jordan. The immigrant-receiving countries, on the other hand, have very high immigrant to population ratios that in 2005 ranged from 26 per cent for Saudi Arabia to a staggering 71 per cent for the UAE and 78 per cent for Qatar (Tzannatos, 2009). There is also a large flow of out-migration from the MENA region to European and north American countries as well as in-migration from outside the MENA region, predominantly from South Asian countries. However, at least half the migrants originating in the MENA countries moved within the region. All these flows are sensitive to international financial crises and economic cycles that drive labour demand and flow of capital in the region and around the world; flows that in turn are reflected in the flow of international remittances, capital and finance.

Financial Flows

Remittances and financial flows, especially FDI and capital flows, are the other major linkages within the MENA and between the MENA and the rest of the world. The MENA countries being one of the main sending and receiving regions of international migration account for a sizeable share of world remittances. In the 2005–09 period it was estimated that the MENA countries received 8.4 per cent of world inflow of remittances (Tzannatos,

2009). As a proportion of national income, the importance of remittances varies greatly across the region, for example in 2006 that for Jordan was estimated to be about 18 per cent and for Lebanon about 22 per cent, whilst the corresponding figure for Egypt was 5 per cent and for Yemen 6 per cent (World Bank, 2009b).

FDI is another major source of finance in the region that in terms of its impact on domestic capital formation and as a share of GDP is far more important, on average, for the resource-poor–labour-abundant countries than resource-rich–labour-deficit countries. In 2006 FDI as a share of gross fixed domestic capital formation for the resource-poor–labour-abundant countries was 42 per cent compared with 10–14 per cent for the resource-rich countries. As it would be expected the ratio of FDI to GDP is higher in the resource-poor countries. The other notable and expected flow of foreign investment in the region is that from resource-rich to resource-poor countries (World Bank, 2009b).

In general foreign investors are attracted to resource-poor–labour-abundant countries to take advantage of cheap labour in order to produce goods for domestic and foreign markets. This has also been confirmed by an analysis of the determinants of FDI to the MENA region between 1985 and 2008 revealing that human and natural-resource bases were more important drivers of the inflow than institutional factors such as promotion of the market forces, property rights or bilateral investment treaties (Mina, 2010).

This type of investment is much more sensitive to short term fluctuations in international markets than FDI that flows to resource-rich–labour-deficit countries that is motivated by the long-term profit of the extractive industries and investment in the manufacturing sector to produce goods for the domestic market of these countries. Given that in the short to medium run there exists a low price elasticity of demand for oil and other minerals and there is relative stability of domestic demand for home-produced goods in the resource-rich countries, FDI flows to these countries may well be more stable than those to the resource-poor–labour-abundant countries. These latter group of countries would experience an increase in unemployment as a result of a gradual decline in FDI.

The 2010 *World Investment Report* of UNCTAD showed that whilst all countries in the region experienced a decline in FDI inflow, the decline was smaller in large resource-rich countries such as Saudi Arabia compared with the small resource-rich countries like UEA (UNCTAD 2010c, Table E, p. 43).

3. THE IMPACT OF THE CRISIS ON MENA COUNTRIES

The region with its relatively open and well integrated economies has not been immune to the 2008 financial and economic crisis, but the impact will be gradual depending on the depth of global integration of various markets and the speed of transmission of the crisis from one market to another.

Given that the global financial markets are the most integrated of all markets it is not surprising that the stock markets in the MENA have been the first casualty of the global financial crisis. Even before the 2009 property crash in Dubai, the Dubai stock market registered one of the highest losses in the region by losing 70 per cent of its value from January to August of 2009 (Tzannatos, 2009, p. 25). It would take time for the stock market losses to work their way into the real economy in terms of loss of output, jobs, etc. This would critically depend on the links between the financial market and the real economy and the availability of liquidity for companies that are hit by global crisis. However, recent evidence on the financial markets in the Persian Gulf region suggests that the financial crisis has made the banks risk-averse, in particular those affected by the collapse in the real estate market and debt problems of Dubai, thus reducing the availability of credit in the region. A decline in sales and profits has also been reported by some leading manufacturers in Egypt (*Financial Times*, 2010).

The resource-rich MENA countries are far better positioned to ride the financial crisis by supporting their companies during the crisis. They run balance of payments surpluses and have substantial foreign exchange reserves (World Bank, 2009b, tables A.21–A.22) despite the occasional dips in the price of oil (that has stabilised since October 2009). Most also have a good international credit rating and can raise money on the international financial markets.

Once the crisis reaches the real economy, the transmission through the labour market will affect the resource-poor–labour-abundant countries which have been sending migrants to the labour-deficit countries of MENA. The labour market impact also affects migrants from the south Asian countries, who are already being laid off in their hundreds in the aftermath of the collapse of the construction industry and collapse of the property market in the Gulf region.

By all accounts remittances at best remain constant. Evidence so far suggests that despite rising unemployment in the labour-deficit MENA and in the immigrant-receiving European countries, some migrants from less developed countries stay put hoping for a quick recovery. The illegal immigrants are in a much precarious situation than the legal ones; the majority of illegal immigrants stay at a destination for quite some time because they cannot easily return once they leave. If migrants decide to ride the recession at their destination by digging into their savings, this would reduce their remittances home. Tzannatos (2009, p. 26) provides a review of available evidence and suggests that remittances are estimated to be declining. This worsens the balance of payments of most of the labour surplus countries which ran large current account deficits, that in the case of Jordan and the Lebanon in 2006 amounted to 13.5 and 16.7 per cent of GDP, respectively (World Bank, 2009b, table A.22). The balance of payments of the labour-sending countries would suffer further if families start sending money to support their unemployed migrant members wherever they are, as the evidence from Latin America reveals.

The way in which the above developments are going to affect the situation of the poor and vulnerable in the MENA countries would depend to a large extent on the policy space of the MENA governments to protect the poor through social policy measures and improved income-earning opportunities, with the latter being related to employment and job creation.

4. GROWTH, POVERTY AND INEQUALITY

The incidence of poverty and vulnerability among the population is very high in the MENA countries despite the region's wealth and good record of economic growth. MENA countries, on average, have experienced a steady annual real GDP growth in the range of 4–6 per cent for much of the past 20 years (Messkoub, 2009, Appendix Tables 1–2). These are respectable rates of growth that should have helped the countries in question to attend to some of the urgent needs of the population such as provision employment and alleviation of poverty. What is important to note is that all countries in the region, whether resource-rich–labour-importing or resource-poor–labour-abundant, have shared in the high growth era of the late 20th and early 21st centuries, in part because of the deep links between the two groups of countries. As will be demonstrated later, these countries achieved very modest gains in reducing poverty and increasing employment. With regard to other basic macroeconomic indicators, real per capita GDP in constant US dollar has also increased in all countries, with inflation being brought down from the double-digit figures of the early 1980s to a single digit by 2000.

In broad terms, the macroeconomic situation looks rather healthy. There is no runaway inflation in MENA countries, public finances seem to be under control, and under the guidance and pressure of international financial institutions and sections of the local elite, all countries have opened up (*Infitah*) their economies, in various degrees, to market forces at national and international levels. Given the increasing role of the private sector and integration of MENA countries in the world economy it would be useful to consider forces that shape this opening up. According to Richards and Waterbury (1990, p. 261)

> 'Infitah' should be seen as the outcome of three interacting set of forces: class actors, often fostered by earlier state-led growth policies; serious economic difficulties, generated both by state-led growth policies and by the international conjuncture; and pressure from international actors [that] does not mean that the public sector is about to be dismantled [nor] state ceding to 'civil society'. Rather than a retreat of the state, *infitah* is better conceived as a restructuring of state activity, always mediating between society and international actors, still responsible for the basic welfare of the population, and continuing to formulate the goals and strategy of economic development and structural change.

These developments have taken place against the background of structural transformation of MENA that has been under way for quite some time. Industry and service sectors have long replaced agriculture as the main source of contribution to GDP. By 2004 the share of agriculture in GDP in most countries under study had dropped to less than 20 per cent, except in Sudan (39 per cent) and Syria (23 per cent). But in most countries agriculture employs a sizable proportion of the labour force, ranging from 27 per cent in Egypt to 54 per cent in Yemen. In general the employment share of agriculture is larger than its GDP share (Messkoub, 2009, Appendix Table 6 and ILO, 2006).

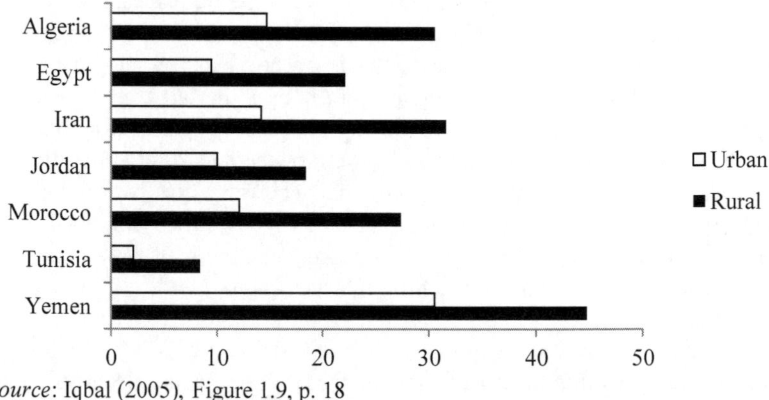

Source: Iqbal (2005), Figure 1.9, p. 18

Figure 11.1 Rural and urban poverty rate, selected MENA countries, 2000

The upshot of the above figures is that a large proportion of the population working in agriculture has to rely on a proportionately low share of GDP for its livelihood, and that would have implications for the incidence of poverty among the rural population. The data on poverty reveal that in most countries of the region poverty rates are higher in rural areas than in urban areas.

According to the national poverty lines in the MENA countries, 22 per cent of Algerians were considered to be poor in 1998. According to a similar indicator in Egypt, 16 per cent of population were poor in 2000. Corresponding figures in other countries were: 19 per cent in Morocco in 1999, 35.4 per cent in Yemen in 1998 and 7.6 per cent in Tunisia in 1995. In all countries a larger proportion of the poor were living in rural than in urban areas. In Tunisia, for example, four times as many poor were living in rural areas than in urban areas. In Morocco, more than twice as many poor were living in rural areas in 1999 than in urban areas (Figure 11.1). The scale of poverty in some of these countries increases dramatically if we use an international poverty line of the percentage of people below $2 a day, that in the case of Egypt in 2000 would be 43.9 per cent. The corresponding figure for Tunisia in 1995 is 12.7 per cent. But in other countries apparently there is not much of a gap between the national and international criteria, since the percentage of population who are poor does not change much when the international poverty line is used.

As far as Jordan is concerned, only studies that use the international poverty line are available. According to the $2 criterion, the proportion of the population who were poor in Jordan in 1997 was 7.4 per cent, but another source (ILO, 2006) reports a higher poverty rate of 21.3 per cent for 1997. The same source also reports a higher incidence of rural poverty compared with urban areas, as observed in other countries. Despite the difference in headcount poverty rates, both sources agree on the reduction in poverty – by 2002 Jordan experienced a 33 per cent drop in poverty rate.

An important aspect of the inter-relationship between poverty and employment in the developing world is the poverty of the employed people whose earnings are not sufficient to provide for their most basic needs of nutrition, sanitation and health (that is usually measured by an absolute poverty line of say $1 or $2 per day). The number of the working poor rises if we use the more appropriate measure of relative poverty (that takes account of distribution of income and expenditure as well as capability to participate in the society by having a voice in the running of ones' affairs). In this chapter the absolute poverty measures are used since the relative poverty measures that are country-specific are not available for all countries concerned.

In the developing countries any employment policy must take into account return to labour if it were to have a poverty reduction objective. Evidence on the working poor in MENA is quite striking. Among the MENA countries in the late 1990s, Egypt and Yemen had the highest share of the working population who were poor: 71.5 per cent in Egypt (1999 figure) and 73.7 per cent in Yemen (1998 figure). In the case of Yemen there was a doubling of the share of the working poor since 1995. The lowest percentage of the working poor belongs to Tunisia at 11.90 per cent in 2000 and Jordan at 12.8 per cent; and those figures were lower than the corresponding figures in the early 1990s. Morocco and Algeria, in contrast, recorded quite a high percentage of working poor – 23.5 per cent (in 1998) and 30.5 per cent (in 1995) respectively (Messkoub 2009, Appendix Table 3).

The poverty of the employed people could be due to many factors such as labour market conditions as well as low productivity and poor skills that in turn lead to low return to labour. An excess supply of labour often pushes wages down that in the absence of minimum wage regulation could lead to the poverty of the employed people. Where minimum wage regulation exists, it is often set at too low a level to prevent people falling below the poverty line. Low productivity could also result in low returns to labour that may well push the working people into poverty. This is often the case of the working poor who eke out a meagre living in the informal sector.

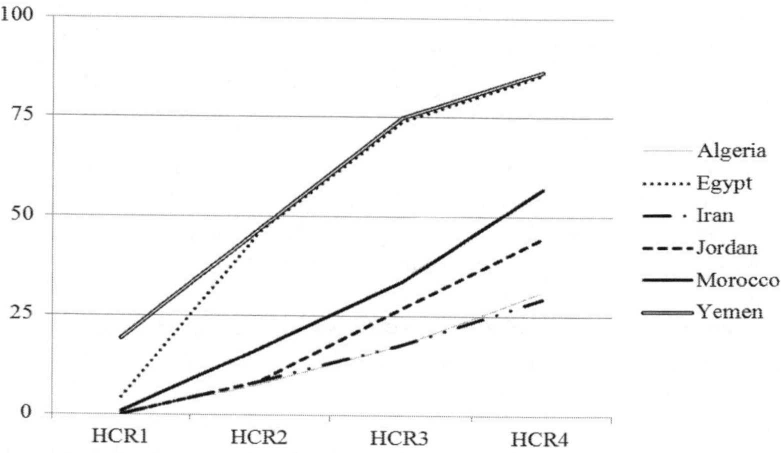

Source: Iqbal (2005), Figure 1.8, p. 13

Figure 11.2 Percentage poor at alternative poverty lines

An important aspect of measurement of poverty based on poverty line is the treatment of those who are just above the poverty line. These are the people who are vulnerable to poverty because any changes in the economy (e.g. increase in inflation that will have price and income effects) would push them below the poverty line. Any anti-poverty policy that is based solely on a poverty line and does not address the problem of vulnerability fails to address the structural causes of poverty that are related to distribution of assets, human capital and skills, ethnic/race/caste and gender discriminations.

To have a measure of vulnerability in the MENA region, let us look at the percentage of poor in population at different poverty lines of $1, $2, $3 and $4 (Figure 11.2). Sharp increases in the percentage of the poor can be observed as we move up from the $1 a day mark. The jump is most dramatic in the cases of Egypt and Yemen where the rates of poverty at $1 are respectively about 3 and 10 per cent that increases to about 42 per cent for both countries at $2. Further jumps in the percentage of the poor can be observed at $3 and $4 but the rate of increase declines. For the richer MENA countries the jump in the percentage of the poor is lower as we move up from $1 to $2 than it is for a move from $2 to $3 and from $3 to $4. In Jordan, for example, the percentage of the poor is below 5 per cent at $1 and goes up to about 5 per cent at $2, but then jumps to about 22 per cent at $3 and 42 per cent at $4.

Table 11.1 Poor in millions at alternative poverty lines, 1987, 2001

Poverty line	$2		$3	
	1987	2001	1987	2001
Algeria	2.3	5.1	6.4	11.2
Egypt	24.2	28.6	38.0	47.6
Iran	7.0	3.5	13.9	10.1
Jordan	0.1	0.3	0.3	1.1
Morocco	3.0	4.1	7.8	9.5
Tunisia	1.3	0.5	2.7	1.7
Yemen	2.2	9.5	4.4	14.1
Total	40.1	51.6	73.5	95.3

Source: Iqbal (2005), Table 1.5, p. 17

The difference in the rate of increase of poverty in the poor and rich group of countries is, in the first instance, due to differences in per capita income and a purely statistical one at that. In other words the high per capita income puts more people above the basic international poverty lines of $1–$4. The lower the per capita income in the country the sharper is the increase in the percentage of the poor as the poverty line is moved up. The MENA countries not only need anti-poverty policies to deal with the sizable number of the poor, they also need to have policies that would monitor and provide cover for the substantial number of people who are just above poverty, whatever the threshold, who could join the ranks of the poor with slightest shifts in the economy that would affect the poor. In Syria, for example, Islam (2005, p. 27) estimates that about 19 per cent are considered vulnerable and go through periods of poverty, that is almost double the percentage of the people who are poor – 11 per cent. In Egypt, in 2001, the number of the poor at $2 was 29 million that would jump to 48.6 million at $3. This vulnerable population of just under 20 million people should be taken into account in the design of pro-poor social policies in Egypt. At the MENA level, with the use of the higher threshold of poverty line – at $3 – the number of poor rises to 95 million, indicating that the vulnerable population at the lower poverty line of $2 is 43 million. Given that the vulnerable population in Egypt accounts for about half the vulnerable population in the MENA region, Egypt should have a strategic position in the regional poverty alleviation programmes of international organisations working in the region.

5. EMPLOYMENT AND LABOUR MARKETS IN MENA

Job creation and gainful employment is a major problem in the region, that will be affected by the impact of the financial crisis on the region. The high natural growth of population due to high past fertility and more recent population momentum in the region has ensured an increase in working age population and labour supply that has outstripped labour demand in all MENA countries. The labour force in the region has been growing at an annual rate of 3–4 per cent since the mid-1980s. The high population growth of the recent past also accounts for the young age structure of the population. At least 30 per cent of the population in the MENA countries are below the age of 15 – a critical challenge in the region is to increase labour demand in the public and private sector.

Unemployment has been a major problem in the region. In countries for which data are available the aggregate unemployment rate for males in 2003 varies between 7.3 per cent in Egypt to 23.4 per cent in Algeria. In between are Morocco with 11.5 per cent and Jordan with 14.7 per cent. The aggregate rates for females are in most cases higher than that for males, with the female unemployment rate in Algeria being 25.4 per cent, in Egypt 23.2 per cent, in Morocco 13.0 per cent and in Jordan 19.7 per cent. A similar picture emerges in Syria where female unemployment is slightly higher than male unemployment, with the largest gap being in the 20–24 age group (Islam, 2005, figure 2, p. 39). Since 1980 the trend in the male unemployment rate has been on the increase in Egypt and Jordan while that in Morocco has been relatively stable. Interestingly enough, female unemployment either has been relatively stable, as in the case of Egypt, or has had a moderate downward trend as in Algeria, Morocco and Jordan.

An important feature of unemployment in the region is a very high rate of youth (15–24 age group) unemployment. However, data are available for only a few countries. In Morocco youth unemployment rates are respectively 17.4 per cent for males and 15.9 per cent for females. In Jordan youth unemployment rates are respectively 28.0 per cent for males and 43.2 per cent for females (ILO, 2009c). ILO's country studies reveal that a large proportion of the young unemployed people are educated at least to secondary level. In some cases the higher the level of education the higher the unemployment rate. In Jordan the female unemployment rate has been highest for those with a bachelor degree (ILO, 2006, p. 3). In Egypt both males and females with 'intermediate' education had the highest rates of unemployment (El Laithy and El Ehwany, 2006, Appendix Table 9, p. 10).

Both supply and demand factors have been responsible for the rise in unemployment. On the supply side the rapid population growth of earlier periods has increased the size of the labour force, especially the young, and on the demand side, economic growth and job creation have fallen far behind the labour supply. An interesting feature of labour supply in the Arab MENA is the decline or stability of the male labour force participation rate (LFPR) in most countries, as against the rise, albeit modest, of the female LFPR. This is the pattern in Algeria, Morocco, Tunisia and Syria (see Messkoub 2009, Appendix Table 4) that poses an important question regarding the problem of female unemployment in these countries. Labour market and job creation policies in the MENA region rarely take note of such gender difference in unemployment rates.

On the demand side it is important to know growth of employment by sector in order to investigate whether sectoral distribution of employment has changed and whether a shift of labour from sectors with low productivity to those with higher productivity has been taking place that could, in turn, help in reducing poverty. As noted earlier there has been a sectoral shift away from agriculture, but the gain in employment in the industrial sector has been very modest in most MENA countries for which data is available. Within the industrial sector the manufacturing sector employment has had a very disappointing record notwithstanding the fact that female employment in manufacturing has gone up, albeit modestly in all the countries concerned. KILM (ILO, 2009c) provides data for the manufacturing employment in a few of the larger countries of the MENA region (Egypt, Iran, Morocco). In all of them, the share of manufacturing in total employment as well as the volume of employment in the manufacturing sector has been stagnant over the years. The data indicates that whatever productivity gain might have taken place in these countries, it has come about more from higher productivity within sectors than a shift from low to high productivity sectors.

The service sector, which has absorbed much of the increase in the labour force in the MENA region, is composed of a diverse range of activities – ranging from high-productivity and high-return sectors such as banking, insurance and finance at one extreme, to very low-productivity and low-return street vendors on the other. To investigate whether the service sector can or will be able to play a major role in poverty reduction we need to see which sub-sectors of the service sector have been growing and have the potential to provide high-productivity and high-wage jobs to the unemployed and under-employed labour force. The available data for the larger countries of MENA that have the most serious unemployment and poverty problems indicate that the high-productivity, high-return sectors are a very small sub-set of the growing service sector, and have also been growing very slowly. The trade and small-scale repair shops (motor vehicles as well as household goods) are the only sub-sectors that have been showing some sign of growth. A large proportion of this sub-sector could be considered informal with low productivity and low returns. However, it would be of interest to know the composition of this sector both in terms of products and skills as well as its linkages with other sectors in order to investigate its potential for productivity growth. Very little information is available on these aspects of the informal sector.

Finally, we should consider the labour demand of the public and private sector and its change over time. There is a large variation in the MENA region in the share of public sector employment in total employment. On the high end of the spectrum are Egypt (with a figure of 60 per cent in 1998) and Jordan (56 per cent in 1998), and on the low end are Algeria (25 per cent in 2004), Syria (26 per cent in 2003) and Yemen (11 per cent in the 2003). In all these countries the share of public sector employment has either been falling over the years or, at best, has been fairly stable (as is the case in Syria and Jordan). The mirror image of these figures is the private sector employment that would employ 89 per cent of the labour force in Yemen, at one extreme, and 40 per cent in Egypt, at the other. This raises very important questions with regard to the role of public and private sectors in creating good quality jobs in the future, in particular when one considers the pressures on the public sector finances. How to improve the capacity of the private sector to increase its supply of high quality jobs would depend on a range of factors: level of demand in the economy, government tax and subsidy policies, labour market rules and regulations, and complementarity between public sector investment (in particular in the areas of education and infrastructure) and private sector investment.

7. POLICY RESPONSES TO THE CRISIS

What can be done to reduce the impact of the crisis on the population? It depends on the fiscal capacity of the state and on the support policy of aid donor countries and international financial institutions (IFIs).

Almost all labour-abundant countries, whether resource-rich or not (Algeria being an exception), have had fiscal deficits since 2006 that by 2007 were expected to deteriorate, particularly in the resource-poor–labour-abundant countries. This raises the all important question of fiscal capacity of the state and the associated social policy space to alleviate the worst effects of the crisis on the population by increasing employment, maintaining access to basic consumption goods, maintaining social expenditure on health and education, and in general preventing poverty from increasing even further.

What states in the region can do to a large degree depends on the policy space that they have, and the way it is interpreted. Interestingly enough, the developed countries in general take a counter-cyclical approach during a downturn by adopting expansionary fiscal and monetary policies (as observed in the north American and in most EU countries) but in the developing countries it is often the opposite. The way fiscal and policy space is interpreted is at the heart of this difference.

An orthodox neoclassical interpretation of fiscal space as favoured by the IMF and other IFIs, is put in terms of 'the room in government's budget that allows it to provide resources for a desired purpose without jeopardising the sustainability of its financial position or the stability of the economy'. (Cavallo and Izquierdo, 2009, quoted in Islam, 2009). This approach usually focuses on the short-term stability of the economy, that could be at the expense of long-term development goals of increasing investment in infrastructure and meeting the basic needs of the population. An alternative interpretation of the fiscal space that is rooted in the structuralist/heterodox macroeconomics and associated with UNDP does not negate the importance of economic stability but focuses instead on the development objectives.

The fiscal and policy space then is as much about the priorities of the state and the economic and development model that it adopts. For example the orthodox approach recommends cuts in public expenditure during a financial crisis because tax and other revenues will be on the decline, whilst its expenditure remains static if not rising in the short to medium run. The alternative approach requires a shift in expenditure away from areas like defence and focuses on health, education, social protection and infrastructure. Countries that have the possibility of accumulating reserves during the boom could pay for their expenditure in the downturn (Islam, 2009). East Asian countries followed this path after the East Asian financial crisis of the 1990s.

The resource-rich countries of the MENA have sufficient reserves to cope with the crisis if they so choose. It is in this connection that social policy space should be added to the fiscal policy space. That is how fiscal policy space could be translated into social policy goals to ensure that social protection is provided on a universal basis for all, especially for the poor and vulnerable. This should be the short-run objective of any policy response to the impact of the crisis on the MENA countries. The resource-poor countries of the region have a more difficult task because of their budget and balance of payments deficit and having to cope with a larger proportion of their population being poor.

In the short run the resource-poor countries would certainly need support to stabilise their external balances, but without the orthodox conditions of cuts in public spending and in general pro-cyclical policies that would worsen the impact of the crisis. Of particular concern is the share of 'vulnerable employment' in total employment that in the MENA region has been put at 33 per cent in 2008 and is expected to increase to 39 per cent in 2009 according to the worst case scenario. The corresponding figures in North Africa are 37 and 42 per cent, respectively (Tzannatos, 2009). Maintaining social expenditure on food subsidies, education and health is not only important from a social and humanitarian point of view, but also from its contribution to demand in the economy.

At a more general level policies should be put in place to maintain employment. In the public sector investment in infrastructure would boost demand and have a counter-cyclical effect on the economy while increasing demand for labour in the short run. The private sector would also need support to maintain employment. In all financial crises the private sector will face cash flow problems as a result of general decline in economic activities and a credit crunch. Not only should the state step in to provide short-term finance, it could also help by giving tax holidays and help to reduce labour costs through social expenditure on health, nutrition and education.

Labour market policies in the region have taken a variety of forms: early retirement in Tunisia (to boost demand for labour and hiring of younger workers); support for small and medium-size enterprises in, for example, Egypt and Jordan; tackling youth unemployment through employment of graduates, the introduction and expansion of training programmes; job sharing as in Tunisia; measures to tackle child labour as in Egypt; and offers of cash transfers to families if they keep their children at school. In the medium to long run job creation and raising the income of the working poor as a policy to reduce poverty remains the main challenge facing the MENA countries. This is perhaps one of the most difficult areas of policy, not only in response to the crisis but also in general (for further details see Messkoub, 2008).

12. Crisis and Exclusionary Growth in Europe's 'East'

Max Spoor

This chapter investigates the structural origins and drivers behind the deep impact the global financial and economic crisis of 2008–2009 has had on the transition economies of Central and Eastern Europe, the Caucasus and Central Asia (EECCA). It argues that while high economic growth rates occurred since the recovery from the Russian financial crisis in 1998, growth has not been 'inclusive'. Growth (and development) is mostly based on specific sectors, such as hydrocarbons (Azerbaijan, Kazakhstan, Russia and Turkmenistan), construction and real estate, or dependency on foreign lending, migrant remittances and official development assistance (to the poorer countries). Only those countries which have managed to have a broad-based and more diversified growth model showed a much less negative impact of the crisis.[1]

The transition countries of the EECCA region have been hit harder than any other region in the world by the global recession (Jahan, 2009). Human development indicators, such as poverty, unemployment, public health and mortality were negatively affected. Economic recovery started in early 2010, but the lasting effects of the crisis on human development in the region might be long-lasting (Horvath et al., 2009). In fact, economic development and recovery during 'transition' has been accompanied by increasing inequality (income, assets and access to social services) and poverty levels. The latter rapidly diminished since the late 1990s, but the recent economic crisis has caused a severe set-back. The structure of the chapter is as follows. Section 1 provides an overview of the impact of the crisis, looking at GDP, but also at the Human Development Index and PPP Income/Capita development during the past two decades. Section 2 looks at the socialist legacy and its influence on the transition period, presenting a periodization in order to understand the development of the various growth and development models of the EECCA region. Section 3 is focused on the growing inequality in income, assets and access during transition, which contributes to the understanding of the severe impact of the recent global crisis. Section 4 provides an analysis of poverty. Poverty increased rapidly until the mid-1990s, reducing substantially since the late 1990s, in particular through the years of rapid growth in the following decade. However, the recent global crisis caused a stagnation in the decline of poverty rates. Section 5 analyzes the various growth models, and their specific characteristics in terms of wealth distribution and spatial concentration of growth. In the concluding section exclusionary growth is linked to the impact of the global financial and economic crisis in the various transition economies of the EECCA region.

1. IMPACT OF THE GLOBAL FINANCIAL AND ECONOMIC CRISIS

The socialist (Soviet and Yugoslav) legacy has had a substantial influence on these transition countries, but they also have developed into various directions, following distinct growth models and transition strategies (Cerami and Stubbs, 2010). Various development models have emerged (Cornia, 2009). Firstly, there are those countries that have managed to build, to strengthen and to consolidate a more broadly shared, diversified (and in part investment-led) economic growth model (such as the Czech Republic, Poland and Slovenia) which saw a relatively limited decline in their GDP growth (see Figure 12.1). In the second group are the countries that have experienced spectacular growth largely founded on a real estate boom and foreign lending (such as the Baltic States, Bulgaria, Moldova, Georgia and others). Mainly because of the credit squeeze and the drop in FDI that followed, and the bursting of the real estate bubble, these suffered much more. The third group, formed by those countries whose growth was based on the extraction and exports of primary commodities (Azerbaijan, Kazakhstan, Russia, Turkmenistan with hydro-carbons), was hit hard by the downfall of the (earlier skyrocketing) prices of oil, natural gas and metals in the world market. The fourth group consists of poorer countries that have been (and still are) dependent on migrant remittances and official development assistance. These were affected primarily by the sudden drop in remittances (such as from workers from the Caucasus and Central Asia in Russia, or from Moldova in Romania and the West) because migrants were the first to lose their jobs, although it seems that in the first quarter of 2010 remittances are growing again. Finally, there are some countries which have mixed sets of 'drivers of growth'. In summary, the drivers of growth in the EECCA region were different, in combination with varying initial conditions, transition strategies and structural features of these economies, and the impact of the crisis is therefore also not the same throughout the EECCA region (Figure 12.1).

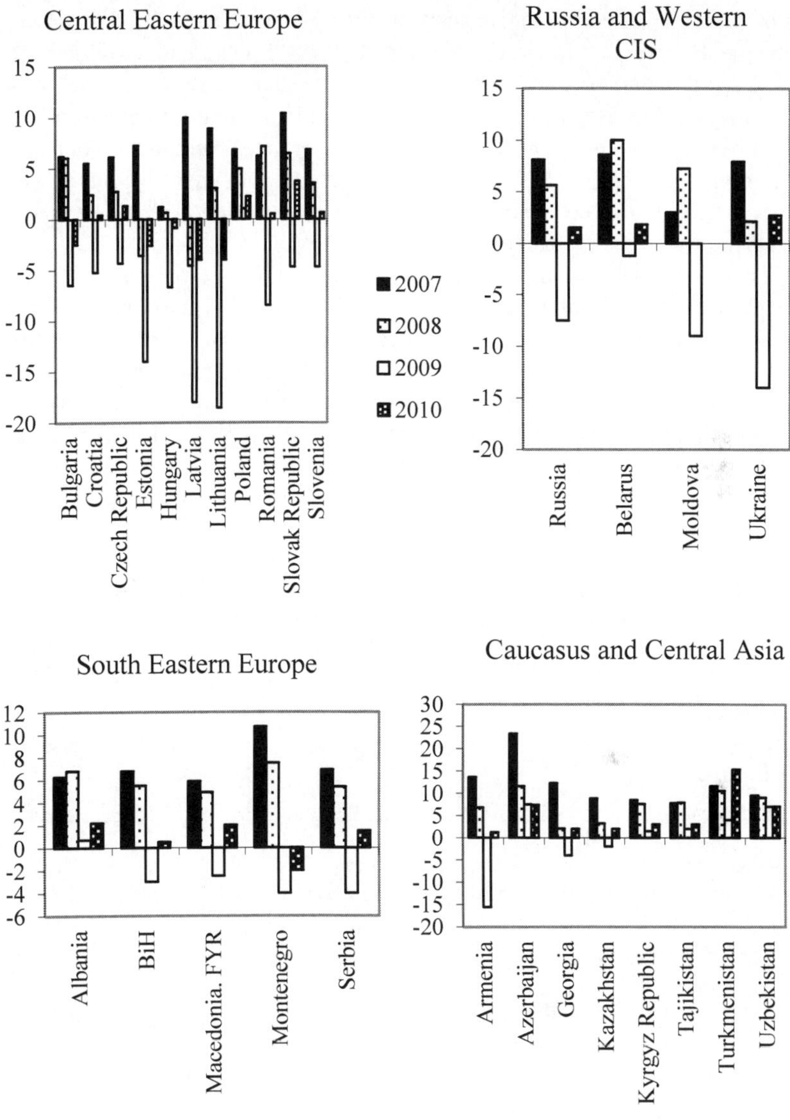

Source: IMF (2010)

Figure 12.1 Gross domestic product growth rates (2007–2010)

If we look further at the 'quality of growth', rather than only at growth rates (see UNDP, 1996), good or even impressive growth can also be 'jobless' and 'ruthless growth'. Growth can only be 'inclusive' when it is *with* poverty reduction (rather than seeing the latter as a 'trickle down' outcome of growth). In order to promote long-term human development, economic growth needs to be inclusive for the vulnerable and poor sections of society. It also needs to be sustainable, in particular reduce inequalities in the sphere of income, non-income (access to services) and assets, but also become more 'green'. Most of the growth and development models of the EECCA transition countries have, however, been shown to be more 'exclusionary' than 'inclusive'.

There is probably no historical comparison for the gigantic impact the fall of the Berlin Wall and the collapse of the Soviet Union had on the livelihoods of its inhabitants, in such a short time-span. Since the 1990s human development is measured by a combination of indicators. The well-known HDI index measures a weighted composition of GDP/Capita (in PPP$), school enrolment and adult literacy, and finally life expectancy. If we compare the movement of the transition countries in the EECCA region during the period 1990–2007, we can see some violent swings (see Table 12.1).

Table 12.1 Shifts in HDI ranking of transition countries in the EECCA region (1990–2007)

	1990	1993	1995	1998	2001	2004	2007
Very High							2
High	14	6	5	6	10	12	17
Medium	6	14	20	19	16	14	9
Total	20	20	25	25	26	26	26

Notes: Increased number is caused by split-up of FYR. Only for 2007 is there a new category of 'very high human development', i.e. with HDI>=0.900

Source: www.undp.org

While in 1990 the estimates for the transition economies in the EECCA region and their predecessors were that 14 were in the High Human Development category and 6 in the Medium Human Development one, during the dramatic initial transition years (whether post-1989 for Central and Eastern Europe or post-1991 for the Former Soviet Union) this relation reversed. By 1995, with the inclusion of the heirs of the Former Yugoslav Republic (FYR) 20 (versus 5) were in the latter group. Furthermore, the HDI ranking was at its worst. In 1990 the highest and lowest ranking ranged from

26 (Czechoslovakia) to 88 (Tajikistan), while in 1995 this had changed from 37 (Slovenia) to 118.

Hence the HDI spread (the highest minus the lowest rank) had risen, and would rise even more during the years of economic recovery and rapid growth. In 2007, the last year before the global economic and financial crisis, the highest position was 29 (Slovenia) and the lowest was 127 (Tajikistan). While with the current global economic crisis HDI indicators have been negatively influenced all over the globe, the EECCA region has most likely suffered more, which will negatively influence HDI indicators in the short and long run (see Horvath et al., 2009). We can observe a process of initial (inter-group) spatial differentiation and worsening between-country income distribution, which seem to have occurred until the late 1990s, where after that a trend of relative convergence is visible.

2. LEGACY AND INITIAL CONDITIONS OF TRANSITION

Transition economies of the EECCA region form a geographically highly diverse region, although in terms of legacies of its socialist past, it is still appropriate to group it together. Nevertheless, differentiation since 1989 has increased, in part due to the regional split into EU-members, countries in process of accession, and non-members (in particular in the CIS). The main 'phases' of crisis, recovery and growth (culminating recently again with a crisis) were the following:

- From 1989/1991 to the early/mid 1990s: severe economic crisis and system disintegration (in which most of the Central European countries had a relatively mild crisis and furthermore recovered growth fairly rapidly, while the Baltic states saw a deep economic downturn). Poverty emerged as a serious problem, and inequality grew.
- The Commonwealth of Independent States (CIS), with the heirs of the former Soviet Union (FSU) as members, saw a deep economic crisis affecting their economies. For some this meant that within the time-span of a few years GDP dropped to well less than 50 per cent of the pre-transition level.
- From the mid-1990s to the late 1990s: economic recovery and positive growth, interrupted by the Russian crisis of 1998, which influenced a short downturn for most of the CIS and the Baltic states, but left Central Eastern Europe largely untouched.
- From the late 1990s to 2007: rapid economic growth, with a strong reduction of poverty rates, albeit with huge spatial inequalities

remaining or even sharpening. This growth lasted until the current global crisis also reached the EECCA region.

- Since mid/late 2008 to 2010, a deep economic recession, with substantial differences for the various individual countries and country groupings, in depth and impact, but overall hitting the EECCA region harder than any other group of countries.

The sub-regional division also takes into account the pre-accession and accession of those that joined the EU in 2004 and 2007 and those who are on its doorstep. Accession to the EU the initial conditions and different strategies of economic growth and recovery have contributed to a much larger differentiation than there was already at the time of 'Die Wende' (1989) or the dissolution of the USSR (1991). Hence, in comparing inequality and poverty, intra-regional comparisons need to be done with the utmost care, in spite of the region's common past and clear signs of common legacies.

The impact of the economic crisis in the early transition process has been practically unparalleled in economic history except for countries that went through violent war periods and social upheaval, in part also occurring in the EECCA region. Again, this impact was not the same across these transition countries. This differential impact is generally explained by a complex set of factors. Firstly, the initial conditions were quite different (Swinnen and Rozelle, 2006). On one end of the spectrum were the relatively well developed Central European economies, which were already partially integrated in the larger European economy, and showing living standards that were within the category of High Human Development. On the other end were the much poorer economies of Central Asia, in particular the Kyrgyz Republic, Tajikistan and Uzbekistan. Secondly, in the Central European countries, where transition had started in 1989, the economic impact has been relatively short-lived and positive growth rates have been realized from 1992–1993 onwards. Thirdly, with the break-out of war in 1992 in former Yugoslavia, in which only Slovenia (and to a lesser extend FYR of Macedonia) was left untouched, the Balkan region was dramatically affected, and the GDP of various of the heirs of the FYR dropped to less than half in the space of a few years. Fourthly, the collapse of the Soviet Union caused a tidal wave of shocks throughout the 15 newly independent states of the FSU.

In particular the smaller peripheral countries of the FSU were hit hardest, as they lost the transfers of the All-Union budget, hardly had any competitive industries, and imported the effects of rampant Russian Ruble inflation of the early 1990s. Those with natural resources that could be exported in hard currency (hydrocarbons, precious metals and cotton) had a buffer to recover, while others resumed economic growth after re-distributive land reforms (such as Albania, Armenia and the Kyrgyz Republic). Some countries or regions in the FSU were doubly hit by domestic and/or external violent conflicts, which led to the destruction of infrastructure and social disruption (refugees and IDPs), such as in Moldova, the Caucasus (Armenia, Azerbaijan and Georgia), Russia (Chechnya) and Central Asia (Tajikistan). Furthermore, there were differences in the implementation of transition and economic reform strategies ('shock', 'gradualist' and mixed forms, but also the overall direction of the society to which it moved), in pace and in sequencing, while the diversity of political transformations was possibly even larger, if one focuses for example on the indicator of democratic governance. In the end this has meant that by the year 2000, some countries had already reached the levels of 1989, while others were still suffering from the disastrous economic contraction during the 1990s.

Most countries, with some exceptions, have indeed shown positive growth rates since 1996, such as Russia (with a formidable financial crisis in 1998), Ukraine (ending consecutive negative growth only in 1999), Moldova (heavily impacted by the Russian crisis, as some of the Baltic states were), and parts of the FYR, mainly because of the Kosovo crisis and NATO's intervention in Serbia. Some Central European economies, such as Poland, already resumed positive growth in the early 1990s. Finally, various groups of countries emerged with comparable development models, with comparative clusters of particular indicators rather than their specific geographical position in the region (Cornia, 2009; *Oxford Analytica*, 2009).

3. INCOME INEQUALITY ON THE RISE

In the first stages of transition, a rapidly worsening income distribution was making the economic crisis even more problematic. From countries in which wage labour had been for long the predominant source of income, with the closing down of factories and overall loss of employment, an income distribution emerged which – in some cases – was comparable with highly unequal Latin American economies. Later on a more sharp division between skilled and un-skilled labour was introduced, and social networks became more important in black and grey markets. Overall there was a transformation of wage labour towards self-employment and informalization of labour, and the increase in capital income. Large-scale privatization programmes, accompanied by policies that made it relatively easy to 'capture' or pillage state resources in industrial and extractive sectors, also caused a highly unequal distribution of assets, one of the causes of social exclusion. The consequence was that there were large groups of employees who became 'lost in transition'. They did not have the skills to adapt to the new markets, and rapidly became the long-term unemployed, sliding gradually into inactivity, and social exclusion. While the ‘cradle to grave’ type of long-term guaranteed employment and ‘workfare’ social services were the foundations of the socialist system, these fell away in the transition. Hence, exclusion from the labour market became the primary vehicle for the occurrence of poverty and social exclusion in the transition period.[2] In a UNDP household survey (November/December 2009), which was done in Kazakhstan, Moldova, FYR Macedonia, Serbia, Tajikistan and Ukraine, a relatively large section of the sample turned to be inactive, and relatively low numbers of employed (lower than the official statistics) were observed.[3]

Countervailing processes were the privatization of housing and small businesses, and also the individualization of agricultural land (such as through a re-distributive land reform in some of the EU-accession countries, and in Albania, Armenia, Georgia, and later Moldova and Azerbaijan (Wegren, 1998; Lerman, 2007; Spoor, 2009). Nevertheless, in spite of these forms of legal empowerment and massive forms of asset distribution, in most transition countries – in only a few years – large groups of ‘have-nots’ emerged (including a rather large group of poor), and fairly tiny groups of ‘haves’, including the ultra rich, or the oligarchs (Milanovic, 1998). A highly unequalizing process of societal transformation took place. While average real incomes dropped dramatically and high inflation rates were discriminatory against wage earners and the real value of transfers such as pensions, income distributions transformed from relatively equal ones to very unequal ones.

However, the passive mentality that was created during the socialist system, in which orders came from above and little initiative was expected and rewarded on the work floor, combined with the already existing ‘hidden’ inequalities in access to commodity distribution, also contributed to exclusionary processes during the painful transition that followed ‘Die Wende’. Income inequality rose dramatically during the transition period, although there were indications that income inequality, as measured by the Gini coefficient, has been leveling off since 2000, except for a few cases.

Income (or expenditure) distribution measured by the Gini coefficient is complex as more than often the data from LSMS or HBS surveys are not completely comparable (because of differences in methodology), which explains that there are substantial variations between different sources. The data available from the ‘Life in Transition Survey’ or LiTS (EBRD, 2007) can also be used for the calculation of the Gini coefficient per country (and for the spatial differentiation between metropolitan, rural and other urban areas). In this case the data provided expenditure for the past 30 days before the survey date. We did recalculate all the Gini coefficients for the extensive database of the LiTS survey, and the outcome is that inequality was higher (on average between 5 to 10 per centage points), than is generally known from the World Bank Development Indicators (also used by the TRANSMONEE database of UNICEF). Some of the most unequal countries are: Armenia, Azerbaijan, Georgia, Moldova, Kazakhstan, Estonia, Latvia and Lithuania. However, in the LiTS data also Belarus, Romania and Ukraine belong to the most unequal group of countries (because of the substantial influence of the in-between sector and spatial inequality in these countries with large rural populations).

Did income inequality go up again as a consequence of global crisis? On the one hand there was a sudden increase in unemployment which had a substantial impact on the incomes of households. However, on the other hand, those with (some) capital income have suffered more in relative terms, which contributed to the lowering of income inequality. In the mentioned recent survey by UNDP, for most of the countries that were surveyed, namely Macedonia, Moldova, Kazakhstan, Serbia, Tajikistan and Ukraine, these Gini coefficients were confirmed.[4] Indeed, in Serbia and Ukraine there is moderate inequality, while the other four (with Moldova at the top of the list) belong to the high-inequality category.

4. POVERTY IN TRANSITION ECONOMIES

Poverty has increased rapidly in the transition countries of the EECCA region, in particular in three sub-regions: (1) Central Asia and the Caucasus; (2) Western CIS (in particular Moldova, Russia and Ukraine); (3) the heirs of the FYR, specifically those affected by the war. Inter-regional income differences were already substantial at the eve of transition, but the emergence of poverty at this scale was rather unexpected (Milanovic 1998; UNDP, 1999; World Bank 2005).

Although reported only in the late 1990s, on the basis of surveys of the period 1993–1995 it was estimated that while before transition (1989) the total number of poor in Eastern Europe and Central Asia was around 14 million, by the mid-1990s this number was more than 10-fold, namely 147 million (Milanovic, 1998). More recent data until 2005 from the World Bank, based on more recently adjusted GDP/Capita figures (1.25, 2.15 and 4.30 PPP$), show lower absolute numbers, although the phenomenon is nonetheless severe (World Bank PovCal Database).

The highest poverty headcount ratio, if we take the poverty line of 2.15 PPP$/Day as a threshold, were found at the end of the 1990s in the following areas and countries. For 1999, firstly, in the EU-10 group, the headcount in Romania was 16.7 per cent, by far the highest in this group which for the rest had relatively low headcount ratios. In the Western CIS, the largest concentration in numbers was in Russia and Ukraine, with poverty headcount ratios of respectively 12.4 and 16.7 per cent. Moldova was the poorest country in that sub-region, with 76.7 per cent of the population below this poverty line. In the sub-region of the Caucasus, the headcount was 43.1 per cent in Armenia, 41.6 per cent in Azerbaijan and 26.0 per cent in Georgia, while in Central Asia there was 16.6 per cent for Kazakhstan, which had a much higher income/capita, and respectively 46.2, 82.0, 53.4 and 63.3 per cent for the Kyrgyz Republic, Tajikistan, Turkmenistan and Uzbekistan. However, by 2005 the headcount poverty rates, again measured with a poverty line of 2.15$ had dropped substantially (World Bank PovCal Database), in particular Moldova (Weeks et al., 2005) and in Azerbaijan.

The most recent data of the World Bank (2010e) now also include the impact of the global economic crisis of 2008–2009. These have been far-reaching in terms of a severe regression in poverty reduction. It has been estimated that while in 2007 it was still expected (taken the very high growth rates) that there would be a continued reduction of poverty until 2010. Actually, using the revised 5.0 PPP$ per day poverty line, the headcount was to be reduced from 160.0 million in 2007 to 119.3 million in 2010. However, the economic crisis changed the scene, and poverty increased again after an initial reduction in 2008 (148.8 million), to a level of 158.7 million in 2009. The expected figure for 2010 is now 153.6 million, which is 34.3 million higher than the pre-crisis estimate (World Bank, 2010e).

Although there are several weaknesses in the data, the overall trend is dramatic during most of the 1990s and was quite positive during the 2000s, in particular caused by very high growth rates since the year 2000 until the entry of the global crisis in the EECCA region. Relative poverty per country is still wide spread, also in those sub-regions (EU-10 and SEE) where hardly any absolute poverty can be observed (as measured by the 2.15 PPP$/day threshold). In particular socially excluded groups, such as refugees and internally displaced persons (IDPs), and certain ethnic minorities (such as the Roma), are generally amongst the relative poor in those countries.

5. EXCLUSIONARY GROWTH MODELS

There is substantial ‘spatial’ inequality in the EECCA countries (and between them), with also regional ‘pockets’ of poverty. This is partly explained by the highly differentiated ‘drivers of growth’, but furthermore by initial conditions, policies and emerging institutions. Here we will concentrate on the ‘exclusionary’ characteristics of certain growth and development models that can be distinguished in the EECCA region. The drivers of economic growth have been very different in several of these transition countries.

Overall we can distinguish more broad-based growth versus unbalanced (spatially and sectorally) growth or 'growth pole'-based. Most of the CIS countries fall in the latter category, while in the EU-10 and SEE transition countries some fall in the former. The growth models can also be distinguished between more open systems (such as the Baltic states) at one side of the spectrum, and semi-closed, with import substitution as a basis (such as Turkmenistan and Uzbekistan) at the other side, in line with Cornia (2009). There are 'shades of grey', with more importance for the role of investment on the one hand, and consumer-led growth on the other. In the transition economies, over the past two decades, there are a number of clear 'drivers' of growth. In order to analyze these more clearly these 'driving' sectors are distinguished.

Extractive Industry and Mining

The hydrocarbon sector in a number of EECCA countries has successfully emerged as a motor of growth in countries such as Azerbaijan, Kazakhstan, Russia and Turkmenistan, often driven by the influx of FDI. However, job creation is minimal, and employment is mostly limited to skilled (or even specialized) labour.

Manufacturing Industry and Services (including SMEs)

For many of the EECCA transition countries the legacy of the socialist past was that employment was primarily in the large industrial state enterprises (with labour hoarding as phenomenon). Little experience existed in the private SME sector, except for those countries where it was present before the transition started, such as in parts of Central Europe. As this driver of growth represents much more labour-intensive production and job growth, less social exclusion is expected to take place through the labour market (such as in some EU-10 countries). Industrial jobs have also been filled with migrant labour.

Agriculture with a Main Cash Crop

In somc of the Central Asian states 'cotton is king', in particular – in order of importance – Uzbekistan, Turkmenistan and Tajikistan, as the crop represents a very important part of exports, and has given rise to the implementation of an import substitution regime in Uzbekistan that financed the development of other industrial sectors and in particular the energy (natural gas) sector (Cornia et al., 2003). Unfortunately, while agriculture-led growth (such as in parts of Central Asia) is normally pro-poor growth, the agricultural sector also houses most of the 'poor jobs', and poverty is more wide spread in rural than in urban areas in countries with a large rural (and agriculture-dependent) population.

Service Sector, Construction and Real Estate

There are many examples in the EECCA region where the rapid growth the past decade was largely due to the development of the service sector (IT in the case of the Baltic states) and the construction sector that boomed with the speculative developments in real estate (in the Baltic states, but also in Central Europe, Bulgaria, Armenia and Georgia), often based on foreign lending. The construction and service sectors were the ones that grew in terms of employment during the 2000s, but are also the ones which show the largest decrease in the current recession.

Migrant Remittances

Remittances of migrants have been a driver of growth. Migration was driven by 'distress push' and 'demand pull' factors. The former originates in poverty, vulnerability and social exclusion, while the latter arises from and is influenced by opportunities in emerging local industries, booming urban economies and demand for labour originating in foreign countries. Remittances very often have a cushioning role in poverty, but migration has also strong social exclusion effects, as family structures are disrupted and migrants are discriminated in the 'receiving' country. Another 'driving' aspect of migration is that migrants fill spaces in labour markets in the receiving countries, because of ageing societies and jobs that are simply not done by the existing labour force. The Russian Federation, Ukraine and Belarus received many migrants from the Caucasus and Central Asia, facilitating this with simplified visa requirements.

Official Development Assistance

Some of the poorest economies have received large amounts of ODA (such as Georgia, Moldova, Kyrgyz Republic and Tajikistan), and this continues to be the case. These economies have also been the recipients of large amounts of remittances. As a number of the EECCA transition countries (even including some of the later EU members) were initially at or fell below the OECD/DAC average income criterion to receive ODA, since the early 1990s official development assistance became important in this region, and turned into an important driver of economic growth for some of the low income countries in the region.

Illegal Activities and Shadow Economy

In various EECCA transition economies the illegal (or shadow) economy is still substantial in size, which weakens the revenue side of the government budget, as tax evasion is inherent in this part of the economy. Illicit activities such as smuggling, human and organ trafficking, drug and arms trade are widespread, with money laundering through the real estate sector. These activities have contributed to the ('virtual') growth of economies, and will need to be tackled to achieve more stable and sustainable growth patterns and income distribution.

The quality of growth has been relatively poor in the countries where this form of highly unbalanced growth took place and in which economic growth rates were not at par with employment growth. Possibly with high growth rates in most of this decade there was no urgency for change, but the current crisis has been hitting 'The East' particularly hard in those cases, giving rise to opportunities to transform into a more sustainable and equitable mode of growth (Ivanov, 2009).

The weaknesses of the growth models, in particular the unbalanced drivers of growth, were amplified by the rapid increase of Euro-nominated debt in several EECCA transition countries, such as the Baltic states (Kattel, 2009). In part this was lending for productive purposes, but in a larger part it represented 'easy money' which financed the ballooning real estate boom (Åslund, 2009). When the crisis struck the financial sector, in particular with the fall of the Lehman Brothers, western banks withdrew capital and stopped further credit lines, which necessitated many countries (but in particular the Baltic states, Hungary, Romania and Ukraine) to ask the IMF for financial bail-out. Contagion had brought the financial crisis to the East. However, a number of EECCA countries were much less affected, although suffering from reductions in foreign direct investment and contractions of their exports.

6. CONCLUSION

The global financial and economic crisis of 2008–2009 has had a severe impact on the national income growth of many transition countries in the EECCA region; worse than any other region of the world. Poverty is more or less at the same level than before the crisis (measured at 5.00 PPP$/day), but this would hide the fact that around 30–40 million people remained poor (or vulnerable to extreme poverty), rather than moving out of poverty, if compared with the trend of the pre-2008 years of the decade. In this chapter, the severity of the crisis impact has been analytically linked with the quality of growth, differentiating between more broad-based and diversified drivers of growth (or growth models) and more exclusionary, specific sector-driven or growth-pole/capital city-driven growth, and its dependency on domestic or external financial sources which influence its sustainability and vulnerability towards external shocks (such as the financial contagion of the current crisis). The impact of the global crisis might lead to a rethinking of the growth models and development models, although there is a danger that few or no lessons will be drawn from the recent past, and similar directions will be taken in the near future. Nevertheless, the restrictions on external lending and the limited fiscal space could provide strong incentives to profoundly reconsider the growth models used until now. It seems that at the moment the oil (and gas)-driven economies are rapidly resuming high growth rates, as oil prices remain high, but that they also use part of their accumulated sovereign funds to invest in the sectors that have lagged behind. This might be a first sign of more fundamental change, 'beyond transition'.

NOTES

1 Although this is outside the scope of this chapter, part of the impact can also be explained by the strength and weakness of the social security system. This chapter, which was part of a paper written for the Regional Human Development Report 2010, focuses only on the 'drivers of growth'.

2 Of course, the new labour markets also became the 'home' of new opportunities, but requiring new skills which many, in particular in the middle-aged groups, did not have, or they had other skills (for example in industry) which were not in demand.

3 Data obtained in the November 2009 RHDR survey.

4 Data obtained from the November 2009 NHDR household survey in these countries.

13. The Crisis in South Asia: From Jobless Growth to Jobless Slump?

Karin Astrid Siegmann

This chapter explores the impact of the global financial crisis on South Asia in terms of qualitative and quantitative aspects of employment. South Asia hosts a quarter of the world's population and a fifth of the global workforce – as well as 40 per cent of the global poor (World Bank 2010d). One contribution is the assessment of the current crisis on the livelihoods of inhabitants of one of the poorest regions in the world. The chapter also provides more general insights about how volatilities in globally integrated markets translate into opportunities for decent work – or the lack thereof.

The past two decades were characterized by a quantum leap in South Asia's integration into the world economy. While the region is less open compared to, for example, East Asia, even the South Asian economies with a large domestic market, such as India, Pakistan and Bangladesh are characterized by significant export orientation. This has contributed to rising rates of economic growth, peaking at 7 per cent in the years before the crisis. However, the growth experience since the 1990s was not matched by proportional employment gains as the trend was away from large enterprises and stable workforces towards flexible production processes associated with precarious employment patterns and pay (MHHDC 2004, p. 122). The inability to provide productive employment to the majority of South Asians caused declining employment-to-population ratios, particularly in India and Bangladesh (World Bank 2010d). This largely jobless growth lowered labour standards in the formal economy and increased the vulnerability of the 90 per cent informally employed (MHHDC 2004, p. 122f). Real wages in South Asia have grown at a much slower pace than labour productivity during the past two decades (MHHDC 2004, p. 48; Ghosh 2008, p. 16f). In 2007, 80 per cent of South Asia's workforce belonged to the category of working poor, generating daily earnings of less than $2 (ILO 2009a, p. 19).

The greater integration into global markets, especially the considerable degree of export-orientation of economies across the region as well as India's connectivity to global financial markets, also increased South Asia's vulnerability to the global financial crisis since September 2008. Stiglitz (2009a, p. 2) distinguishes three main channels through which the crisis was transmitted from the US to the rest of the world. Firstly, the direct transmission took place through financial markets: foreign direct investment (FDI) inflows to the region shrank by more than a fifth between 2008 and 2009 (World Bank 2010d). Secondly, transmission occurred through the fall in trade from October 2008 (see Figure 1.1 on page 9). Given the specialization in labour-intensive manufacturing in the global South, this drop in demand hit producers in developing countries hard. The most dramatic dips occurred in Bangladesh and India. Furthermore, the movement of international labour migrants matters. While aggregate remittances to South Asia increased between 2008 and 2009 for reasons to be discussed below, the crisis heightened the obstacles for labour migrants' international movements.

In the macro-economic analysis of the crisis in South Asia, employment has often remained a footnote. Even contributions that directly focus on poverty impacts of the crisis often ignore that labour markets are the main channels that translate macro shocks into poverty outcomes (e.g. McCulloch and Sumner 2009b). So it is important to investigate how the crisis impacts on opportunities for productive employment under decent working conditions in South Asia. Section 1 provides a patchwork of survey data, published and grey literature as well as media reports for the largest South Asian economies (Bangladesh, India, Pakistan and Sri Lanka) in order to investigate how trade with, financial markets in and labour migration from the region work out in labour markets. In Section 2, regional patterns regarding employment and workers' social security are discussed, with special attention being given to gender dimensions. The discussion leads to answers to how to strengthen workers' resilience against volatilities of a globalized economy in Section 3.

1. IMPACT ON SOUTH ASIA'S LABOUR MARKETS

Given the considerable degree of export-orientation of South Asian economies at the onset of the crisis and its dramatic decline during 2009 resulting from it, the transmission of the global crisis via the drop in export demand from industrialized countries had the most significant impact on employment and decent work in South Asia.

1.1 Transmission through Exports

In Bangladesh, export growth decelerated steadily from 42.5 per cent (2008 Q3) to –11.7 per cent (2009 Q3) (Rahman et al. 2010, p. 4). This was chiefly due to weak foreign demand for garments, the dominant item (80 per cent in 2009, Ahmed and Mujeri 2009, p. 6) in Bangladesh's export basket. Some 90 per cent thereof was shipped to the US and the EU (Rahman et al. 2009, p. 14). While the employment of the more than two million workers in the garment sector was largely sustained, a number of entrepreneurs adopted cost-cutting measures that ranged from increasing working hours, reducing fringe benefits and utilizing the firm's capacity, to shutting down. While owners reported that fresh recruitments slowed down significantly since mid-2008, the Bangladesh Garments Manufacturers and Exporters Association claimed that up to 30,000 workers faced job losses since 2009 Q3 (Rahman et al. 2010, p. 18ff). Hossain (2009, p. 61) perceived a shift of employment from formal to informal units since 2008 Q4. These smaller units are described as sweatshops that do not comply with legal labour standards, in which managers misbehave with workers, beat and abuse them and in which there is no job security. Besides, 12 out of 341 spinning mills shut down and most of the other mills reduced their level of operation by about 30 per cent. As a result, many workers lost their jobs (Rahman et al. 2009, p. 22).

All other major export items, such as frozen food, jute goods and leather, were affected by a slowdown and partially negative growth in external sales between mid-2008 and mid-2009 (Ahmed and Mujeri 2009, p. 6). In jute enterprises producing hessian, the sluggish trend was due to a drop in demand from the construction sector. During the second half of 2008, 10–20,000 seasonal workers were dismissed from jute mills as a result. The loss of jobs may have reached 50,000 by mid-2009. The informal nature of their contracts possibly implied that they would not be targeted under any support programme (Rahman et al. 2009, p. 21ff). Ahmed and Mujeri (2009, p. 11) speculate that the contraction of the shrimp sector that employs one million people (the majority are women) could lead to job losses in large numbers for female unskilled workers, who have very limited employment opportunities.

Economies with larger domestic markets, such as India and Pakistan, were less susceptible to the decrease in export demand that hit the region in 2009. The argument was even put forward that India's robust growth trajectory since the 1990s was decoupled from international developments and hence shielded from the crisis. The developments since 2008 proved this assumption wrong (Ghosh and Chandrasekhar 2009). The OECD countries were the destination of 42 per cent of India's merchandise exports and nearly its entire services export in 2008 and the slowdown in OECD growth constituted the most important factor constraining India's exports.

Merchandise exports in 2008Q4 were more than 10 per cent lower *vis-à-vis* 2007Q4 (Ghosh and Chandrasekhar 2009, p. 728). Since October 2008, key export sectors (automotives, gems, jewellery and textiles) experienced significant declines in sales (Department of Commerce 2010).

By early 2009, the adverse employment effects of this decline were evident. The reduction in sales abroad was associated with increasing reports of Indian manufacturing companies adopting reductions in the number of working days. UNCTAD India (2009, p. 38f) simulated the employment effects of the economic crisis. While predicted employment growth was positive for all sectors in 2010–11, with a net loss of about 750,000 jobs, the simulated employment change was negative for 2009–10. According to UNCTAD, in 2008–09 and 2009–10, the most negatively affected sectors were ores and minerals (814,000), textiles and clothing (T&C) (813,000) and gems and jewellery (722,000). (On the latter, see Chapter 14 by Kapoor.)

Quarterly surveys of the Labour Bureau corroborate the anticipated effect on T&C in particular (Labour Bureau 2010, p. 12). From September to December 2008, the related survey that covered the manufacturing, mining, construction, transport and the business process outsourcing/information technology (BPO/IT) sectors, indicated job losses of half a million (Labour Bureau 2009a, p. 10). Mostly, exporting units were characterized by greater decreases compared to establishments serving the domestic market (Labour Bureau 2009a, p. 13). The Indian granite and natural stone industry was struggling as a result of its major market – the US – being badly hit by recession. As a consequence of the stalling of production in hundreds of processing units and the closure of quarries, the livelihoods of thousands of labour migrants hailing from the most backward districts of India were at stake (Mahajan 2009, p. 41). With the exception of the gems and jewellery sector, direct workers were affected more severely by job losses. For instance, in the T&C and BPO/IT sectors the response to the crisis appears to have included the replacement of direct workers by contract workers (Labour Bureau 2009c, p. 7). Manual employment declined in most sectors covered in the survey (Labour Bureau 2009b, p. 15). This category is probably the most poorly paid and hence most vulnerable if unemployed.

During the early period of the crisis, a mix of supply and demand responses seem to have caused the employment decline. While, for instance, workers in export units of the T&C sector in Chennai left their establishments for better employment avenues, in the Tirupur knitwear cluster many of the units informed that export orders were either not coming or their value had declined. Employers felt that, if the situation did not improve, they would be compelled to lay off workers during the forthcoming months or would shift to production for the domestic market (Labour Bureau 2009c, p. 12). During the first quarter of 2009, a slight recovery was noted.

Employment increased by roughly a quarter million in the surveyed sectors, with the rise being more pronounced in non-exporting establishments (Labour Bureau 2009a, p. 10). The T&C sector showed a mixed performance during the first quarter of 2009. Whereas employment in spinning, weaving and finishing experienced a slight recovery, the downward trend in the more labour-intensive garment production continued (Labour Bureau 2009a, p. 24). With orders halving during that period for the Tirupur cluster, there were job losses also in the woollen garments cluster in Ludhiana as well as in the Bangalore garment industry of 500–800,000 workers. Besides job losses, reductions in wages and fringe benefits were other forms of reducing labour costs (Kumar 2009, p. 9f). Earnings declined by an average of 1.3 per cent in 2009 (Labour Bureau 2009c, p. 13). The Labour Bureau's estimates are conservative given that they are based on a survey of units employing ten or more workers only (Labour Bureau 2009c, p. 6). Hence, the effects on many micro, small and medium enterprises and their largely informal employment may have not been captured.

Compared to manufactures, services exports had a greater role in India's growth of the 1990s (Ghosh and Chandrasekhar 2009, p. 727). India had emerged as the largest exporter of IT services in the world economy after the EU (WTO 2009, p. 145). Although they came with a lag due to the longer duration of services contracts, this exposure implied adverse effects of the crisis on BPO/IT firms. By the first quarter of 2009, several software and BPO/IT services firms in India predicted lower revenue growth, cut back on recruitment and even started laying off workers (Ghosh and Chandrasekhar 2009, p. 728f). For the retained workforce, the cancellation of orders implied a higher workload (Narasimhan 2009, p. 3f). While sectoral growth rates remained positive and BPO/IT companies remained net hirers between 2008 and 2010, especially from the fourth quarter of 2008 onwards, export demand grew slower than the years before: Indian BPO/IT exports totalled 40 billion USD between April 2007 and March 2008, 47 billion USD during the same period in 2008–09 and 50.1 billion USD during 2009–10 (NASSCOM 2008, 2009 and 2010). During 2008–09, about 70,000 fewer workers were hired (Narasimhan 2009, p. 3f). Mahajan (2009, p. 43) perceives indirect employment effects due to lower demand in previous boom sectors like the BPO/IT industry, e.g. on the retail sector and domestic work. This took the form of job losses as well as falling wages for shop assistants and support staff. Outside the labour market, Narasimhan (2009, p. 4) reports that dismissals also caused a rise in domestic violence.

In Pakistan, the drop in foreign demand caused by the financial crisis coincided with – possibly more influential – domestic factors troubling export sectors. The contraction in industrial production of 3.6 per cent between July 2008 and June 2009 was also ascribed to power shortages that have plagued the country (SBP 2009, p. 28). Similar to the situation in Bangladesh and India, mainly the T&C sector (which produces about half of Pakistan's export value) was affected by slow or stagnant orders since the first quarter of 2009. Both the quantities of orders and their unit values decreased (PTJ 2009b, p. 12), resulting in a total drop in sectoral exports by 9.3 per cent in July 2008–April 2009 in comparison with the previous year (Ministry of Finance 2009, p. 120). As a compound result of the expiry of the quota system for T&C exports in 2005, the financial crisis since 2008 and other domestic and external factors, almost a third of knitwear units (PTJ 2009a, p. 16ff) and a fifth of all spinning mills closed down until the beginning of 2009 (SBP 2009, p. 37). In Southern Punjab, 30 out of 50 textile mills were reported to be closed, with 100,000 workers laid off (PTJ 2009a, p. 9). Especially small or informal units were facing problems (SBP 2009, p. 37). Siddiqui (2009, p. 1) reports a total loss of 300,000 jobs until May 2009.

The negative effect of the crisis on T&C manufacturing runs as a red thread through the South Asian region. Also in Sri Lanka, the garments sector, with 43 per cent of foreign sales the largest export engine (Gunatilaka 2009, p. 8), was affected severely by the crisis in terms of declining employment and deteriorating working conditions. Between September 2008 and March 2009, 220 factories closed (Sunil 2009, p. 1). During the first quarter of 2009, a total of approximately 200,000 jobs were lost, of which 31,000 were in the garments industry and 64,000 in construction. The majority of those were semi-skilled, unskilled and skilled operators rather than executive positions (Gunatilaka 2009, p. 23ff). The largest employment losses for male workers were amongst elementary occupations, affecting about 80,000 workers in this category until the first quarter of 2009 (DCS 2009a, p. 20). Similar to Bangladesh, India and Pakistan (Siegmann 2007, p. 4; Hirway 2008; p. 16, Khosla 2009, p. 289), Sri Lanka's garment industry is a major employer of women (Kelegama 2009, p. 581). While absolute and relative job losses for male workers were more significant, the shrinking workforce in the garment sector meant that a major formal employer for women was no longer available to accommodate job seekers. This is particularly worrying given that unemployment in Sri Lanka is more severe among females than that of males (DCS 2010, p. 21).

Similar to employers' strategies in other South Asian countries, retrenchments were used as firms' last option for cost cutting. They were catalysed by the re-establishment of the tripartite National Labour Advisory Council (NLAC) in Sri Lanka (Sunil 2009, p. 1). The NLAC suspended the operation of procedures under the Termination of Employment of Workman Act, thus allowing companies speedy lay-offs and reduction in working hours. Freezing recruitment, natural labour attrition, reducing overtime and the number of days of work, as well as eliminating allowances and wage cuts were reported as alternative ways of reducing labour costs in face of the crisis (Gunatilaka 2009, p. 33). Compared with dismissals, these strategies had a significant impact on the working conditions of a far larger group of workers in terms of their income and social security.

The employment decline in Sri Lanka's manufacturing and construction sectors was paralleled by the creation of 203,000 jobs in the agricultural sector as well as 129,000 new jobs in services during the same period (Gunatilaka 2009, p. 23). They are likely to be expressions of a growing informalization of employment resulting from the drop in external demand. Retrenched workers entered sub-contracted employment in the same value chain, took up urban informal employment in services or migrated back to rural areas in search of agricultural employment. However, agriculture was hardly able to offer productive employment even before such return migration. What is more, one aspect of the crisis itself was the significant decrease in agricultural exports by about 20 per cent between 2008 and 2009 (Export Development Board 2010). In comparison with an average of 62 per cent informal employment in the Sri Lankan economy, agriculture employs more than 84 per cent of the workforce informally (DCS 2009b, p. 2).

1.2 Squeeze in Financial Markets

In comparison with the export channel discussed above, the less pronounced role of FDI and the poorer development of stock markets in South Asia implies that the transmission of the crisis through financial markets can be considered less relevant for labour market developments in the region. With the exception of India, the stock markets of most South Asian economies are largely isolated from the global economy. In Bangladesh only about 2 per cent of the market capital is sourced from abroad. FDI in Bangladesh has always been low compared with its South Asian neighbours, accounting for only 4.4 per cent of total investment. Resultantly, the global crisis had little direct effect on capital market developments (Rahman et al. 2010, p. 16f).

This contrasts with the situation in India. Employment declines in non-export sectors suggested that the transmission of the international crisis to India went beyond external trade, (Ghosh and Chandrasekhar 2009, p. 729f). The immediate effects on financial markets were plummeting stock prices, a net outflow of foreign capital, a large reduction in foreign reserves and a sharp tightening of domestic liquidity (World Bank 2009a, p. 2). This choked an important financing source for Indian companies and led to a slowdown in business and consumer expenditure. Hence, besides the direct effects caused by a drop in demand in major export markets, the lack of credit constituted another bottleneck for Indian exporters. Small producers and traders who contribute more than 30 per cent of exports and employ the majority of workers in export-related sectors were particularly hard hit. The smallest segment of informal enterprises, which obtained less than 2 per cent of all bank credit before the crisis, received a meagre 1.2 per cent in 2008. This segment is now in danger of being rationed out of the credit market altogether since banks' usual unwillingness to lend to them is reinforced by strong competing demand from the organized sector in a situation of acute credit shortage (NCEUS 2008, p. 3). Small producers' economic difficulties directly translate into reduced employment. Ghosh and Chandrasekhar (2009, p. 729) emphasize the growing difficulties for agriculturalists, in particular. They had seen prices for their export crops collapse and input costs rise. The liquidity shortage resulting from the ongoing financial crisis came on top of their financial problems and large debt burdens.

In sum, while the growth period since the neoliberal reforms of the 1990s had been driven by credit financed purchases encouraged by easy liquidity and low interest rates, the curtailment of credit further reduced consumption and investment demand, increased inventories and led to job losses in domestic sectors like housing, construction, consumer durables and the BPO/IT sector (Ghosh and Chandrasekhar 2009, p. 729f; World Bank 2009a, p. 2). This lack of fresh capital was also felt in Sri Lanka, where foreign investors were unable to complete construction projects, while at the same time the squeeze in bank lending negatively affected small and medium enterprises (Gunatilaka 2009, p. 12). In Pakistan, the banking sector was affected significantly by employment declines (Siddiqui 2009, p. 1).

1.3 The Crisis and International Labour Migration

In comparison to financial flows, workers' remittances are considered more resilient to financial crises, amongst others due to the fact that they are being sent by the cumulative number of migrants, rather than by new migrants alone (Ratha et al. 2009a, p. 4). Remittances' resilience does not mean, though, that South Asian labour migrants were sheltered from the economic shock of the financial crisis. On the contrary, due to their weaker position in the host countries' labour markets, migrant workers are often the first victims of an economic crisis (Stiglitz 2009a, p. 2).

The populous and poor countries of South Asia have historically been migrant-sending regions. Resultantly, India, Bangladesh and Pakistan have been part of the top 10 recipients of remittances, with India leading the list (Ratha et al. 2009c, p. 3). Nepal and Bangladesh figure prominently in the ranking of countries whose GDP is most dependent on workers remittances (Ratha et al. 2010, p. 2). Migration and remittances have played a stabilizing role in previous economic and political crises. Yet, the origin of the financial crisis that started in 2008 was in the wealthy nations of North America and

Europe, which are important destinations for many South Asian migrant workers (McCulloch and Sumner 2009b, p. 5). While it is likely that crisis-induced economic turmoil in some of the sending countries' labour markets provided yet another 'push' factor for international labour migration (Abella and Ducanes 2009, p. 1), annual growth in workers' remittances to South Asia, which peaked in 2007 with 32.6 per cent, decelerated rapidly to 4.9 per cent in 2009 and a predicted 4.7 per cent in 2010 (Ratha et al. 2010, p. 18).

Ratha et al. (2009b, p. 7) perceived rising protectionist tendencies in the major destination countries of international migrant workers. Many host countries reduced immigration quotas or imposed tougher standards for immigrant workers. Businesses' efforts to adjust their workforce to a drop in demand was often fulfilled through lay-offs of a less protected migrant workforce. Singapore's foreign workers, for example, represent about a third of the country's labour force. More than 80 per cent of these are low-skilled workers, from India and Sri Lanka amongst others. It has been reported that more foreign workers in Singapore complained about pay cuts, not being paid on time, having their working days reduced, and not being provided food, shelter and healthcare, which employers are legally obliged to provide. Also, in Malaysia, host to many migrant workers from Bangladesh in particular, many firms adjusted to the crisis by reducing the number of working days, overtime, and in some instances forcing workers to use their annual leave (Abella and Ducanes 2009, p. 1f).

Overall, the Gulf Cooperation Council (GCC) countries have been the main destination of South Asian labour migrants. It is estimated that 90 per cent of the Indian state of Kerala's 1.85 million overseas workers are employed in the Middle East. Similarly, 80 per cent of Sri Lanka's 1.5 million migrant workers as well as the same share of Bangladesh's international workforce's deployment during the past three decades was to Middle Eastern countries. Some 400,000 workers from Pakistan are estimated to work in the Gulf countries (Abella and Ducanes 2009, p. 2f). The slowdown in the construction sector in Dubai, which was harder hit by the crisis than oil-rich, recession-sheltered Saudi Arabia has impacted migrant workers (Fix et al. 2009, p. 94; Ratha et al. 2009b, p. 7). About 20,000 construction workers from India had lost their jobs in the Gulf up to 2009 (Debroy 2009, p. 22). Labour migrants in GCC countries are particularly vulnerable due to the temporary nature of their contracts. As a result of the crisis, several of the labour-receiving countries in the region stopped issuing new work permits to or renewing work permits of foreign workers. Besides, in a move to counter the rising unemployment of local workers, some are providing companies with incentives to replace foreign with national workers (Abella and Ducanes 2009, p. 9).

While no large-scale return migration to the sending countries in South Asia was recorded, the global recession's pinch on labour markets was felt. After a record rise of migrants' outflows from Bangladesh to the Gulf region in 2007, about 10 per cent of Bangladeshi migrants have not had their three-year contracts renewed and were sent home in 2008–09 (Fix et al. 2009, p. 41f). Saudi Arabia and Kuwait stopped issuing work permits to Bangladeshi nationals; these two destinations had received 40 per cent of the total migrant workers from Bangladesh (Rahman et al. 2009, p. 23). Malaysia cancelled work visas for 55,000 Bangladeshi workers in March 2009 and 12,000 Bangladeshi workers were retrenched. Malaysia is also attempting to restrict the entry of new and returning workers (Ratha et al. 2009a, p. 5; Rahman et al. 2010, p. 10). Resultantly, the volume of emigration in the first month of 2009 was already 40 per cent lower than the monthly average from January to November 2008. The effects of the crisis also depended on the skill level and sex of the workers. While the deployment of semi-skilled and low-skilled workers declined, that of professionals and skilled workers increased (Abella and Ducanes 2009, p. 5). While there is no evidence of a large-scale return of low-skilled migrants to India, in Pakistan, in contrast, the difficult situation in the domestic labour market appeared to have further catalysed emigration. Anecdotal evidence points to the return migration of skilled employees from IT and software designing departments abroad, though (Siddiqui 2009, p. 1).

The situation in Sri Lanka mirrors the dynamics in Bangladesh and India. Net emigration slowed down by 1.4 per cent from a high of 250,000 in 2008 to 247,000 in 2009 (SLBFE 2010, p. 3). Anecdotal evidence suggests that skilled and semi-skilled workers in the garments and construction sectors returned home during 2009, while migrant domestic workers' correct and timely wage payments were affected negatively. In 2009, the Sri Lanka Bureau of Foreign Employment ceased training workers for the Korean labour market as South Korea terminated its labour-contracting arrangements with Sri Lanka following the economic slump (Gunatilaka 2009, p. 11). The bleak growth outlook for the United Arab Emirates in particular, where approximately 150,000 workers were employed, worried policy makers in Sri Lanka (Abella and Ducanes 2009, p. 7f).

2. DISCUSSION

This section identifies and discusses regional patterns in the effects of the global financial crisis on major South Asian countries' labour markets. The focus is on qualitative and quantitative aspects of employment on the one hand, and on workers' social security as well as on the gender dimensions of the impact of the crisis on the labour market, on the other hand.

2.1 The Impact of the Crisis on Employment

The chapter took the nexus between economic growth and employment creation in the period of liberalization of South Asian economies as a starting point. It highlighted the decoupling of macro-economic developments and employment during two decades of accelerated growth since the beginning of the 1990s. The review of the preceding sections has shown that, while this disconnect held for a period of upswing, it did not during the recession caused by the global financial crisis. South Asian employers' main response to the drop in export demand of major markets in the North was to reduce labour costs. Amongst others, this has led to employment losses in the main export industries, such as T&C. Resultantly, the South Asian unemployment rate was estimated to grow from 4.8 to 5.1 per cent between 2008 and 2009 (ILO 2010a, p. 46), despite the simultaneous fall in – mainly female – participation rates in the region (ILO 2010a, p. 50).

However, job losses are just the tip of the iceberg of the labour market impact of the crisis (ILO 2010a, p. 9). The projected increase in unemployment rates in South Asia, particularly among workers in globally-oriented industries, is small in comparison with the effects on the masses of the region's workers engaged in low-productivity, vulnerable employment. Given the lack of public social safety nets in the event of job loss, workers in the global South commonly cannot afford to stay unemployed.

Two processes that are not captured in unemployment statistics can be distinguished. First, workers who are threatened by job losses due to the impact of the crisis faced a deterioration of their working conditions in terms of lower benefits, overtime payments and wages. Besides the effect of the crisis on the domestic workforce, the space for decent work for South Asian international labour migrants has narrowed in the host economies' labour markets. Most of them stayed in their destinations despite a more hostile climate towards non-nationals. Yet, the ongoing crisis has reduced their earnings and has added to their vulnerability. Ironically, a 3 per cent increase in labour productivity has been recorded in South Asia during the first year of the crisis (ILO 2010a, p. 49). This may reflect the higher GDP growth compared to employment, but possibly also the work intensification for the retained workforce. Many of them belong to South Asia's 80 per cent working poor who can scarcely afford further deterioration in their working conditions. Second, informalization increased. The share of informal employment in India is estimated to be more than 92 per cent (NCEUS 2009, p. 13). In Bangladesh, Pakistan and Sri Lanka these shares are 78, 73 and 60 per cent of the workforce, respectively (Bangladesh Bureau of Statistics 2006, p. 4; Ministry of Labour Relations and Manpower 2009, p. 10; Ministry of Finance 2010, p. 251). The crisis added to this. In some sectors, such as the T&C industry, directly employed workers were replaced by a casual workforce. In India, such informal workers in registered establishments represent about 45 per cent of the workforce in formal units (NCEUS 2009, p. 2). Dismissed workers often found new employment in the same industry, but in informal workshops characterized by poorer working conditions and less protection. Possibly more importantly, informal employment in the urban services sector as well as return migration to agricultural employment served as questionable 'buffers' for the loss of livelihoods. While informal employment is not systematically and regularly reported in South Asia, the share of vulnerable workers (i.e. own-account workers and contributing family workers, see ILO 2010a, p. 18) is projected to grow to nearly 79 per cent of total employment in the most pessimistic scenario (ILO 2010a, p. 53).

2.2 Implications for Social Security

With large shares of the labour force being employed informally preceding the crisis, most workers in South Asia did not enjoy the security that wage and salaried jobs could provide (ILO 2010a, p. 19). The recession seems to have hit these vulnerable workers first and hardest. The credit squeeze reduced the profitability of informal enterprises. Informal home-based workers (HBWs) faced greater income insecurity due to the drop in demand, a risk passed on by their employer. In many cases, casual workers were the first to be laid off. Ironically, informal workers are largely invisible in the monitoring of the impact of the crisis (Ghosh 2009b, p. 30). Establishment-based surveys tend to ignore informal enterprises as well as informal workers in formal establishments. The examples above have indicated that the latter category represents a significant share of the workforce in registered units. Resultantly, these vulnerable workers are not (adequately) targeted in policy responses. Rather, the focus on trade and financial flows in official statistics does not support an adequate and timely assessment of the effects of the crisis on people's livelihoods. This in turn is likely to lead to an anti-labour bias in the policy options considered to address the impact of the crisis.

The coping strategies available, especially reverting to self-employment in agriculture and services, do not promise social security in any meaningful sense of the word, given the poor earnings and high risks associated with these jobs. International labour migration and the associated remittances have often been considered an important pillar of family-based forms of social security that offer buffers in times of economic shocks – not just by households themselves, but also by South Asian policy-makers. The global scale of the ongoing financial crisis has revealed the precariousness of this reliance on anti-cyclical international as well as urban remittances as migrants' destinations have been hit hard by the recession.

Public provision of social security for workers is unknown or poorly developed in most South Asian countries. In India, for example, of the present workforce of around 500 million, no more than 40 million are covered by formal social security arrangements. One ambitious scheme, the Indian National Rural Employment Guarantee Scheme (NREGS), does not necessarily cover those affected by the effects of the global meltdown. Often, returning migrants that were laid off in export-oriented industries in India are not classified as rural workers – a prerequisite for NREGS – making them ineligible for this form of protection (Debroy 2009, p. 23f).

2.3 Gendered Labour Market Dynamics

While both women and men were affected, it is useful to illuminate the gender dimensions of the crisis more explicitly, amongst others, in order to allow more well-targeted responses to the crisis. Many of the sectors, such as T&C, that were hit are characterized by a female-dominated workforce. While these women workers' educational and skill levels are often poor, as are their working conditions, employment in the garment industry represents one of the few opportunities for paid and – often – formal employment for women. By far the largest number of South Asian women work as unpaid family helpers in agriculture, while the rest are concentrated in a few sectors and occupations. The decline in demand for T&C in the course of the current crisis means that women have been hit first by dismissals (ILO 2009b, p. 7). This is possibly reflected in the faster increase in female as compared to male unemployment rates in the region between 2008 and 2009. In view of the comparatively low labour force participation of South Asian women of around 35 per cent in 2008 (ILO 2010a, p. 50) and their comparatively higher exposure to unemployment, these job losses are very worrying. The World Bank (2009b, p. 3f) estimates that gendered income inequality is likely to further deteriorate as a result.

In recent years, the IT industry in India has become a major employer of a female workforce. In contrast to employment in the garment industry, it offers jobs associated with comparatively good earnings and other working conditions. As said, the crisis caused a major drop in demand for IT services. Case study evidence points to gendered effects on employees in the IT industry (Narasimhan 2009). Dismissals affected mainly male employees. This is being rationalized with the construction of women as being more 'conscientious' workers. While men's lay-offs led to domestic violence as they conflicted with perceptions of the stereotypical role of men as the family's breadwinner; for the retained, the reduction in the workforce implied an increased workload. Indirect job losses for domestic workers also had distinct gender dimensions given the high concentration of female workers in this occupation. More than half of all regular non-agriculture jobs for women in India are comprised of domestic work (NCEUS 2009, p. 142).

These indirect effects suggest that the crisis impacted on informal employment which dominates South Asian labour markets. In India and Bangladesh women work relatively more in the informal economy, but not so in Pakistan (Bangladesh Bureau of Statistics 2006, p. 4; NCEUS 2009, p. 23; Ministry of Finance 2010, p. 251) and Sri Lanka where women are comparatively well represented in formal jobs (Ministry of Labour Relations and Manpower 2009, p. 10). HBWs constitute a large portion of informal employment in India, most of which relates to women (NCEUS 2009, p. 149). Their work caters for both domestic and foreign markets. The marginal utilization of women in manufacturing is typically at the poorest-paid parts of the production chain. Such women workers are effectively deprived of all the benefits that may accrue from outside employment except for the low nominal returns that they receive from piece-rate work which excludes them from any security of contract (Ghosh 2009b, p. 32). So, while they belong to the poorest strata of Indian society, as a result of the crisis, HBWs' incomes, especially in export-oriented work, were affected by a pincer movement of shrinking labour demand and a progressive reduction in piece rates (AIDWA 2009).

All in all, the recession is likely to further marginalize South Asian women economically. Gender inequalities within and outside the South Asian labour market are very high in global comparison. Regional female labour market participation is the second lowest after North Africa and the Middle East and the gender gap in participation is second widest (ILO 2010a, p. 50). Inequalities are mediated by social norms that marginalize women in the wider society. Given their segregation in a few sectors and occupations, this loss of paid and often formal employment opportunities can potentially contribute to their further marginalization in and outside the labour markets.

3. CONCLUSION

This chapter has highlighted asymmetries in the labour market consequences of growth and recession in South Asia. The period of higher economic growth since the beginning of the 1990s had not been paralleled by growth in productive employment opportunities, but the global financial crisis has translated into job losses and deteriorating working conditions, especially in export-oriented industries. Vulnerable segments of the labour force had to bear the greatest risks: women with few employment alternatives as well as informal workers whose livelihoods are characterized by poor earnings, a lack of jobs and social security. The coping strategies of poor households in the face of economic shocks, such as labour migration, have become unreliable during the present crisis; sectors and destinations in which domestic and international migrant workers are employed have been hit hard.

A common response to the current crisis of South Asian countries also was to strengthen public investment with the aim of compensating for the fall in foreign demand and to provide public safety nets. In Bangladesh, for example, existing safety nets were strengthened and new programmes, including an enhanced employment generation scheme for the poor, were introduced (ADB 2009, p. 121). Other measures included an increase in the coverage or level of old-age pension as well as steps to protect migrant workers (ILO 2009b, p. 19). Public expenditure in India was planned to rise by 16.1 per cent in response to the crisis, including large increases for public investment, e.g. in infrastructure and the NREGS (ADB 2009, p. 131), and interest subventions for most employment-oriented export sectors. Similarly, in Pakistan, spending on infrastructure was increased during 2009 with the aim of generating employment (ILO 2009b, p. 17).

In the past, international financial institutions were hesitant to counter an economic crisis with more public spending, this way effectively reducing developing countries' policy space. This time, both the World Bank and the IMF have supported the provision of fiscal stimuli (e.g. World Bank 2009a, p. 5f; IMF/ILO 2010) – at least at the rhetoric level. Such investment has been at the heart of many reform proposals for South Asia after the crisis. Ghosh (2010c, p. 2) pleas for a re-orientation towards wage-led growth that focuses on inclusivity: the allocation of public resources to sectors in which the poor work, the areas in which they live, their factors of production and the goods they consume. The viability of informal production should be guaranteed through better access to credit, and greater integration into supply chains as well as through technology improvements. Besides the provision of a minimum wage floor through increases in public employment, public funding for wider coverage with social protection should be a policy priority. The preceding sections have shown that, apart from wages, setting and enforcing standards for decent working conditions, especially for the most vulnerable workers, is crucial. In the case of migrant workers, bilateral cooperation agreements, like the ones signed in 2009 between trade unions from Sri Lanka and their counterparts in migrant-receiving countries in Bahrain, Jordan and Kuwait for the protection of migrant workers' rights, are examples of such standard-setting (ILO 2010b, p. 175). Last but not least, tax receipts are to be channelled into the public delivery of housing and other infrastructure, health, education etc. Strengthened and expanded investment in human development of the poor and vulnerable (NCEUS 2009, p. 4ff) would differ significantly from the current reaction of the private sector to the crisis which focuses on cost-cutting rather than pro-active strategies like multi-skilling, greater functional mobility and alternative work schedules (Gunatilaka 2009, p. 35).

A 'Jobs Pact' (ILO 2009d) for South Asia comprising the measures outlined above may go a long way to strengthen workers' resilience against the volatilities of a globalized economy and to redress the anti-labour bias in the current form of globalization.

14. Diamonds are for Never: The Economic Crisis and the Diamond Polishing Industry in India

Astha Kapoor

The focus of this chapter is a description of the impact of this crisis in an economic sector of a country that has been hailed as an upcoming superpower: India. Political leaders have been claiming that the impact of the crisis on India will not be as severe as in other countries. It is believed that since the country is said to be growing at the rate of 6.7 per cent (*Times of India*, 2009), the effect of the crisis will resonate much less. However, this is not true. The recession has caused much trouble in India as elsewhere, especially in sectors of the economy that are directly connected with the global market. One such industry is diamond polishing in India, the focus of this chapter. It is intricately linked to the international market and has its roots in the small towns of Western India. Even though the diamond is a sign of luxury, the roots of its sheen lie in squalid conditions across the world. The Indian diamond industry, in Surat, is one such place. The current financial crisis shocked the industry and had serious repercussions for everyone involved with it. In light of the economic crisis, the research explores various coping mechanisms that are employed by the labourers and analyses how these are a function of the industry, its structure and its informality.[1]

1. BACKGROUND TO THE CRISIS

The gem industry in India was hit significantly by the economic crisis.[2] The government of Gujarat says that there are 6547 diamond processing units employing approximately 800,000 people (Reserve Bank of India, 2009), but the numbers may be higher since smaller factories employing thousands of workers are not registered. The Gems and Jewellery Export Promotion

Council (GJEPC) newsletter *Ideal Cut* (December 2008, p. 1) claims that there was a 15 per cent fall in demand from the US alone, which is one of the largest markets for Indian diamonds. In 2007, the jewellery sales for the holiday season accounted for $100 billion to which India contributed 34 per cent (Rediff India Abroad, 2008). The GJEPC (2008, p. 2) also notes that in boom time 20 per cent retail growth leads up to 40 per cent growth in employment whereas in recessionary times the inverse holds true: 10 per cent fall in demands can lead to 30 per cent slump in employment.

1.1 The Surat Diamond Industry

Over 200,000 diamond cutters lost their jobs after November 2008 (*Telegraph*, 2009) when over 1000 units shut down. Newspapers reported about the plight of the diamond workers in Surat, including worker suicides on an almost daily basis. All this elaborated on an existing reality: the Surat diamond industry has been crippled by the crisis and no help was being extended to it. The Surat diamond industry is dominated by a system of reliance on kith and kin. The phenomenon makes it very hard to breach the space, in which only the trusted are permitted, for research. The stone in question is extremely precious, security levels are high and not everyone is allowed to enter the factory. The diamond trade in India relies heavily on export. About 90 per cent of the stones polished are meant for external consumption. Until the financial year 2003–04, the Government of India followed an export promotion policy. This benefitted the industry heavily as it did not have to pay income or excise tax. Profits were presented as soaring in an attempt to lure in even more governmental incentives. However, in 2003–04, the Government levied a tax on the export of diamonds. The diamond companies then showed very little profit to evade tax. As a result of this industry-wide tax evasion there are no reliable records of value added in the industry as a whole. The diamond industry relies on trust and most transactions are verbal. Most dealings happen with people previously known, as credit-based transactions are the primary way of doing business. It is also impossible to assess with certainty the number of workers in Surat. There are close to no records. Most factory owners show their workers as labour contractors instead of acknowledging them as *karigars*. A labour contractor means that the worker is a freelancer with no need to be included in factory or labour laws meant for salaried employees. Consequently, the number of *karigars* is not recorded. Business owners ensure a certain informality of the labour force in order to tie workers to the business, without a platform to put forward their grievances. Even before the crisis hit, the conditions of the labourers in the diamond industry were not up to the standards of the Indian government. Engineer (1994) wrote that the day was 12–16 hours long and the owners of the factories used blind faith to search out 'thieves'. He also reported that some factories kept torture rooms to deal with workers accused of stealing diamonds. Also some factories are unregistered, they rely on stolen electricity and water for their sustenance. It is important to clarify that this is not the case of all factories but a majority of them. The big factories follow registration of workers and guarantee provident funds and insurance. Big factories also give their work on contract to the thousands of smaller factories that exist around Surat but do not take responsibility for what happens to workers there.

1.2 The Lawless Trade

The caste distribution in Surat is interlinked with the diamond industry. The management and production of the stone in Surat is controlled by two major caste groups: the *Palanpuri Jain* (hailing from Palanpur in Gujarat state) which established the first production units in 1960s and the *Kanbi Patels* (*Kathiawaris* in the industry). The Patels were originally farmers from Saurashtra, who were forced to leave their native land because of poor rainfall, no prospects of agriculture and conflict with other caste groups in the area. The Patels came to Surat looking for work and were employed by the Palanpuri Jains in the diamond manufacturing units as *karigars*. Gradually the Patels became managers of units and factories. They began bringing people from their own family and caste to the city. Business was growing and the Palanpuri Jains began contracting work to the Kathiawaris. Soon, they became owners of factories. Recent unofficial estimates say that today the Patels make up 80 per cent of the labour force in the industry. Most of the older, bigger factories are still owned by the Palanpuri Jains but the majority of the factories are small, employing 50–100 workers all under the management of the Patels. According to Richman (2009) the Patels embody the spirit of globalisation. It is through the global demand for a good that the skills of an obscure people have become a tool for success. The success of the Patels in the industry reveals that 'ethnic trading networks can flourish in a globalising economy' (Richman, 2009, p. 11). Richman notes that the Patels were oriented around ethnic extralegal mechanisms, quickly adapted to the industry structured around the same and integrated into its global network.

The Patels dominate 'sight holding' in traders' offices in London and Antwerp, even though the Palanpuri Jains remain important. All Gujarati families trading with DTC have offices, usually occupied by close family members in New York (the export out-post), London (DTC Headquarters), Antwerp (large trading ground) and Mumbai (trading out-post). When brought back to Surat, the diamonds are given on contract to smaller factories, or sold in open diamond markets where middle men sell them to small diamond factories.

1.3 Wages

The wages are paid on piece rate. How many stones they work on depends on the quality of the stone. A good quality diamond will take less time to polish. It is hard to give an average wage for the *karigars* due to the heterogeneous nature of the profession. Diamond polishing is easy to learn, it takes about 2–3 months to understand the work and then it is up to the worker to increase skill and more importantly speed. The stone goes through many hands. Each level requires a different level of skill which determines the pay.

2. FROM BOOM TO BUST: THE CRISIS HITS SURAT

The Surat diamond industry has flourished without any serious hurdles since the 1970s. Production usually gathers pace before the Indian festival of Diwali, after which the workers are given a short holiday and they come back for full production for Christmas and New Year, given the export-orientated nature of the industry. The price of the rough diamonds was very high before the Diwali season in 2008 was setting in. The diamond merchants bought roughs at high prices in speculation of high diamond demand for Diwali, Christmas and New Year. The Lehmann Brothers' crash in September had shaken the confidence of the industry. Yet there was a sense of optimism in the market since the holiday season of Christmas and New Year was approaching; the diamond industry sells the majority of its produce during this time and the hope was that despite the crisis demand would not fall. The crisis ended up staying longer than expected; resultantly the demand of the polished diamonds fell steeply. DTC did not lower their prices of roughs, instead what they did was reduce production in mines. Diamonds being luxury goods were the first to be effected by the economic downturn. The factory owners had already bought roughs at high prices and felt it was best to hold on to them until the price of the polished diamonds rose again. This meant that the *karigars* no longer had access to the stone, their only source of livelihood.

The GJEPC requested the international mine owners retrench the supply of the diamonds for a while so that Indian companies do not lose their trading licenses and in order to maintain stability in the industry during this time of crisis. The GJEPC stated that the import of rough diamonds would be on hold for a month beginning 25 November, 2008, as stocks were deemed sufficient to minimize the impact on their labour force. GJEPC further stated that by moving fewer roughs through the diamond pipeline producer companies would share the financial burden contributing to faster restoration of an otherwise healthy business (ibid.).

Diwali was on 4 November, 2008. Workers packed up their work and returned to their villages for their yearly holiday. When they came back in at the end of December they found that the factories had not reopened. No prior information had been given to the *karigars* about the impending crisis. Some of the bigger factories claim to have informed their workers but this was not corroborated by the workers. For three months, the *karigars* had no information as to what had happened and when it would be over. The Labour Ministry of Gujarat surveyed about 1700 diamond units in December and found approximately 1200 of them shut.[3] The Ministry claims it pressured the factory owners to open shop even if that meant running it at reduced capacity. The Labour Commissioner asked the owners to reduce wages and make the *karigars* work in shifts, but warned them not to take away their livelihood entirely. The Ministry also claims that it put continuous pressure on the owners and it was decided that all factories would open by 22 January, 2009. However, thousands of the smaller factories did not open and thousands were left without jobs. It appeared that workers in smaller units as opposed to bigger ones suffered relatively greater losses (remember, however, that no records exist). Aagam Sanghvi, the head of Sanghvi Exports said that wages were not reduced but the quantity of work did fall by about 30–40 per cent.[4] He also said that in his surroundings there were about 160 small and big diamond factories out of which only four had managed to reopen on time.

The diamond firms lobbied the state and central governments for a bailout package. The state government urged the central government to mobilise resources to provide relief. In the tussle between the central and the state governments the diamond industry seems to have suffered.[5] The central government was vehemently against bailouts and did not give in to the demands of the diamond industry. As a result, none were given. The factories remained closed until the end of January. Workers were forced to fend for themselves. When the factories reopened the initial sense of hope disappeared when the workers realised that the functioning at reduced capacities meant that even people who had jobs could not rely on that job for their survival. Workers were forced to find other means of livelihood.

Even though the workers were the worst hit, others in the diamond industry also felt the impact of the crisis. The owners of the factories were forced to abandon their shops. The middle-men had nothing to sell and dipped into their savings to sustain themselves while they waited for the crisis to pass. However, the workers were the only ones who did not have savings for a time like this. They relied on social networks to survive the worst economic downturn they had ever seen. Around May 2009, the effect of the crisis seemed to subside yet the workers believed otherwise. A large number of interviewees said that they were getting a full day of work but the time they spent on each stone was longer because the supervisors were stricter than before, the standards of acceptance had gone up since the crisis had hit. Close to 15 interviewees claimed that the stones they would usually polish in 10 minutes now took close to 40 minutes. There was also a sense of impending doom despite having survived the worst. The workers knew that the goods were not moving beyond Mumbai to the foreign market which makes up 90 per cent of the market. Diamonds were being produced at a higher rate but the market was depressed. A lot of workers feared another recession after Diwali as they realised the importance of external markets.

In July and August 2009 things had seemingly got better. The worst of the crisis was over and people were back in the factories working full days. Yet, closer observation showed differently. In the residential areas of the *karigars*, there were many houses with big locks, indicating that a number of people had been forced to abandon their big city lives and choose a more economically viable option of waiting out the crisis in the villages. The locks confirm the phenomenon of recession refugees. The fieldwork, to which we now turn, enabled me to make the necessary closer observations.

3. IMPACT AND SURVIVAL STRATEGIES

In most houses visited, the women are engaged in embroidery work. This points to the fact that men, the primary breadwinners of the house, are no longer able to earn enough to support the house which means that women have to take up a means of employment to sustain the household.

Ved Road, one of the older parts of the city, which was where the diamond industry began in Surat, also bears signs of the distress in the industry. The diamond *ghantis* crowd the back alleys, while the noise of large machinery consumes the surroundings. Many small diamond factory owners,[6] suffering from the loss of demand in diamonds, abandon their work and switch to a less lucrative but more stable textile industry. They use their savings to invest in this machinery. This change in occupation is evident from the change in machinery. It also indicates a certain sort of abandonment of diamonds once and for all, as diversification to a new industry requires investment which will probably be for the long term.

The first casualty is the standard of living, which falls as a crisis sets in. Most crises lead to large-scale job cuts and reduced wages. People cut corners in luxuries and then in necessities. People who belong to the low income groups and do not have a fixed income suffer the most. Expenditure on health and education is reduced for the duration of the crisis. Illnesses are ignored and children (mostly girls) are pulled out from school and pushed into the labour market. Women workers are the first to be retrenched during a recession. Women also take on more burdens within the household, their nutrition levels fall and they are forced to work informally in order to substitute for the loss of income. As large parts of population belong to the unorganised sector, social security has very limited reach. Therefore, people are forced to look elsewhere to sustain themselves through hard times. A large variety of coping mechanisms are employed by the interviewees, the most popular is family. Households that are most vulnerable to economic volatility are those that employ risky coping mechanisms like informal insurance systems and informal credit. Income diversification is seen as a likely option to overcome the crisis; low investment (even if returns are low) is seen as a viable option.

3.1 Employers

The diamond industry treats its workers with carelessness and has not put in any measures to ensure the safety and security of the workers. Yet, the feeling the workers have towards their employer is not that of rebellion and anger but of kinship and respect. The patron–client relationship as elucidated by Scott (1972, p. 96) is a 'dyadic relationship between a person of higher socioeconomic power who uses his influence to provide protection or benefits, or both, for a person of lower status (client) who, for his part, reciprocates by offering general support and assistance.' This relationship can be extended to the relationship between the employers (patron) and the employees (client) in the diamond industry. The relationship is symbiotic as employers provide protection to the employees in times of trouble in return for their services.

This relationship of protection extends only during the good times. When the crisis hit, the employers of the smaller factories absconded without word. Not only were there no formal, institutionally binding measures of protection for the workers, there were none from the revered employers either. Krishnabhai Patel had worked in a factory of about 30 workers for 15 years. He had a personal relationship with the owner of the factory. When the crisis hit, the owner was not to be found, and he felt abandoned as the employers had played no role in attempting to rescue their workers.

3.2 Labour Unions

Labour unions have existed to support workers but in Surat they are almost invisible. The ones that do exist are not considered reliable enough to provide help to those who need it. Historically, there have been close to no trade union movements in Gujarat. The people are not stirred into action; despite the sense of community as organised by caste affiliations, organisation on the basis of class is not visible. The workforce is largely fragmented and this factionalism is perpetuated by the employers.

Firstly, each worker is paid differently depending on the amount and quality of the work they do. This breeds competition within the workers and makes them unwilling to organise towards a common cause. As Engelshoven (1999, p. 373) points out,

> the high degree of specialisation, the competition between workers for good roughs and the resulting turnovers of workers between workshops makes it very difficult for workers to come together and to organise strikes and mass protests.

Satyendra Kumar, of Socialist Unity Centre of India (SUCI) is of the belief that the owners perpetuate the idea of small entrepreneurship. They make one out of four workers the overseer of his table, which gives him a sense of power and distinguishes him from the rest. This factionalism makes organisation close to impossible. He also thinks that the Gujarati people are business minded; any activity which steers them away from their business is considered not worth their time. The difference between a trade union and a company has been blurred over the years and the Gujaratis are more inclined towards the latter.

Second, the employers use fear to discourage worker organisation. Anyone who attempts to organise is beaten up or tortured and loses his job. The owners are very powerful. The names of those who go to union offices are given to the police who in turn beat them up. All *karigars* when questioned said that even attempting organisation was close to impossible. Girdharbhai who has worked in the industry for over 12 years told the story,

> If the managers even hear us talking about forming an organisation they separate us from the table. That's the first warning. After that, we just get beaten up. They can also falsely accuse us of stealing in case they feel the need to justify their actions. The problem is primarily this, the owners are united and the workers aren't so it's best that we just mind our own business and do our work.

Third, ties of kinship exist because the industry is organised in patron–client relationships. The diamond workers have compassion for the owners. Most factory owners today began as diamond *karigars* in factories. The workers respect the toil that the owners have put into building their empires. At another level there is their own desire to be owners one day. For this reason, employees feel the need to remain in the factory and struggle like the owners. Girishbhai, who hopes to start his own business in the next five years, says,

> It's easy to protest and organise a strike. It is difficult is to stick through your job. The owner of my factory came to the city in the 1970s within nothing, now he is such a big man. It's very easy to criticise him but he worked hard for it. I have no complaints; I get what I deserve at the end of the day much like he did and look where he is now. The point is to make money, and you have to struggle before you can kick your feet back and relax. No good comes out of a strike in any case; all that happens is a loss of wages.

Vijay Shenmare, Communist Party of India member in Surat confessed that it was close to impossible to organise the people.

> What is needed for organisation is a large scale factory with a significant number of workers. The diamond industry doesn't have that. They are all scattered in tiny factories across the entire city. There is no place to get them together. The diamond workers had a really comfortable existence for about three decades before this crisis. When the factories shut down after Diwali, we believed that something would happen. There were some movements in other parts of the state, sporadic movements which went unreported but nothing really came off it. A lot of them didn't want to organise then as well because they feared that when the factories would open, they would not get rehired.

For the above reasons, the existence of trade unions in not only harder to ensure but also looked upon as undesirable for the trade.

3.3 Government Support

The people believe that the central government did little for the diamond workers, even though the opinion on the streets is that they should have organised some sort of package for the industry. The social security measures that exist were never enforced in Surat. The Income Tax Department said,

> The government has never really benefitted from the diamond industry. The fall in exports of diamonds doesn't really hamper the revenues of the government. There are no records. No one pays tax. It is highly secretive and organised on rules that are outside the law.

Needless to say, this is not a good enough reason for the inactivity of the government with regard to the situation. The Labour Ministry in Delhi says,

> Often times we have tried to introduce our national schemes in the diamond industry. We have Factory Laws and Labour Laws that should be enforced, but because the diamond industry was making so much money in the last three decades, nobody wanted the government's intervention. The government is seen as the 'party pooper' in neo-liberal surroundings such as the diamond industry.

The state government did begin a programme for unemployed diamond workers. The programme was administered by the Indian Diamond Institute (IDI) in Surat. The state government gave the diamond institute a grant to train unemployed diamond workers for three months. The lure of this training was not only to upgrade skills while waiting out the crisis but those who chose to enrol in this three-month programme would also get Rs 100 per day as a stipend. The workers learn how to chisel the stone through laser machines. Sameer Joshi, the deputy manager of the Institute, said that there were only 150 workers who had enrolled in the programme. Classes are held five times a week which means no payment for the weekends. The classes were in the afternoons so it was impossible for the enrolled to work in the earlier part of the day. The government scheme was largely taken up by the younger generation in the diamond industry, mostly belonging to families where they were not the sole breadwinners. Godrachinbhai, 22 years old, has been working in the industry for about two years. He had been asked to give up his studies and acquaint himself with diamond work as the financial conditions of the house were bad. His brother and father are also employed by the diamond industry. When the crisis set in, Godrachinbhai's factory shut down.

> After the crisis, my brother and father were having troubles finding a job, so I had no possibilities with my limited experience and skills. A government sponsored scheme to train workers and pay them for the training sounded like a really good idea to spend three months. I could acquire skills and be paid for doing so. I am doing the course on jewellery design. I also restarted my Bachelors in Commerce through correspondence. I feel like to survive in the Surat diamond industry it is essential to diversify. I don't want to be in a state that my father is in where the only thing you know how to do is to polish diamonds and if that is taken away then you have no other option. I want to start my own business and what I am doing right now fits into the larger scheme of things.

Prachinbhai, also 22, has worked in the industry for four years. His father, a diamond polisher, initiated him in the trade.

> I was learning the skill of planning when the recession hit. When I came in for my old job, I was told that my work was not up to the mark and I couldn't be rehired. I feel like the real reason was the fact that the factory had no work for me. Then I applied for this program. I felt like I could hone my planning skills further and use the newest machinery to do it and get paid Rs 100 per day.

The younger generation having seen such a crisis early in their careers, have decided to step away from the usual *karigari* of the industry and diversify. The government scheme provided them the opportunity to polish their skills and wait out the crisis in a safe environment. All the students seem to really appreciate the programme and had only good things to say about the quality of teaching. A course that costs close to Rs 15,000 for three months was being given to them for free and they were aware of the opportunity that presented. It is a luxury which was only afforded by 150 out of the alleged 800,000 workers in Surat.

3.4 Fall in Consumption

It is believed that high income risk, as seen during the crisis months in the industry, is reflected in household consumption levels which fluctuate and bear an imprint on nutrition, health and education (Dercon, 2000, p. ii). This was seen in Gujarat but even as consumption on luxuries fell the expenses on education remained stable. Education is now perceived as a necessity instead of a luxury. Govindbhai, a factory worker said,

> In the earlier months we stopped consuming milk, it is our biggest luxury and we indulged in it uninhibitedly. We also stopped going out to eat. We don't eat meat or consume alcohol but the quality of food deteriorated just a little. I thought it was better to make these sacrifices instead of pulling my children out of school. If they keep going to school, at least they will have more of a chance at a better life.

The diamond workers in Surat, despite the hard times, decided to prioritise differently for the future of the young generation.

3.5 Family Networks

The family network formed the strongest coping mechanism during the crisis. The diamond workers are still seen as strugglers, so it is almost impossible for them to get loans from mainstream credit channels. The workers most badly affected had no assets to give as collateral, so the only real means of getting a loan was the family, even though, since the entire community is involved in the diamond business, everyone was struck by the crisis and faced the same liquidity loss. Most workers turned to well-off relatives in the village for a short-term loan. Alkesh Bhai, who started work in the diamond industry seven years ago, said that the only source of money for him was his extended family in the village.

> We had gone to the village hoping to wait out the crisis but this didn't seem like a solution. My family and I decided to come back to the city but we had to borrow Rs 10,000 from my uncle to sustain the family while we figured out what was to be done next. We borrowed it for our daily expenses and rent since we had no savings.

When asked why people think the crisis has come to the diamond industry, many believed that it is because women were allowed to touch the stone and must have jinxed the trade which had done so well for so long. Yet, when the men lost their jobs it was the women who took up the mantle of supporting the household. The society is conservative and women are traditionally supposed to be confined to the household and care for the home and children. However, since the crisis took away the means of livelihood from the sole breadwinner of the family and it was hard to find a new means of sustaining themselves, the women were forced to take up employment. The wives of the diamond workers began taking up home-based work to contribute to the finances of the house. Even in times of crisis the society remained conservative, so most women were still expected to care for the house and did not explore the option of more profitable employment.

Sangitaben, a diamond worker's wife took up home-based embroidery work to earn some money while her husband was waiting for his factory to reopen. She borrowed money from her father and bought an electric sewing machine and got her brother, a textile worker, to source her some work.

> I have to cut the threads at the back of each one and hem the sides. Each piece takes about half an hour and I get paid Rs. 0.50 per piece. I do about 20 pieces every day, which amounts only to Rs10 per day. I also give out pieces to women in my neighbourhood, and get a commission from my brother for working as a middle-man. Unfortunately, we aren't paid for the thread, or electricity for the machine and it is hard work which isn't remunerated properly but it is more than nothing so I do it.

Amleshbhai, also a diamond worker in one of the bigger factories in Surat, encouraged his wife to pick up embroidery work after he lost his job in November when the factory shut down and he couldn't find a job. She sows the sequins on to saris.

> Someone comes and drops off the maal and she is supposed to sew the sequins on the saris. She already had a machine so there was no investment ... She makes Rs 5 per piece and can make up to Rs 100 per day if she gets the work and can find enough time to make 20 pieces. Her income helped the house immensely.

The family networks emerged as the greatest source of security during the crisis. They were not only an economical but also an emotional cushion which helped see many workers through the crisis.

3.6 Caste Ties

Caste is the strongest tie in the diamond industry. It is used for the extension of the business, sifting of employees and as a tool of control. Since the industry is run like a large family business, it would be easy to assume that caste played a definite role in the coping as well. However, this was not entirely true. The Patels did not feel that being from the dominant caste had benefitted them in coping but others, outside the caste, did. Again, caste was used as a tool of exclusion from which drawbacks and benefits emerge. Arvindbhai is from the scheduled caste, his family has been in Surat since the 1960s. He got involved in the diamond industry through a family member but his lower caste has always been an issue when trying to find a job. When the industry was in boom, he could manage to get employment because there was a need for workers skilled in diamond polishing. However, things changed significantly for the diamond industry when the crisis came in and even more so Arvindbhai and others like him who did not belong to the Patel caste,

> When applying to sit in the factory, I was asked my caste and as soon I said I was a scheduled caste they would refuse me work. They would say that the Patels don't like sitting for 8–10 hours next to an 'untouchable'. I began lying about my caste to get work then. Since I was a skilled worker, even if they found out later the managers would ignore it. When the crisis set in, I asked my Patel friends to recommend me for jobs in their factories and they would say that in this crisis, when upper castes are not getting work, it's almost impossible for a lower caste to do so.

Satish Bhai, a diamond worker who belongs to the Patel caste, lost his job like everyone else. His old factory is still closed and he has found a job in another factory through the recommendation of a family member.

> I did lose my job, but so did everyone else. The crisis was so bad that it didn't matter what caste you belong to. Being a Patel doesn't really help in Surat in any case and it definitely didn't help during the crisis. My landlord (who is also a Patel) did give us a waiver in the rent for two months. Caste affiliations make a difference but not when everyone is in the same rocky boat.

3.7 Mass Migrations

When the factories did not reopen in November after Diwali, many of the workers left for their villages. These people were mostly those who were living in Surat in rented accommodations. Return migration, a rare phenomenon in developing countries, was a logical option in this case because the cost of living in the city is significantly higher than that in the villages. Most of the people who moved back had land to go back to, which means that the ties to the city are often superseded by the ties to the village because of the existence of agricultural land. The idea was to find employment through the NREGA which has now become a popular scheme in large parts of rural India.

However, it is interesting to note that even though the realisation of the crisis had set in by December, the masses only moved back in April (*Indian Express*, 2009b) after the school exams of the children finished. This implies that a number of workers chose to struggle for a few months for the sake of their children's education.

3.8 From Diamond Polishing to Tea Stalls

A large number of diamond workers, after having given up on the trade as a means of earning a livelihood, began looking at other options. Notably, most people who branched out to other trades were those who were outsiders to the Patel community, the city of Surat and the state of Gujarat.

Rammahurat came from Uttar Pradesh in 1991. He has worked in the diamond industry ever since. His wife and children were with him until March, but after the children finished their exams, they left for their village where they go to school now. Rammahurat's factory owners kept the workers hanging. He says they kept postponing the date of opening. Finally the factory opened at the end of January. He was not happy with the state of affairs and decided to open a small tea stall in a quaint corner of the city. For now business was slow but he seemed hopeful.

Many see diversification of income as a viable option. Interestingly, all respondents who chose to diversify did so within the informal sector.

3.9 Suicides

Some people chose to end their lives in face of the recession. In April a Gujarati film called, 'Have Mare Heera Nathi Ghasva', translated 'I do not want to polish diamonds anymore' was produced. The film was catering to the unemployed workers of the diamond industry, trying to encourage them not to commit suicide and to return back to their villages. This is a small indication of the number of suicides that were taking place in Surat and other parts of Gujarat as the crisis was beginning to set in and it was seen that it was going to stay. Much like most numbers in the diamond industry, the numbers of suicides are hard to calculate. *Pragoti* magazine (February, 2009) put this number at 71. However, the field research brought up a number close to 200. Comrade Dhar, a member of the CPI, Delhi went for a reconnaissance in Surat in July, 2009 and said, '200 people have committed suicides in Gujarat state and about 90 of them are in Surat'. However, the local Member of Legislative Assembly (MLA) for Surat, completely denied the correlation between the suicides and the recession. He was of the belief that most of the displaced workers had been absorbed in other parts of Surat's economy or had left for their villages. He also stated that even when the crisis was in full swing in December and January, the question of survival had not really been the concern. The people had savings which they had dipped into. As to suicides, the MLA believed that brouhaha was media hype. In his belief, the crisis was not bad enough to provoke suicides, the factories were closed only for two months and that was not a long enough time to push people to the brink.

Even though it was not possible to talk to the families of the deceased, most diamond workers had heard of stories of people who were in debt and had no option but to kill themselves along with their entire families. These were not workers who had been in the trade for many years who could rely on their savings, nor the ones who had land in their villages to go back to; these were not workers who lived in small rented accommodations in austerity. The research proved that those who died were not really the poorest of the lot, they were usually the middle income group who had taken loans to buy a house in the city and had no link with the villages.

4. CONCLUSION: THE INDUSTRY TWO YEARS ON

A year after the crisis set in, the Surat diamond industry had begun to show signs of recovery. Newspaper reports at the time suggested that the industry was regaining its lost lustre and demand for polished diamonds was increasing (*Indian Express*, 2009c). One year after the field visit, this remains true. There is an increase in demand for diamonds internally along with from the Middle East and East Asia. There was a real increase of 20 per cent in cut and polished diamonds in February–March, 2010 compared with 2009 (*Business Line*, 2010). However, it is interesting to note that the quality of diamonds being sold in the markets was lowered in order to make them more affordable. Since the trade has picked up, and the workers who moved back to the villages during the recession have still not returned to Surat, there is a severe shortage of labour (ibid.). This has increased the bargaining power of the workers who went on strike at the beginning of June, 2010 when the owners of the factories decided to reduce the piece rate of the stone (in light of lower quality) (DNA, 2010).

NOTES

1. The research (an MA thesis at ISS) aims to understand the workings of an informal industry and to examine the surrounding labour relations.
2. Chapter 10 by Karin Siegmann provides a general background of informal labour and developments in India and elsewhere in Asia.
3. The report was being filed when the research was taking place.
4. Sanghvi Exports is a sightholder and one of the biggest exporters of diamonds to the United States of America.
5. The state government of Gujarat is led by the Bharatiya Janta Party and the Central government is led by the Congress Party. Both these parties belong to different ideological groups and do not see eye to eye on many issues.
6. Small factories with just a few *ghantis,* which employ about 10–15 workers.

15. Defending Vulnerable Workers in South Africa after the Crisis: What Role for COSATU?

Freek B. Schiphorst

The crisis did not spare South Africa. Employment showed an increase until the last quarter of 2008, but then plunged. The economy shrank by 1.8 per cent with mining and manufacturing particularly hard hit showing a decrease in output of 7 and 12 per cent respectively (Gordhan 2010, p. 5). By the middle of 2010 over 1.1 million people had lost their job since the beginning of 2009 (Statsa 2009 and 2010, p. vi). Unemployment rose to 25 per cent and if one includes the people who are discouraged from looking for a job, even to 36.5 per cent (Statsa 2010, p. v; see also Verick 2010a). The coverage of the Unemployment Insurance Fund (UIF) is very uneven and the benefits small.[1] Rising unemployment and discouragement thus mean that people have to resort to vulnerable jobs to secure their livelihood. This begs the question what vulnerable workers can expect from organised labour to give them voice and representation, if not something more tangible. This chapter will explore this question by looking at what COSATU has done to defend the interest of vulnerable workers in South Africa. I will first explore the size of the vulnerable workforce in South Africa. Then I will analyse official COSATU documents on its policy towards the informal economy. Then I will present two attempts to give voice to vulnerable workers in South Africa and examine the role played by the COSATU in each of them. These cases are: the Self Employed Women's Union (SEWU) and Sikhula Sonke, an independent trade union organising farm workers in the Western Cape.[2]

1. TRADE UNIONS AND VULNERABLE WORKERS

For quite some time now, trade union leaders, policy advisers and organisers the world over are concerned with the growing importance of informal work and the decline of formal sector employment (Adu-Amankwah 1999). This concern has many facets: a loss of membership and resources is certainly one, but not the only one. The representativeness of the trade union movement also became an issue; with the dramatic decline in formal sector employment what claim could a trade union have to be 'the voice of working people' if it was engaged only with formal work? Finally, with the often degrading conditions of work in the informal economy notions of labour solidarity played a role. So, despite a few odds (elaborated below), a trade union seems to be an obvious candidate to redress the voice deficit of the working poor in the informal economy.

There are at least three arguments that seemingly stop trade unions from engaging constructively with (and for) vulnerable workers in the informal economy. Traditional views have it that a union should only organise wage workers, and since workers in the informal economy often are own account workers these count as entrepreneurs. An equally antiquated view holds that a trade union should first organise completely the formal sector and only once that has been achieved turn its attention to workers in the informal economy. The view is antiquated, not only because it totally ignores the basic tenet of worker organisation (i.e. labour solidarity) but also because – as in the case of South Africa – it is based on the outdated view that the informal economy is small in size and therefore does not yet need the full attention of the trade union. We shall return to question of size shortly. A third objection is more difficult to counter, since it is not based on dogma but on unruly reality. Some fear that by organising the working poor the interests organised by a trade union become too heterogeneous. These diverse interests might now even become directly opposing. Suppose a union would organise both the workers in a large factory as well as the working poor in the small and micro establishments with whom this large firm has cut-throat contracts to supply it with parts and half-products. Any improvement in the condition of these working poor will directly be debited to the wages and conditions of the union members in the large firm. This is a zero-sum game: the gain of one is the loss of the other. And thus, it is better not to bring such opposing interests into the fold of one organisation and complicate matters. Indeed, convincing existing trade union members of the need to extend union services to informal workers is a major obstacle. This is compounded by the fact that informal workers often are not able to meet the subscription requirements that ordinary trade union members face (Adu-Amankwah 1999).

We will turn to South Africa now and first sketch an overview of the magnitude of the phenomenon of the vulnerable workers there. The main focus in this chapter is on COSATU, arguably one of the strongest and best endowed central labour organisations in Sub Saharan Africa (with the Nigerian Labour Congress being at least numerically stronger). With a membership of 1.8 million, COSATU by far outnumbers the other national centres in the country,[3] and as a member of the national Tripartite Alliance – with the ANC and SACP – it is close to the powers that be.

2. VULNERABLE WORKERS IN SOUTH AFRICA

Compared to other countries on the African continent the size of the informal economy is relatively small. Three-quarters of non-agricultural employment in Sub Saharan Africa is informal and over 90 per cent of new jobs are in the informal economy. And with informal work I refer – following the ILO usage of the term – to work which is not registered, recognised or protected within legal and regulatory frameworks (Table 15.1).

Table 15.1 Labour market indicators and employment by sector (1000s)

Population 15–64	31,399	Total employed	12,742
Total economically active	17,054	Formal (non-agric)	8,845
Total employed	12,742	Informal (non-agric)	2,124
Total unemployed	4,312	Agriculture	618
Discouraged work-seekers	1,907	Domestic	1,155
Other not active	12,438		

Source: Data for June 2010 according to Statsa 2010, p.vi

At first glance, the number of the informally employed is less than 20 per cent of total employment and thus far less than the average for Sub-Saharan Africa. However, this is misleading. In the absence of social security protection we have to assume that the unemployed as well as the discouraged work-seekers will have to find some income in the informal economy. Work in the domestic service as well as in agriculture is widely recognised as vulnerable (see King 2007 and Vavi 2010) and, thus we have to add those categories as well (Table 15.2).

A narrow focus on people in informal employment obscures the magnitude of vulnerable workers. This could easily create the impression that with a relatively small size the urgency is also small. This seems to be the picture that COSATU paints for its members. In its report to the Congress in 2006, COSATU's secretariat uses phrases like 'the share of informal employment has remained fairly stable since 1996' and 'the decline compared to 1999' above a table which shows that the informal sector only has 23 per cent of total employment (COSATU 2006, p. 39). The report for the Congress in September 2009 is silent about its role in the informal economy and it almost seems that the only type of vulnerable worker recognised by COSATU is the contract worker hired by labour brokers.

Table 15.2 Vulnerable workers, June 2010 (1000s)

	Total	Female	Male
Total unemployed	4,312	2,152	2,160
Discouraged work-seekers	1,907	1,070	837
Informal	2,124	933	1,190
Domestic	1,155	910	244
Agriculture	618	214	404
Vulnerable	10,116	5,279	4,835
Formal	8,845	3,590	5,256

Source: Statsa 2010, p.vi and 2–3

3. COSATU

The first time COSATU was squarely confronted with the question of what to do with vulnerable workers was when the September Commission tabled its report to the Congress in 1997. In its chapter 'New Workers, New Members: Organising New Sectors and New Layers of Workers', the report identifies two options regarding the 'vulnerable sectors', the first one being:

> COSATU could continue as it currently does [i.e. with no change]. The result could be weak affiliates in many vulnerable sectors. The affiliates that are currently strong and well-organised would remain so. But overall, COSATU's position in the labour market would be weakened, and this would be likely to affect its influence. (September 1997, p. 6)

The second option is carried by the particularly poignant vision regarding the role of a trade union *vis-à-vis* workers in the informal economy.

> Most of those who work in the informal sector do so outside the protection of state regulation or union organisation. This makes them vulnerable to many different kinds of exploitation and oppression. Their weakness also impacts on the power and conditions of formal sector workers, weakening the position of trade unions in the labour market. Their plight therefore concerns COSATU, both from the point of view of promoting human rights and social justice in general, and from the point of view of protecting the strength of the trade union movement. (September 1997, p. 8)

The September Commission (1997, p. 8) recommends in particular two options. Firstly, to encourage affiliates to expand their activities to include workers in informal sector activities in their industrial sectors. Secondly to encourage organisations of informal sector workers to affiliate to it or even initiate the formation of informal-sector affiliates. The Commission urges COSATU to develop a strategy to encourage affiliates to extend their services to vulnerable workers. While it recognises that unions in these efforts may face financial problems – after all vulnerable workers are not able to contribute substantial dues – the Commission recommends COSATU:

> to develop a strategic focus on the vulnerable sectors. Strategies could include the internal transfer of resources from strong to weak affiliates... [and] ... a modest 'solidarity levy' could be levied on all affiliates. (1997, p. 9)

The report of the September Commission was subsequently duly adopted by Congress as a guideline for the future direction of the COSATU (Bonner 2004, p. 4). The Congress of COSATU in 2000 resolved that a special commission be established to prepare an organisational review. This high powered commission presented a report in 2001 to the First Central Committee of COSATU which called for efforts to 'expand existing membership and to reach out to workers in non-standard jobs and the informal economy' (COSATU 2001, p. 21). The report then proposes a two-pronged approach. On the one hand, it suggests (as 'the best way') that the government takes the lead improving conditions for vulnerable workers. On the other hand the commission urges that a study explores the feasibility

> of establishing service centres in the regions to reach out to workers in the informal sector as well as domestic and farm workers. Advice centers would both help reduce the cost of serving these workers, and let workers get help from unions even if vulnerability at work means they cannot join. (COSATU 2001, p. 22).

The Organisational Review report to the National Congress in 2003 is not very explicit on the extension to the informal economy or vulnerable workers. The closest it comes to an appeal to its affiliates to devote attention to these workers is couched in general terms as follows:

> Given downsizing in the formal sector, recruitment is critical. Every affiliate should aim for 10% growth every year. In particular, we must ensure much higher density for COSATU unions in the formal sector, while continuing to support recruitment in the informal sector. (COSATU 2003, p. 22)

Rather than a two-pronged strategy for the long term, i.e. one in which simultaneously (vulnerable) workers in the formal and in the informal economy are targeted, it now seems that the focus is squarely put on recruitment in the formal sector.

Then NALEDI, COSATU's think-tank, picked up the gauntlet. It sourced funds for a review study and asked Chris Bonner – a well respected figure within COSATU – to produce an overview of the developments in organisational renewal. She wrote a critical yet constructive report painfully showing the slow progress COSATU has made since the September report in 1997. Bonner observes that:

> Extending the boundaries beyond 'traditional' membership type does not appear high on the agenda of many established affiliate organizational renewal programmes. Whilst the September Commission, as early a 1997, set out recommendations for organizing workers in the informal sector, and COSATU Congress of 2000 set out a programme to do so, unions have not generally prioritized this in their organizational renewal programmes. (2004, p. 34)

Bonner (2004, p. 34) explains how a few affiliates have gone to some length to support workers in informal employment and subsequently puts her finger on the crux of the matter:

> [the affiliates] have targeted 'atypical' or 'non-standard' workers in waged employment, such as casual and outsourced workers, workers employed through labour brokers and the like, rather than those who more clearly form part of the informal economy, such as street vendors.

As for the role of COSATU in organisational renewal, Bonner warns against having a lackadaisical attitude. Despite the fact that seven years had passed since the September Commission pointed the way, and with two national Congresses since then urging the organisation to take an active stance, no progress could be reported. Her study is based on interviews with the leadership of the affiliates and from these she reports:

> However, serious reservations have been expressed about the ability of COSATU and individual affiliates to successfully implement resolutions on organizational renewal and sustain the work, unless COSATU actively keeps it on the agenda, continuously 'whips' affiliates into action, and provides more support for affiliates processes. Since the 8th Congress it has failed to do this. COSATU leadership has influence, weight and authority with affiliates, which it is failing to maximize to promote and monitor affiliate organizational renewal work. (Bonner 2004, p. 61)

In February 2005 COSATU convened a strategic planning workshop which decided that COSATU would launch a new trade union 'for workers in the burgeoning informal economy (...) in a move aimed at boosting its stagnating membership' (Robinson 2005). The new union was to organise street vendors and producer groups, including home-based workers. It is clear from the two available reports of this meeting (Horn 2005, and Robinson 2005) that care had to be taken not to tread on the toes of existing affiliates. The new union was only to deal with self-employed workers outside the scope of existing affiliates, and so it would not affect 'workers in other sectors of the economy, including the taxi industry, construction and manufacturing, [who] will be absorbed into existing COSATU affiliates' (Robinson 2005).

It was decided at the workshop that prospective members would pay dues but it was also reported that a COSATU official thought that 'the new union will be supported financially by the foreign donors that sustained SEWU' (Robinson 2005). The workshop also agreed to have a dedicated National Co-ordinator to see to the implementation of the project (Horn 2005, p. 2). A year passed and COSATU's secretariat proposed the same to the Congress in 2006 (COSATU 2006, p. 42). Devenish and Skinner (2006, p. 256) optimistically report that COSATU committed itself to 'assist in establishing a new informal economy union [which] may well hire former SEWU staff'. Since then, little has been made public about this new project and by the end of 2010 nothing had materialised yet. At the tenth national Congress of COSATU out of a total 129 resolutions covering a total of 188 pages, only one resolution dealt with organising the unemployed and vulnerable workers. The resolution tabled by NUMSA called on COSATU to 'champion the struggle for vulnerable workers, by organising these workers and providing a service to them. The Department of Labour must assist in terms of resources for this to happen' (COSATU 2009, p. 141).[4]

Another topic of heated debate is the role of labour brokers. A long-standing phenomenon in South Africa, it became a very topical issue when in November 2008 the Supreme Court in Namibia ruled that a ban on them was not against the constitution (Ndungu 2009, p. 9). Within a month the South African Minister of Labour pronounced that the ANC planned to ban labour brokers as well, a statement welcomed by COSATU's spokesperson. Already in 2006 the Congress of COSATU had adopted resolutions for the federation to combat the abuse by labour brokers 'but no action was actually undertaken' (Ndungu 2009, p. 8). During 2009, COSATU rallied behind the Minister's call. At the Congress, four affiliates called for 'stringent regulation, if not outright outlawing of the labour broker industry and practices' (COSATU 2009, p. 79). Interestingly, the same resolution does not call on COSATU to step up its efforts to *organise* externalised workers. Instead the resolution calls on COSATU to fight for a change in the law that would convert 'all temporary, contract and casual jobs into permanent quality jobs' (COSATU 2009, p. 80).

All in all, one cannot escape the conclusion that COSATU is amply aware of the need to become engaged with informal work, both as a result of casualisation, informalisation and externalisation of formal workers and as a result of the growing number of people eking out a living without access to income out of the formal economy. However, it does not seem that COSATU leadership feels a sense of urgency, despite repeated recommendations from its own think-tank or resolutions from its own Congress. The result of such an approach can be seen in two cases to which we will now turn: the rise and fall of SEWU and the experience of Sikhula Sonke.

4. THE SELF EMPLOYED WOMEN'S UNION – SEWU

Easily the most cited example of organising workers in the informal economy in South Africa is the Self Employed Women's Union – SEWU (see Lund and Skinner 1999, 2004; Skinner 2000; Motala 2002; Bennett 2003; Chen et al. 2004; Devenish and Skinner 2004, 2007; Kabeer 2008; Theron 2010). This is quite extraordinary for a movement that existed only ten years: established in 1994, it closed down in 2004.

Inspired by the model set by SEWA in India, Pat Horn, a trade unionist of long standing in South Africa, decided to organise women in the informal economy. According to SEWU's constitution membership was only open to women who were working without regular waged employment, were involved in an economic activity not covered by any other trade union and who did not employ more than three others (Bennett 2003, p. 34). Although never registered as a trade union, SEWU's organisational model and practice were based on direct democracy (of workers controlling their own organisation) and its organisational form resembled that of a trade union (see Devenish and Skinner 2006, pp. 260–62).

SEWU's members were active at the lower end of the labour market in 'survivalist activities', with incomes of members being very low. Where initially membership was drawn from street vending, this over time broadened to include also home-based work and small-scale farming, for the major part in urban areas. The initial dominance of street vendors in its membership gave way over time to a dominance of home-based workers (Devenish and Skinner 2004, p. 17). After three years, in 1997, SEWU also opened offices in the Western Cape and in the Eastern Cape, and in 2001 offices were opened in two more provinces (Free State and Mpumalanga). These moves were only possible thanks to foreign donor funds.

Membership records for SEWU are difficult to gauge, in retrospect. SEWU had the habit of recording not only paying members but also 'lapsed' members, i.e. all those former members who had not paid their dues for six months. When figures are quoted it is not always clear whether reference is to paying members or to a combination of paying and lapsed members (see Motala 2002, p. 30; Devenish and Skinner 2004, p. 17). In the first three years of existence SEWU grew rapidly to 2,425 in 1997, and another three years later a peak was reached of 3,169 members[5] (Devenish and Skinner 2004, p. 16). In the following year a decline set in, the depth of which is unclear; one source gives 2,645, another 2,276 members for 2001. At this low point, SEWU reports 10,645 'lapsed' members (Motala 2002, p. 30). From then onwards the picture is ambiguous. Devenish and Skinner (2006, p. 261) claim that membership rose again to 4,930 in 2003, but another report speaks of a 'dramatic decline in membership in 2003' and a financial situation that could only be improved thanks to a reduction of staff in all provincial offices from three to one (Roos 2004, p. 2). At the peak of SEWU existence (in 2003) eight international donors were supporting SEWU with one organisation contributing 65 per cent of its annual budget.[6] However, at the end of that year all but this one major donor had left. One can imagine that in such a situation annual reports are beautified by an organisation desperately looking for a financial life-line.[7] Be this as it may, in the beginning of 2004, paid up membership stood at 1,967 and provincial offices were closed. The last remaining donor was by that time dissatisfied with the way in which SEWU and its leadership stumbled from crisis to crisis unable to stop the downward trend. The regional structures no longer functioned properly and also the head office lacked the managerial competence to keep financial administration in order. The nail in SEWU's coffin is reported to have been 'a decision of the CCMA,[8] the effect of which was to reinstate in its employ two dismissed officials. SEWU could simply not afford the cost of the accumulated back-pay consequent to this decision' (Theron 2007, p. 252). However, in an interview with a policy advisor of the last remaining donor it was mentioned that the fact that after ten years it had proven to be impossible to establish close working relationships with COSATU was felt as a major disappointment. Coupled to the sorry state of the organisation in 2004 (according to this policy advisor) it was not possible any more to continue the support in the absence of a strong local partner.[9] It seems that if COSATU had made a move, it might have been able to save SEWU!

With her own history in the formal trade union movement the founder of SEWU, Pat Horn, had realised how important the relations with COSATU would have been, for reasons of worker solidarity and for strategic reasons. As Devenish and Skinner (2006, p. 264) report:

> From the beginning the founder stressed that it was strategically necessary to position SEWU and its aims within the broader union movement. This was in fact critical to SEWU securing funding from the international trade union movement. COSATU head office acknowledged SEWU from the outset but

> ironically only at the time of SEWU's closure did national staff pay much attention to this small union. Prior to this, national SEWU staff expressed much frustration at the numerous meetings they tried to schedule with COSATU head office staff, that were either cancelled or no one arrived.

It seems that at one point in time there was rapprochement between SEWU and COSATU when the two shared the same donor and 'due to an interest in SEWU by COSATU's former president J. Gomomo. However, this relationship ended when Gomomo left COSATU' (Dlamini 2002, p. 76). Thereafter, according to the same study COSATU gave SEWU the cold shoulder, not even responding to correspondence from SEWU (Dlamini 2002, p. 77). COSATU shop stewards showed disdain for SEWU's representatives and two SEWU officials also provide a reason for this:

> They see SEWU as a sexist union – when you are at meetings they will say 'self employed workers union' and when you correct them they are upset ... some say yes we understand your position but we do not know why you want to be a union, why are you not an ordinary organisation, why are you not including men' and the officials [with whom the interview was held] add: 'They do not think that one day they might be self-employed or might be informal sector workers'. (Dlamini 2002, pp. 77–8)

Significant for SEWU was the progress it made in providing women with leadership. Membership training was an important activity, with activities in skill training directly relevant for its members' activities (e.g. sewing or business skills), as well as more general education and training in broader issues, e.g. literacy and English language (Devenish and Skinner 2004, pp. 25–8). These activities were particularly successful in empowering women members. SEWU thus pursued two approaches to serve its members: representation and empowerment. Jan Theron, who labels the latter as 'conventional empowerment strategies', queries whether 'the pursuit of empowerment and trade union-type demands can be reconciled within one organisation' (2007, p. 252).

5. GRASS ROOTS TRADE UNIONISM: SIKHULA SONKE

Sikhula Sonke was registered as a trade union in December 2004. It is the offspring of the work done by an NGO, the Women on Farms Project. By March 2006 it had 2,500 members (Jara 2006, p. 4), by November 2006 this had risen to 3,336. In March 2008 its website reports a membership of 3,600.[10] The annual report over 2008 lists a membership of 3,977 (Vehicle 2008, p. 7), while in 2010 a membership of 'nearly 5,000' is quoted (White 2010, p. 674).[11] Sikhula Sonke organises seasonal farm workers and it is open to male members, but it insists on women leadership 'because issues that affect women are largely neglected by mainstream unions' and 'because we believe that women must lead the efforts for change in their lives' (Sikhula n.d., p. 1). It is a membership-based organisation and in the first two years of its existence dues were 8 ZAR per month. This was raised to 15 ZAR at its Congress in September 2006 (interview data 2006).[12] It wants to operate as a social movement trade union and its focus, therefore, is not only on labour issues, but on 'all livelihood challenges of farm dwellers'. In this it wants to establish an 'integrated approach addressing the full range of farm workers problems' (interview data 2006). Sikhula Sonke sees itself as 'a vehicle for the voices of workers, a school where farm workers are educated and a sturdy house that protects workers' Sikhula Sonke (n.d., p. 1) wants

> to improve the living and working conditions of members and their dependants, including the youth and elderly and enhance the status of women and protect their interests. It wants to do this through collective bargaining on behalf of its members for improved wages and other working conditions, including housing. And it wants to improve the economic conditions of members by developing work and other economic opportunities.

By 2008 it had twelve branches (Vehicle 2008, p. 9). The Branch Executive holds monthly meetings with farm reps where organisers report on activities. In addition it created farm committees whose members (similar to shop stewards) receive training from Sikhula Sonke. The members elect a 'Resource Agent' who can assist farm workers to deal with their problems. There are weekly forums for organisers where plans are discussed and experiences shared (interview data 2006). From the range of 'common problems' Sikhula Sonke identified for farm workers it is clear that indeed it adopts a broad vision. On the one hand there are 'labour issues' like unfair dismissals, unsafe working conditions and non-payment of minimum wages or illegal deductions from wages. There is bad housing and intimidation of worker leaders. On the other hand Sikhula Sonke also wants to address the high school drop-out rates, food insecurity, gender-based violence and the legacy of alcoholism (interview data 2006).

The fight against evictions from farms was a main initial focal point of action, and this was broadened later to include legal assistance to workers challenging e.g. dismissals before court or through direct intervention with the employer. Sikhula Sonke also enters into collective agreements with individual farms and it tries to create a platform for farm committees to communicate regularly with employers. There are an increasing number of recognition agreements with farms which sometimes result also in a check-off arrangement. It also meets with individual employers regarding intimidation or the prevalence of alcoholism on their farms – on the latter score it is proud to report some success (interview data 2006).

Fiona White (2010) explains that Sikhula Sonke aims at building a democratic movement that challenges the paternalistic employer–employee relations and the highly unequal gender relations at the farms as well as the unfair labour practices. She concludes: 'Sikhula Sonke has made inroads into reducing social inequality between farmers and workers, between women and men and between different races' (2010, p. 680). However, she also reports that neither the branch meetings nor the meetings of the farm committee are held regularly and that their effectiveness varies.

A key reason for this, White argues, is 'the lack of organizational experience' (White 2010, pp. 676–7). Together with Women on Farms Sikhula Sonke also engages in collective action and campaigns – for example it participated actively in a campaign in 2005 targeting Tesco. As one of its challenges it lists that now bargaining is done on a one-on-one basis and it would like to see the formation of a bargaining council to get all the employers around the table (interview data 2006). It organises training and education sessions for shop stewards to equip them with skills to negotiate, and to give them legal knowledge so that they can represent members in hearings. Where, in all of this, one could wonder, is COSATU? Wendy Pekeur, the General Secretary of Sikhula Sonke, said that a COSATU rep attended the congress in 2006 and praised: 'You achieved what not even our affiliate could do' (interview data 2006). More specifically asked about the links with COSATU she explained: 'We're nervous by the politics in COSATU. We are a bit scared, with this support for Zuma, it is confusing. We prefer a non-political trade union.' As for affiliation to COSATU she said: 'At the moment we want to consolidate ... maybe in the future' (interview data 2006).

Fiona White reports that by 2007 the COSATU Western Cape Provincial Secretary claimed to have a 'good relationship' with Sikhula Sonke and indeed both organisations shared public platforms, e.g. demonstrating against evictions with a march to Parliament in 2007. But this co-operation does not go beyond the recognition of Sikhula Sonke's existence, and possibly some moral support, i.e. no material support (in whatever form) is given. COSATU does not open up its educational programmes to Sikhula Sonke.[13] COSATU also does not facilitate the participation of Sikhula Sonke members in the training programmes DITSELA offers.[14]

6. EXPLANATIONS FOR COSATU'S RELUCTANCE

Despite numerous calls from its own affiliates COSATU, as the main national umbrella organisation for labour failed to pick up the gauntlet thrown by globalisation and flexibilisation in the form of ever-increasing numbers of vulnerable workers. Reasons for this reluctance could be numerous. A first clue could be found if one realises that there is an ever growing gap between earnings of union members and non-members. An analysis of trends in 50 wage settlements in the collective agreements of eight sectors in 2006/7 show average monthly salaries of ZAR 8,500 (Ndungu 2007, pp. 5–7), with incomes in the informal economy well below 2,000 ZAR. An earlier survey showed that the average income for COSATU members was one-and-a half times the income of non-members (NALEDI 2006, p. 55). Further, union members stood a better chance of receiving benefits such as medical aid, retirement fund, paid leave and a written contract of employment.

So, it could well be that union members affiliated in COSATU are more and more distancing themselves from the working poor. However, this is not very likely. On the one hand, every wage earner maintains up to five dependants, and so the reality of livelihood struggles is vividly present in almost every household. On the other hand, COSATU affiliates do try and reach out to vulnerable workers, whether in the formal or informal sectors. Affiliates are attempting to organise in their respective sectors: construction workers, casual shop workers, industrial home workers, minibus drivers, security guards and cleaning workers (Horn 2008, p. 4). It is COSATU itself – as a national centre – that does not make a move. An explanation for this could be inspired by the sociological theory of opportunism, suggested by Offe and Wiesenthal (1985). The argument is that a trade union at a certain stage of its development depends for its continued success on openings offered by the state rather than on extending and mobilising its membership base. COSATU leadership seems so keen on its position within the tripartite alliance and the influence this has yielded in many a tripartite national forum that it neglects calls for an organisational renewal. Not that these calls are easy to heed. Theron (2010, p. 88) recently referred to a 'wage culture' which now blocks the emergence of solidarity. Such a wage culture locks the established trade unions in a logic of collective action which is only focussed on collective bargaining. Dealing with vulnerable workers (a substantial part of whom are not wage workers but basically entrepreneurs) then not only becomes an ideological anathema, but would also require a behavioural split. Theron argues for a paradigm shift as 'the prospect of waged employment is increasingly unrealistic for ever larger numbers'. Such a shift should again render membership-based organisations meaningful for the poor.

A glimmer of hope could be found in the approach which makes especially Sikhula Sonke successful. It has a broad agenda, and uses a wide array of approaches: collective action and individual mediation, through representation as well as membership empowerment. Contrary to Theron's fears (see Theron 2007, p. 252) such a combined approach is not only possible for a trade union but seems also to be successful for union and members alike. It could well be, though, that it is especially this combination of representation and empowerment that makes it difficult for COSATU to follow, locked as it seems to be in an exclusive representational mode – a mode that is focussed at representation at national levels at the expense of local levels.

7. CONCLUSION

This chapter has examined the approach of COSATU towards vulnerable workers, both as informalised workers linked to the formal sector as well as workers engaged in informal work. The record of the federation is not positive. Despite numerous resolutions at its national congresses, COSATU seems to face major internal hurdles to get something off the ground. This could be partly because of the problems inherent in engaging with vulnerable workers and partly because of an inclination to deal first and foremost with the formal sector. It would seem that a rejuvenated commitment is required for the national centre to take up the plight of the vulnerable workers.

The comparison between COSATU, on the one hand, and on the other hand SEWU and Sikhula Sonke – two cases of organising for vulnerable workers – shows that a combination of different modes of collective action (representation and empowerment) seems to offer changes for success. In SEWU's case COSATU's absence contributed to its downfall. What COSATU's arm's-length practice will mean for Sikhula Sonke is something the future only will tell. However, with a more prominent role in collective bargaining in the future it would seem that a partnership of some sorts would allow the negotiators of Sikhula Sonke to draw on the vast experience of COSATU in this respect. Such a partnership could be mutually valuable in that COSATU could learn to broaden its range of collective action modes to include empowerment strategies. And from this, so it seems, vulnerable workers whose ranks have grown so dramatically after the crisis hit South Africa could benefit.

INTERVIEWS

Wendy Pekeur, General Secretary Sikhula Sonke, 4 November 2006, Cape Town.

Elijah Mutemeri, Informal Economy Programme Coordinator, ZiCTU, 22 February 2010, Harare.

Vimbai Mushongera Zinyama, Parliament, Advocacy & International Affairs (previously Informal Economy Programme) ZiCTU, 22 February 2010, Harare.

Miriam Chikamba, Head Education Department, ZiCTU, 24 February 2010, Harare.

NOTES

1 A worker registered and contributing for four years to the UIF can claim a maximum of 58 per cent of a day's salary for 218 days (www.capegateway.gov.za/). Verick (2010b, p. 28) concludes: 'employment protection legislation (EPL) in South Africa is relatively weak. Thus, workers are neither provided protection of jobs through EPL nor protection of income via unemployment benefits.'

2 Fieldwork was undertaken in South Africa in 2006. Subsequent interviews were held in Harare in February 2010 with officials of the Zimbabwe CTU.

3 NACTU (400,000 members in 2003), FEDUSA (515,000 in 2003) and CONSAWU (240,000 in 2006) (Schiphorst et al. 2007). These four federations (and 250 independent trade unions) had a union density in 2004 of close to 40 per cent. After the onset of the crisis this dropped to just under 30 per cent.

4 NUMSA is the National Union of Metal Workers in South Africa that proudly calls itself the 2nd largest trade union in South Africa. It is remarkable that a trade union of this stature calls on the government to fund organisational renewal. It contrasts sharply with earlier calls for the stronger affiliates to assist the weaker ones. It is, however, fully in agreement with the attitude that government should take the lead and/or should pick up the tab.

5 The authors claim that these figures are based on SEWU's annual reports. Motala reports a figure of 3,095 for 2000 (2002, p. 30).

6 'Members' fees [are] 5% of SEWU's costs. The rest [is] from international donors, … trade unions and foreign governments' (Budlender 2003, p. 17).

7 It is more difficult to understand why after the collapse of SEWU authors who should know better also push membership figures for SEWU to mythical heights. Devenish and Skinner (2006, p. 261) report a maximum of 4,930 members by the end of 2003, but later write that SEWU had 10,000 members (2007, p. 54). Chen et al. (2004, p. 161) even mention a figure of 25,000.

8 Commission for Conciliation, Mediation and Arbitration.

9 Given the amounts involved the donor would have easily been able to pick up the costs of two years' salary of the verdict (interview data 2006).

10 See: http://www.sikhulasonke.org/, 12 March 2008; see also the Women on Farms Project at http://www.wfp.org.za/, 14 January 2008. Additional information was obtained during an interview with the General Secretary in 2006. In 2009 the URL of Sikhula Sonke changed to www.ssonke.org.za.

11 'Drawn from over 200 different farms in ten geographical locations in the Western Cape' (White 2010, p. 674).

12 The 2008 annual report (total membership 3,977; membership income ZAR 140,420) suggests that monthly dues are 3 ZAR (Vehicle 2008, pp. 7–37). The report shows that membership fees account for 6 per cent of operating and programme costs, the remainder covered by (foreign) grants and donations.

13 This is what the union centre in Zimbabwe did: accept the organisation of informal workers as an affiliate and invited its members to ZCTU education events. It produced a manual for para-legal training for informal workers.

14 DITSELA is the Development Institute for Training, Support and Education for Labour, formed by the labour movement and the Ministry of Labour in 1996 and is highly regarded for the quality education and training it offers. Although created to serve the whole labour movement in South Africa COSATU tends to see it as an 'extension of its own education department over which it has exclusive control' (see Schiphorst et al. 2007, p. 58).

16. How China Managed the Impact of the Financial Crisis: Globalization and Public Policy Responses in an Emerging Economy

Arjan de Haan and Sen Gong*

In May 2010, at a time with mixed prospects of a recovery of the global economy, possibly a second part of the double-dip recession in the making, and continuously heated debates on the rights and wrongs and sustainability of the Keynesian policies of the last two years, *The Economist* summarised the fears around the health of the world economy as follows: 'the global recovery will falter as Europe's debt crisis spreads, China's property bubble bursts and America's stimulus-fuelled rebound peters out.'[1] The significance of this statement was not in the prediction of the direction of the global economy, uncertain as it was, nor its analysis of the adequacy of governments' responses, but in the fact that the reference to the US, Europe and China as the pillars of the global economy confirms the importance of the emergence of a country that was poorer than most African countries only 30 years ago, and for which the global financial crisis presented the 'opportunity' to reassert the global role it has been assuming over the past decades, even though China was understandably keen to downplay its emerging global role.

After a brief discussion of the financial crisis, how it impacted China, and the recovery over the last 12 months or so, this chapter focuses on the role that China's public policy played in managing the impact of the financial crisis. This has a number of components. First of all, there are indications that China was well-prepared for the crisis, probably having learnt the lessons from the 1997–98 crisis. This appears directly in line with China's pragmatic reform policies which had become its hallmark since 1978. Second, the crisis response – 'pragmatic' as this is – can be conceptualised as a double balancing act, of domestic and international politics, and of economics and politics, including managing the expectations and fears around China's global rise. Third, while the fiscal stimulus package has been celebrated as a key ingredient of China's successful response, this chapter describes how this stimulus was fiscally sustainable in a way that Keynesians can only dream of, and its composition was very much in line with China's previous productivist-focused social policies, while continuing the gradual upward trend of investment in social sectors which had been initiated in the 1990s and reinforced under the 'harmonious society' project of the Hu-Wen administration. In this context, we discuss how the fiscal stimulus package was dwarfed by the size of bank loans that followed central government directives. By themselves, however, these measures are unlikely to address the structural challenges that China's development model faces. In the conclusion we ask the question whether there are lessons from the way China's public policies have addressed the financial crisis.

1. GLOBAL FINANCIAL CRISIS, RECOVERY AND ASIA

The financial crisis of 2008 was, according to Krugman (2009d, pp. 165–6), rather than being like nothing that had been seen before, 'like everything we've seen before': a combination of real estate bubble, wave of bank runs, liquidity trap, and crisis in international financial intermediation, capital flows and currencies. Cracks in the system had appeared in August 2007 with subprime mortgage problems and the French bank BNP suspending withdrawals, and this turned into a full-blown financial crisis in September 2008 with the default of Lehman Brothers. Stock markets may have declined by around 50 per cent and global GDP was expected to decline by 3 per cent in 2009. In the same year, global trade fell, for the first time in almost three decades.

Of course, the impacts on the rest of world have been highly heterogeneous, across countries and within countries, through impacts on trade, investments, capital flows, migration and remittances, and with varying time lags. Outside the OECD, the immediate impact was perhaps no more visible than in China, particularly in the areas that were previously the most dynamic parts of the global economy. The limited openness of China's financial sector helped to reduce the direct impact of the global financial crisis on China, but the stock market was affected. Exports declined, in the last months of 2008, and by about 20 per cent in the first half of 2009. Manufacturing firms resorted to massive de-stocking. FDI into China saw a decline of 20 per cent in the first seven months of 2009 compared to the same period in 2008. In coastal areas an estimated 20 million jobs were lost, and tens of thousands of factories reportedly closed down throughout 2008.

While the potential for social unrest among laid-off workers was closely monitored by Chinese officials, throughout the latter part of 2008 and 2009, senior policy makers and most analysts remained optimistic that China would be able to weather the crisis well (see for example World Bank 2009a). President Hu Jintao stressed: 'Crisis creates opportunities, and we shall put more efforts in technological upgrading, and build up technology reserves for the future.'[2] Despite heavy blows to the export industry, China had the fiscal and macroeconomic space to implement a substantial stimulus, and does not rely on external financing. There are doubts about available data – regarding GDP, bank information, figures on unemployment and new jobs – but this does not have a big impact on the assessment that China was managing the effects of the global crisis, and the optimism (and some nationalist sentiments) was consciously fuelled in the public debate.

In August 2009 the global news was getting better: France, Germany and Japan were exiting from recession – but with continued doubts whether this was a recovery of the real economy or driven by government stimulus – and unemployment figures in the US started to appear less bad than expected. Predictions emerged that the world economy would reach positive growth in 2010, and while uncertainty continues to exist particularly in Europe, growth figures have again become slightly positive, though living standards are generally not improving. Private capital flows to emerging markets which had fallen from a peak of 1,200 billion in 2007 to 435 billion in 2009, picked up again slightly (Institute of International Finance, 2010).

Table 16.1 Growth rate of GDP (% per year)

	2007	2008	2009	2010 (expected)
Developing Asia	9.6	6.6	5.2	7.5
East Asia	10.4	7.3	5.9	8.3
China	13.0	9.6	8.7	9.6
Global		2.0	−1.9	3.4
Global excluding China		1.5	−2.6	3.0

Source: ADB (2010, p. 8); last two rows World Bank (2010g).

Asia, and China in particular, led the recovery, though the recovery is thought to be fragile with risks of early withdrawal of fiscal stimulus, price deflation and volatile capital flows. China's growth rate never dropped below 6 per cent and reached the 8 per cent target again in 2009, when its economy grew by 8.7 per cent, while East Asia's expanded by 5.9 per cent (ADB 2010; see Table 16.1). While FDI declined during 2008 and 2009 (World Bank 2009a), and exports declined throughout 2009 by about 10 per cent, the external economy too rebounded in the second part of the year (World Bank 2010b). China's trade surplus has again been on the rise, though with fluctuations, experiencing the effects of uncertainty in European markets.

The migrants in China's coastal zones who lost their urban jobs in large numbers in late 2008 had almost all found new urban employment by mid-2009, although not necessarily in the same workplace (OECD 2010), and in early 2010 reports started to appear that shortages of (semi-skilled) labour had re-appeared. It is likely that the crisis led to the worsening of labour conditions of many in the export-oriented industries, as the trend of improving conditions was reversed in the early phase of the economic crisis. In May–June 2010 a wave of labour protests occurred in export-oriented factories (including a series of suicides by Foxconn workers), but it is not clear whether this is related to the economic crisis (as the violence in the toy factory which prompted the violence in Xinjiang was) and recovery since, or a continuation of a rising trend of protests over the last decade.

The overall positive story about how China has managed the crisis should not stop us from looking at the process very carefully, as it may tell us important stories both about the Chinese development 'model' and its growing global role; the crisis did not initiate or even fundamentally change any of the directions, but arguable has articulated some of these more clearly, as discussed in the following two sections.

2. CHINA, THE GLOBAL ECONOMY AND CRISES

> U.S. finance is closely connected with the Chinese finance. If anything goes wrong in the U.S. financial sector, we are anxious about the safety and security of Chinese capital. That's why ... I have made it clear that the financial problems in this country [China] not only concerns the interests of the United States but also that of China and the world at large. (Premier Wen Jiabao in CNN interview, 23 September 2008)

Globally, governments' responses to the economic crisis have been forceful, and apparently very different from the crisis of the 1930s, or indeed different from the advice that was given to East Asian governments after the 1997–98 crisis. The focus has been to restore global financial stability, through large-scale government interventions across the world, and a range of micro-level measures has been introduced in response to increasing unemployment and, for example, to promote housing markets. All these have contributed to a large increase in public debt in many countries, which are now at the heart of the debate on continuing or ending the fiscal stimulus, with the G20 meeting in June 2010, for example, urging the reduction of budget deficits, and cuts starting to bite even in the moderately-affected OECD countries.

The crisis once again highlighted the extent of global interconnectedness, but also with a strong commitment – unlike after the 1929 crisis – to ensure global policy coordination, and attempts to avoid or limit protectionism. One of the issues that received even more attention than before the financial crisis was the role of the emerging economies. Early post-crisis analysis stressed correctly that emerging economies would be able to overcome the (impact of the) crisis in a short period of time, as their banks generally had not been directly impacted, due to the build up of resilience after the Asian crisis and because of the counter-cyclical packages put in place.[3] Moreover, the size of the emerging economies like Brazil, India, Indonesia and China also enabled them to have more isolation from global fluctuations (Addison et al. 2010).

The inter-connectedness is forcefully demonstrated by China, in our view contradicting ideas of de-coupling which resurged after the crisis.[4] The interconnectedness was directly the result of the reform path China has followed since 1978, in turn increasingly shaping the global economy, including through investments in the 'forgotten' continent Africa, and through an impact on commodity prices. The figures of China's growing global economic importance are well known, as are the heated debates related to the Chinese currency and 'savings glut', for example (see Andrew Fischer, Chapter 6 in this volume). While still a lower–middle-income country, it has experienced three decades of high levels of even, though not uninterrupted, growth. Recent years saw almost uninterrupted economic growth of over 10 per cent per year, similar to the East Asian miracle countries earlier, and China has thus become the world's second largest economy, and the fastest growing one, even though tens of millions of people still live in extreme poverty.

Like East Asian growth performances, China's has been based on developing industrial capabilities, with strategic industrial policies and using transfer of technology from foreign firms (Rodrik 2009), and growing shares and already high technology levels in exports. While agriculture and later rural industrialisation drove the restoration of China's economy in the 1970s and 1980s, exports have been a main driver of subsequent economic growth (alongside capital formation), forming over one-third to 40 per cent of GDP before the crisis (see Yang 2008). China's share in world trade rose to 7 per cent by 2005, with exports to the US about one-third of China's total.[5] Foreign investments in China have played an increasingly important role for its exports, and over time policy moved from joint ventures towards allowing wholly foreign owned companies. Fairly suddenly, as Figure 16.1 demonstrates, China also has become an important investor abroad (reinforced after the crisis, for example, in the oil sector), by both private and state companies, and supported by government policy. China developed large surpluses in current, capital and financial accounts, and accumulated huge international reserves (estimated at over $2 trillion) – which with the financial crisis have become a major concern and point of debate.

Events since the financial crisis and the dramatic pictures of millions of Chinese migrant workers returning home indicate that the way China is integrated in the global economy is changing less radically than suggested in the judgement by *The Economist* (13 June 2009), that we had witnessed the end of export-led growth, a view shared by some Chinese officials. Data since mid-2009 – arguably a turning point for China's economic crisis – are gradually emerging, with economic growth now at about 9 per cent (World Bank 2010a). Exports increased rapidly during 2009, faster than the growth of external demand, with exporters increasing competitiveness. But the trade surplus continued to decline, with imports increasing and declining terms of trade. While the government stimulus has gradually been withdrawn, household consumption has continued to increase, alongside heavy investment in real estate; we discuss these recent changes below, asking whether they imply a break in China's development model, but first discuss China's pattern of reforms over the last 30 years and the role of social policies in this.

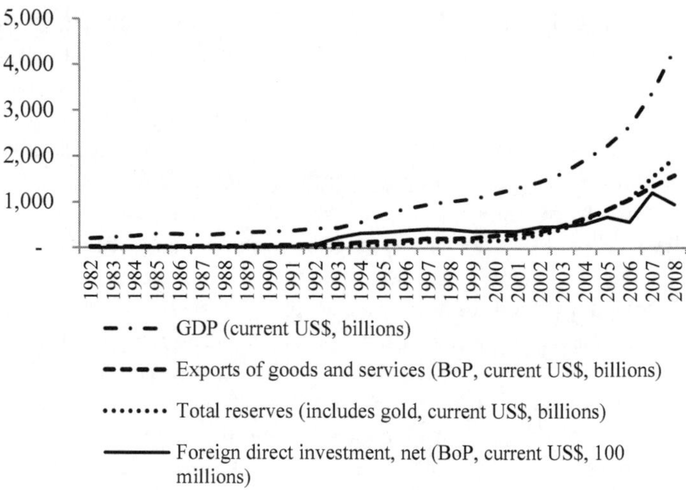

Figure 16.1 China's growth, reserves and exports

3. 'CROSSING THE RIVER ...'

China's development path thus appears directly linked to the world economy's phase of 'supercapitalism' (Reich 2008). For example, Hung

(2009) emphasises the extent to which China's economy tightened links to the US economy, financing its financial deficits (even if it cannot be held responsible for this, as is implicit in the 'savings glut' argument) by providing cheap credit and low-cost imports. Development and international studies are only beginning to conceptualise this new role of China in the global economy and politics, hindered by a relative lack of knowledge about China's development paths.[6] Perspectives are predictably diverse, and so are the political pressures on and expectations from China, for example highlighted in discussion around China's currency exchange rate.[7]

While a full discussion of these questions is well beyond the scope of this chapter, it is important that we get a better understanding of the Chinese agency, with all its internal contradictions and debates.[8] These economic successes, including the enormous privatisation of the Chinese economy (which was temporarily reversed after the crisis as SOEs (state-owned enterprises) benefited more from the stimulus package), have happened under the guidance of what may be termed a developmental state (though one that unlike other East Asian countries had privatisation of SOEs as core to its economic strategy), which carefully managed China's transitions in agriculture, rural industrialisation and export promotion. In the external arena, capital flows and exchange rates continue to be controlled, and as indicated the still-limited openness of the financial sector has helped to reduce the direct impact of the global financial crisis on China.

China's relatively austere social policies, despite the ideology of Communism, illustrate the guiding role of the state in the promotion of capitalist development. Like other East Asian social policies, China has had a very strong 'productivist' focus and maintained congruence between economic and social policy. Social policies have been pro-actively – but selectively – designed to play a key role in its pattern of economic growth and entry to global markets. Social policies also have played a key role in nation-building processes. Egalitarian norms predominate in public debate, often under authoritarian practices and with a focus on productive opportunities, while social polices remain based in a perception of the family as the main provider of welfare. Social spending has remained low and often skewed to particular sections of the working population, including in urban areas. The model of social policy is challenged by the rapid demographic shift from rural to urban areas, and is of course directly influenced by the economic reforms, privatisation of the economy and collapse of the social services previously provided through communes and SOEs.

China's economic success has been led by a number of favourable initial conditions in 1978, such as increasingly mobile capital from OECD countries, a relatively stable nation state which had provided broad-based education and health, and a very wealthy ethnic-Chinese business community in East and South-east Asia ready to invest in China. Its reform strategies effectively mobilised these potentials, while finding a middle road through uncertainty and political differences. Deng Xiaoping's mottos of 'crossing the river while touching the stones', and 'it doesn't matter whether the cat is black or white, as long as it catches mice' sums up much of the spirit with which reforms in agriculture, rural industries and other areas have been implemented. The key aspects of policy reforms have been their gradual and decentralised nature. Policy reforms are piloted in specific areas and scaled up when successful, and even then usually with locally-specific rules. Policy making is strongly evidence-based, and development consciously 'de-politicised'. Besides economic reforms, and while the basics of China's political system may have remained unchanged – at least comparatively to the collapse of the Soviet Union – policy makers have responded to political and citizens' pressure, including through natural and economic crises.

The response to the financial crisis appears to be directly in line with this gradual and pragmatic reform practice. At a time when the cracks in the international financial system started to appear, China's economy was perceived to be overheating for some time already, at least since 2003/04. Efforts to slow down the economy through changes in interest rates, bank lending and exchange rate had been in place at least since 2006, and had become a high priority in 2008 – but also criticised in the export-dependent areas.[9] China's crisis response and its public policies were also informed by learning from other experiences with crises (including their political fall-out). This also included China's own experience with the financial crisis of 1997, in which China was not affected as heavily as Thailand and South Korea and did not devalue its currency but, as Jia (2009) described, about ten million jobs were lost, and Premier Zhu Rongyi reinforced a promise to maintain 8 per cent growth and use fiscal stimulus. We now focus the discussion on the way China's current crisis response balances the political–economy within China with the way it is positioned in the global system.

4. BALANCING ACT OF AN EMERGING ECONOMY

> China is NOT a superpower. Although China has a population of 1.3 billion and although in recent years China has registered fairly fast economic and social development since reform and opening up, China still has this problem of unbalanced development between different regions and between China's urban and rural areas. China remains a developing country. (Premier Wen Jiabao in CNN interview, 23 September 2008, emphasis in original)

While China's growth performance over the last 30 years is not exceptional in comparison with other East Asian 'miracles', China's size makes the impact it is having on the global economy – including the developing world – unique, and its different political system and relative isolation (compared to India, for example) during Mao's period makes its international rise particularly noted in the international press and politics. It is therefore critical that we understand the crisis response as a double balancing act, of domestic and international politics, and of economics and politics, including the management of the expectations and fears around China's global rise.

With China's economic success, it has created formidable development challenges, many of which have had significant international impacts. Of particular relevance are the enormous internal inequalities that have emerged. While on the one hand the large, relatively poor rural masses provided the source for growth in the township-village enterprises and subsequently export-oriented economies, the growth model also has created inequalities deemed to be unsustainable under the leadership of the Communist Party. While the model under Deng Xiaoping was clearly one of 'growth first' and an explicit acceptance of growing inequalities, the issue of inequality and justice was never entirely off the radar screen; it arguably contributed to the unrest at the end of the 1980s and academics pointing at a justice gap, and such forces finally led to the political project by the Hu-Wen administration to build a harmonious society. In March 2007, Premier Wen admitted that China's economy was 'unstable, unbalanced, uncoordinated and [had] unsustainable problems'.[10]

Some of the causes of inequalities are very deeply rooted within China's public policies and will require thorough reforms of the public administration, of course often encountering large opposition. First, the fiscal capacity of the state of course had become limited as a result of the extensive privatization; while this has been gradually addressed since the mid 1990s, and total fiscal revenue may be higher than figures suggest (because of extra-budgetary revenue), the country's fiscal system remains very regressive, posing challenges for the poorest areas and lowest levels of government. Second, personal inequality is worsened by high costs and personal savings for health-care and old-age provisions, and low spending in social sectors, particularly in rural areas, which is now gradually being addressed. Third, migration, despite having been considered one of the motors of the Chinese economy, continues to be essentially unfree, with the hukou system still in place and a continued urban bias in provision of public services (reform of this is thought to be blocked by city officials afraid of ballooning costs for public services, among others). The financial crisis of 2008 was presented as an opportunity by the Chinese administration to change China's developmental model, including to invest in greening the economy. International observers were happy with the announcements of these policies; in the context of the concerns over external balances, internal divisions of course existed over the appropriate government response, for example expressed in the push to reduce the wages of workers in export sectors and roll back labour legislation introduced just a year before the crisis.

China's internal inequalities are directly related to the global imbalances which preceded and continued through the 2008–09 crisis. Its phenomenal export and economic growth performance is of course concentrated in coastal areas, and fuelled by the existence of an enormous labour surplus of relatively poor rural workers, who have become migrants without obtaining the right to services in industrial and urban areas, while their move is promoted through pro-active policies including training of migrants. The collapse of the social services provided during the pre-1978 period was directly linked to the process of privatisation, and no general system of social security has been promoted in the export industry, with the rural hinterland remaining the safety valve during periods of crises. The surplus generated through China's export-oriented model was invested only to a small extent in inward-oriented development, and to a significant extent in foreign reserves.

China's emerging global role is perceived as an attempt to re-take the position that it lost 150 years ago under the influence of colonialism, and to some extent the result of its needs for natural resources in a global economy that had already divided the access to most of these resources. This drives China to explore possibilities in physically and politically more challenging corners of the world, in turn leading to a common critique that China is plundering Africa and supporting regimes that abuse human rights. While China's foreign policy principles drafted in the 1950s still serve this new global strategy to a large extent, since the 1990s it has started to reformulate this to take account of China's status as a 'comprehensive power' (Zheng and Tok 2007), and it has been forced to respond to critiques regarding its engagement in Africa, while simultaneously becoming more assertive. Similarly, China's huge build up of reserves and control ('manipulation') of its currency have attracted a great deal of criticism, to which the Chinese government has responded with a characteristic mix of assertiveness (such as the remarks through an essay on the website by the Governor of the People's Bank of China, Zhou Xiaochuan, for the need to replace the US dollar as the single international reserve currency[11]) and acceptance.

Internationally, China appears to be adopting the same pragmatic attitude that has become the core of its internal reforms. For example, it has continued with its policies started in the early 1970s to enhance its position in UN organisations, and has made its voice ever-better heard in debates around reforms of the international financial system (including regional). But simultaneously Chinese leaders seem careful not to become too assertive in international fora, for example highlighted in the limited contribution provided to IDA15 in 2007/08 (seemingly designed to be in line with other newcomers; its voting power was increased in 2010), and increasing collaboration with old aid donors even though it continues to stress the distinctiveness of its own aid programme. China has become part of and been proactive in creating new international networks, for example in ASEAN+3, etc., while ideologically it continues to commit to the spirit of the 1950s Non-Aligned Movement. In its relations with Africa, including in the debates on aid, China continues to assert its distinctiveness and reject western criticism, but simultaneously is incorporating international practices and participating in the international fora like that of the OECD.

On the surface, perhaps, none of these actions seem remarkable. However, they are part of a very rapidly changing field of international relations and arguably a new phase of globalisation with a uniquely rapid rise of such a large country, which the rest of the world is gradually getting accustomed to. Simultaneously, China is undergoing a dramatic international transformation, economically, demographically and institutionally. Continued Party control relies not just on managing this internal transformation, but also China's international repositioning, and arguably the two are increasingly inter-connected. This inter-connectedness was intensified during the recent economic crisis, as we describe next.

4. KEYNES, OR BLACK AND WHITE CATS

The rest of the world looked with admiration at China's crisis response, but internal reactions typically were more reserved. In the new *Journal for Global Development* celebrating the return of Keynesian policies, Yu Yongding underscored that it is unremarkable that a country with China's reserves could implement the crisis response it did, and Chinese researchers were among the first to highlight the new challenges that emerged.

China was among the first to feel the impact of economic trouble in 2007 – while it was already busy slowing down its economy – and throughout 2008, culminating in drastic declines in exports (Yang 2008) and rising unemployment in the first half of 2009. While its banking sector generally appeared to be little affected,[12] the stock market was heavily affected.[13] Soon after the global crisis unfolded, and with its heavy impact on skilled and unskilled employment, China introduced a range of economic measures which have subsequently been adjusted.[14] Taxes were reduced to boost private consumption, particularly in rural areas (Schmidt and Heilmann 2010, p. 15), but also value-added tax rebates that were previously used to slow down the economy were adjusted to promote exports. In June 2010 the Ministry of Commerce announced the tax rebates would be reduced again. Second, credit policies were adjusted, with China exiting from the 'moderately tight policies' adopted since 2003. Interest rates were cut, and lending rules were adjusted, including the encouragement of lending by commercial banks, leading to a large injection in the financial system, with total new loans in the first quarter of 2009 reaching a level of the whole of 2008 (Zhang et al. 2009). Very soon, this was seen to lead to a bubble and was followed by reductions in lending in mid-2009. For 2010 a less expansionary monetary policy was proposed, and China continues to focus on keeping inflation low. Third, measures were introduced to stabilise housing and stock markets. Controls on mortgage loans were reduced to stimulate the purchase of residential property (mortgage rates, support to first-time buyers), with local governments benefiting significantly from higher property prices and land sale revenues. This was seen to contribute to the speculative bubble, and in 2009 measures were put in pace to try to limit the diversion of investments to the property market, to contain price increases – for example through raising the mortgage interest rate – and by promoting the construction of low-cost housing.

Fourth, the value of the (pegged) yuan has been the subject of much discussion, and even though the yuan has appreciated over the last couple of years, its current level is still thought to be relatively low, supported by China's interventions to support the dollar and contributing to promoting China's exports. As indicated above, by mid-2010 it seemed that Chinese policy would let the yuan resume its appreciation again.

Fifth, China's large stimulus package of 4 trillion yuan over two years, by some calculations 12 per cent of 2008 GDP,[15] has been seen as the core of China's crisis response. Most commentators agree that the real size of the package is less clear than the precise figures in yuan suggests; while on the other hand as explained below the package is only partly a financial injection from the central government, as central funding is matched by contributions from private sources and lower-level government and bank financing, amounting to two-thirds of the total stimulus. There were doubts about how much of the money was new money, or was public funding that had been committed earlier. Though there were questions regarding whether an injection of 6 per cent of GDP (on an annual basis) would be sufficient to stabilise the economy, and while there was little change in China's budget deficit, an immediate positive impact was felt.

The following aspects of the fiscal response are noteworthy. While investing in infrastructure has been one of the strengths of China's economic model, the stimulus package too had a heavy emphasis on investment, following a need to insert money into the economy quickly, and increasing the powers of big-spending bureaucracies.[16] But this emphasis also came under criticism,[17] as China's growth model already was skewed heavily towards investment (more than half of GDP in the decade). While households are saving about a quarter of their disposable income and private consumption is only about one-third of GDP, the positive economic impact of investing in infrastructure would likely be only temporary, physical investments might have little effects on increasing employment, and these form of investment might be high-polluting, energy-intensive and have low efficiency.

Table 16.2 China's stimulus package

	Billions of yuan	In per cent
Public infrastructure	1500	38
Earthquake reconstruction	1000	25
Social welfare	400	10
Rural development	370	9
Technology advancement	370	9
Sustainable development	210	5
Educational and cultural	150	4
Total	4000	100

Source: NDRC March 2009; http://www.eeo.com.cn/

At the same time, the government promised more than just more of the same in infrastructure. The crisis was also presented as an opportunity to invest in long-term objectives of skill development and green technology, for example. The stimulus package was seen as a means towards more inward-oriented development, partly through funding rural infrastructure, but also through promises for social sectors, though too little for many commentators,[18] and it appears the government responded to criticism by increasing or highlighting the commitments to social spending. In January 2009 the government announced spending of 123 billion to promote a universal health care system. Education, particularly vocational training and education of migrant workers was emphasized, for example, during the China Development High Level Forum in March 2009. As described elsewhere (de Haan 2010a, 2010b), the directions of China's social policy as part of the fiscal package did not fundamentally differ from those of the past and was used as a reinforcement of previous attempts to build a 'harmonious society' (with some indications the growth of inequalities has been halted; OECD 2010) while maintaining the magic 8 per cent growth target. In fact, some of the improvement in labour was reversed temporarily.

As important as the content of the stimulus package is the way it was funded, as this is likely to impinge heavily on China's internal fiscal system that has been undergoing large reforms since the mid 1990s. Central government funded one-quarter of the 4 trillion yuan directly, and additionally issued government bonds and bonds on behalf of local governments. But for local governments – responsible for three-quarters of total spending – bank lending has been the main source. The fiscal stimulus package was dwarfed by the size of bank loans that followed central government directives – with banks keen to lend for government-guaranteed projects and local partly leaders competing with each other to provide funding – leading to a rapid rise of indebtedness of local governments.

While the 1930s crisis in the US led to radical changes in regulation, fiscal relations and social sector spending (Mitchener 2009), the changes in China appear less dramatic, and to be reinforcing some of its older problem. China appears to have been well-prepared for the crisis, possibly assuming its export-led growth would always be vulnerable, and having built up the reserves that makes its response less remarkable than may have been suggested. The measures that were introduced by and large seem to have had their intended effects, and were a pragmatic combination of and response to different constituencies (in line with the 'black-or-white-cat' pragmatism promoted under Deng Xiaoping): to promote exports, while simultaneously reinforcing its shift towards more inward-oriented development through investing in rural infrastructure, and reinforcing its commitment to social sectors. By themselves these measures are unlikely to address the structural challenges that China's development model faces: institutional change will be gradual, expansion of social spending will continue to remain controlled, and the fiscal relations between centres and local governments have now been further stretched by increased indebtedness.

5. CONCLUSION

Are there lessons from the way China's public policies have addressed the financial crisis? As always, China's development path is unique – all countries' paths are, but China's is more remarkable than many others' – and so is the way the crisis response has evolved, and it is thus critically important that we come to a better understanding of China development path, and the inevitable complicated political economy this entails.

A first lesson is that global economics is changing drastically. Emerging economies' growth rates are indeed 'decoupled', with China and India having much higher growth rates than OECD countries, but this happens in close connectedness with global economics, finance and politics. The basic economic principles under which China has achieved this success and weathered the financial crisis appear unremarkable, but it is by now evident that it is China's relative autonomy in setting out the path that has allowed it to elevate from developing country status: while Amsden (2007) emphasises how countries in the developing world had less space to define their own economic policies after the 1970s, China, while integrating actively into the global economy, defined its own route, and has thus started to change the rules of the game amidst continued global uncertainties.

Second, China's response shows the importance of understanding the policies and politics of emerging economies as a balancing act, with Chinese scholars the first to highlight that directions are far from evident or undisputed. While China needs to assert its global role, partly for internal political reasons, partly to ensure its huge economic interests overseas, it is careful also not to push too hard (and certainly does not seem keen to challenge development orthodoxy, as Duncan Green remarked in his OXFAM blog on Justin Lin Yifu). Internally, China continues to balance the interests and constituencies of the export sector on which its growth has depended heavily, with the needs and pressure to strengthen inward-oriented development and to reduce inequalities. The way China manages these challenges are worth in-depth study, not only because China's development is increasingly critical to global prosperity, but its path(s) of development is also increasingly seen as a model for other countries.

NOTES

* This chapter builds on discussions and presentations at a workshop organised by the two authors, for the Development Research Centre, and DFID China, in Beijing, March 2009; and Gong Sen (2009) and de Haan (2010b).

1 *The Economist*, 29 May 2010, p. 9. This leader repeated the by-now familiar analysis that 'China needs to accelerate the rebalancing of its economy towards domestic consumption, with the help of a stronger currency'.

2 *China Daily*, 30 June 2009.

3 Naudé (2009) and Llaudes et al. (2010) analyse the diverse impact of the crisis on 50 emerging economies.

4 The notion of decoupling of emerging economies came back a little while after the onset of the crisis (Kose and Prasad 2009). Some observers saw signs of greater independence of emerging economies, or 'deglobalisation' (van Bergeijk 2009c).

5 China's economic policies have reduced external risks, at the cost of increasing internal ones (Prasad 2009, p. 120).

6 See de Haan (2010c) on development studies, McCulloch and Sumner (2009a), and report of an ISS-BNU workshop held in Beijing, July 2010 (http://www.iss.nl/Conferences-Seminars-Public-Debates/30-Years-Reform-in-China-July-2010).

7 China's currency has been appreciating by about 20 per cent over the last few years; this was halted in response to the crisis, and Chinese policy may let the Rmb resume its appreciation against the dollar.

8 The essays collected in Zhang et al. (2010) provide views on the dynamics of the various aspects of transformation.

9 Wong (2008). According to Zhang et al. (2009) tightening of money supply started in the 3rd and 4th quarters of 2003.

10 Whyte (2010), on the basis of a unique nation-wide survey, criticises the idea that the rising inequalities would be propelling China toward a social volcano. De Haan (2010a) discusses the internal debates on inequalities.

11 In fact, specific proposals were rather more modest: Zhou Xiaochuan (2009) stressed: 'The crisis again calls for creative reform of the existing international monetary system towards an international reserve currency with a stable value, rule-based issuance and manageable supply, so as to achieve the objective of safeguarding global economic and financial stability.' See also Xu (2009) and Zhang et al. 2009, pp. 21–2.

12 Though there were doubts about the quality of information about banks (Fan 2008); Yao et al. (2010) describe the problems of the Chinese housing market and bank lending during 2007–08, and reasons why the stability of the Chinese financial sector was relatively little affected.

13 The Shanghai stock market fell by 48 per cent between May and November 2008, compared to New York's and London's fall by 68 and 69 per cent respectively (in Sharma 2009, p. 2); see also Yao et al. (2010, p. 405).

14 Zhang et al. (2009) provide a time-line of government responses, starting from June 2008 for which there is an indication that the leadership assessed how the global financial crisis would affect China.

15 Or 6 per cent on an annual basis. This would reduce China's reserves but still keep them well out of the red. China's current account balance was 10 per cent of GDP in 2008, and expected to decline to 7–8 per cent in 2010 and 2011.

16 The 2010 budget proposed a total budget increase by 10 per cent, with education and health spending rising somewhat faster (14 per cent) and social security spending not more than the average (World Bank 2010, p. 14).

17 Alongside this, there was criticism regarding the transparency in appropriation of government funds, which government agencies were forced to respond to (Schmidt and Heilmann 2010, pp. 17–18).

18 Tang Min argued that funding for social welfare should go up to 35 per cent of government revenue (CDRF report, quoted in *China Daily*, 3 April 2009). Guan Xinping suggested the government needs to invest more to educate and train youth and unemployed, speed up the establishment of a basic social security system and strengthen public services (*China Daily*, 24 June 2009). Ding Yuanzhu of CASS argued for creating an effective social demand permanent cure for crisis (*China Daily*, 24 June 2009). Some argued that the investment in hardware might even reduce access to, for example, health-care facilities (because of institutions' incentives to recover costs).

17. Thailand from Crisis to Crisis: Do We Ever Learn?

Karel Jansen

The Asian crisis which started in 1997 has had a profound impact on Thailand's economy and society, an impact that can still be seen today, so many years after the crisis. This chapter will argue that the crisis has substantially changed the accumulation pattern underlying Thai economic growth. It is important to understand the various elements of the economic structure that emerged after the Asian crisis in order to assess whether and how Thailand will be able to cope with the current global financial crisis.

The chapter is organized as follows: the next section will analyze the Asian crisis as it started and evolved in Thailand. The main part of the chapter is devoted to an analysis of the aftermath of the Asian crisis. The final section speculates on how Thailand will be affected by the global financial crisis and, in particular, assesses how the legacy of the Asian crisis affects the ability of the country to cope with these new challenges.

1. THE ASIAN CRISIS OF 1997

The Asian crisis led to an extensive literature on the causes of the crisis. Some emphasized the structural weaknesses and policy mistakes in Thailand while others emphasized the volatility of global financial markets (two early and representative studies are Radelet and Sachs 1998 and Corsetti et al. 1998). The Asian crisis is a typical boom–bust story with years of double-digit growth in the early 1990s followed by collapse in 1997/98. The current financial crisis has led to a revival of interest in the work of Hyman Minsky who introduced the 'Financial Instability Hypothesis' according to which the modern capitalist economy is subject to an instability that is inherent and endogenous to advanced financial systems (Minsky 2008). Similar approaches to analyzing financial crises can be found in Akerlof and Shiller

(2009), Kindleberger (1978), Rogoff and Reinhart (2009) and Roubini and Mihm (2010).

The Minsky model is built on the interaction between profit expectations leading to investment; the realization of profits validates further investment. These investments need to be financed but the rising profit expectations and realized profits make banks willing to provide the credit. In the process the indebtedness of firms increases resulting in fragile financial structures. Obviously, this process cannot go on forever; at a certain moment expectations turn around and the crisis sets in. The special nature of the Asian crisis arises from financial globalization – access to global finance fed the credit boom but also made the collapse more spectacular.

This approach can serve very well to interpret the 1997 Asian crisis in Thailand. The Thai economy went through a difficult patch during the 1980s. Growth remained subdued up until 1986. It could be argued that what lifted the Thai economy out of its growth recession was the upturn in FDI, the outcome of the restructuring of global (in particular Japanese) production with the yen appreciation after the 1985 Plaza agreement. This started a real boom; the average growth rate of real GDP over the period 1987–1995 was close to 10 per cent.

In this same period Thailand liberalized its financial markets. In the late 1980s the latest restrictions on domestic financial markets were removed and in the early 1990s the capital account was opened, culminating in the creation of an off-shore market in 1993 to link Thai financial markets to global markets.

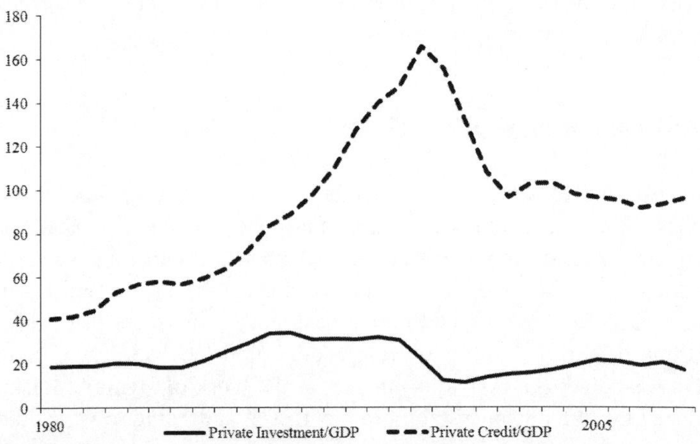

Source: NESDB and Bank of Thailand

Figure 17.1 Private investment and credit to GDP in per cent

This period can be interpreted as a Minskyan cycle. The surge in foreign investment started the process of growing profit expectations. Domestic investment followed closely. Figure 17.1 shows how the private investment ratio had hovered around 20 per cent in the 1980s but started to shoot up from 1987 onwards to reach a high level of over 30 per cent in the 1990s. The boom was financed by a rapid growth of domestic credit.

The private domestic credit/GDP ratio shot up from below 60 per cent before 1987 to over 160 per cent by 1997. On top of this, the larger Thai firms obtained direct access to global financial markets. The external debt of private enterprises increased from 15 per cent of GDP in 1994 to 30 per cent in 1997. Taking domestic and external indebtedness together, the total debt of the Thai private sector increased from around 70 per cent of GDP in the mid-1980s to close to 200 per cent at the peak in 1997, surely a credit boom. The booming investment, credit and profits suggest that the mood in these days was very optimistic. Growth was around 5 per cent during the early 1980s; it shot up after 1986 and there were a series of years with double-digit growth, an exceptional period in Thai economic history. Asset prices were rising fast. Good times create confidence and lower risk perception. In the early 1980s the Stock Market of Thailand (SET) index was hardly above the 100 level at which it had been started in 1975. But after 1986 the index shot up to a peak of over 1600 in 1993. After that year the index declined; a decline that set in long before the crisis hit Thailand. A similar story on asset prices can be shown in the real estate sector. The Bank of Thailand price indexes for single detached houses including the land increased from 100 in 1991 to 144 in 1997.

Source: Bank of Thailand

Figure 17.2 Foreign assets/foreign liabilities, commercial banks 1985–2004

But financial fragility started to build up. Driffield et al. 2004 give some data for Thailand and other Asian countries on the basis of Worldscope firm level data that show that the debt–equity ratio of Thai firms increased rapidly between 1989 and 1997. Another aspect of the fragility is the currency mismatch. Figure 17.2 gives the ratio of foreign assets over foreign liabilities of commercial banks between 1985 and end 2004. It shows that there was initially some balance – up to the late 1980s the ratio fluctuated around 100 per cent. But with the financial liberalization banks got into foreign borrowing and their foreign liabilities far exceeded the foreign assets. This open position implied a severe exchange rate risk.

Other indicators of the currency mismatch can be obtained from Goldstein and Turner (2004). They use a standard indicator for reserve adequacy: short-term external debt as a percentage of international reserves; the ratio was above 100 per cent and increased from 1995 to 1997.The trigger for the crisis is difficult to identify. It could have been the stagnation of exports in 1996 which suggested an upcoming depreciation. It could have been the problems of finance companies in late 1996/early 1997 mainly due to excessive exposure to the real estate sector where prices started to decline. Certainly the trigger came suddenly since capital inflows went on until just before the floating of the Thai baht. But, in the Minsky way of thinking the trigger is not so important. The fragility that has been built up during the boom inevitably will lead to a correction.

When the crisis hit it was extreme. In July 1997 the central bank had to let the baht float. In the past one would have seen a depreciation to take care of the trade balance problems, but in the era of globalized finance things are different. The shock of the crisis led to a halt in international credit and firms and banks had to repay their short-term debt. The outflow of funds resulted in a dive of the exchange rate. In an effort to protect the exchange rate (and under pressure of the IMF) the central bank increased interest rates. Firms were now hit by higher interest rates on domestic loans and higher local currency costs of servicing external loans due to the depreciation. On top of that, the credit supply dried up. Foreign creditors stopped lending and local banks were all bankrupt as they were confronted with the high cost of settling external debt and with a rapid growth in non-performing loans on local markets. The outflow of funds led to a collapse of asset prices (stock market, real estate, exchange rate). The bail-out cost of the financial system led to an increase in government debt. Moreover, once the economy dived automatic stabilizers ensured that government revenue declined so that the budget moved into deficit. Public debt increased sharply, also due to the borrowing from the IMF.

2. AFTER THE CRISIS

The Asian crisis was an enormous, abrupt and unexpected shock to the Thai economy. In the almost half century between 1952 and 1996 there had been only one year with negative growth. The average growth rate over this period had been 7.3 per cent. Even during the global recession and debt crisis of the early 1980s, when Thailand also suffered a financial crisis, growth had remained around 5 per cent. By contrast, in 1998 the economy contracted by more than 10 per cent.

The crisis brought home the dangers of financial globalization. During the earlier financial crisis of 1984, relative external debt levels had been comparable to those of 1997 but most of the debt was long-term public-sector debt and private financial flows were still controlled. There was thus no capital flight. In 1997 most of the debt was short-term and private and international creditors wanted their money back. In addition local investors were now free to move their money around. This resulted in a huge capital outflow. The 1997 crisis also exposed Thailand to the rapaciousness of multinational capital. Multinational firms used the crisis to increase their share in joint ventures and to take over failing firms at fire-sale prices. And Thailand learned that the IMF is not on your side when you need a friend.

The impact of and response to the Asian crisis can be captured under two headings: (1) greater caution on the part of Thai economic agents, and (2) a deeper integration into the global economy. It is useful to analyze these trends in some more detail as they also determine how Thailand is affected by the sub-prime crisis.

Caution

The greater caution is reflected in reduced levels of private investment and in de-leveraging in the private sector. It is not surprising that the crisis led to a sharp fall in private investment, but it is remarkable that even more than a decade after the crisis the ratio of private investment to GDP has hardly recovered; it still hovers around the level of the early 1980s which was a rather poor period in Thai economic history (see Figure 17.1 above).

The result of the lower level of investment is a decline in the trend level of economic growth. Over the period 1952–96 the average growth rate was 7.3. Over the post-crisis period 2000–09 average growth was 4.8 per cent.[1]

Related to the fall of private investment is a radical reduction in credit (see Figure 17.1). The continued low level of private investment is surprising as corporate profits have recovered well. Table 17.1 uses the Flow-of-Funds data to analyze the account of the 'Incorporated Business', the main part of the private sector. Table 17.1 shows how corporations finance their investment and compares the averages for the six years before the crisis with the years after the crisis.

Table 17.1 Accumulation and financing of corporate sector (period averages)

	Shares of total investment		Shares in GDP	
	1991–96	2000–07	1991–96	2000–07
Investment	100	100	27.0	18.8
Gross savings	47.3	98.5	12.7	16.8
Net loans	32.9	−8.3	8.9	−0.7
Commercial bills	15.5	1.1	4.2	0.5
Share capital	13.5	22.5	3.6	3.8
Debenditures	2.2	4.6	0.6	0.9
Net foreign liabilities	17.9	−12.4	4.9	−2.0
Others	−29.3	−5.5	−7.9	−0.4

Note: The 'others' category includes financial assets that firms are acquiring

Source: NESDB, Flow of Funds

We observe:

- After the crisis the level of corporate investment fell significantly.
- Corporate savings increased to almost the level of investment. The profit share is now larger than it was before the Asian crisis.
- Before the crisis corporations invested much more than their own savings. The gap was financed mainly by bank loans and by foreign borrowing.
- After the crisis firms have restored profitability (savings) but they are using these savings to run down bank loans and foreign debt. New capital is sourced by issuing equity and debenditures (bonds).

The picture is one of financial disintermediation. Figure 17.1 traced the development of the ratio of outstanding private credit to GDP. This ratio peaked at 166 per cent in 1997 but has declined to 96 per cent by the end of 2009.

It is also interesting to look at the balance sheet of the commercial banks. Table 17.2 shows the structure of total assets and liabilities. Comparing December 1996 with recent years leads to important observations:

- Banks hold far more reserves, now over 10 per cent of total assets compared to just 3 per cent before the crisis.
- There is an increased holding of foreign assets.
- In contrast, the share of assets for claims on the private sector (i.e. loans to the private sector) has fallen significantly.
- On the liability side, foreign liabilities (at 22 per cent before the crisis) have almost disappeared as a source of funds.
- Own capital has been strengthened.

Table 17.2 Assets and liabilities of commercial banks (per cent and per ultimo)

	1996	2005	2006	2007	2008	2009
Reserves	2.9	7.4	8.9	10.0	14.0	14.8
Foreign assets	3.2	8.0	10.0	9.4	5.3	5.8
Claims						
on government	0.1	3.7	4.4	4.1	3.8	5.1
non-financial state enterprises	2.0	2.6	2.4	2.6	2.1	2.0
household and private business	82.4	65.2	58.7	58.3	58.2	56.5
Other assets	9.4	13.0	15.7	15.7	16.6	15.9
Total Assets	*100.0*	*100.0*	*100.0*	*100.0*	*100.0*	*100.0*
Deposits	59.9	66.7	68.2	64.7	63.3	62.1
Foreign liabilities	22.0	3.9	3.3	2.6	2.8	2.7
Own capital	8.9	13.4	9.3	9.8	9.9	10.1
Other liabilities	9.2	16.0	19.2	22.9	24.0	25.2
Total liabilities	*100.0*	*100.0*	*100.0*	*100.0*	*100.0*	*100.0*

Source: Bank of Thailand

The balance sheet of the commercial banks looks stronger: higher reserves, higher capital coverage, lower leverage and less dependence on foreign loans. But one could question whether the level of reserves and capital coverage is not too high; they appear to be above the standard norms and may reflect risk avoidance on the side of banks.

The low level of private investment and the drastic decline in leverage suggest a reduced willingness to take risks (ADB 2007). The distinguished Thai economist Ammar Siamwalla observed:

> Our entrepreneurs have learned the lesson of the crisis, but perhaps they have learned it too well. Before the crisis they took many risks. Now they seem to take too few risks, or none at all. The appetite for risk taking has almost disappeared. The banks, in particular, spent the years after the crisis learning

> how to manage risk and installing new systems for evaluating the risks of each loan. The amount of credit they make now available to the productive sector of the economy is half what is was in real terms prior to the crisis. The banks are swamped by excess liquidity. Perhaps they are now being too careful. (Siamwalla 2008, p. xi)

The willingness to take risks may have been further reduced by the political instability of recent years. Since 2006 the country has been in almost constant turmoil with widespread street demonstrations, a military coup in September 2006, a number of short-lived and ineffective governments, the occupation of the Bangkok airport in November 2008, the disruption of the ASEAN summit in April 2009 and the street protest in Bangkok and its violent repression in May 2010.

It is not just the private sector that exhibits caution, also government policies shifted in the direction of greater caution. Directly after the crisis stringent IMF conditionality determined fiscal policies. The Thaksin government, which came to power in 2001, formulated a dual track approach to macroeconomic management under which fiscal stimulus is used when other elements of demand, such as exports or private investment, are weak. Fiscal stimulus was provided through a number of grassroots programmes, including the programme in which each of the 77,000 villages received 1 million baht for village projects, a public works programme, subsidized health care, a moratorium of farmers' debt, etc.[2] Real primary government expenditure increased rapidly in 2001 and 2002. However, the recovery of the economy also led to an increase in government revenue and the fiscal deficit was falling in 2002.

The policy debate in 2002, however, shifted to the question whether this fiscal stimulus was sustainable in view of the rising government debt. Total public sector debt was only 15 per cent of GDP before the crisis in 1996, the result of a series of fiscal surpluses during the boom years. The crisis implied falling revenue and increasing deficits that required financing in addition to the borrowing necessary to bail out the financial institutions. The public debt ratio had peaked at over 57 per cent in 2000–01. The concern was that public debt may rise to 60 per cent of GDP, a limit above which, according to many, it would be dangerous to go. Whatever the merits of these discussions (see Jansen 2004) the upshot was a shift back to more cautious fiscal policies. The best illustration of the reluctant use of fiscal policy is the fact that total real government spending (at 1988 prices) exceeded its 1997 peak only in 2006.

Caution also informed other macroeconomic policies. In 2000 the Bank of Thailand introduced inflation targeting as its new monetary policy regime. The target ceiling for inflation was set at 3.5 per cent – rather ambitious in view of the fact that in the decades preceding the Asian crisis average inflation had been over 5 per cent per year.

After the Asian crisis Thailand was forced to abandon the fixed exchange rate regime and move to a more flexible arrangement. Still, the central bank clearly intervened in the foreign exchange market to control the level of the exchange rate, leading to the rapid accumulation of international reserves.

Globalization

The Asian crisis brought home to Thailand the dangers of globalization. The financial liberalization exposed Thailand to volatile global financial markets with disastrous results. It is perhaps surprising that there was not more of an anti-globalization backlash after the crisis. As a matter of fact, the crisis served to draw the country more into the global markets, and foreign investment and trade intensity increased significantly.

Table 17.3 shows FDI inflows as a percentage of total investment. In the early 1980s this was quite low and even when FDI inflows started to rise they accounted for less than 5 per cent of total investment but after the crisis the share increased to a much higher level. The foreign-owned capital stock as a percentage of GDP shows a similar trend. In the period 1990–96 the share was about 10 per cent. After the crisis it increased sharply to about 35 per cent in recent years. Foreign ownership increased in the more sophisticated sectors, such as automotive, electronics and banking. Foreign firms increased ownership shares in joint ventures or took over Thai firms at fire-sale prices and much of the Thai export manufacturing became foreign-owned. The Thai economy became more export dependent. Table 17.3 gives period averages of the export/GDP ratio which had been gradually increasing from around 25 per cent in 1980 to 40 per cent in 1996. In the years after the crisis it jumped to 76 per cent in 2008. As investment spending remained low, and with a cautious fiscal and monetary policy, exports became the main driver of growth, making Thailand more vulnerable to the state of the world economy.

Table 17.3 Globalization of the Thai economy

	1980–86	1987–96	1997–99	2000–08
Export/GDP	23.1	37.8	55.1	70.1
FDI inflow/GDP	2.5	4.5	20.4	15.0
FDI stock/GDP		10.2 [1]	14.5	28.8[2]

Notes: [1] 1990–96 [2] 2000–07

Source: Bank of Thailand and UNCTAD

3. THE SUB-PRIME CRISIS IN THAILAND

The Asian crisis brought a collapse of confidence and an increased awareness of risk which translated into declining levels of investment and leverage. Regulations for financial institutions and corporate governance were tightened. Macroeconomic policy was re-calibrated with a shift in the exchange rate regime towards more flexibility and a renewed emphasis on cautious fiscal and monetary policies. The crisis resulted in a significant opening to foreign investment and foreign trade.

These changes determine how Thailand is affected by and can deal with the current global financial crisis. Some elements will help Thailand in coping with the crisis but other elements will increase the challenges. The Asian crisis invited more caution, leading to de-leveraging of banks and firms and accumulation of international reserves. This helped Thailand cope with the financial shock of the sub-prime crisis. But the Asian crisis also resulted in an increased reliance on exports as an engine of growth. This makes Thailand more vulnerable to the global recession that followed the sub-prime crisis.

The great strength of countries like Thailand is that they went into the sub-prime crisis with healthy corporate and financial sector balance sheets.

That does not mean that the financial crisis does not affect Thailand. There were sharp outflows of portfolio investment funds in the second and third quarters of 2008 when global investors sold out to transfer liquidity back home. Foreign bank loans were repaid in the third and fourth quarters of 2008 and foreign trade credit fell sharply in the fourth quarter of 2008 and first quarter of 2009. Foreign banks needed funds to restore their own balance sheets and withdrew these funds from emerging markets. This time, however, the financial impact was limited as Thailand had ample international reserves. Actually, the current account remained in surplus and this kept adding to the reserves.

Moreover, local financial institutions were rather liquid and could easily replace external credit, but the crisis increased their risk awareness and may have induced credit rationing: the outstanding loans of commercial banks have stagnated since the end of 2008 and started to increase only modestly in 2010. Of course, it is difficult to assess whether the stagnation in loans and the decline in foreign loans and trade credit are due to the reluctance of banks to give loans or to a fall in the demand for loans as the economy is declining.

Thailand entered the crisis with healthy fiscal balances and moderate government debt. Moreover, the government did not need to support financial institutions. The recession is undermining government revenue. Moreover, the government announced and started to implement fiscal stimulus packages which will further add to the deficit and increase government debt. It is, however, likely that debt will remain sustainable. It would thus seem that the adjustments inspired by the Asian crisis mean that the financial fall-out of the sub-prime crisis will be limited.

Since the Asian crisis economic growth in Thailand is increasingly driven by exports, in the coming years demand for Thai exports may be relatively weak. Current predictions are for a slow recovery of the world economy and continued financial fragility. Four aspects can be mentioned.

1. The sub-prime crisis, like the Asian crisis, was the outcome of a credit boom that was focused on the household sector where mortgage and credit card debt rose to finance consumption. The adjustment after the crisis will thus weaken consumption expenditure as households have to cut back spending since their access to credit is restricted and their asset values have declined.

2. The sub-prime crisis showed again high levels of leverage within the financial sector. Some of the highly leveraged financial institutions have closed down (e.g. some big investment banks and many hedge funds); others were saved. Financial institutions will have to restore their balance sheets and this is likely to lead to slow credit growth in years to come. Moreover, it is likely that, as in Thailand after the Asian crisis, regulation will tighten which may further reduce the availability of or increase the cost of credit.

3. The Asian crisis affected a few emerging market economies but had hardly any impact on the state of the global economy. The Asian countries could thus use exports as the way out of the crisis assisted by the sharp depreciation of their currencies. The sub-prime crisis is indeed a global crisis and thus the level of global demand has fallen sharply

4. One significant difference between the two crises is the roles of the government and central bank. In the Asian crisis the government could not do much to fight the recession as it was constrained by IMF conditionality. The central bank was ineffective because a large part of the debt of banks and corporations were in dollars and because the IMF insisted on tight monetary policy. During the current crisis governments and central banks in the OECD countries have opened all sluices to insert demand and liquidity in the economy. Even the IMF has known a remarkable change of heart and is now supporting expansionary fiscal and monetary policies and it has inserted significant funds into the global economy through its new Flexible Credit Lines and through the issue of special drawing rights (SDRs). These actions have certainly helped to soften the recession. But now questions are arising. At the start of the sub-prime crisis the USA, Japan and many Western

countries had weak fiscal balances. Fiscal deficits were high even during boom years and many governments were carrying high levels of debt. The cost of bailing out financial institutions and the fiscal stimulus packages have further increased government debt. It is likely that future years will see fiscal retrenchment to bring debt levels under control. Central banks that have lowered interest rates to historically record low levels and have invented 'quantitative easing' to insert liquidity into financial markets are now starting to worry about the inflationary impact this may have in the medium term. It is thus likely that the stimulating roles of the government and central bank will reduce in the near future.

These points suggest that the aftermath of the sub-prime crisis may be a long period of rather slow global growth. The adjustments after the Asian crisis have made Thailand more dependent on exports and global demand and thus more exposed to the impact of the sub-prime crisis. Merchandise exports fell sharply in Q4 2008 and Q1 2009 and have since been slowly recovering. In Q2 2010 they were still below their Q3 2008 peak. As a result, economic growth in 2008 was only 2.5 per cent mainly due to contraction in the fourth quarter and in 2009 the economy contracted with 2.3 per cent.[3]

4. CONCLUSION: WHAT DO WE LEARN?

From the above it is clear that Thailand learned lessons from the Asian crisis. It learned that financial globalization is risky. Since the crisis Thai financial institutions have introduced better risk management. The government has introduced stricter regulation and tighter supervision of financial institutions. Corporations have reduced credit exposure and the government has built up safety cushions in the form of large international reserves.

The current crisis is again a learning experience. While the Asian crisis exposed the dangers of financial instability, the current crisis exposes the vulnerability due to the excessive dependence on exports. Even before the crisis Thailand's mercantilist development model, based on export growth and the accumulation of reserves, had been questioned. The crisis made these questions more urgent. There are at least three points on the sustainability and desirability of this strategy.

Delinkage is Doubtful

The first follows from the observations above on the prospects of global trade. Thai exports are not much directed at the centres of the current recession, the USA and EU (taking in a quarter of Thai exports). Optimists argue that East Asia can de-link from the West and become an economic powerhouse on its own. Indeed, Thai exports to China are growing rapidly and in 2009 accounted for about 10 per cent of exports. Exports to the ASEAN+3 countries[4] accounted for 44 per cent of Thai exports but a considerable part of these exports are part of global production networks the end products of which end up in Western countries, and the slow-down of demand in the West is thus likely to also affect the intra-regional trade. The current crisis may also increase protectionist pressures in the West. Even before the crisis the USA was pressuring Asian countries – particularly China but also Thailand – to allow their exchange rates to appreciate to improve the trade balance. This pressure is likely to increase. In any case, the dollar may weaken when the deficit persists. The relative appreciation of the exchange rate will weaken Thailand's export competitiveness.

External Surpluses and Reserve Accumulation

The Asian crisis brought a radical shift in the accumulation pattern in Thailand. In the long period 1955–97 there were only three years in which Thailand had a (small) current account surplus; in all the other years there were deficits. Such deficits were considered normal for developing countries that needed to invest to grow and received inflows of foreign investment, aid and external credit to finance investment. Since 1998 Thailand experienced substantial current account surpluses at an average of 4.6 per cent of GDP over the period 1998–2009; the result of booming exports and moderate growth of imports due to the slow recovery of domestic demand. The current account surpluses have been accompanied by continued net inflows of external capital (FDI, portfolio investment, loans) and the result is a rapid accumulation of international reserves. The holdings of international reserves have increased from $21 billion in 2000 (4 months of imports and 18 per cent of GDP) to $138 billion at the end of 2009 (11 months of imports and 52 per cent of GDP). Such high levels of international reserves are: (i) unnecessary – they are more than enough to take care of any imaginable external shock; (ii) undesirable – the purchase by the central bank of international currencies increases liquidity on financial markets and the central bank loses control over monetary policy; (iii) inefficient – reserves are invested in low-yielding assets, such as the US treasury.

Wolf concludes that the current account imbalances and the low global real interest rates are 'in important respects the consequences of deliberate policies of export-led growth and self-insurance against the risk of financial crises that result in the huge accumulations of foreign-currency reserves' (Wolf 2009d, p. 58). Bernanke in his famous 'savings glut' speech identified this accumulation of reserves in response to the financial crisis as the main source of the global imbalances (Bernanke, 2005). These imbalances, in turn, are one factor behind the financial excess that resulted in the sub-prime crisis.

It was a shock for Thailand to find that when it was in deep trouble in 1997 it was on its own. Global banks and investors fled the country. The IMF extended a loan but the conditions were harsh and unhelpful and were resented. Wolf argues that this experience explains the rapid accumulation of international reserves after the crisis. But this requires some qualification. As we have seen, after the Asian crisis profits and savings recovered but investment remained at a consistently lower level. The surplus of (private) saving over investment is the counterpart of the current account surplus and this is the outcome of private sector decisions, not of government policy.

It is government policy to take the dollars arising from current account surpluses and capital inflows out of the market and to add them to the reserves. Here one can assume two motivations. The first is the experience of the Asian crisis when the Thai authorities were running out of reserves to defend the baht and when Thailand was forced to go to the IMF. The lesson drawn from this unpleasant experience is that much higher levels of reserves are needed. A second, and for Wolf more important, reason for the accumulation of reserves is the intervention by monetary authorities in currency markets to avoid the appreciation of the exchange rate. After the Asian crisis, the East Asian countries quickly went back to their export-led growth model. As most of the export goods of East Asian countries are relatively simple products, even small cost differences can undermine competitiveness and this makes the exchange rate an important policy target.

The real effective exchange rate index (REER) of the Bank of Thailand hovered around 100 in the period 1990–95 and appreciated in 1996 and 1997 to around 106 which contributed to the stagnation of exports in 1996. The Asian crisis brought a sharp depreciation and the REER then stabilized around 80 in the years 2000–05 and started to appreciate again in 2006. This fuelled concerns amongst exporters with the result that in December 2006 the central bank even introduced capital controls to stop the appreciation. These controls invited much criticism and were later withdrawn.

Domestic Sources of Growth

When the current account surplus and reserve accumulation is unsustainable and export prospects dim, it is imperative to search for domestic sources of growth. Before the Asian crisis the investment boom had driven growth but since the crisis investment has been subdued. Government spending is low in Thailand – total government expenditure are about 17 per cent of GDP – and does not contribute much to growth. That means that the only element of domestic demand that can push growth is consumption demand.

Consumption expenditure in GDP is relatively low in Thailand. In the 1970s the share hovered around 65 per cent. With the investment and growth boom that started in the late 1980s the share not surprisingly declined and stabilized around 55 per cent. What is surprising is that when investment spending declined so much after the Asian crisis, the share of consumption did not recover; it remains at the low level of around 55 per cent of GDP.

This is related to the very unequal income distribution which, in turn, is related to the export-led growth strategy. Thai exports are now dominated by manufactured goods (with a share of 90 per cent in 2009), but the sector does not create much employment. The manufacturing sector (exporting firms and firms producing for the domestic market) employ only 15 per cent of the total labour force.[5] And those working in this sector do not earn very good wages. The average monthly wage in the manufacturing sector in 2009 was just 7,700 baht (about $240). Over the period 2001–09 the nominal average wage in the sector had grown by 24 per cent, while inflation ran at 22 per cent, implying that real wages were largely stagnant over a period in which real GDP grew by 39 per cent. Thus, growth depends on exports but exports do not generate much employment and income for consumers. It should be noted that Thailand is not just an exporter of merchandise goods but also an important exporter of services – tourism. This sector accounts for about 6 per cent of GDP and is more labour-intensive than the industrial export sector. Also in this sector average wages are very low. The wage share in national income was around 35 per cent in the 1980s and with the modernization and formalization of the economy it increased to around 43 per cent in the early 2000s, but in recent years it has fallen back to 39 per cent. Despite rapid growth and modernization still around 50 per cent of the labour force is engaged in the informal sector (as own account workers and as unpaid family workers). More than one third of the labour force is active in agriculture, which contributes only 12 per cent of GDP; a large share of the labour force is engaged in rather low-productivity activities earning only modest incomes.

Economic progress in Thailand is not equally shared. According to the *2007 Household Socio-economic Survey* the richest quintile earned 49 per cent of all household income and the average per capita income of the top quintile is 13 times that of the bottom quintile (NSO 2007). In 1990 this multiple was 8.5 times and in 2000 9.3 times. This reflects sharp increases in income inequality. The wealth distribution is even more unequal. Phongphaichit (2009) quotes figures that show that in 2006 the richest quintile owned 69 per cent of household assets. The stagnating real wages in the modern sector, the fact that most workers are still engaged in the informal sector and the increasing concentration of income and wealth in the top quintile all explain the low and declining consumption share. But it should be recognized that a development strategy driven by export competitiveness based on low labour cost and undervalued exchange rate has its limits.

First, the need to keep wages and other costs and taxes low undermines domestic demand as a source for growth. Low wages and poor employment conditions may keep wage costs down and employment up, but also reduce productivity growth. The poor employment conditions lower the motivation of workers and reduce their incentive to invest in education. Low labour costs also reduce the incentives to invest in labour-saving and more productive capital goods and allow low-productivity firms to survive. Kleinknecht et al. (2006) use survey data on Dutch companies to show that the wage restraint and other labour market reforms agreed to by trade unions to defend employment did indeed result in lower wage costs and an expansion of employment but also resulted in reduced labour productivity growth. In the long run, therefore, such low labour cost strategies will lead to low and stagnating growth (see also Lucidi and Kleinknecht 2010).

Second, the social acceptance of the growing inequalities inherent to the strategy decreases. Interestingly, some interpret the current social and political unrest in Thailand as a struggle between different socio-economic groups. Montesano (2009) points at the changing economic structure that disadvantages rural areas and at the inadequate attention for quality mass education and an elite-dominated political system as factors behind widening social disparities. The resentment about this was activated by the populist policies and rhetoric of the Thaksin governments. Although the current Thai political conflict is highly complex, certainly one element in it is the confrontation between the 'haves' and the 'have-nots'.

NOTES

1. The trend decline in growth is not specific to Thailand; it affects all countries directly hit by the Asian crisis: Indonesia, Malaysia and Korea (ADB 2007).
2. In 2001 57 billion baht was spent on the programmes (about 1 per cent of GDP). For 2002 expenditure of 92 billion was foreseen (*Nation*, 3 July 2002).
3. The *Economic Monitor* of June 2010 (World Bank 2010a) notes that the economic growth in 2010 is fully driven by export demand. Note that this export growth is, so far, just the recovery from the trade collapse of 2008/09 and may not be sustained in the future if external demand remains weak.
4. The 10 ASEAN countries plus China, Japan and South Korea.
5. Data on employment and wages are drawn from the Labor Force Surveys conducted by the National Statistical Office (see http://web.nso.go.th).

PART IV

Preparing for the Next Crisis?

18. The Global Economic Crisis and the Future of Globalization

Rob Vos

Having fallen into the most severe post Second World War recession, the world economy appeared to be recovering in 2010. Following a contraction of 2.0 per cent in 2009, the UN (2010a) projected world gross product (WGP) to grow by 3.0 per cent in 2010 and 3.1 per cent in 2011. By mid-2010, systemic risks in the world financial system that were at the root of the crisis seemed to have abated and risk premia in most credit market segments had dropped to pre-crisis levels. Major equity markets had recovered on average about half of the losses incurred during the crisis, while banks and other financial institutions had managed to rebuild their capital. Capital inflows were gradually returning to many developing economies, and prices of primary commodities had rebounded after steep declines from the start of the crisis to 2009Q2. Propelled by fiscal stimulus packages and expansionary monetary policies, most economies registered positive growth in late 2009 and early 2010. The increase in policy-engendered public spending and the restocking of inventories, which were curtailed precipitously during the crisis, were major factors in the growth recovery.

Yet, during 2010 the world economy continued to show important weaknesses. Despite huge amounts of liquidity injected into the financial system, credit flows to non-financial sectors, especially in the developed economies, remained subdued. While the rebound in equity prices mitigated the losses of financial institutions, the process of establishing sounder balance sheets through write downs of troubled assets and de-leveraging was still far from complete. At the same time, the public finances of many developed countries deteriorated rapidly. In Greece, Portugal, Spain and Ireland they turned out to be a new source of financial instability, causing a strong downfall of the euro and most European governments to initiate a retreat from their stimulus measures. The recovery of economic activity at the global level has been weaker and slower than observed after previous recessions of recent date. Economic recovery also has been very uneven across countries and regions (see Table 18.1). In most developed countries, two years after the start of the global downturn, private sector activity was still lacklustre and unemployment rates high. World economic recovery mainly relied on the new poles of growth, especially in developing Asia, led by China and India. Robust growth in Asia helped pull up many economies in Africa and Latin America, though to strongly varying degrees.

Table 18.1 Growth of world output, 2004–2011 in per cent

	2004–07	2008	2009	2010[a]	2011[a]
World	3.8	1.8	−2.0	3.0	3.2
Developed economies	2.6	0.4	−3.4	1.9	2.1
USA	2.6	0.4	−2.4	2.9	2.5
Japan	2.1	−1.2	−5.2	1.3	1.3
European Union	2.7	0.8	−4.2	1.0	1.8
Economies in transition	7.6	5.4	−6.7	3.9	3.4
Developing economies	7.2	5.3	2.2	4.3	5.8
Africa	5.7	5.0	2.4	5.8	5.3
North Africa	5.2	4.9	3.6	4.7	5.3
Sub-Saharan Africa	6.0	5.0	1.9	4.6	5.3
East and South Asia	8.5	6.2	4.8	7.1	6.9
China	11.7	9.0	8.7	9.2	8.8
India	9.2	7.3	6.4	7.9	8.1
Western Asia	6.0	4.3	−1.0	4.2	4.0
Lat. Am. and Caribbean	5.3	4.0	−2.1	3.8	4.1
Brazil	4.4	5.1	−0.2	5.5	6.0
Mexico	3.9	1.3	−6.5	3.5	2.8
Least developed countries	7.8	7.1	4.0	5.6	5.6

Note: a. UN forecast

Source: UN (2010a)

The crisis and its aftermath raise a myriad of questions about future sources of global economic growth, whether such growth will be sustainable (both from economic and environmental perspectives), and what challenges this poses to existing mechanisms of global economic governance. These questions are addressed following a discussion of the origins of the crisis.

1. HOW DID WE GET INTO THIS MESS?

In 2008, an unprecedented though short-lived period of broad-based global economic growth ended. During 2002–08, developing countries averaged 5 per cent of per capita GDP growth per year, outpacing welfare increases in developed countries by far. Also many of the poorest countries witnessed strong per capita income growth (Figure 18.1), leading some observers to make the contradictory claims that globalization was effectively working to enhance living standards worldwide and that some kind of "decoupling" was taking place with strong endogenous growth in developing countries having become less sensitive to downturns in developed economies.[1]

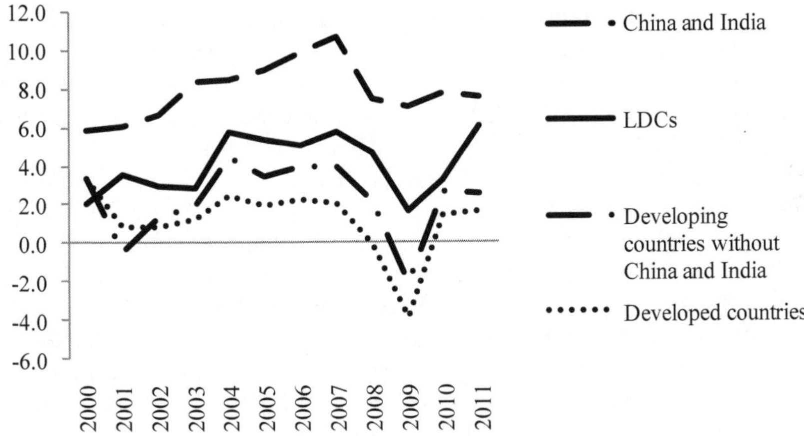

Source: UN/DESA, database for World Economic Situation and Prospects 2011

Figure 18.1 Growth of per capita GDP by main country groups, 2000–2010, (in per cent)

Both claims were proven utterly wrong. The present crisis emerged on the back of an intrinsically unsustainable global growth pattern. This pattern was characterized by strong US consumer demand, funded by easy credit and booming house prices. Far-reaching financial deregulation facilitated a massive and unfettered expansion of new financial instruments, such as securitized sub-prime mortgage lending, sold on financial markets worldwide. This pattern of growth enabled strong export growth and booming commodity prices benefiting many developing countries. Growing US deficits in this period were financed by increasing trade surpluses in China, Japan and other countries accumulating large foreign-exchange reserves and willing to buy dollar-denominated assets, thus fuelling mounting global financial imbalances and the indebtedness of financial institutions, businesses and households. In some countries, both developed and developing, domestic financial debt has risen four- or fivefold as a share of national income since the early 1980s. This rapid explosion in debt was made possible by the shift from a traditional 'buy-and-hold' banking model to a dynamic 'originate-to-sell' trading model (or 'securitization'). Leverage ratios of some institutions went up to as high as 30, well above the ceiling of 10 generally imposed on deposit banks. In the context of a highly integrated global economy without adequate regulation and global governance structures, this risky pattern of financial expansion implied that the breakdown in one part of the system would also lead to failure elsewhere. This systemic failure was at the root of the Great Recession of 2008–09. The deleveraging that followed brought down established financial institutions and led to rapid evaporation of global liquidity directly affecting the real economy in developed countries, while the developing countries were hit through collapsing global trade, plunging commodity prices and reversals of capital flows, thus falsifying the 'decoupling' hypothesis.

Until September 2008, all parties seemed to benefit from the boom, particularly major financial institutions in developed countries, despite repeated warnings, such as those highlighted in successive issues of the UN *World Economic Situation and Prospects*, that mounting household, public sector and financial sector indebtedness in the US and elsewhere, and reflected in wide global financial imbalances would not be sustainable over time. The interconnectedness of excessive risk-taking in financial markets with the problem of the global imbalances, vast dollar reserve accumulation (especially in parts of the developing world), volatile commodity prices and declining trends in productive investment explain why the crisis was systemic in origin and quickly spread to the world at large.

The recent recovery has been led by emerging market economies, especially those in Asia. This raises the subsequent question whether income divergence among developing countries will increase further and become the main characteristic of rising global inequality in the foreseeable future. At current trends, East Asia and India (not South Asia as whole) are likely to be among the more dynamic poles of the new world economy. This implies more serious thinking is needed about the specific mechanisms through which the most dynamic poles of the developing world are going to disseminate their growth to the developing world at large.

2. TOWARDS A SUSTAINABLE RECOVERY?

Following the intensification of the financial crisis in September 2008, governments worldwide took bold actions. Massive public funding was made available to recapitalize banks, taking partial or full government ownership of ailing financial institutions and providing ample guarantees on bank deposits and other financial assets. Worldwide, publicly guaranteed funding for financial sector rescue operations made available during 2008 and 2009 is estimated to amount to about $20 trillion, or some 30 per cent of WGP (UN, 2009a). Monetary and fiscal policies have been strongly counter-cyclical in most major economies (for example, liquidity injections and fiscal stimulus packages totalled about $2.6 trillion or 4.3 per cent of WGP) to be spent during 2008–10. These policies proved effective in as far as they helped stabilize global financial markets, supported global effective demand and alleviated some of the economic and social impact of the crisis. The policy responses were coordinated to some extent, in particular at the level of the Group of 20 (G20) of major developed and developing countries. At their London and Pittsburgh summits in April and September 2009 the leaders promised to continue the stimulus and other extraordinary measures as long as necessary and pledged to deliver on all international development commitments and fight off protectionist tendencies.

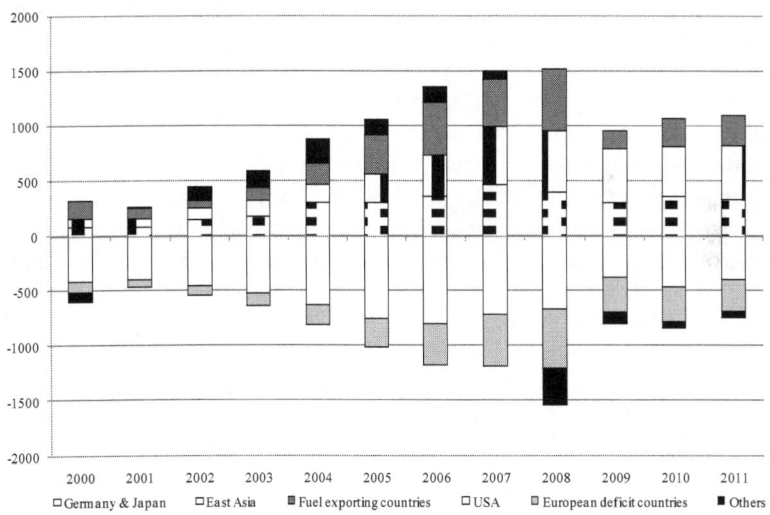

Source: IMF World Economic Outlook database for observed trends for 1996–2009 and UN projections for 2010–2011

Figure 18.2 Global imbalances, 1996–2011(billions of US dollars)

World leaders also facilitated a significant increase in resources for countries with external financing problems. The G20 by and large lived up to its promise to provide $1.1 trillion for this purpose, including through tripling the resources available to the IMF, facilitating additional lending by multilateral development banks and supporting trade finance. The IMF and the World Bank have in effect significantly stepped up lending operations.

At the Pittsburgh Summit, leaders further agreed to establish a policy coordination framework for 'strong, sustainable and balanced growth' of the world economy. G20 members with significant external deficits, the US in particular, pledged to pursue policies to support private savings and to undertake fiscal consolidation over the medium run. Surplus countries, including China, Germany and Japan, would strengthen domestic sources of growth. Although these steps towards effective coordination and a more balanced global recovery are encouraging, more concrete details with clear policy targets and time horizons have to be worked out and the policy actions that have been undertaken thus far have by no means been fully concerted.

As indicated, two years from the start of the crisis, the response did not appear to have been strong enough to induce a self-sustained process of recovery, let alone having set off a benign rebalancing of the global economy. Four key concerns are detailed in the sub-sections below. First, the pattern of recovery so far has been one of a resurgence of the global imbalances that characterized the pre-crisis period. This may well augur for renewed financial and exchange rate instability, in particular because the systemic causes of the global crisis are yet to be dealt with in earnest. Second, as a consequence of the crisis and the stimulus measures, fiscal deficits have widened and indebtedness has increased dramatically, especially among developed countries, compounding dramatically the problem of the global imbalances and has raised concerns about the feasibility of further stimulus which has led to retreats into fiscal austerity. Critics, in contrast, see great risks attached to withdrawal from stimulus now as it could cause a double-dip recession and would miss the opportunity for a redirection of growth patterns onto a more sustainable path. Third, the Southern engines of growth may not be strong enough to pull up the global economy and, moreover, if Southern economies like China and others would more forcefully shift towards domestic sources of growth, international trade could well become the weaker link in the recovery over the medium run. Fourth, the cooperative spirit among major economies has been waning during 2010, as was apparent at the Toronto and Seoul summits of the G20. The concerns over rising public debt shifted policy priorities to fiscal consolidation, combined in some cases with aggressive new quantitative monetary easing in some major economies. These shifts in policy stances were not coordinated and not only risked weakening the recovery, but also further complicated the prospects for a benign global rebalancing. The consequences felt during 2010 were enhanced exchange instability among major reserve currencies and more speculative capital flowing toward merging market economies, causing responses in the form of heavy interventions in foreign exchange markets and capital controls, which could be followed by rounds of trade protectionist measures.

Resurging Global Imbalances and the Reserve Currency Problem

As the crisis unfolded, the global imbalances narrowed markedly (see Figure 18.2). The large external deficit of the US declined from $700 billion in 2008 to about $420 billion in 2009, approximately 3 per cent of its GDP. This was mirrored by smaller surpluses in China, Germany, Japan and a group of oil-exporting countries. This adjustment, however, was a pure effect of the recession with the sharp retrenchment in imports of deficit countries and the collapse in exports of surplus countries, especially in early 2009.

In the US, declining import demand was closely linked to lower household consumption and a precipitous fall in both residential and business investment. The household savings rate increased from 1.7 per cent in 2007 to 4.2 per cent of disposable household income in 2009.[2] Government savings, in contrast, declined along with the widening budget deficit which surged from 1.2 per cent in 2007 to 9.9 per cent in 2009. Adjustments in savings and investment balances of major surplus economies vary across countries, but falling government savings were a common trend. Among the surplus countries that entered into recession, like Germany and Japan, falling tax revenue and higher fiscal spending as part of stimulus measures are key factors for the decline in their aggregate surpluses. The decline in investment demand in Germany and Japan only partly offset this trend. In China, in contrast, fiscal stimulus and a strong increase in investment demand were the main factors behind the reduction in its savings surplus in 2009. Consumption demand in China also increased markedly, but compared with other major economies total consumption relative to GDP still remains extremely low.

In the short-to-medium term outlook the global imbalances are set to widen again. The large US budget deficit will remain high and is likely to decrease only gradually as a share of GDP. The private sector in the US is not expected to generate large enough savings surpluses to finance the government deficits, implying that the economy will rely on foreign borrowing. As the recovery proceeds, business confidence will improve and output gaps will close, and private investment demand is likely to pick up ahead of growth in private savings. Consequently, even with a gradual rebalancing from public to private demand during the recovery, the US external deficit stands to increase further in the medium term. In Europe, the recovery may show a similar pattern of rebalancing, assuming that an ongoing recovery will induce a phasing out of the fiscal stimulus while private consumption and investment demand will pick up again from 2011. Such trends in Europe and the US would need to be matched by increasing surpluses elsewhere. In major surplus countries, the savings–investment patterns have not been fundamentally changed. All other things being equal, continued recovery will sustain the rebound in oil prices and thereby savings surpluses in major oil-exporting countries. Most countries in Asia have resumed their export-led growth paths. China is taking policy measures to rebalance growth towards domestic demand, particularly by stimulating household consumption growth, but in such a large economy structurally altering the basic drivers of growth will take a long time. In the case of China, where the current-account surplus has continued to rise in terms of level but moderated slightly in terms of a percentage of GDP, the persistent surplus is a reflection of two factors. In the external sector, the large proportion of China's 'processing trade' (about 60 per cent of total trade), lay at the root of a synchronized decline in China's exports and imports: as the orders for China's exports dropped, China's orders for the imports of raw materials and intermediate goods, which are used as inputs for manufacturing the exports, also dropped. On the domestic front, the large stimulus package of 2008 has boosted domestic demand to offset some of the dragging effects from the weakening external demand. However, the stimuli have had more effect on boosting fixed investment than household consumption, leaving the household consumption-to-GDP ratio below 40 per cent. In the short run, one should expect that China's external surpluses will continue to increase, as in 2010, as China's net investment income on foreign assets is an increasingly important contributor to the country's foreign-exchange earnings.

Table 18.2 presents such a possible pattern of global imbalances under a scenario of a continued slow global recovery for the world as a whole beyond the baseline forecast for 2011. The results are based on simulations with the UN Global Policy Model.[3] It is uncertain whether such a scenario will actually materialize, but what it shows is the risks associated with a path of largely uncoordinated economic recovery that has been set in. Public debt ratios in Europe and the US would continue to increase over the medium run and the net external liability position of the US, which is already large, would increase further. This will increase the cost of borrowing in deficit countries and enhance the likelihood of much larger exchange rate volatilities. The fundamentals are for a much weaker US dollar which could strengthen export growth. But, in combination with a continued high public debt overhang in both Europe and the US, the risks for a disorderly adjustment and volatility in currency and financial markets at large would increase substantially. With the continued global financial imbalances, the net foreign liability position of the US has increased substantially over the past two decades, reaching $2.1 trillion in 2007 (Nguyen 2009). The position worsened further and surged to $3.5 trillion by the end of 2008, or 25 per cent of GDP. The increment of about $1.4 trillion is approximately double the current account deficit registered in 2008, implying that half of the increase can be explained by a revaluation of assets and liabilities to the disadvantage of US investors and debt holders. The abrupt adjustment of the global imbalances and the further worsening of the net foreign investment position of the US are associated with the volatile and erratic movement of the exchange rate of the US dollar *vis-à-vis* other major currencies.

The resurging external indebtedness of the US following a renewed widening of the twin deficits will keep downward pressure on the dollar and a hard landing of the world's main reserve currency remains a clear and present danger. Intrinsic shortcomings of the present global reserve system are at the heart of the continued exchange rate volatility and risk of a future financial meltdown. The use of the US dollar as the major reserve currency suffers from a number of systemic flaws that have been well documented.[4]

First, the present global reserve system suffers from the deflationary bias characteristic of any system in which the burden of macroeconomic adjustment falls on deficit countries. High debt ratios or lack of external financing typically put greater external pressure on deficit countries to adjust than on surplus countries. As demand contraction in the deficit country tends to take the more typical form of asymmetric adjustment, it can be called a deflationary bias. The second flaw relates to the instabilities associated with the use of a national currency as an international currency. For other countries to accumulate reserves, the reserve currency country must run an external deficit. Over time, this may lead to an undesirable level of external indebtedness of the reserve-currency country, followed by an erosion of confidence in the value of that currency. The accumulation of vast amounts of foreign-exchange reserves by developing countries was to an important degree a response to the perceived need for increased 'self-protection' against pro-cyclical capital flows in the aftermath of the Asian crisis and other crises in emerging market economies. The response was logical in the absence of more adequate collective insurance mechanisms to manage balance-of-payments crises. However, by contributing to the problem of significantly widening global imbalances, related volatility and weakening of the value of the major reserve currency, the response itself became part and parcel of the factors that caused the present crisis.

Table 18.2 UN Global Policy Model: medium-term scenario of risk of resurging global imbalances

	Average 04-07	2009	2011	2013	2015
World economic growth	3.9	−2.0	3.8	4.4	4.1
United States					
Economic growth	2.8	−2.4	3.4	3.9	2.6
Bank loans (private)	86.8	77.6	56.2	69.4	89.2
Government debt	49.3	71.8	92.8	95.9	94.8
Private savings–investment	−2.7	6.9	4.8	0.7	−3.0
Govt. savings–investment	−3.1	−10.2	−8.9	−6.2	−4.7
Current account	−5.8	−3.3	−4.1	−5.5	−7.6
Europe					
Economic growth	2.6	−4.0	2.7	3.2	3.5
Bank loans (private)	117.1	106.8	84.5	97.1	113.0
Government debt	61.1	81.9	96.7	96.0	87.3
Private savings–investment	1.6	4.0	3.5	1.2	−1.3
Govt. savings–investment	−1.5	−4.4	−4.0	−2.7	−1.5
Current account	0.1	−0.4	−0.5	−1.4	−2.8
Japan and Other Developed					
Economic growth	2.5	−4.2	2.2	2.8	2.6
Bank loans (private)	149.9	155.8	149.7	156.7	164.3
Government debt	126.4	135.2	129.9	123.1	116.5
Private savings–investment	−1.3	1.4	1.2	1.8	2.6
Govt. savings–investment	3.3	−0.6	0.0	0.5	0.4
Current account	2.0	0.8	1.1	2.3	3.0
Russia and other Economies in Transition					
Economic growth	7.4	−6.7	6.3	6.3	7.1
Bank loans (private)	33.0	61.7	43.2	39.9	38.1
Government debt	17.5	17.3	27.4	32.8	32.8
Private savings–investment	1.7	7.9	10.3	9.6	7.7
Govt. savings–investment	4.3	−5.3	−6.7	−5.9	−4.6
Current account	6.0	2.5	3.6	3.7	3.1
China					
Economic growth	11.2	8.7	8.2	8.9	8.5
Bank loans (private)	125.1	108.8	120.5	130.8	142.8
Government debt	11.9	13.8	16.8	18.1	18.9
Private savings–investment	11.4	9.3	8.9	7.9	9.2
Govt. savings–investment	−3.9	−3.5	−3.1	−1.7	0.0
Current account to GDP	7.5	5.9	5.9	6.2	9.2

Table 18.2 continued

	Average 04-07	2009	2011	2013	2015
India					
Economic growth	9.0	6.4	9.8	8.6	7.8
Bank loans (private)	42.2	51.4	51.4	53.1	55.0
Government debt	67.8	71.2	70.2	63.7	53.4
Private savings–investment	2.9	7.4	6.4	5.9	5.8
Govt. savings–investment	−3.3	−8.8	−7.1	−4.6	−2.7
Current account	−0.4	−1.4	−0.7	1.3	3.2
Other Developing Asia					
Economic growth	6.1	−0.1	3.7	5.2	5.9
Bank loans (private)	55.2	68.3	65.4	67.4	70.0
Government debt	50.3	55.8	46.0	39.2	34.9
Private savings–investment	5.2	4.7	4.1	4.5	5.4
Govt. savings–investment	1.0	0.1	0.3	0.4	0.4
Current account	6.3	4.8	4.3	5.0	5.8
Latin America					
Economic growth	5.6	−2.1	4.4	4.9	5.3
Bank loans (private)	32.3	55.9	52.4	51.4	51.1
Government debt	30.7	36.5	36.4	34.4	30.9
Private savings–investment	0.5	0.3	0.2	1.2	1.9
Govt. savings–investment	0.1	−1.6	−1.5	−1.3	−1.0
Current account	0.6	−1.2	−1.3	−0.1	1.0
Africa					
Economic growth	6.5	2.4	6.0	5.8	5.5
Bank loans (private)	40.1	59.6	56.2	58.5	60.7
Government debt	46.0	48.8	36.1	31.3	28.9
Private savings–investment	6.2	2.6	3.2	4.5	4.9
Govt. savings–investment	−1.1	−4.4	−3.1	−2.7	−2.7
Current account	5.0	−1.9	0.0	1.9	2.2

Source: UN (2010a)

Note: All variables with the exception of economic growth in per cent of GDP

Till Debt do us Part?

While the fiscal stimulus packages were critical for stabilizing individual economies in 2009, their contribution to the recovery has been uneven due to large differences in the nature and size of the stimulus packages across countries and in the timing of their implementation. The discretionary fiscal measures contributed to widening budget deficits, though the direct impact of the recession (via lower tax revenues and/or higher unemployment benefit payments) has been larger. According to IMF estimates, the stimulus packages account for some 40 per cent of the increase in structural primary balances in the developed G20 countries and 30 per cent for the G20 developing countries (IMF 2010a).[5] Levels of public indebtedness have increased significantly, especially among developed countries (Figure 18.3). During 2010, the perception of increased risk of sovereign debt default impacted on smaller European countries, including Greece, Ireland and Portugal, but concerns also extended to Spain. These problems transmitted to turmoil in global currency and financial markets.

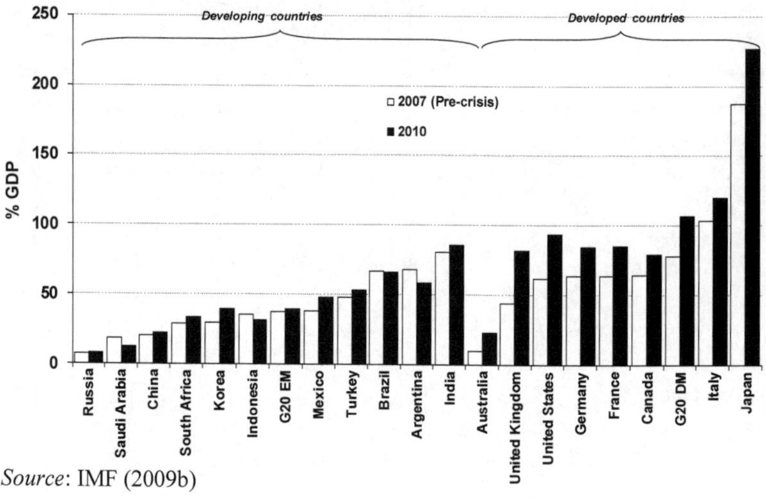

Source: IMF (2009b)

Figure 18.3 Public debt of G20 countries, per cent of GDP, 2007 and 2010

With the exception of Japan, Greece, Iceland, Italy and Portugal, even by conservative estimates most developed countries are rated to still have significant fiscal space for further stimulus according to a recent IMF study (Ostry et al. 2010). The IMF assessment does not take into account, however, the positive growth impact which fiscal policy can have in the presence of high unemployment rates or hysteresis. The latter concept refers to a situation where the 'natural rate' of unemployment has increased as a result of persistent cyclical weakness in the economy. With hysteresis, fiscal stimulus will provide a stronger impulse to aggregate demand if it can counteract unemployment and bring output back to potential. Past experience has shown that long-lasting demand expansions were able to achieve this, as well as that they can lower public debt-to-GDP ratios from both the added output growth and the high tax revenues (Ball 2009). Similarly, counterfactual model simulations with the UN Global Policy Model showed that premature fiscal consolidation while economic recovery is still feeble likely will cause lower growth and falling tax revenue, thereby exacerbating fiscal difficulties and causing the public debt ratio to rise even further (UN 2010c). Both such findings suggest that a prolonged demand stimulus by governments focused on job creation is not only necessary to avoid a weak and protracted recovery, but that this can be done without endangering fiscal sustainability.

Southern Global Growth Engines?

As said, the global economic recovery has been strongly based in the rebound in emerging market economies. Indeed, in modern history the world has never before experienced a situation in which, given the current weakness of industrial countries, major developing countries have become the principal engine of world economic growth. Continuing expansion of these economies is therefore crucial for the world. But that said, the question that needs to be raised is about the current and future capacity of developing economies to transmit their growth dynamics to the rest of the world.

China holds the largest share of global trade among developing countries, which makes it a test case. China's ability to induce growth in the rest of the world inevitably depends on its capacity to turn its large trade surplus into a balance or even a trade deficit. This problem is absent in other large developing countries, like Brazil and India, which run current account deficits. In the case of China, the transition from export-led to domestic-led growth raises a myriad of questions, including the capacity to shift domestic demand dynamics from investment to consumption and therefore substantially increase wage shares and reduce the significant overcapacity generated by the highest investment rate ever recorded in history. Also, as already mentioned, given that large parts of its trade links are associated with the demand for inputs for its export sector, the shift from export-led to domestic demand-led growth may actually reduce Chinese import demand.

Under any scenario, however, it is essential that we do not throw the baby out with the bathwater as China reorients its pattern of growth. In particular, although some real appreciation of the renminbi should be part of this process, a very strong and disorderly appreciation could seriously affect Chinese economic growth. Looking back in history, a strongly appreciating currency to reduce export surpluses is one, not implausible interpretation of how Japan's dynamic growth came to a halt and its costly financial crisis was incubated. In any case, it is the one interpretation that Chinese authorities seem to have in mind when trying to avoid repeating that history. The more desirable scenario is a Chinese economy that transmits its stimulus to the rest of the world through rising imports generated more by the income effect (through rapid economic growth and real wage increases) than by the substitution effect (through strong real exchange rate appreciation). Opening more space for Chinese investment abroad should also be an essential part of this strategy.

But even if and when other major surplus countries manage to rebalance their economies while sustaining robust growth, it may well be at the cost of weaker international transmission of their growth. The reorientation of the Chinese and other large surplus economies towards greater dependence on domestic demand could slow their import demand. But also many of the poorer economies would need to refocus their economies away from their high dependence on primary exports or footloose manufacturing export production and toward a strengthening of the backward and forward linkages of their export industries. Countries that have more diversified trade and stronger links with their own or regional economies are less prone to trade shocks (Figure 18.4) and grow faster in the long run as they gain more from trade (Figure 18.5). Along with the increased spending on non-tradables (including, on infrastructure, sources of renewable energy and education), creating such links may require slowing export growth during the process of structural adjustment. If so slowing of world trade would be transitory, but benign.

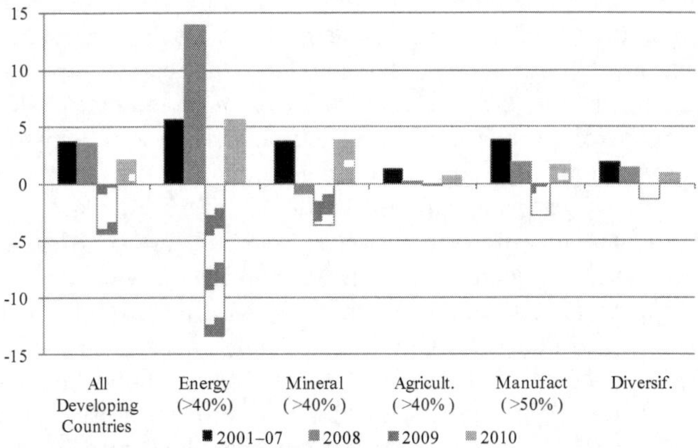

Source: UN/DESA (2010a)

Note: Export specialization: share in total merchandise exports exceeding 40 per cent.

Figure 18.4 Trade shocks in developing countries by product-based export specialization, 2007–10 (per cent of GDP)

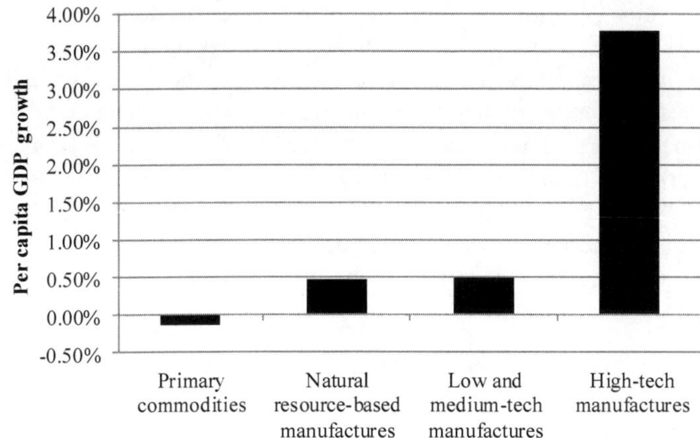

Source: UN (2006)

Figure 18.5 Developing countries per capita GDP growth by dominant technology content of export specialization, 1960–2000

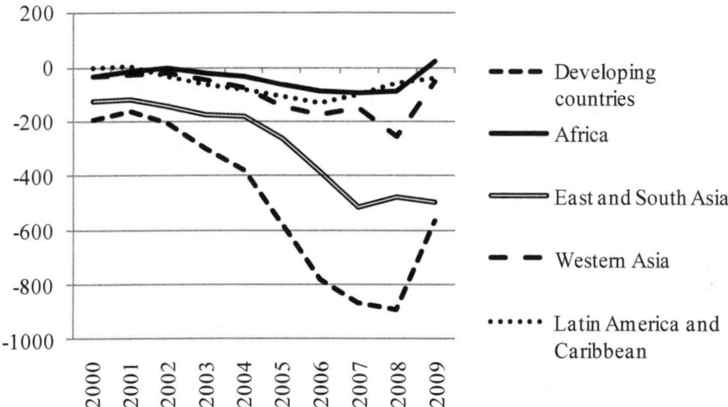

Source: UN (2010c), table III.1

Figure 18.6 Net financial transfers to developing countries, by region, 2000–09 (billions of US dollars)

For this scenario to emerge, low and middle-income countries will need to benefit not only from greater market access but also from greater breathing space in WTO rules and regional and bilateral free trade agreements to apply temporary support measures so that they can climb up the trading ladder. Easing impediments to technology transfers, especially those affecting access to green technologies, would need to be part of the same package (UN

2010b: Ch. II and IV). In this scenario, direct investment and further development of the technologies to be transferred to developing countries could become more important in developed country growth to compensate for the possible weakening of international trade dynamics. There will be major impediments for such a scenario. The principal one may well be in the task to shift corporate strategies of multinational companies which dominate global value chains and global trade to facilitate greater value added generation and new technology adaptation in developing countries by making their production less footloose and more strongly rooted in local economies.

3. IS SUSTAINABLE REBALANCING FEASIBLE?

Going forward, the worst global scenario would be one in which all or most countries, including the industrial countries, aim at improving their current accounts through fiscal consolidation or otherwise, since this is nothing but a scenario of weak global demand and even a new recession. A more desirable global scenario thus would be one in which most developing countries run current account deficits. This would require continued strong growth in developing countries and allow for dealing with global poverty and climate change. For that, not only the large-scale infrastructure investments to support economic diversification, but also substantial increases in public expenditures are needed for achieving the millennium development goals (MDGs) as well as new investments in renewable energy and sustainable agriculture. Similarly, all the calls for additional development financing and enhanced international cooperation point in the same direction. Moving towards a world of multi-polar growth consistent with income convergence across all nations, consistent with broad-based poverty reduction and with the greening of global growth, would require not a balancing, but in fact a reversal in the pattern of global imbalances over the medium run.

The counterpart trend would consist of a reversal of the present pattern of net transfers of financial resources flowing from developing countries to those industrial countries that are running large deficits. In 2008, those transfers bordered $1 trillion. The major surplus countries in East Asia and Western Asia of course contributed most, but also Africa saw more financial resources flowing out of its region than flowing in (see Figure 18.6). Because of the crisis, the UN estimate net financial outflows fell back to around $600 billion in 2009 (UN, 2010c). Because of the present pattern of the recovery and the return of massive, mostly short-term capital flows towards emerging markets, however, all other things being equal, one should expect the amount of net transfers from poor to rich countries to increase again in the coming years. This return to pre-crisis patterns of international financial flows runs the risk of generating future busts, following well-known patterns.

Rebalancing across countries is needed because, as discussed, one of the key drivers of pre-crisis growth, consumer demand in the US, is likely to remain sluggish in the immediate outlook. Moreover, from the perspective of the problem of global imbalances, it would be undesirable to have to rely on this source of growth again for the recovery. Private investments are also expected to remain subdued in the near future in the US (as well as in other major developed economies) as rates of capacity utilization were still at historic lows in 2010. If fiscal stimulus is to be phased out, net exports of the major deficit countries would need to increase. Rising exports by these countries would need to be absorbed by major surplus countries, starting with China and other parts of developing Asia. This could be achieved in part through a further strengthening of domestic demand by way of fiscal stimulus, which, along with a weaker US dollar, would push up import demand in that part of the world. Since not all Asian trade is with the US, other countries would also need to contribute to the rebalancing. Germany and Japan, other major surplus economies, could seek to strengthen investment and productivity growth in domestic production sectors, while major oil exporters could further step up domestic investment plans to diversify their economies. Additional financial transfers to developing countries with weak fiscal capacity would be needed to complete the rebalancing process and would enable these countries to increase domestic investment in infrastructure, food production and human development so as to support growth, poverty reduction and sustainable development.

They would also encourage global import demand. Stepping up public and private investment to address climate change could well be an integral part of the process. Large-scale investments in energy efficiency and renewable energy generation will need to be made now in order to achieve the scale effects needed to lower the cost of green technologies and effectively achieve low-emission growth paths. Such investments will also be needed in developing countries, where energy demand should be expected to increase starkly along with their efforts to reach higher levels of development. By leapfrogging to green technologies, they could contribute to emission reductions while sustaining high-growth development trajectories (UN 2009b). Substantial investments will need to be made for climate change adaptation, especially in developing countries which are already being affected by the adverse effects of global warming. As developed countries currently possess a comparative advantage in the development of green technologies and related capital goods, the increase in world demand for these goods should thus contribute to reducing the aggregate external deficit of these economies. Such a sustainable rebalancing of the world economy will not be easy. It will be demanding on our mechanisms for global economic governance (UN 2010b) and it will require fundamental reforms to the functioning of the global financial system.

Strengthening International Policy Coordination

An orderly rebalancing of the world economy will require much stronger international policy coordination built around common principles and goals and sustained over the long run. But, as may be clear from the above analysis, such coordination cannot be merely about managing exit strategies from the extraordinary stimulus measures or about managing aggregate demand. It is even more important to address such issues in conjunction with industrial and energy policies, poverty reduction strategies, strategies for international development financing and cooperation, and trade policies. The G20 framework for strong, sustainable and balanced global growth thus should comprise all of the above.

In this context, the framework proposed by the G20 is a first step towards international policy coordination – at least among the major developed and emerging economies – to prevent a recurrence of the large global imbalances. The success of this framework, however, will depend not only on how to institutionalize the mechanism delineated above (which so far is still carried out on an ad hoc basis), but also on progress in the broad reforms of the international financial architecture and global economic governance.

To support the enhanced framework for policy coordination, further progress on global economic governance reforms will need to be made on four related fronts. First, multilateral surveillance by the IMF will need to be extended well beyond the traditional emphasis on exchange rates, to address broader macro-financial surveillance and also to monitor the 'sustainable rebalancing' process of the global economy as outlined. Second, more pervasive progress on governance reform of the IMF will be needed to add legitimacy to the institution's enhanced role in this respect and also for mediating multi-annual agreements. Mediation to achieve consensus on the main targets for policy coordination is unlikely to be successful where doubts exist about the impartiality of the mediator. In this context, the reform of the governance of and representation in the IMF has become all the more urgent and important so that seats in the Executive Board and votes in the Fund better represent developing country interests in the decision-making process that is under way.

Third, while the ongoing crisis has given strong impetus to macroeconomic policy coordination, there is no guarantee that all parties will remain committed to the agreed joint responses. Having clear and verifiable targets for desired policy outcomes will help make parties accountable, and the possible loss of reputation through non-compliance should be an incentive to live up to policy agreements.

Fourth, sustainable rebalancing of the global economy will require close coordination with other areas of global governance, including those related to development financing and the multilateral trading system, as well as with the UN Framework Convention on Climate Change (UN 2010b). No specific mechanism for such coordination exists at present, and the creation of such a mechanism would need to be considered.

Reforming the International Financial System

The second main reason why sustainable rebalancing will be most demanding is that it cannot be done without major reforms in the global financial system. Reversing the pattern of global imbalances will remain difficult without touching the global reserve system. Continued reliance on the dollar and the perceived need of countries to accumulate strong reserve positions as self-insurance against world market instability is bound to sustain the current pattern of global imbalances rather than reverse it.

The risk of exchange-rate instability and a hard landing of the dollar could be reduced by having a global payments and reserve system which is less dependent on one single national currency. One way in which the system could naturally evolve would be by becoming a fully multi-currency reserve system. The present system has already more than one reserve currency, but the other currencies remain a secondary feature in a system where most reserve assets by far are held in dollars and where most of the world's trade and financial transactions take place in the major reserve currency. The advantage of a multi-reserve currency arrangement is that it would provide countries with the benefit of diversifying their foreign-exchange reserve assets. However, it would not solve the problem of the tendency towards the emergence of important global imbalances and the related deflationary bias in the macroeconomic adjustment between deficit and surplus countries.

Such deficiencies could be more readily overcome by pursuing the transition to a reserve system based on a true form of international liquidity, such as by expanding the role of special drawing rights (SDRs). Doing so would, in fact, fulfil the objective included in the IMF Articles of Agreement of 'making the special drawing right the principal reserve asset in the international monetary system' (Article VIII, Section 7, and Article XXII). The G20 decided, in April 2009, on a general SDR allocation equivalent to $250 billion in recognition of the need to boost international liquidity using an international reserve unit. Further advances could result from making SDR issuance automatic and regular, and linked to the demand for foreign-exchange reserves and the growth of the world economy. A key criterion for

SDR issuance, withdrawal and allocation would be the provision of counter-cyclical finance. Thus, both key deficiencies of the present system – its deflationary bias and the inherent instability of the value of the reserve currency – could be overcome. An SDR-based reserve system would also provide a basis for a better pooling of international reserves, as international liquidity could be made available on a counter-cyclical basis, reducing the need for individual countries to hold costly amounts of reserves on their own.

There will be important practical hurdles to be overcome en route to such a system, and they will need to be discussed and addressed in conjunction with other reforms, in particular those of existing mechanisms for financial regulation and supervision. Some emerging market countries have already responded to the return of speculative capital flows by introducing capital controls, a logical response to avoid their macroeconomic policy space being overridden by boom–bust capital flows that can be so devastating for growth and poverty reduction. Yet a serious discussion of capital account regulations in the world is still surprisingly missing at the forefront of the current discussions of global financial reform. The effectiveness of any international policy coordination mechanism would also greatly benefit from overcoming these and other systemic deficiencies, as tendencies towards excess risk-taking in financial markets would be reined in and the inherent tendency of the current system towards global imbalances and an unstable value of the major reserve currency would be addressed.

The Role of the G20

Progress on all these fronts has been slow at best. The G20 provided a strong impulse in the early stages of the crisis. Fear of a complete global meltdown and a new great depression brought leaders of major economies together and, cognizant of the increased importance of major developing economies, the G20 replaced the G7/G8 as the key platform for deliberating internationally concerted solutions. Important progress has been made in terms of coordinating enhanced availability of international liquidity and promoting financial regulatory reform, leading to agreement on a new set of internationally agreed standards (Basel III). Along the way the IMF was much empowered, after having fallen into virtual oblivion just prior to the crisis. Its resources for crisis responses more than tripled and its surveillance role has strengthened. The G20 also played a decisive role in reaching agreement on a 5 per cent shift in voting power and more seats on the IMF's executive board in favour of the developing countries.

As mentioned, however, the cooperative spirit among the G20 members waned during 2010 over disagreements about the role of fiscal policy in keeping up the momentum of the recovery and contentious discussions about exchange rate policies of China and other major emerging market economies and the spillover effects of the expansionary monetary policies of major reserve currency countries. Consequently, also little progress was made in making the framework for 'strong, sustainable and balanced global growth' more operational. The credibility of international policy coordination and, more broadly, the mechanisms of global economic governance is at stake. It is not only the lack of a defined framework for policy coordination that is undermining the credibility of the process. Also, the present dominance of ad hoc decision making at the level of the G20 over more institutionalized multilateral decision making through the IMF or the UN remains problematic.

The agility of decision making by a limited number of key players will only be of lasting advantage if is given legitimacy through more representative decision-making processes. Notwithstanding its flaws, the multilateral trading system no doubt provided a key role in avoiding beggar-thy-neighbour trade protectionist responses that were a factor in turning the crash of 1929 into a prolonged global depression. Similarly, a clear and broadly accepted set of rules for keeping global imbalances in check and a strengthened international financial architecture should help ensure commitment to sharing the responsibility to preserve global financial stability and sustainable development.

NOTES

1. Both IMF and World Bank, while recognizing trends towards rising global inequality, sustained the decoupling hypothesis till shortly before the present crisis (see e.g. IMF 2007, 2008a; World Bank 2008).
2. As a share of GDP, personal savings in the US increased from 1.3 to 3.3 per cent between 2007 and 2009.
3. See: http://www.un.org/esa/policy/publications/ungpm.html.
4. See, for example, Clark and Polak (2004), UN (2005), Eichengreen (2009), Ocampo (2009), UNCTAD (2009a), and United Nations Commission of Experts of the President of the UN General Assembly (2009: 92–102).
5. The stimulus has a much more modest impact (less than 5 per cent) to the rise in debt-to-GDP ratios, which is mostly on account of revenue losses.

References

Abella, M. and G. Ducanes, 2009, 'The effects of the global economic crisis on Asian migrant workers and governments' responses', ILO/SMC Workshop on Building a Comparable, Up-to-date, and Sustainable Database on Labour Migration, 21–22 January 2009.

Abugre, C., 2009, 'The Financial Crisis and Social Development in Africa: An Opportunity for Strategic Change', paper presented at the CODA Conference on the Impact of the Financial Crisis on Africa, Tunis.

ADB (Asian Development Bank), 2007, 'Ten Years After the Crisis: The Facts about Investment and Growth', in *Asia Development Outlook*, Asian Development Bank, Manila, pp. 46–65.

ADB, 2009, *Asian Development Outlook 2009 Update: Broadening Openness for a Resilient Asia*, ADB, Manila.

ADB, 2010, *Asian Development Outlook 2010: Macroeconomic Management Beyond the Crisis*, ADB, Manila.

Addison, T., C. Arndt and F. Tarp, 2010, 'The Triple Crisis and the Global Aid Architecture', *UNU WIDER Working Paper 2010/01*, UNU-WIDER: Helsinki.

Adu-Amankwah, K., 1999, 'Trade unions in the informal sector: finding their bearings: nine country papers: Ghana', *Labour Education* **116** (3), pp. 1–14.

AfDB, 2009, 'Impact of the Global Financial Crisis and Economic Crisis on Africa', *Working Paper No.96*, pp. 7–12.

Agosin, M., 2008, 'Is Foreign Investment Always Good for Development?', *Working Group on Development and Environment in the Americas, Discussion Paper No. 9*, April.

Aguiar, M.A., 2005, 'Investment, devaluation, and foreign currency exposure: The case of Mexico' *Journal of Development Economics* **78**, pp. 95–113.

Ahmed, N. and M.K. Mujeri, 2009, 'Social Impacts of Global Economic Slowdown: The Case of Bangladesh', paper presented at the ABD Conference on The Impact of the Global Economic Slowdown on Poverty and Sustainable Development in Asia and the Pacific, September 28–30, Vietnam.

Ahmed, M., T. Lane and M. Schultz-Ghattas, 2001, 'Refocusing IMF conditionality', *Finance and Development*, (December), International Monetary Fund (IMF), Washington, DC.

AIDWA (All India Democratic Women's Association), 2009, *Report on the Condition of Work of Home-based Workers in Delhi*, AIDWA, New Delhi.

Akerlof, G.A. and R.J. Shiller, 2009, *Animal Spirits, How Human Psychology Drives the Economy and Why it Matters for Global Capitalism*, Princeton University Press, Princeton.

Akyüz, Y., 2002, 'Crisis Management and Burden Sharing' in Y. Akyüz (ed.), *Reforming the Global Financial Architecture: Issues and Proposals*, ZED Books/UNCTAD/TWN, London, pp. 118–34.

Akyüz, Y. and K. Boratav, 2003, 'The making of the Turkish financial crisis', *World Development* **31** (9), pp. 1549–66.

Akyüz, Y. and A. Cornford, 1999, 'Capital flows to developing countries and the reform of the international financial system', *UNCTAD Discussion Paper, 143*, Geneva.

Amsden, A.H., 2003, *The Rise of 'The Rest': Challenges to the West from Late-industrializing Economies*, Oxford University Press, Oxford.

Amsden, A.H., 2007, *Escape from Empire. The Developing World's Journey through Heaven and Hell*, MIT Press.

Arbache, J. and J. Page, 2007, 'More growth and fewer collapses? A new look at long run growth in Africa', *World Bank Policy Research Paper No. 4384*, World Bank, Washington, DC.

Åslund, A. (2009), 'Implications of the global financial crisis for Eastern Europe', *Development & Transition* **13**, pp. 2–4.

Athukorala, P., 2007, *Multinational Enterprises in Asian Development*, Edward Elgar, Cheltenham, UK and Northampton, MA, USA.

Athukorala, P. and N. Yamashita (2009). 'Global production sharing and Sino–US trade relations', *China and World Economy* **17** (3), pp. 39–56.

Auboin, M. 2009, 'Restoring trade finance during a period of financial crisis: Stock-taking of recent initiatives', *WTO Staff Working Paper ERSD-2009-16*, WTO, Geneva.

Ball, L.M., 2009, 'Hysteresis in Unemployment: Old and New Evidence', *NBER Working Paper No. 14818*, National Bureau for Economic Research, Cambridge, MA.

Bangladesh Bureau of Statistics, 2006, 'Key Findings of Labour Force Survey 2005–06', BBS, Dhaka.

Beckman, B., 2009, *Trade Unions and the Politics of Crisis*, Draft paper, November 2009.

Bennet, M., 2003, 'Organizing in the Informal Economy: A Case Study of the Clothing Industry in South Africa', *Seed Working Paper No. 37*, ILO, Geneva.

Bergeijk, P.A.G. van, 2009a, 'Expected extent and potential duration of the world import crunch', *Kyklos* **62** (4), pp. 479–87.

Bergeijk, P.A.G. van, 2009b, 'Some Economic Historic Perspectives on the 2009 World Trade Collapse,' *ISS Working Paper 476*, ISS, The Hague.

Bergeijk, P.A.G. van, 2009c, 'I Come to Bury Globalization, Not to Praise It', Inaugural address at the International Institute of Social Studies, Erasmus University (ISS), 29th October 2009.

Bergeijk, P.A.G. van, 2009d, *Economic Diplomacy and the Geography of International Trade*, Edward Elgar, Cheltenham UK and Northampton, MA, USA.

Bergeijk, P.A.G. van, 2010, *On the Brink of Deglobalization: An Alternative Perspective on the Causes of the World Trade Collapse*, Edward Elgar, Cheltenham UK and Northampton, MA, USA.

Bernanke, B., 2005, 'The Global Saving Glut and the US Current Account Deficit', http://www.federalreserve.gov/boarddocs/speeches/2005/200503102/.

Bhutta, Z.A., F.A. Bawany, A. Feroze, A. Rizvi, S.J. Thapa and M. Patel, 2009, 'Effects of the crises on child nutrition and health in East Asia and the Pacific', *Global Social Policy* **9**, pp. 119–43.

Bijleveld, J., 1939, 'Memorie van Overgave van den aftredende Gouverneur van Jogjakarta', National Archive, The Hague, Archive of the Ministry for the Colonies MMK 144.

BIS, 2008, *Annual Report*, BIS, Basel.

BIS, 2009, *Statistics on Amounts Outstanding of OTC Equity-Linked and Commodity Derivatives, by Instrument and Counterparty*, BIS, Basel.

Bond, P., 2009, *African Reaction to Global Finance*, Draft paper.

Bonner, C., 2004, *Organisational Renewal in COSATU & Affiliates: An Overview*, NALEDI, Johannesburg.

BPS (Biro Pusat Statistik), (various issues, 1999–2003), *Laporan Perekonomian Propinsi DI Yogyakarta*, Biro Pusat Statistik Propinsi DI, Yogyakarta

Brecher, R. and J. Bhagwati, 1987, 'Voluntary Export Restraints versus Import Restraints: A Welfare Theoretic Analysis', in H.K. Kierzkowski (ed.), *Protection and Competition in International Trade. Essays in the Honour of W.M. Corden*, Oxford, Basil Blackwell, pp. 41–53.

Budlender, D., 2003, *Street Traders and their Organisations in South Africa*, ILO, Geneva.

Busse, M. and P. Nunnenkamp, 2009, 'Gender disparity in education and the international competition for foreign direct investment', *Feminist Economics* **15** (3), pp. 61–90.

Büthe, T. and H.V. Milner, 2008, 'The Volatility of Foreign Direct Investment Flows into Developing Countries: Impact of International and Domestic Institutions', Mimeo.

Cali, M., and S. ell'Erba, 2009, 'The global financial crisis and remittances: what past evidence suggest', *Working Paper 303*, Overseas Development Institute (ODI), London.

Cali, M., I. Massa and D.W. te Velde, 2008, 'The global financial crisis: financial flows to developing countries set to fall by one quarter', *ODI Report*, ODI, London.

Candelon, B. and F.C. Palm, 2010, 'Banking and debt crises in Europe: The dangerous liaisons?', *De Economist* **158** (1), pp. 81–99.

Carstens, A. and M.J. Schwartz, 1998, 'Capital flows and the financial crisis in Mexico', *Journal of Asian Economics* **9** (2), pp. 207–26.

Cavallo, E. and A. Izquierdo (eds), 2009, *Dealing with an International Credit Crunch: Policy Responses to Sudden Stops in Latin America*, Inter-American Development Bank, Washington, DC.

Cazes, S., S. Verick and C. Heuer, 2009, 'Labour Market Policies in Times of Crisis', *Employment Working Paper No. 35*, ILO, Geneva.

Cerami, A. and P. Stubbs, 2010, 'The Political Economy of Child Poverty and Exclusion in Countries in Transition', Draft study for UNICEF CEE/CIS region.

Cerra, V. and S.C. Saxena, 2005, 'Growth Dynamics: The Myth of Economic Recovery', *IMF Working Paper No. 05/147*, IMF, Washington, DC.

Chandrasekhar, C.P. and J. Ghosh, 2006, 'Macroeconomic Policy, Inequality and Poverty Reduction in India and China', in G.A. Cornia (ed.), *Pro-poor Macroeconomics: Potential and Limitations*, Palgrave Macmillan, Basingstoke, pp. 248–81.

Chang, H.J., 2004, 'Regulation of foreign investment in historical perspective', *The European Journal of Development Research* **16** (3), pp. 687–715.

Chen, M.A., J. Vanek and M. Carr, 2004, *Mainstreaming Informal Employment and Gender in Poverty Reduction: A Handbook for Policy-Makers and Stakeholders*, Commonwealth Secretariat, London.

Cheru, F., 2002, *African Renaissance: Roadmaps to the Challenge of Globalization*, Zed Press, London

Chhibber, A., J. Ghosh and T. Palanivel, 2009, 'The Global Financial Crisis and the Asia Pacific Region', Mimeo, UNDP Colombo.

China Daily, 2009a, 'Government Spending on Social Welfare Must Rise', 3 April 2009. Accessed at www.chinadaily.com.cn/cndy/200904/03/content _7644949.htm, on 4 May 2010.

China Daily, 2009b, 'Experts Call for Stimulus Package for Social Welfare', 24 June, 2009. Accessed at www.chinadaily.com.cn/cndy/2009-06/24/ content_ 8315474.htm, on 4 May 2010.

Choong, C.K. and V.K. Liew, 2009, 'Impact of foreign direct investment volatility on economic growth of ASEAN-5 countries', *Economics Bulletin* **29** (3), pp. 1838–50.

Cinquetti, C.A., 2000, 'The real plan: Stabilization and destabilization', *World Development* **28** (1), pp. 155–71.

Clark, P.B. and J.J. Polak, 2004, 'International liquidity and the role of the SDR in the international monetary system', *IMF Staff Papers* **51** (1), pp. 49–71.

Cockburn, J., I. Fofana and L. Tiberti, 2010, 'Simulating the Impact of the Global Economic Crisis and Policy Responses on Children in West and Central Africa', *Innocenti Working Paper No. 2010-01*, UNICEF Regional Office for West and Central Africa, Dakar and UNICEF Innocenti Research Centre, Florence.

Collingwood, V., 2003, 'Indispensable or Unworkable? The IMF's New Approach to Conditionality', Bretton Woods Project, Washington, DC.

Committee of African Finance Ministers and Central Bank Governors (2009), 'Impact of the Crisis on African Economies – Sustaining Growth and Poverty Reduction', African Perspectives and Recommendations to the G-20, (March 21) available at www.afdb.org.

Copestake, J., M. Greeley, S. Johnson, N. Kabeer and A. Simanowitz, 2005, *Money with a Mission. Microfinance and Poverty Reduction*, Intermediate Technology Publications, London.

Cornford, A., 2002, 'Standards and Regulation', in Y. Aküyz (ed.), *Reforming the Global Financial Architecture: Issues and Proposals*, UNCTAD/TWN/ZED Books, pp. 29–77.

Cornia A.G., D. Kotz, M. Spoor and T. McKinley (2003), *Growth and Poverty Reduction in Uzbekistan: An Overall Strategy for Pro-Poor Growth*, UNDP, Tashkent.

Cornia, A.G., 2009, 'Structural divergence in economies in transition', *Development and Transition* **14** (December), pp. 2–4.

Corsetti, G., P. Pesenti and N. Roubini, 1998, 'What Caused the Asian Currency and Financial Crisis?,' *Papers 343*, Banca Italia, Roma.

COSATU, 2001, 'Transforming Ourselves to Transform Society, Report of the Organisational Review Commission to the 1st Central Committee', COSATU, Johannesburg.

COSATU, 2003, Organisational Review: Report to the 8th National Congress, COSATU, Johannesburg.

COSATU, 2006, COSATU Secretariat Report to the Ninth National Congress 18–21 September 2006, Gallagher Estate, Midrand, at llnw.creamermedia.co.za/articles/attachments/03082_cosatusecreta.pdf.

COSATU, 2009, 'Final Draft Consolidated Resolutions to the COSATU 10th National Congress' COSATU, Johannesburg.

CSY (Chinese National Bureau of Statistics), 2009, *China Statistical Yearbook 2009*, China Statistical Press, Beijing.

Damill, M., R. Frenkel and R. Maurizio, 2002, 'Argentina: A Decade of Currency Board – An Analysis of Growth, Employment and Income Distribution', *ILO Employment Paper No. 2002/42*, International Labour Office (ILO), Geneva.

Dang, H., S. Knack and H. Rogers, 2009, 'International Aid and Financial Crises in Donor Countries', *Policy Research Working Paper 5162*, Washington DC, World Bank.

Daseking, C., A.R. Ghosh, A.H. Thomas and T.D. Lane, 2004, *Lessons from the Crisis in Argentina*, IMF, Washington, DC.

Davies, R.B. and A. Voy, 2009, 'The effect of FDI on child labor', *Journal of Development Economics* **88**, pp. 59–66.

DCS (Department of Census & Statistics), 2009a, *Quarterly Report of the Sri Lanka Labour Force Survey. First Quarter 2009*, Ministry of Finance and Planning, Colombo.

DCS, 2009b, *Bulletin of Labour Force Statistics of Sri Lanka 47*, Ministry of Finance and Planning, Colomo.

DCS, 2010, *Sri Lanka Labour Force Survey. Annual Report 2009*, Ministry of Finance and Planning, Colombo.

Debroy, B. (2009) 'Growth Downturn and its Effects', in R. Kumar, B. Debroy, J. Ghosh, V. Mahajan and K.S. Prabhu (eds), *Global Financial Crisis: Impact on India's Poor*, United Nations Development Programme (UNDP) India, Delhi, pp. 14–24.

Demir, F., 2004, 'A failure story: Politics and financial liberalization in Turkey, revisiting the revolving door hypothesis', *World Development* **32** (5), pp. 851–69.

Department of Commerce, 2010, 'Foreign Trade Performance Analysis: Commodity Group-Wise 2007–2009' (webpage of Government of India).

Devenish, A. and C. Skinner, 2004, *Organising Workers in the Informal Economy: The Experience of the Self Employed Women's Union, 1994–2004*, School of Development Studies, University of KwaZulu-Natal.

Devenish, A. and C. Skinner, 2006, 'Collective Action in the Informal Economy: The Case of the Self-Employed Women's Union, 1994–2004', in R. Balland, A. Habib and I. Valodia (eds), *Voices of Protest: Social*

Movements in Post-Apartheid South Africa, University of KwaZulu-Natal Press, Scottsville, pp. 255–77.

Devenish, A. and C. Skinner, 2007, 'SEWU and Sikhula: Tips on organising informal workers', *South African Labour Bulletin* **31**(3), pp. 54–6.

Dhanani, S. and I. Islam, 2004, *Indonesian Wage Structure and Trends, 1976–2000*, ILO, Geneva.

Dingemans, L.F., 1926, 'Nota inzake den welvaartstoestand ten plattelande en ter hoofdplaats van het gewest Djokjakarta', in L.F. Dingemans (ed.), *Gegevens over Djokjakarta 1926*, Magelang, Maresch, pp. 6–9.

Diwan, I., 2001, 'Debt as Sweat: Labour, Financial Crisis, and the Globalization of capital', mimeo, World Bank, Washington, DC.

Dlamini, A., 2002, 'Mainstreaming the Informal Economy in South Africa: A Gender Perspective of Trade Union Policy Responses (1994–2001)', Mini-Dissertation, Rand Afrikaans University, Johannesburg. Accessed at http://ujdigispace.uj.ac.za:8080/dspace/bitstream/10210/101/1/Draft1.pdf, on 4 March 2008.

Driffield, N., V. Mahambare and S. Pal, 2004, 'Dynamic Adjustment of Corporate Leverage: Is there a Lesson to Learn from the Recent Asian Crisis?', *EconWPA Finance 0405007*, ideas.repec.org/e/ppa99.html.

Dwor-Frécaut, D., F.X. Colaco and M. Hallward-Driemeier (eds), 2000, *Asian Corporate Recovery: Findings from Firm-Level Surveys in Five Countries*, World Bank, Washington, DC.

Easterly, W., R. Islam and J. Stiglitz, 2001, 'Shaken and stirred: Volatility and macroeconomic paradigms for rich and poor countries,' in B. Preskovic and N. Stern (eds), *Annual Bank Conference on Development Economics 2000*, World Bank, Washington, DC, pp. 191–212.

EBRD, 2007, *Life in Transition: A Survey of People's Experiences and Attitudes*, European Bank for Reconstruction and Development, London.

ECLAC, 2010, *Economic Survey of Latin America and the Caribbean 2009–2010*, ECLAC.

Edison, H.J., M.W. Klein, L.A. Ricci and T. Sløk, 2004, 'Capital account liberalization and economic performance: Survey and synthesis', *IMF Staff Papers* **51** (2), pp. 220–56.

Eichengreen, B., 2009, 'Out of the Box: Thoughts about the International Financial Architecture', *IMF Working Paper WP/09/116*, IMF, Washington, DC.

El Laithy, H. and N. El Ehwany, 1996, 'Employment–Poverty Linkages Towards a Pro-Poor Employment Policy Framework in Egypt', unpublished (restricted) paper presented to the ILO, Cairo.

Elson, D., 2009, 'Gender and the Economic Crisis in Developing Countries: A Framework for Analysis', paper presented at the Gender and the Economic Crisis Workshop, Oxford, UK, 15–16 September 2009.

Emmett, B., 2009, 'Paying the Price for the Economic Crisis', *Oxfam International Discussion Paper*, www.oxfam.org.

Engelshoven, M., 1999, 'Diamonds and Patels: A report on the diamond industry of Surat', *Contributions to Indian Sociology* **33**, pp. 353–377.

Engineer, I., 1994, 'Backward communities and migrant workers in Surat riots', *Economic and Political Weekly* **29** (22), pp. 1348–60.

Export Development Board (Last updated 2010), 'Export Performance by Major Sectors January to March 2008, 2009 & 2010' (webpage of EDB).

Fan, M., 2008, 'The Global Financial Crisis and China', *IDS Briefings on the Financial Crisis* (www.ids.ac.uk).

FAO, 2009, *The State of Food Insecurity in the World. Economic Crises – and Lessons Learned*, FAO, Rome.

FAO, 2010, *National Food Prices Situation, 25 January*, FAO, Rome.

Financial Times, 2010, 'The dog that hasn't barked', 22 October, p. 2.

Fischer, A.M., 2009, 'Putting aid in its place: Insights from early structuralists on aid and balance of payments and lessons for contemporary aid debates', *Journal of International Development* **21**, pp. 856–67.

Fischer, A.M., 2010a, 'The Great China Currency Debate: For Workers or Speculators?', *G24 Policy Brief No. 56.*

Fischer, A.M., 2010b, 'Is China turning Latin? China's balancing act between power and dependence in the lead up to crisis', *Journal of International Development* **22** (6), pp. 739–57.

Fix, M., D.G. Papademetriou, J. Batalova, A. Terrazas, S.Y.Y. Lin and M. Mittelstadt, 2009, *Migration and the Global Recession*, Migration Policy Institute, Washington, DC.

Friedman, J. and N. Schady, 2009, 'How Many More Infants are Likely to Die in Africa as a Result of the Global Financial Crisis?', *Policy Research Paper No.5023*, World Bank, Washington, DC.

G20 Trade Finance Expert Group, 2009, 'G20 Trade Finance Experts Group August Report – US–UK Chairs' Recommendations for Finance Ministers', available from www.g20.org.

Gallagher, K.P. and D. Chudnovsky, 2009, *Rethinking Foreign Investment for Sustainable Development: Lessons from Latin America*, Anthem Press, London.

Gems and Jewellery Export Promotion Council, 2008, *Ideal Cut*, Newsletter Volumes 19, 20, 21, GJEPC, Mumbai.

Gesseler Verschuir, P.R.W. van., 1939, 'Memorie van Overgave van den aftredenden Gouverneur van Jogjakarta', National Archive, The Hague, Archive of the Ministry for the Colonies MMK 141.

Ghosh, J., 2008, 'Growth and Employment Dynamics in India', *Working Paper No. 92*, ILO, Geneva.

Ghosh, J., 2009a, 'Adjustment, Recovery and Growth after Financial Crisis: A Consideration of Five "Crisis" countries of East and Southeast Asia', in J. Ghosh and C.P. Chandrasekhar (eds), *After Crisis: Adjustment, Recovery and Fragility in East Asia*, Tulika Books, New Delhi, pp. 65–86.

Ghosh, J., 2009b, 'Global Crisis and the Indian Economy', in R. Kumar, B. Debroy, J. Ghosh, V. Mahajan and K.S. Prabhu (eds), *Global Financial Crisis: Impact on India's Poor*, UNDP India, Delhi pp. 25–35.

Ghosh, J., 2010a, 'The unnatural coupling: Food and global finance', *Journal of Agrarian Change* January: Symposium on Global Food Crisis.

Ghosh, J., 2010b, 'Global crisis and beyond: Sustainable growth trajectories for the developing world', *International Labour Review* **149** (2), pp. 209–25.

Ghosh, J., 2010c, 'What Does Wage-Led Growth Mean in Developing Countries with Large Informal Employment?', available from amandlapublishers.co.za/ home-menu-item/500.

Ghosh, J. and C.P. Chandrasekhar, 2009, 'The costs of "coupling": The global crisis and the Indian economy', *Cambridge Journal of Economics* **33** (4), pp. 725–39.

Goldman, T., 2003, 'Organizing in South Africa's Informal Economy: An Overview of Four Sectoral Case Studies', *SEED Working Paper 60*, ILO, Geneva.

Goldstein, M. and N.R. Lardy, 2009, 'The Future of China's Exchange Rate Policy', *Policy Analyses in International Economics 87*, Peterson Institute for International Economics, Washington, DC.

Goldstein, M. and P. Turner, 2004, *Controlling Currency Mismatches in Emerging Markets*, Institute for International Economics, Washington, DC.

Gong, S., 2009, 'Lessons for China – a reflection', presentation at the Workshop 'Social Policy Responses to Economic Crises', 23–24 February 2009, Beijing.

Gonzalez-Vega, C. and D.H. Graham, 1995, 'State-Owned Agricultural Development Banks: Lessons and Opportunities for Microfinance', Mimeo, Ohio State University, Dublin, Ohio.

Gordhan, P., 2010, 'Budget Speech 2010', Minister of Finance, National Treasury, www.treasury.gov.za, Pretoria.

Gottschalk, R., 2004, *How Financial Crises Affect the Poor*, DFID, London.

Green, D., R. King and M. Miller-Dawkins, 2010, 'The global economic crisis and developing countries: Impact and response', *Oxfam Research Report*, Oxfam, London.

Gregorio, J. de, S. Edwards and R.O. Valdés, 2000, 'Controls on capital inflows: Do they work?', *Journal of Development Economics* **63** (1), pp. 59–83.

Grossman, G.M. and E. Helpman, 1994, 'Protection for sale', *American Economic Review* **84**, pp. 833–50.

Guha, K., 2009, 'Bernanke warns on imbalance risks', *Financial Times*, 19 October.

Gunatilaka, R., 2009, *Rapid Assessment of the Impact of the Global Economic Crisis on Employment and Industrial Relations in Sri Lanka*, ILO, Geneva.

Haan, A. de, 2010a, *Towards a New Poverty Agenda in Asia: Social Policies and Economic Transformation*, Sage, New Delhi.

Haan, A. de, 2010b, 'The financial crisis and China's "harmonious society"', *Journal of Current Chinese Affairs* **2**, pp. 69–99.

Haan, A. de, 2010c, 'A defining moment? China's social policy response to the financial crisis', *Journal of International Development* **22** (6) pp. 758–71.

Habib, B., A. Narayan, S. Olivieri and C. Sanchez, 2010, 'The Impact of the Financial Crisis on Poverty and Income Distribution: Insights from Simulations in Selected Countries', *World Bank Economic Premise 2010, No. 7*.

Hausman, R. and E. Fernández-Arias, 2000, 'Foreign Direct Investment: Good Cholesterol?', *Inter-American Development Bank Working Paper No. 417*, Washington DC.

He, X. and Y. Cao, 2007, 'Understanding high saving rate in China', *China and World Economy* **15** (1), pp. 1–13.

Hirway, I., 2008, 'Trade and Gender Inequalities in Labour Market: Case of Textile and Garment Industry in India', International Seminar on 'Moving Towards Gender Sensitization of Trade Policy', February, New Delhi.

Hoeven, R. van der, 2010, 'Income inequality and employment revisited: Can one make sense of economic policy?', in *Journal of Human Development and Capabilities* **11** (1), pp. 67–84.

Hoeven, R. van der and M. Luebker, 2007, 'Financial Openness and Employment: The Need for Coherent International and National Policies', in J.A. Occampo and K.S. Jomo (eds), *Towards Full and Decent Employment* , London, Zed Books, pp. 22–53.

Hoeven, R. van der and L. Taylor, 2000, 'Introduction: Structural adjustment, labour markets and employment: Some considerations for sensible people', *Journal of Development Studies* **36** (4), 57–65.

Horn, P., 2005, 'COSATU Strategic Planning Workshop: Organising Workers in the Informal Economy', *StreetNet News* 5. Accessed at http://www.streetnet.org.za/englsih/cosatu5.htm.

Horn, P., 2008, 'Realising Decent Work in Africa: A Shared Vision of Growth and Improved Quality of Life in a Globalized World', Paper prepared for the 5th African Regional Conference of the IIRA, 26–28 March 2008, Cape Town.

Horvath, B., A. Ivanov, M. Peleah, with M. Pospisilova, 2009, 'The Human Development Impact of the Global Crisis in Central, Eastern and Southern Europe, and the CIS', Mimeo, UNDP, Bratislava.

Hossain, N., 2009, 'Crime and social cohesion in the time of crisis: Early evidence of wider impacts of food, fuel and financial shocks', *IDS Bulletin* **40** (5), pp. 59–67.

Hossain, N. and R. Eyben (eds), 2009, *Accounts of Crisis: Poor People's Experiences of the Food, Fuel and Financial Crises in Five Countries*, Institute of Development Studies, Brighton.

Hossain, N., R. Fillaili, G. Lubaale, M. Mulumbi, M. Rashid and M. Tadros, 2010, *The Social Impacts of Crisis: Findings from Community-Level Research in Five Developing Countries*, Institute of Development Studies, Brighton.

Hu, A., 2000, 'On China Reforms and the Go-West Policy (an Interview with Hu Angang by Laurent Malvezin)', *China Sustainable Industrial Development Network.*

Hung, H.F., 2009, 'America's head servant? The PRC's dilemma in the global crisis', *New Left Review* **60**, pp. 5–25.

Hutchison, M.M. and I. Noy, 2006, 'Sudden stops and the Mexican wave: Currency crises, capital flow reversals and output loss in emerging markets', *Journal of Development Economics* **79** (1), 225–48.

Ibarra, C.A., 1999, 'Disinflation and the December 1994 devaluation in Mexico', *International Review of Applied Economics* **13** (1), pp. 55–69.

ILO, 2004, World Commission on the Social Dimensions of Globalization, *A Fair Globalization: Creating Opportunities for All*, ILO, Geneva.

ILO, 2005, *World Employment Report 2004–05: Employment, Productivity and Poverty*, ILO, Geneva.

ILO, 2006, 'Employment Poverty Linkages and Policies for Pro-poor Growth in Jordan (1990–2003)', Second Draft (restricted document), ILO, Geneva.

ILO, 2008a, *World of Work Report 2008. Income Inequalities in the Age of Financial Globalization*, ILO, Geneva.

ILO, 2008b, *Global Employment Trends*, ILO, Geneva.

ILO, 2009a, *Global Wage Report: Minimum Wages and Collective Bargaining Towards Policy Coherence*, ILO, Geneva.

ILO, 2009b, *The Financial and Economic Crisis: A Decent Work Response*, ILO, Geneva.

ILO, 2009c, *Key Indicators of the Labour Market*, 5th edition, ILO, Geneva.

ILO, 2009d, *Global Employment Trends for Women 2009*, ILO, Geneva.

ILO, 2009e, *Protecting People, Promoting Jobs*, ILO, Geneva.

ILO, 2009f, 'A Global Jobs Pact', ILO, Geneva.

ILO, 2009g, *World of Work Report 2009. The Global Jobs Crisis and Beyond*, ILO, Geneva.

ILO, 2010a, *Global Employment Trends January 2010*, ILO, Geneva.

ILO, 2010b, *International Labour Migration. A Rights-Based Approach*, Geneva, ILO.

IMF, 2000, *Report of the Acting Managing Director to the International Monetary and Financial Committee on Progress in Reforming the IMF and Strengthening the Architecture of the International Financial System*, IMF, Washington, DC.

IMF, 2007, *World Economic Outlook: Spillovers and Cycles in the Global Economy*, April, IMF, Washington DC.

IMF, 2008a, *World Economic Outlook: Housing and the Business Cycle*, April, IMF, Washington DC.

IMF, 2008b, 'The Great Sub-Saharan African Growth Takeoff: Lessons and Prospects', in *Regional Economic Outlook: Sub-Saharan Africa*, Washington, DC, pp. 23–51.

IMF, 2009a, 'World Economic Outlook Update', January 2009.

IMF, 2009b, 'The State of Public Finances Cross-Country', Fiscal Monitor, *IMF Staff Position Note SPN/09/25*, November, IMF, Washington, DC.

IMF, 2009c, 'Impact of the Global Financial Crisis on Sub-Saharan Africa', Africa Department, IMF, Washington, DC.

IMF, 2009d, 'The Implications of the Global Financial Crisis for Low-Income Countries', March, IMF, Washington, DC.

IMF, 2010a, 'Navigating the Fiscal Challenges Ahead', *Fiscal Monitor*, 14 May, IMF, Washington, DC.

IMF, 2010b, *Regional Economic Outlook: Sub-Saharan Africa, Back to High Growth, World Economic and Financial Survey*, IMF, Washington, DC.

Indian Express, 2009a, 'Social Security Net can do Little for Diamond Workers', 14 February. Accessed at www.expressindia.com.

Indian Express, 2009b, 'Diamond Polishers Leave Surat After Board Exams', 17 April, 2009. Accessed at www.expressindia.com, on 11 October 2009.

Indian Express, 2009c, 'Surat Diamond Units Cut Short Diwali Break to Regain Lustre', 3 October, 2009. Accessed at www.expressindia.com, on 11 October 2009.

Institute of International Finance, 2010, 'Capital Flows to Emerging Market Economies', *IIF Research Note*, IIF, Washington, DC.

Iqbal, F., 2005, *Sustaining Gains in Poverty Reduction and Human Development in the Middle East and North Africa*, World Bank, Washington, DC.

Islam, I., 2005, 'Managing without Growth: Challenges Confronting the Syrian Labour Market', Unpublished manuscript, ILO, Geneva.

Islam, I., 2009, 'The Global Economic Crisis and Developing Countries: Transmission Channels, Fiscal and Policy Space and the Design of National Responses', *Working Paper No. 36*, ILO, Geneva.

Islam, R., G. Bhattacharya, S. Dhanani, M. Iacono, F. Mehran, S. Mukhopadhya and P. Thuy, 2001, 'The Economic Crisis: Labor Market Challenges and Policies in Indonesia', in G. Betcherman and R. Islam (eds), *East Asian Labor Markets and the Economic Crisis*, World Bank and ILO, Washington, DC, and Geneva, pp. 43–96.

Ivanov, A., 2009, 'The economic crisis as a human development opportunity', *Development & Transition* **13**, pp. 22–24.

Jahan, S., 2009, 'Global Economic Crisis: Transmission, Impact and Responses. A Comparative Review of Selected Developing Regions', Mimeo, United Nations, New York.

Jansen, K. 2004, 'The scope of fiscal policy: A case study of Thailand', *Development Policy Review* **22** (2), pp. 207–28.

Jara, M.K., 2006, *Monitoring Compliance with the Sectoral Determination for Farm Workers in Five Westerns Cape Farming Districts: Report of an Exploratory Study,* Women on Farm Project, Stellenbosch.

Jia K., 2009, 'The Active Fiscal Policy in China during the Eastern Asian Crisis', (in Chinese), Paper presented at the Workshop 'Social Policy Responses to Economic Crises', 23–24 February 2009, Beijing.

Jomo, K.S., 2001, *Financial crisis and macroeconomic policy responses to the 1997–8 financial crisis in Malaysia*. Paper prepared for the workshop on macroeconomic policies and employment, Bangkok, December 2001, Mimeo, ILO, Bangkok.

Jomo, K.S., 2005, 'Malaysia's September 1998 Controls: Background, Context, Impacts, Comparisons, Implications, Lessons', *G-24 Discussion Paper Series No. 36*, UN, Geneva and New York.

Kabeer, N., 2008, *Mainstreaming Gender in Social Protection for the Informal Economy*, Commonwealth Secretariat, London.

Kaminsky, G.L., C. Reinhart and C. Végh, 2004, 'When it Rains, it Pours: Procyclical Capital Flows and Macroeconomic Policies', *NBER Working Paper No. 10780*, NBER, Cambridge, MA.

Kang, S.H., J. Keum, D.H. Kim, and D. Shin, 2001, 'Korea: Labor Market Outcomes and Policy Responses After the Crisis', in G. Betcherman and R. Islam (eds), *East Asian Labour Markets and the Economic Crisis*, World Bank and ILO, Washington, DC and Geneva, pp. 97–139.

Kapsos, S., 2004, 'Estimating Growth Requirements for Reducing Working Poverty: Can the World Halve Working Poverty by 2015?', *ILO Employment Strategy Paper No. 2004/14*, ILO, Geneva.

Kattel, R., 2009, 'The rise and fall of the Baltic states', *Development & Transition*, **13**, pp. 11–13.

Kaufman, H., 1992, 'Ten reasons to reform', *Euromoney*, November, p. 57.

Kawai, M., I. Lieberman and W.P. Mako, 2000, 'Financial Stabilization and Initial Restructuring of East Asian Corporations: Approaches, Results, and Lessons', in C. Adams, R.E. Litan and M. Pomerleano (eds), *Managing Financial and Corporate Distress: Lessons from Asia*, Brookings Institution Press, Washington, DC, pp. 77–136.

Kelegama, S., 2009, 'Ready-made garment exports from Sri Lanka', *Journal of Contemporary Asia* **39** (4), pp. 579–96.

Keynes, J.M., 1936, *The General Theory of Employment, Interest and Money*, Macmillan, London.

Khanna, G.D. Newhouse and P. Pacci, 2010, 'Fewer Jobs or Smaller Paychecks? Labor Market Impacts of the Recent Crisis in Middle-Income Countries', *World Bank Economic Premise 2010, No. 11*.

Khosla, N., 2009, 'The ready-made garments industry in Bangladesh: A means to reducing gender-based social exclusion of women?', *Journal of International Women's Studies* **11**, pp. 289–303.

Kindleberger, C.P. (1978) *Manias, Panics and Crashes: A History of Financial Crises*, Basic Books, New York.

King, A.J., 2007, *Domestic Service in Post Apartheid South Africa: Deference and Disdain*, Ashgate, Aldershot.

Kleinknecht, A., R.M. Oostendorp, M.P. Paradhan and C.W.M. Naastepad, 2006, 'Flexible labour, firm performance and the Dutch job creation miracle', *International Review of Applied Economics* **20** (2), pp. 171–87.

Kose, E. and M.A. Prasad, 2009, 'The decoupling debate is back', *Foreign Policy*, 15 June, www.foreignpolicy.com.

Kose, M.A., E. Prasad and M. Terrones, 2003, 'Financial integration and macroeconomic volatility', *IMF Staff Papers* **50**, pp. 119–42.

Kregel, J., 2008, 'Financial Flows and International Imbalances: The Role of Catching-Up by Late Industrializing Developing Countries', *Working Paper No. 528*, Levy Economics Institute of Bard College, Annandale-on-Hudson.

Kregel, J., 2010, 'No Going Back: Why we Cannot Restore Glass-Steagall's Separation of Banking and Finance', Paper presented at IDEAs Conference on Re-Regulating Finance, Muttukadu, India, 25–27 January 2010.

Krugman, P., 2009a, 'China's dollar trap', *New York Times*, 2 April.

Krugman, P., 2009b, 'China and the liquidity trap', *New York Times*, 15 May.

Krugman, P., 2009c, 'The Chinese Disconnect', *New York Times*, 22 October.

Krugman, P., 2009d, *The Return of Depression Economics and The Crisis of 2008*, W.W. Norton & Company, New York.

Krugman, P., 2010a, 'Taking on China', *New York Times*, 14 March.

Kumar, R., 2009, 'Global Financial and Economic Crisis: Impact on India and Policy Response', in R. Kumar, B. Debroy, J. Ghosh, V. Mahajan and K.S. Prabhu (eds), *Global Financial Crisis: Impact on India's Poor*, UNDP India, Delhi, pp. 7–13.

Kutanegara, P.M. and G. Nooteboom, 2002, 'Forgotten Villagers? The Effects of the Crisis in Rural Java and the Role of the Government', in C. Holtzappel, M. Sanders and M. Titus (eds), *Riding a Tiger: Dilemmas of Integration and Decentralization in Indonesia*, Rozenberg, Amsterdam, pp. 248–77.

Kwartanada, D., 2002, 'Competition, patriotism and collaboration: The Chinese businessmen of Yogyakarta between the 1930s and 1945', *Journal of Southeast Asian Studies* **33** (2), pp. 257–77.

Labour Bureau of India, 2009a, *Report of Effect of Economic Slowdown on Employment in India: January–March*, Ministry of Labour, Chandigarh.

Labour Bureau of India, 2009b, *Report of Effect of Economic Slowdown on Employment in India: April–June*, Ministry of Labour, Chandigarh.

Labour Bureau of India, 2009c, *Report of Effect of Economic Slowdown on Employment in India: October–December*, Ministry of Labour, Chandigarh.

Labour Bureau of India, 2010, *Report on Effect of Economic Slowdown on Employment in India (January–March 2010)*, Ministry of Labour, Chandigarh.

Lau, L. and J. Stiglitz, 2005, 'China's alternative to revaluation', *Financial Times*, 24 April.

Laursen, S. and L.A. Metzler, 1950, 'Flexible exchange rates and the theory of employment', *Review of Economics and Statistics* **32**, pp. 281–99.

Lee, E., 1998, *The Asian Financial Crisis. The Challenge for Social Policy*, ILO, Geneva.

Lee, K. and A. Jayadev, 2005, 'Capital Account Liberalization, Growth and the Labor Share of Income: Reviewing and Extending the Cross-country Evidence', in G. Epstein (ed.), *Capital Flight and Capital Controls in Developing Countries*, Edward Elgar, Cheltenham, UK and Northampton, MA, USA, pp. 15–57.

Lensink, R. and O. Morrissey, 2001, 'Foreign Direct Investment: Flows, Volatility and Growth in Developing Countries', *CREDIT Research Paper*, University of Nottingham.

Lerman, Z., 2007, 'Land Reform, Farm Structure and Agricultural Performance in CIS Countries', Paper presented at the CESE Conference

Economic Transition in Midlife: Lessons from the Development of Markets and Institutions, Portoroz, 11–13 May.

Li, H., P. Huang and J. Li, 2007, 'China's FDI net inflow and deterioration of terms of trade: Paradox and explanation', *China and World Economy* **15** (1), pp. 87–95.

Lin, J., 2008, 'Coping with the Crisis: Risks, Options, and Priorities for Developing Countries', QFINANCE, the 2007–2008 Marshall Lecture, Cambridge University.

Llaudes, R., F. Salman and M. Chivakul, 2010, 'The Impact of the Great Recession on Emerging Markets', *IMF Working Paper, WP/10/237*, IMF, Washington, DC.

Loungani, P., and A. Razin (2001) 'How beneficial is foreign direct investment for developing countries?', *Finance & Development* **38** (2), http://www.imf.org/external/pubs/ft/fandd/2001/06/loungani.htm.

Lucidi, F. and A. Kleinknecht, 2010, 'Little innovation, many jobs: An econometric analysis of the Italian labour productivity crisis', *Cambridge Journal of Economics* **34**, pp. 525–46.

Lund, F. and C. Skinner, 1999, 'Promoting the Interests of Women in the Informal Economy: An Analysis of Street Trader Organisations in South Africa', *Research Report 19*, School of Development Studies, Durban.

Lund, F. and C. Skinner, 2004, 'Integrating the informal economy in urban planning and governance: A case study of the process of policy development in Durban, South Africa,' *International Development Planning Review* **26** (4), pp. 431–56.

Majahan, V., 2009, 'Impact of the Economic Downturn on Non-Farm Sector Workers', in R. Kumar, B. Debroy, J. Ghosh, V. Mahajan and K.S. Prabhu (eds), *Global Financial Crisis: Impact on India's Poor. Some Initial Perspectives*, United Nations Development Programme (UNDP) India, Dehli, pp. 36–44.

Mahmood, M. and G. Aryah, 2001, 'The Labor Market and Labor Policy in a Macroeconomic Context: Growth, Crisis, and Competitiveness in Thailand', in G. Betcherman and R. Islam (eds), *East Asian Labour Markets and the Economic Crisis*, World Bank and ILO, Geneva, pp. 245–92.

Mansor, N., T. Eu Chye, A. Boerhanoeddin, F. Said and S.M. Said, 2001, 'Malaysia: Protecting Workers and Fostering Growth', in G. Betcherman and R. Islam (eds), *East Asian Labor Markets and the Economic Crisis*, World Bank and ILO, Washington, DC and Geneva, pp. 141–94.

Marconi, R., 2010, *The Global Crisis: A Threat or an Opportunity for Microfinance Providers and their Clients?* Hivos, The Hague.

McCulloch, N. and A. Grover, 2010, 'Estimating the National Impact of the Financial Crisis in Indonesia by Combining a Rapid Qualitative Study with Nationally Representative Surveys', *IDS Working Paper 346*, (www.ids.ac.uk).

McCulloch, N. and A. Sumner, 2009a, 'Will the global financial crisis change the development paradigm', *IDS Bulletin* **40** (5), pp. 101–8.

McCulloch, N. and A. Sumner, 2009b, 'Introduction: The global financial crisis, developing countries and policy responses', *IDS Bulletin* **40** (5), pp. 1–13.

Messkoub, M., 2008, 'Economic Growth, Employment and Poverty in the Middle East and North Africa' *Working Paper Series 19*, ILO, Geneva.

Messkoub, M., 2009, 'The Impact of Global Financial Crisis on Employment and Poverty in the MENA Region', Paper presented at the UN-ESCWA expert meeting on the global financial and economic crisis: the social impact and responses in the region, 8 December, Beirut.

MHHDC (Mahbub ul Haq Human Development Centre), 2004, *Human Development in South Asia 2003*, Oxford University Press, Oxford.

Milanovic, B., 1998, *Income, Inequality and Poverty during the Transition from Planned to Market Economy*, World Bank, Washington, DC.

Mina, W., 2010, 'Institutional Reforms Debate and FDI Flows to MENA Region: Is Debate Relevant?' Nordic Conference on Development Economics, Helsinki, 18–19 June 2010.

Ministry of Finance, 2009, *Pakistan Economic Survey 2008–09*, Government of Pakistan, Islamabad.

Ministry of Finance, 2010, *Pakistan Economic Survey 2009–10*, Government of Pakistan, Islamabad.

Ministry of Labour Relations and Manpower, 2009, *Labour and Social Trends in Sri Lanka 2009*, ILO, Colombo.

Minsky, H., 2008, *Stabilizing an Unstable Economy*, McGraw-Hill, New York.

Mishkin, F.S., 1999, 'Lessons from the tequila crisis', *Journal of Banking and Finance* **23**, pp. 1521–33.

Mitchener, K., 2009, 'Experience from the Great Depression', Paper presented at the Workshop 'Social Policy Responses to Economic Crises', 23–24 February, Beijing.

Mittelman, J., 2010, 'Crisis and global governance: money, discourses, and institutions', *Globalizations* **7**, (1–2) (March), pp. 151–166.

Montesano, M.J., 2009, 'Contextualizing the Pattaya Summit debacle: Four April days, four Thai pathologies', *Contemporary Southeast Asia* **31** (2), pp. 217–48.

Morandé, F.G. and M. Tapia, 2002, 'Exchange Rate Policy in Chile: From the Band to Floating and Beyond', *Central Bank of Chile Working Paper No. 152*, Banco Central de Chile, Santiago de Chile.

Motala, S., 2002, 'Organizing in the Informal Economy: A Case Study of Street Trading in South Africa', *SEED Working Paper 36*, ILO, Geneva.

Mundell, R., 1961, 'Flexible exchange rates and employment policy', *Canadian Journal of Economics and Political Science* **27**, pp. 509–17.

Murphy, S., 2010, 'Changing Perspectives: Small-Scale Farmers, Markets and Globalization', *Hivos Knowledge Programme. Report 2010*, International Institute for Environment and Development (IIED), Centro Mainumby and Hivos, The Hague.

Murshed, S.M., 1992, 'Commercial and monetary policy in a North–South macroeconomic model: Tariffs and VERs compared', *Australian Economic Papers* **31**, pp. 414–26.

Murshed, S.M., 1997, *Macroeconomics for Open Economies*, Dryden Press, London.

Murshed, S.M. and S. Sen, 1999, 'Macroeconomic effects of a voluntary export restraint in a two country monetary model', *Greek Economic Review* **19**, pp. 63–80.

NALEDI, 2006, *The State of COSATU: Phase One Report*, NALEDI, Johannesburg.

Narasimhan, S., 2009, 'Impact of the Global Financial Meltdown on Women in Developing Economies. Case Studies from India', International Association for Feminist Economics 2009 Annual Conference, 26–28 June.

National Statistical Office of Thailand (NSO) (2007) The Household Socio-economic Survey 2007, see http://web.nso.go.th/survey/house_seco/socio.htm.

NASSCOM, 2008, *Strategic Review 2008*, NASSCOM, New Delhi.

NASSCOM, 2009, *Strategic Review 2009*, NASSCOM, New Delhi.

NASSCOM, 2010, *IT-BPO Sector in India: Strategic Review 2010*, NASSCOM, New Delhi.

Naudé, W., 2009, 'The Financial Crisis of 2008 and the Developing Countries', *Discussion Paper No. 2009/01*, UNU-WIDER, Helsinki.

NCEUS (National Commission for Enterprises in the Unorganised Sector), 2008, *The Global Economic Crisis and the Informal Economy in India: Need for Urgent Measures and Fiscal Stimulus to Protect Incomes in the Informal Economy*, NCEUS, New Delhi.

NCEUS, 2009, *The Challenge of Employment in India: An Informal Economy Perspective*, NCEUS, New Delhi.

Ndungu, S.K., 2007, 'Surviving below the margin: Recent trends in collective bargaining and wage settlements,' *Naledi Policy Bulletin* **8** (2), pp. 4–8.

Ndungu, S.K., 2009, 'Labour Brokers: Should they be Banned or Regulated?' *Naledi Research Working Report 1*, Johannesburg.

Nguanbanchong, A., 2010, *Beyond the Crisis: The Impact of the Financial Crisis on Women in Vietnam*, Oxfam, London.

Nguyen, E.L., 2009, 'The international investment position of the United States at year end 2008', *Survey of Current Business* **89** (7), pp. 10–19.

OECD, 2009, *Development Co-Operation Report 2009*, OECD, Paris.

OECD, 2010, *Economic Survey of China*, OECD, Paris.

Offe, C. and H. Wiesenthal, 1985, 'Two Logics of Collective Action', in C. Offe (ed.), *Disorganized Capitalism*, Polity, Cambridge, pp. 170–220.

O'Malley, W., 1977, Indonesia in the great depression: A study of East Sumatra and Yogyakarta in the 1930s', PhD dissertation, Cornell University, Cornell.

Ortiz, I., J. Chai, M. Cummins and G. Vergara, 2010, *Prioritizing Expenditures for a Recovery for All*, UNICEF.

Ostry, J.D., A.R. Ghosh, J.I. Kim, and M.S. Qureshi (2010), 'Fiscal Space', *IMF Position Note SPN 10/11*, IMF, Washington, DC.

Oxfam, 2010, *The Global Economic Crisis and Developing Countries*, Oxford, Oxfam.

Oxford Analytica, 28 July 2009. Accessed at http://www.oxan.com, on 1 June 2010.

Papadimitriou, D., G. Hansen and G. Zezza, 2009, 'Sustaining Recovery: Medium Term Prospects and Policies for the American Economy', *Levy Institute Strategic Analysis*, Levy Economics Institute of Bard College, Annandale-on-Hudson.

Papanek, G. and D. Dowsett, 1975, 'The cost of living 1938–1973', *Ekonomi dan Keuangan Indonesia* **23** (2).

Patnaik, P. (2009) 'A Perspective on the Growth Process in India and China', *IDEAs Working Paper 2009/5*, www.networkideas.org.

Patunru, A. and C. von Luebke, 2010, 'Survey of recent developments', *Bulletin of Indonesian Economic Studies* **46** (1), pp. 7–31.

Pettis, M., 2009, 'China's September Data Suggest that the Long-Term Overcapacity Problem is Only Intensifying', *Emerging Markets Monitor, Roubini Global Economic Monitor*, 21 October 2009.

Pettis, M., 2010. 'How Will an RMB Revaluation Affect China, the US, and the World?' *Roubini Global Economics Monitor*, 17 March 2010.

Phongphaichit, P., 2009, 'Towards a Fairer Thai Society', Speech at 11th King Prajadhipok's Institute (KPI) Congress on Conflict, Legitimacy and Government Reform: Equitable Allocation of Resources in Thai Society, Bangkok, November 2009.

Poerwosoedirdjo, I., 1932, *Roengokno tjirtane nêgara woetah gêtihmoe. Boekoe kanggo kanca Jawa sing ana ing sebrang bab loeroe dalam oerip ing nêgara*, Kantoor van Arbeid, Batavia.

Prabawa, T.S., 2010, *The Tourism Industry under Crisis: The Struggle of Small Tourism Enterprises in Yogyakarta,* PhD thesis, Free University Amsterdam.

Prasad, E.S., Rogoff, K., Wei, S. and Kose, M.A., 2004, 'Financial globalization, growth and volatility in developing countries,' *NBER Working Paper No. 10942*, National Bureau of Economic Research, Cambridge, MA.

Prasad, E.S., 2009, 'Is the Chinese growth miracle built to last?', *China Economic Review* **20**, pp. 103–123.

Prasad, N. and M. Gerecke, 2010, 'Social policy in times of crisis', *Global Social Policy* **10** (2), pp. 218–247.

Pratikno, F., 2000, *Gerakan Rakyat Kelaparan: Gagalnya Politik Radikalisasi Petani*, Media Pressindo, Yogyakarta.

PTJ (*Pakistan Textile Journal*), 2009a, 'Knitwear Industry in Dire Straits', (March), p. 16.

PTJ, 2009b, 'Textile Demand Shrinking in USA and Western Markets', (April), p. 12.

Radelet, S. and J. Sachs, 1998, 'The East Asian financial crisis: Diagnosis, remedies, prospects', *Brookings Papers on Economic Activity 1*, pp. 1–74.

Raffer, K., 1990, 'Applying Chapter 9 insolvency to international debts: An economically efficient solution with a human face', *World Development* **18** (2), pp. 301–11.

Raffer, K., 2002, 'Sovereign Debt Workout Arrangements', Paper presented at the Alternatives to Neoliberaism Conference sponsored by the New Rules for Global Finance Coalition, Washington, 23–24 May.

Rahman, M., M.A. Iqbal, T.I. Khan and S. Dasgupta, 2010, 'Bangladesh Phase 2', *Global Financial Crisis Discussion Series Paper 12*, Overseas Development Institute and Centre for Policy Dialogue, London.

Rahman, M., K.G. Moazzem and S.S. Hossain, 2009, *Impact of the Global Economic Crisis on the Employment and Labour Market of Bangladesh: A Preliminary Assessment*, CPD, Dhaka.

Rajan, R., 2008, 'Global imbalances, or why are the poor financing the rich?', *De Economist* **156**, pp. 3–24.

Rajan, R.R., 2010, *Fault Lines. How Hidden Fractures Still Threaten the World Economy*, Princeton University Press, Princeton.

Ratha, D., 2009, 'Remittances expected to fall by 5 to 8 percent in 2009', http://blogs.worldbank.org/peoplemove/remittances-expected-to-fall-by-5-to-8-percent-in-2009.

Ratha, D. and S. Mohapatra, 2009, *Migration and Development Brief 9*, World Bank, Washington, DC.

Ratha, D., S. Mohapatra, A. Silwal, J. Irving and S. Plaza, 2009a, *Migration and Development Brief 10*, World Bank, Washington, DC.

Ratha, D., S. Mohapatra and A. Silwal, 2009b, *Migration and Development Brief 11*, World Bank, Washington, DC.

Ratha, D., S. Mohapatra and A. Silwal, 2010, *Migration and Development Brief 12*, World Bank, Washington, DC.

Ravallion, M., 2009, 'The Crisis and the World's Poorest', in World Bank, *Growing out of Crisis*, World Bank Institute, New York, pp. 16–19.

Rediff India Abroad, 2008, 'Pre-Christmas Jewellery Exports to US Decline 15%', 22 November, www.rediff.com.

Reich. R., 2008, *Supercapitalism. The Battle for Democracy in an Age of Business*, Icon Press, Cambridge.

Reinhart, C.M. and V. Reinhart, 2010, 'After the Fall', Paper for the Federal Reserve Bank of Kansas Symposium Macro Economic Policy, Post Crisis and Risk Ahead, Jackson Hole, Wyoming.

Reinhart, C.M. and K.S. Rogoff, 2009a, 'The Aftermath of Financial Crises', *NBER Working Paper 14656*, NBER, Cambridge, MA.

Reinhart, C.M. and K.S. Rogoff, 2009b, *This Time is Different, Eight Centuries of Financial Folly*, Princeton University Press, Princeton.

Reserve Bank of India, 2009, *Report of the Task Force for Diamond Sector*, Reserve Bank of India, Ahmedabad.

RGE (2009), 'Is Another Bubble in the Making? Could Central Banks Lose Control?' *RGE Monitor*, 21 November 2009.

Richards, A. and J. Waterbury, 1990, *A Political Economy of the Middle East: State, Class and Economic Development*, Westview Press, Boulder, CO.

Richman, B., 2009, 'Ethnic Networks, Extralegal Certainty, and Globalisation: Peering into the Diamond Industry', in V. Gessner (ed.), *Legal Certainty Beyond the State*, Hart Publishing, Oxford.

Robinson, V., 2005, 'COSATU to launch new union', *Cosatu Weekly* 15 July.

Rodriguez, C. A., 1979, 'Short-run and long-run effects of monetary and fiscal policies under flexible exchange rates and perfect capital mobility', *American Economic Review* **69**, pp. 176–82.

Rodrik, D., 1998, 'Who needs capital-account convertibility?' *Princeton Essays in International Finance* **207**, pp. 55–65.

Rodrik, D., 2003, 'Growth Strategies', *NBER Working Paper No. 10050*, NBER, Cambridge, MA.

Rodrik, D., 2006a, 'The Social Cost of Foreign Exchange Reserves', *NBER Working Paper No. 11952*, NBER, Cambridge, MA.

Rodrik, D., 2006b, 'What's so special about China's exports?' *China and World Economy* **14** (5), pp. 1–19.

Rodrik, D., 2009, 'Growth After the Crisis', Mimeo, Harvard Kennedy School (paper prepared for the Commission on Growth and Development).

Roodman, D., 2008, *History says Financial Crisis will Suppress Aid*, Center for Global Development.

Roos, W., 2004, 'Notitie: SEWU in Trouble, Mimeo, FNV Mondiaal, Amsterdam.

Rothermund, D., 1996, *The Global Impact of The Great Depression 1929–1939*, Routledge, London and New York.

Roubini, N. with S. Mihm, 2010, *Crisis Economics: A Crash Course in the Future of Finance*, Alan Lane, London.

Sarkar, P., 2007, 'Does Foreign Direct Investment Promote Growth? Panel data and Time Series Evidence from Less Developed Countries, 1970–2002', *MPRA Paper no. 5167*, http://mpra.ub.uni-munchen.de/5176/.

SBP, 2009, *The State of Pakistan's Economy: Third Quarterly Report 2008–2009*, State Bank of Pakistan, Karachi.

Schiphorst, F.B., G. Farred and T. van der Rijken, 2007, *Country Report South Africa: Evaluation Trade Union Co-Financing Programme*, Inspectie Ontwikkingssamenwerking en Beleidsevaluatie, The Hague.

Schmidt, D. and S. Heilmann, 2010, 'Dealing with the Economic Crisis in 2008–09: The Chinese Government's Crisis Management in Comparative Perspective', China Analysis 77, Trier University, Triest.

Scott, J., 1972, 'Patron–client political change in Southeast Asia', *American Political Science Review* **66** (1), pp. 91–113.

Selosoemardjan, 1962, *Social Changes in Jogjakarta*, Cornell University Press, Ithaca.

September Commission, 1997, *The Report of the September Commission on the Future of the Unions to the Congress of South African Trade Unions*, COSATU, Johannesburg, www.cosatu.org.za.

Sharma, S.D., 2009, 'Dealing with the contagion: China and India in the aftermath of the subprime meltdown', *China and World Economy* **17** (2), pp. 1–14.

Siamwalla, A., 2008, 'Foreword', in P. Phongpaichit and C. Baker (eds), 2008, *Thai Capital after the 1997 Crisis*, Silkworm Books, Chiang Mai, pp. xi–xii.

Siddiqui, S., 2009, 'Recession Renders 300,000 Pakistanis Jobless', *The News International*, 19 May.

Siegmann, K.A., 2007, 'Gendered Employment in the Post-Quota Era: The Case of Pakistan', in *At the Crossroads: South Asian Research, Policy and Development in a Globalized World*, SDPI and SAMA, Islamabad and Karachi, pp. 3–15.

Sikhula Sonke, n.d., 'Sikhula Sonke Project: Who We Are', sikhulasonke.org/.

Singh, A., 2003, 'Capital account liberalization, free long-term capital flows, financial crisis and development', *Eastern Economic Journal* **29** (2), pp. 191–216.

Skinner, C., 2000, 'Securing Livelihoods: A Gendered Analysis of Support Interventions Available to Street Traders in the Durban Metropolitan Area', *CSDS Research Report 34*, University of KwaZulu Natal, Durban.

SLBFE, 2010, *Annual Statistical Report of Foreign Employment 2009*, Sri Lanka Bureau of Foreign Employment, Battaramulla.

Solimano, A. and G. Larraín, 2002, 'From Economic Miracle to Sluggish Performance: Employment, Unemployment and Growth in the Chilean Economy', Paper prepared for the ILO multidisciplinary Team Santiago de Chile, Santiago de Chile.

Spoor, M., 2009, *The Political Economy of Rural Livelihoods in Transition Economies: Land, Peasants and Rural Poverty in Transition*, Routledge, London and New York.

Standing, G., 2007, 'How Cash Transfers Boost Work and Economic Security', *UN DESA Working Paper No. 58*, UN, New York.

Statsa, 2009, *Statistical Release P0211*, Statistics South Africa, Pretoria.

Statsa, 2010, *Statistical Release P0211*, Statistics South Africa, Pretoria.

Stiglitz, J., 2000, 'Capital market liberalization, economic growth, and instability', *World Development* **28** (6), pp. 1075–86.

Stiglitz, J., 2006, *Making Globalization Work*, Allen Unwin, London.

Stiglitz, J., 2009a, 'The global crisis, social protection and jobs', *International Labour Review* **148** (1), pp. 1–13.

Stiglitz, J., 2009b, 'The Imperative for Improved Global Economic Coordination', in World Bank, *Growing out of Crisis*, World Bank Institute, New York, pp. 39–42.

Stok, E.M., 1939, 'Memorie van overgave van den Controleur bij het Binnenlandsch Bestuur, Hoofd van het Kantoor voor Agrarische Zaken', National Archive, The Hague, Archive of the Ministry for the Colonies MMK 144.

Sugwara, N., V. Sulla, A. Taylor and E.R. Tiongson, 2010, 'The Crisis Hit Home: Stress-testing Households in Europe and Central Asia', *World Bank Economic Premise 2010, No. 12*.

Sumitro, Djojohadikusumo, 1952, *Het volkskredietwezen in de depressie*, Noordhoff – Kolff NV, Jakarta.

Sun, H., 2009, 'Autonomy and effectiveness of Chinese monetary policy under the de facto fixed exchange rate system', *China and World Economy* **17** (13), pp. 23–38.

Sunil, W.A., 2009, 'Sri Lankan Government Reactivates Tripartite Labour Council to Impose Mass Sackings' (webpage of World Socialist Web).

Swinnen, J.F.M. and S. Rozelle, 2006, *From Marx and Mao to the Market*, Oxford University Press, Oxford.

Teivainen, T., 2002, 'The World Social Forum and global democratization: learning from Porto Alegre', *Third World Quarterly* **23** (4), pp. 621–32.

The Economist, 2009, 'Economic Focus: Fatalism v Fetishism. How will developing countries grow after the financial crisis?', 13 June, p. 78.

The Economist, 2010, 'Fear returns: Governments were the solution to the crisis. Now they are the problem', 29 May, p. 9.

The Hindu Business Line, 2010, 'Rise in Rough Diamond Prices Cause for Concern', 31 August 2010. Accessed at http://www.thehindubusinessline.in/2010/08/31/stories/2010083150441600.htm, on 10 September 2010.

The Nation, 2002, 3 July 2002. Accessed at www.nationmultimedia.com.

The Telegraph, 2009, 'Global Financial Crisis Wrecks India's Diamond Industry', 22 Febuary. Accessed at http://www.telegraph.co.uk/finance/financialcrisis/4781041/Global-financial-crisis-wrecks-Indias-diamond-industry.html, on 16 August 2009.

Theron, J., 2007, 'Membership-Based Organizations of the Poor: The South African Experience', in M. Chen, R. Jhabvala, R. Kanbur and C. Richards (eds), *Membership-Based Organizations of the Poor*, Routledge, London, pp. 240–60.

Theron, J., 2010, 'Informalization from Above, Informalization from Below: The Options for Organization', *African Studies Quarterly* **11** (2/3), pp. 87–105.

Third World Network, 2009, 'The IMF's Financial Crisis Loans: No Change in Conditionalities', Penang, Malaysia, www.twnside.org.sg/title2/IMF.Crisis.Loans-Overview.TWN.March.2009.doc.

Tily, G., 2010, 'The critical steps in the transition from the Treatise to the General Theory: an alternative interpretation', *History of Economic Issues* **18** (1), pp. 64–93.

Times of India, 2009, 'Economy to grow at 6.7%', 30 July.

Trivelli, C., J. Yancari and C. De Los Ríos, 2009, *Crisis y pobreza rural en América Latina*, Rimisp-Centro Latinoamericano para el Desarrollo Rural, the International Fund for Agricultural Development (IFAD) and the Instituto de Estudios Peruanos (IEP).

Tzannatos, Z., 2009, *The Global Financial, Economic and Social Crisis and the Arab Countries: a Review of the Evidence and Policies for Employment Creation and Social Protection*, ILO Regional Office for Arab States, Beirut.

UN (United Nations), 2005, *World Economic and Social Survey 2005: Financing for Development*, UN, New York.

UN, 2006, *World Economic and Social Survey: Diverging Growth and Development*, UN, New York.

UN, 2009a, *World Economic Situation and Prospects 2009*, UN, New York.

UN, 2009b, *World Economic and Social Survey: Promoting Development, Saving the Planet*, UN, New York.

UN, 2010a, *World Economic Situation and Prospects as per Mid-2010*, UN, New York.

UN, 2010b, *World Economic and Social Survey: Retooling Global Development*, UN, New York.

UN, 2010c, *World Economic Situation and Prospects 2010*, UN, New York.

UNCTAD, 2001, *Trade and Development Report 2001*, UNCTAD, Geneva and New York.

UNCTAD, 2007, *Trade and Development Report 2007*, UNCTAD, Geneva.

UNCTAD, 2008, *World Investment Report: Transnational Corporation and the Infrastructure Challenge*, UNCTAD, Geneva.

UNCTAD, 2009a, *The Global Economic Crisis: Systemic Failures and Multilateral Remedies*, UNCTAD, Geneva.

UNCTAD, 2009b, *Economic Development in Africa: Strengthening Regional Economic Integration for Africa's Development*, UNCTAD: Geneva

UNCTAD 2010a, *Global Investment Trends Monitor No. 2*, UNCTAD, Washington and Geneva.

UNCTAD, 2010b, *Trade and Development Report: Employment, Globalization and Development*, UNCTAD, Geneva.

UNCTAD, 2010c, *2010 World Investment Report*, UNCTAD, Geneva.

UNCTAD India, 2009, *Impact of Global Slowdown on India's Exports and Employment*, UNCTAD India, New Delhi.

UN/DESA, 2007, *Report on the World Social Situation 2007: The Employment Imperative*, UN, New York.

UN/DESA, 2010a, 'World Trade Recovers, but Developing Country Vulnerability to Commodity Price Swings Remains', *World Economic Vulnerability Monitor, No. 3*, UNDESA, New York.

UN/DESA, 2010b, *Rethinking Poverty: Report on the World Social Situation 2010*, UNDESA, New York.

UNDP, 1996, *Economic Growth and Human Development, Human Development Report*, UNDP, New York.

UNDP, 1999, *Human Development Report for Europe and the CIS*, Regional Human Development Report, UNDP, New York.

UNDP, 2009, *Human Development Report 2009*, UNDP, New York.

United Nations Commission of Experts of the President of the UN General Assembly, 2009, *Report on the Reforms of the International Monetary and Financial System*, UN, New York

Vavi, Z., 2010, 'Address to the National Farm Workers Summit 30–31 July 2010 in Somerset West'.

Vehicle, 2008, *A Vehicle for Women's Voice to be Heard: Annual Report 2008 Sikhula Sonke*. Accessed at http://www.ssonke.org.za, on 12 September 2010

Velde, D.W. te et al., 2009, *The Global Financial Crisis and Developing Countries: Synthesis of the Findings of 10 Country Case Studies*, ODI, London.

Verick, S., 2010a, 'Unravelling the Impact of the Global Financial Crisis on the South African Labour Market', *Employment Working Paper 48*, ILO, Geneva.

Verick, S., 2010b, 'The Global Financial Crisis and South Africa: What has Been the Impact on the Labour Market?' Paper for the DPRU/EPP/TIPS conference 'The Global Economic Crisis and South Africa: Lessons, Long-Run Economic Growth, and Development', Johannesburg, October.

Volkstelling, 1934, *Volkstelling 1930 Vol. II*, Landsdrukkerij, Batavia.

Vreede, A.G., 1931, 'De omvang der werkloosheid in Nederlandsch-Indie over de periode December 1930/Juni 1931', *Koloniale Studieën* **15** (II).

Wade, R., (2009). 'From global imbalances to global reorganisations', *Cambridge Journal of Economics* **33**, pp. 539–562.

Wahl, P., 2009, *Food Speculation: The Main Factor of the Price Bubble in 2008*, Briefing Paper, World Economy, Ecology and Development, Berlin.

WCSDG, 2004, *A Fair Globalization: Creating Opportunities for All. World Commission on the Social Dimension of Globalization*, ILO, Geneva.

Weeks, J., T. McKinley, A.G. Cornia, M. Spoor and M. Reynolds, 2005, *Economic Policies for Growth, Employment and Poverty Reduction: Moldova in Transition*, UNDP, Chisinau.

Wegren, S., 1998, *Land Reform in the Former Soviet and Eastern Europe*, Routledge, London and New York.

Wen, J., 2009, Transcript of interview with Chinese Premier W. Jiabao by Fareed Zakaria, 23 September.

White, F., 2010, 'Deepening democracy: A farm workers' movement in the Western Cape', *Journal of Southern African Studies* **36**, pp. 673–91.

Whyte, M. K., 2010, *Myth of the Social Volcano: Perceptions of Inequality and Distributive Injustice in Contemporary China*, Stanford University Press, Stanford.

Wolf, M., 2008a, *Fixing Global Finance*, Johns Hopkins University Press.

Wolf, M., 2008b, 'Keynes offers us the best way to think about the crisis', *Financial Times*, 24 December 2008.

Wolf, M., 2009a, 'It is in Beijing's interests to lend Geithner a hand', *Financial Times*, 9 June 2009.

Wolf, M., 2009b, 'Why China must do more to rebalance its economy', *Financial Times*, 22 September 2009.

Wolf, M., 2009c, 'Grim truths Obama should have told Hu', *Financial Times*, 17 November 2009.

Wolf, M., 2009d, *Fixing Global Finance, How to Curb Financial Crises in the 21st Century*, Yale University Press, New Haven.

Wong, J., 2008, 'China's economy in 2007/2008: Coping with problems of runaway growth', *China and World Economy* **16** (2), pp. 1–18.

World Bank, 1999, *Global Economic Prospects 1998/1999 Beyond Financial Crisis*, World Bank, Washington, DC.

World Bank, 2005, *Growth, Poverty and Inequality, Eastern Europe and the Former Soviet Union*, World Bank, Washington, DC.

World Bank, 2008, *Global Economic Prospects 2008*, World Bank, Washington, DC.

World Bank, 2009a, *Global Economic Prospects 2009*, World Bank, Washington, DC.

World Bank, 2009b, *2008 Economic Development and Prospects: Regional Integration for Global Competitiveness. Middle East and North Africa Region*, World Bank, Washington, DC.

World Bank, 2009c, *Impact of Global Financial Crisis on South Asia*, World Bank, Washington, DC.

World Bank, 2009d, *The Global Financial Crisis: Assessing Vulnerability for Women and Children*, World Bank, Washington, DC.

World Bank, 2009e, *Global Development Finance 2008*, Online Database, World Bank, Washington, DC.

World Bank, 2009f, *China Quarterly Update March*, World Bank, Beijing.

World Bank, 2009g, *China Quarterly Update June*, World Bank, Beijing.

World Bank, 2009h, *China Quarterly Update November*, World Bank, Beijing.

World Bank, 2010a, *Thailand Economic Monitor*, June 2010, World Bank, Bangkok Office.

World Bank, 2010b, *Global Economic Prospects 2010*, World Bank, Washington, DC.

World Bank, 2010c, *The MDGs after the Crisis Global Monitoring Report 2010*, World Bank, Washington, DC.

World Bank, 2010d, *World Development Indicators and Global Development Finance Database 2010*, World Bank, Washington, DC.

World Bank, 2010f, *China Quarterly Update March*, World Bank, Beijing.

World Bank, 2010g, *China Quarterly Update June*, World Bank, Beijing.

World Bank, 2010h, *China Quarterly Update November*, World Bank, Beijing.

Wray, R.L., 2009, 'The Social and Economic Importance of Full Employment', *Working Paper 560*, Levy Economics Institute of Bard College, Annandale-on-Hudson.

WTO (2009), *International Trade Statistics 2009*, WTO, Geneva.

Xu, M., 2009, 'How to Reform the International Financial System? A Chinese Perspective', *FES Briefing Paper 11*, September.

Yang, D., 2008, 'The Impact of the Financial Crisis in China', *IDS Briefings on the Financial Crisis*, www.ids.ac.uk.

Yao, S., 2009, 'Why are Chinese exports not so special', *China and World Economy* **17** (1), pp. 47–65.

Yao, S., D. Luo and S. Morgan (2010), 'Impact of the US credit crunch and housing market crisis on China', *Journal of Contemporary China* **19** (64), pp. 401–17.

Zakaria, F., 2008, *The Post-American World*, W.W. Norton & Company, New York.

Zhang, X., S. Fan and A. de Haan (eds), 2010, *Narratives of Chinese Economic Reforms: How Does China Cross the River?* World Scientific Publishing, Singapore.

Zhang Z., W. Li and N. Shi, 2009, 'Handling the Global Financial Crisis: Chinese Strategy and Policy Response', available at http://ssrn.com/abstract=1377049.

Zheng, Y., and S.K. Tok, 2007, '"Harmonious Society" and "Harmonious World": China's Policy Discourse Under Hu Jintao', *Briefing Series 26*, China Policy Institute, University of Nottingham.

Zheng, Y. and J. Yi, 2007, 'China's rapid accumulation of foreign exchange reserves and its policy implications', *China and World Economy* **15** (1), pp. 14–25.

Zhou X., 2009, 'Reform the International Monetary System'. Accessed at http://www.pbc.gov.cn/english/detail.asp?col=6500&id=178.

Index